Unifying China, Integrating with the World

Studies in Asian Security

A SERIES SPONSORED BY THE
EAST-WEST CENTER WASHINGTON

Muthiah Alagappa, Chief Editor

The aim of the Asian Security series is to promote analysis, understanding, and explanation of the dynamics of domestic, transnational, and international security challenges in Asia. The peer-reviewed books in this series analyze contemporary security issues and problems to clarify debates in the scholarly and policy communities, provide new insights and perspectives, and identify new research and policy directions related to conflict management and security in Asia. Security is defined broadly to include the traditional political and military dimensions as well as the nontraditional dimensions that affect the survival and well-being of political communities. Asia, too, is defined broadly, to include Northeast, Southeast, South, and Central Asia.

Designed to encourage original and rigorous scholarship, books in the Asian Security series seek to engage scholars, educators, and practitioners. Wide-ranging in scope and method, the series welcomes an extensive array of paradigms, programs, traditions, and methodologies now employed in the social sciences.

*   *   *

The East-West Center, with offices in Honolulu, Hawaii, and in Washington, D.C., is a public, nonprofit educational and research institution established by the U.S. Congress in 1960 to foster understanding and cooperation among the governments and peoples of the Asia-Pacific region, including the United States.

Unifying China, Integrating with the World

SECURING CHINESE SOVEREIGNTY
IN THE REFORM ERA

Allen Carlson

SPONSORED BY THE EAST–WEST CENTER WASHINGTON

Stanford University Press • *Stanford, California 2005*

Published with the partial support of the
Sasakawa Peace Foundation (USA).

Stanford University Press
Stanford, California

Printed in the United States of America on acid-free, archival-quality paper

Library of Congress Cataloging-in-Publication Data

Carlson, Allen, 1968–
   Unifying China, integrating with the world : securing Chinese sovereignty in the
reform era / Allen Carlson.
      p.   cm. — (Asian security)
   Includes bibliographical references and index.
   ISBN 0-8047-5060-2 (cloth : alk. paper)
      1. China—Foreign relations—1976– 2. China—Boundaries. 3. China—
Relations—Tibet. 4. Tibet (China)—Relations—China. 5. China—Relations—
Taiwan. 6. Taiwan—Relations—China. 7. Sovereignty—Case studies. I. Title.
II. Series: Studies in Asian security.

JZ1734.C37 2005
320.1'5'0951—DC22

                                                                    2005013721

Original Printing 2005

Last figure below indicates year of this printing:
14   13   12   11   10   09   08   07   06   05

For Jing

Contents

Figures

Preface

I began work on this book in the early 1990s when I was a graduate student in Yale University's Political Science Department. At that time I received invaluable advice from Shaoguang Wang, and especially from my dissertation chair, Alexander Wendt. Subsequently, Alastair Iain Johnston generously shared with me his expertise on both security studies and China's foreign relations, and his extensive list of contacts.

While conducting field research in China from 1995 through 1998 I benefited from the assistance of a diverse group of scholars in Beijing and Shanghai. During this period I conducted interviews with ninety-nine members of China's growing community of foreign policy and national security experts. These interviews were conducted with the promise of confidentiality, and included talks with both senior and junior scholars and policy analysts. During this period I discussed the issue of sovereignty with academics affiliated with the Foreign Affairs College, Fudan University, Peking University, People's University, and Qinghua University. I also met with a number of scholars working at various institutes within the Chinese Academy of Social Sciences (CASS) (including the Institute of American Studies, the Institute of Asian-Pacific Studies, the Legal Studies Institute, the Institute of Taiwan Studies, the Research Center for the Study of Borderland History and Geography [RBHG], and the Institute of World Economics and Politics). In addition, I interviewed individuals affiliated with the Beijing Academy of Social Sciences, the Center for Peace and Development Studies, the China Reform Forum, the China Society for Strategy and Management Research, the Chinese Institute of International Studies (CIIS), the Chinese Institute of Contemporary International Relations

(CICIR), the Foundation for International Strategic Studies, the PLA's Academy of Military Sciences and National Defense University, the Shanghai Academy of Social Sciences, and the Shanghai Institute of International Studies (SIIS). Moreover, I was particularly fortunate to hold even more extensive conversations with a number of China's most distinguished students of foreign policy and international relations working at the Foreign Affairs College, the Institute of World Economics and Politics, and Peking University.

Utilizing interview data from China, and taking advantage of both Yale's library's and Bob Ross's comprehensive, personal collection of Chinese foreign policy journals, I then completed my first attempt to come to terms with the Chinese stance on sovereignty in 2000 when I submitted my dissertation ("Constructing a New Great Wall: Chinese Foreign Policy and the Norm of State Sovereignty") to Yale University.

While at Yale, I was the beneficiary of generous financial support from the National Science Foundation, Yale's Political Science Department, and the East Asian Studies Program. In addition, as I was completing the dissertation, both Alexander Wendt and Iain Johnston played instrumental roles in encouraging me to sharpen my conceptualization of the theoretical and empirical aspects of the project.

After finishing the Ph.D., I began to revise the dissertation for publication after I joined the Government Department at Cornell University in the fall of 2000. At Cornell I benefited enormously from discussing the manuscript with my colleagues, including Matt Evangelista, Jonathan Kirshner, Jeremy Rabkin, J. J. Suh, and especially Peter Katzenstein. Outside Ithaca, Amitav Acharya, Tom Christensen, M. Taylor Fravel, and Adam Segal all reviewed chapters of the manuscript. In addition, the comments of anonymous reviewers for the *Journal of Contemporary China* and the East-West Center Washington's Policy Studies series provided me with valuable insights into how to improve the arguments I make here.

With the assistance of the National Committee on U.S.-China Relations, and the support of Cornell's Government Department, I then conducted follow-up field research for the book in China in the winter of 2001–2. Cornell's Peace Studies Program and East Asia Program provided me with additional funds to conduct supplemental fieldwork in Taiwan in the spring of 2002.

After I finished revisions of the manuscript in the fall of 2003 Muthiah Alagappa expressed his interest in the work and played a central role in facilitating its consideration for inclusion in the East-West Center Washington's newly established Asian Security series. The anonymous reviews of the manuscript and the suggestions forwarded by the series editorial board then helped to make the book stronger. In addition, Muriel Bell and Carmen Bourbon-

Wu at Stanford University Press assisted me in navigating my way through the publication process. This task was professionally facilitated by the outstanding research assistance of Duan Hong, and especially Sarah Tarrow's help with editing.

Finally, over the years it took to complete this project, I benefited enormously from the support of my parents, Jane and Russ Carlson, and my wife's parents, Zheng Tongli and Liang Wujun. More importantly, the book would not have been completed without the patience and understanding of my wife, Jing (who left China for the United States while I was writing it), and the happiness that our boys (Ned and Ethan) gave to me as I worked to complete it.

September 2004
Beijing, China

Unifying China, Integrating with the World

Introduction

This book describes and explains the evolution of Beijing's relationship with the rest of the international system since the start of China's reform era in the late 1970s, by analyzing the prominent, yet poorly understood, role of sovereignty within this dynamic process. As discussed in more detail in the following chapter, sovereignty is a bundle of mutually recognized rights and obligations that states possess via their status as sovereign members of the contemporary international system. More specifically, it comprises four distinct components (territory, jurisdiction, authority, and economic rights) that form the lines between states. In this sense, sovereignty makes international politics possible by providing it with structural underpinnings. However, as the rights that constitute sovereignty are constantly being produced by the words and actions of states in ways that either reinforce or transgress the boundaries it creates, its specific meaning is never a given, but rather always in the process of being substantiated and refined.

Sovereignty is thus placed at the center of this book because of its contested and variable role in international politics, and because of the prominence of sovereignty-related concerns within each of the most contentious foreign policy issues facing Beijing as China has moved along the transformative path of economic opening set in motion in the late 1970s. Indeed, securing China's territorial borders, defining the status of Taiwan and Tibet—and to a lesser extent Hong Kong—as a part of China, and navigating the terms of China's involvement with the international human rights system and the global economy are all exercises in articulating sovereignty.[1] Each issue revolves around the type of sovereign boundaries being created between China and the rest of the world.

The book, then, is about how and why Chinese foreign policy and national security makers and analysts have attempted to draw the line between what is inside China and what is outside (the international system, community, or society) during a period of rapid change within both spheres. It seeks to cut through the controversies surrounding this issue by addressing the following questions: Has China's stance on sovereignty changed since the late 1970s, what factors have most directly influenced the Chinese position, and is the Chinese story then different from that being constructed by other states?

I addressed these questions via a five-step research process. First, I sought to advance our understanding of sovereignty through developing a new conceptual framework for analyzing its role in international politics. Second, I collected empirical data that add new specificity to the discussion of sovereignty's changing role in international politics. Third, I selected a series of cases directly related to the Chinese position on each of the main components of sovereignty. The general rationale for case selection was two-fold. To begin with, cases were chosen that constituted China-specific manifestations of issues that had already been identified in the new literature on sovereignty as key sites, or nodal points, in the construction of its role in international politics. Following initial research, I then chose issues that showed variation within Chinese sovereignty-related behavior (from boundary transgression, or soft policies, to boundary reinforcement, or a hard stance). The issue areas I selected, then, include China's stance on territorial boundaries; its relationship with Taiwan, Tibet, and Hong Kong; its involvement in the international human rights system; and its economic concerns, including globalization and participation in the major multilateral economic organizations (the World Bank, International Monetary Fund, and especially the General Agreement on Tariffs and Trade [GATT] / World Trade Organization [WTO]). Fourth, I collected and analyzed a comprehensive set of documents, primarily in Chinese, on all four issue areas. This involved (1) analysis of all sovereignty-related statements in official Chinese publications such as *Beijing Review* and *Zhongguo Waijiao Gailan* (Survey of China's Diplomacy); (2) examination of the universe of articles on sovereignty published in China's main academic journals of international relations and national security;[2] and (3) review of specific policy decisions made by Beijing. Finally, I carried out extensive interviews with ninety-nine members of China's elite foreign policy and national security circles in 1997 and 1998.[3] The interviews focused on the informants' views of the role of sovereignty in international relations. Interviewees were asked questions intended to identify their receptiveness to the prospect of change in such a role.

This research reveals that the Chinese position on sovereignty is not what it used to be. Through the mid-1970s, China's stance was absolutist, unyielding, and stood in sharp contrast to the changes beginning to take shape in the international arena at the time. Since then, both subtle and substantive changes in the Chinese position have occurred. Initially, during the 1980s, the Chinese approach continued to be relatively constant and boundary reinforcing, but placed a greater emphasis on cooperation and compromise than had been the case during the first thirty years of the People's Republic of China (PRC). In contrast, during the 1990s the Chinese position shifted, became more varied, and in the process also became the subject of intense debate within foreign policy and national security circles in China. More specifically, Chinese policies preserved a static interpretation of territorial sovereignty, promoted an unyielding and increasingly combative stance on jurisdictional sovereignty, and permitted a transgression of the lines created by the economic and authority components of sovereignty. In light of such developments, and lending specificity to the book's general framing questions, the central analytical task I confront in the following chapters is to explain the relatively uniform changes in Chinese policies affecting sovereignty in the 1980s, and the divergence of policies in the 1990s.

I argue that China's shifting stance on sovereignty is a product of the changing relationship between relatively persistent and historically conditioned sovereignty-centric values, rational cost-benefit calculations, and external pressures (both material and normative) inadvertently brought to bear on China by reform and opening. During the 1980s, Deng Xiaoping's pragmatic call for strengthening China through a controlled integration with the international political and economic system provided the impetus for limited changes in the Chinese stance on each aspect of sovereignty (by overcoming the reticence to change caused by historical and ideological influences). Yet, over the course of the reform era, it was external factors that pushed newly emerging interpretations of sovereignty from the international arena into China.

More specifically, Chinese policies during the 1990s were shaped by the increasing salience of two different trends created by China's increasingly complex interdependence with the rest of the international system. First, material pressures for change (bilateral demands and enmeshment in multilateral institutions) became more pronounced than was the case during the 1980s. Second, new ideational influences for change were introduced in the process of norms diffusion and the advent of new image concerns in Beijing about portraying China as a responsible power. The combined weight of these forces caused substantial changes in two key facets of the Chinese approach to sovereignty (economic and sovereign authority), left one other largely untouched (territory), and triggered a prolonged battle to preserve the status quo vis-à-vis another component of the norm (jurisdictional sovereignty).[4]

These findings speak directly to a host of controversial issues in the "new sovereignty" debate in international studies and in recent analyses of Chinese foreign policy and national security making. To begin with, key aspects of Chinese behavior are puzzling when viewed solely within the distinct strands of the secondary literature on sovereignty that have forwarded relatively parsimonious arguments about the causes of sovereign change. Along these lines, my explanation of Chinese behavior is intended to contribute to the general constructivist turn in international relations theory (by bringing a consideration of historically framed, domestic ideational constraints into the discussion of international norms diffusion). However, it is also eclectic in integrating collective memory, pragmatic interest calculations, and external normative influences within its frame.[5] In this sense, the book is part of a movement in international relations and security studies to bridge the apparent divide between rationalist and ideationalist accounts of international politics.

For students of Chinese foreign relations and Asian security, documenting the emerging heterogeneity of policy in the 1990s, in contrast to the homogeneous policies of the 1980s, is of inherent interest since the finding challenges current conventional wisdom. Chinese sovereignty is not as unyielding and monolithic as is commonly asserted. In addition, the patterns of sovereign change highlighted in the book have not been adequately documented or explained in the few sophisticated analyses previously published. Furthermore, by placing the issue of sovereignty at its core, the book sheds new light on how and why new interpretations have emerged (and are being contested) in China about the location of the boundaries between the PRC and the rest of the international system. The book reveals just how precarious the process of drawing such lines has become. Indeed, it shows a profound bifurcation within China between those who accept the erosion of Chinese sovereign rights and those who will make heroic efforts to resist such a trend. This being said, I am not advancing an alarmist thesis about the "coming collapse of China," but rather exposing the extent to which "old" Chinese approaches to sovereignty are being increasingly buffeted by new and unexpected domestic and international challenges.

Although the specifics of this struggle are unique, the dilemma of participating in an increasingly interdependent and densely layered international system while maintaining independence and individuality in such a community is not. On the contrary, foreign policy and national security elites in most states are intimately familiar with the difficulties inherent in grappling with this dilemma. In this sense, to return to one of the questions raised at the outset, the development of the Chinese stance on sovereignty since the late 1970s is not all that unusual. It is embedded in the historical evolution of China's relationship with the rest of the international system, and parallels the struggles of other new states that won admission to the system over the course of the last century. Nonetheless, over the last two decades sovereignty has become an increasingly controversial issue in China's relationship with the rest of the world, one that during the 1990s posed unprecedented difficulties for China's leaders, and has the potential (vis-à-vis Taiwan) to place Beijing in direct conflict with other powerful members of the international system (especially the United States).

In short, changes in the Chinese approach to sovereignty during the reform era were impressively deep, but defined more by a divergence in positioning than by the consolidation of a single unified stance. Such behavior is reflective of China's evolving relationship with the rest of the international system during this period. While Beijing has allowed China to become ever more deeply incorporated into the world economy and polity since the late 1970s, it has also striven to maintain the lines that separate China from this system. In other words, China is both integrating with, and differentiating itself from, the international community in which it is now firmly embedded. This is the central characteristic of Chinese foreign relations and national security policy over the last two and a half decades, and, despite mounting challenges to such a position, will continue to be so in the future.

1

Reconsidering Sovereignty's Role
in International Politics

The founding figures of modern international law long ago traced the roots of sovereignty back to the 1648 Peace of Westphalia and the protocols for diplomatic exchange that developed between the new European states in the 1700s and 1800s. Moreover, over the course of the last century, students of international politics devoted a great deal of attention to its role in the broader international system. Much of their analysis centered on the question of whether sovereignty would survive within a rapidly changing international system. The first wave of such scrutiny began following World War I, as scholars examined the impact on sovereignty of popular nationalism and the principle of self-determination that Woodrow Wilson had so famously endorsed. Subsequently, in the early 1950s, political theorists anxiously grappled with the normative and ethical implications of a principle that appeared to place the domestic abuses of Nazi Germany beyond the rebuke of the international community; many called for an end to the sovereign prerogatives of states. At the same time, Hans Morganthau's realist classic, *Politics Among Nations*, explored sovereignty within the context of a broader survey of the limitations facing international law in an arena dominated by power politics and found little reason to expect change in the sovereign framework of such a system.

In contrast to this assessment, during the 1970s a diverse group of scholars argued that economic interdependence and political integration were indeed beginning to erode the sovereign boundaries between states. Yet, despite such claims, by the end of the decade the conventional wisdom within the field of international studies was that sovereignty constituted a relatively static anchor for the contemporary international system. Not surprisingly, this consensus resulted in a brief lull in work on sovereignty. However, the main debate in international relations theory that emerged out of this period, along with the growing interest in international studies in the process of globalization and the prospects for systemic change, soon replaced this calm with yet another wave of scholarly analysis and political debate on sovereignty. Indeed, it is now seen as both a compelling and controversial issue. This book grew out of such a turn. This chapter contributes to the "new sovereignty" debate by developing a more sophisticated framework for analyzing the role of sovereignty in the international system.

Sovereignty's Foundational Role in International Politics

Contributors to the "new sovereignty" debate have argued that sovereignty is a central, and relatively fluid, feature of the contemporary international system. However, for the most part, the work that makes this point has also been plagued by conceptual imprecision and a relatively pervasive failure to ground abstract theoretical considerations of structural change with more concrete empirical referents. This section, after briefly reviewing this literature, argues that the first step toward addressing these shortcomings, and more effectively identifying how sovereignty's role in the international political system varies, is to disaggregate its component parts. It then demonstrates that over the course of the post–World War II era—but especially since the late 1960s—systemic trends began to gather momentum in a manner that, to varying degrees, challenged, or at the very least raised new questions about, the meaning of the boundaries between states established by each facet of the norm.

From Discussing Anarchy to Thinking about Sovereignty: The "New Sovereignty" Debate in International Relations Theory

Recent international relations theory initially identified the significance of sovereignty's role in the contemporary international system via the debate that has dominated the field since the early 1980s about the anarchic nature of international politics. Despite forwarding starkly contrasting understandings of the meaning of anarchy and its effect on state behavior, the contributors to this debate collectively agreed that it was sovereignty that made possible the defining feature of the system, the distinction between internal hierarchy and international anarchy.

The pivotal figure in this trend was Kenneth Waltz. Within his work, sovereignty, at first glance, appears to be of little significance. Indeed, Waltz touched upon it only in passing in his canonical *Theory of International Politics*. However, upon closer inspection, it is also clear that his approach to international relations was actually grounded by a conceptualization of sovereignty that treated it as a fundamental principle of the contemporary international system. For Waltz, the state was sovereign insofar as "it decides for itself how it will cope with its internal and external problems" (Waltz 1986: 90). Moreover, because "each state, like every other state, is a sovereign political entity," each is also a member of the same category—sovereign states—and therefore functionally similar. Thus, "national politics consists of differentiated units performing specified functions. International politics consists of like units duplicating one another's activities" (p. 92). In other words, sovereignty, understood to be synonymous with autonomy, made all units within the system alike. This assumption then freed Waltz to focus on the international system's anarchic structure and the order that exists within it due to the material distribution of power between states.

This influential thesis quickly generated an outpouring of critical scholarship. Such work was remarkably diverse in its theoretical and methodological foundations, but at the same time was broadly unified in its tendency to emphasize the narrowness of the neo-realist approach to the possibility of structural change within international politics. The crux of this critique was that anarchy was less of a constant, constraining feature of international relations than Waltz had posited, and sovereignty was more malleable than he had portrayed. The point of contention was not that Waltz had overstated sovereignty's foundational position within the international system. Indeed, there was nearly universal agreement that it was pivotal. Rather, Waltz's critics argued that his conceptualization of sovereignty did not accurately reflect either its historical evolution or its place within current international politics.[1]

Writing against the backdrop of such claims, students of international politics began to devote more direct attention to sovereignty in the early 1990s. Such a turn was initially animated by a surge of interest in the extent to which globalization and the end of the Cold War were creating a new era of sovereign change, one that would lead to the "end of sovereignty."[2] However, while interest in globalization grew exponentially over the course of the decade, the core of the sovereignty debate quickly moved beyond this fascination with its possible demise. The first facet of this turn was primarily conceptual, as a wide array of scholars took issue with earlier definitions of sovereignty for being overly general and failing to accurately capture how its role had evolved historically and was now being secured within the current international system. Instead, the contributors to the "new sovereignty" debate forwarded a series of what Michael Fowler and Julie Bunck (1995) have called "basket" approaches, analytical definitions designed to more accurately describe the multiple aspects of sovereignty's place in international politics.

The most influential proponent of such a move was Stephen Krasner. After he initially identified sovereignty as a set of institutions, or conventions, he then cataloged four uses of the term: internal public authority of a state; control over transborder flows; international legal sovereignty; and the Westphalian model ("an institutional arrangement for organizing political life that is based on territoriality and autonomy") (Krasner 1988, 1995/96, 1999). Krasner's broad intent in taking apart sovereignty in this way was to cut through what he saw as the conceptual haze surrounding the issue by forcing those talking about sovereignty to be more precise. He also contended that within such a framework, it was clear that the loss of one of sovereignty's aspects did not necessarily affect its other facets (Krasner 1999: 24). The key dynamic element in this reconceptualization of sovereignty was then located in Krasner's attempt to trace how sovereign institutions had been violated over time via four distinct "modalities of compromise" (conventions, contracts, coercion, and imposition) (p. 25). In an intriguing inversion of Waltz's neo-realist thesis, Krasner found that sovereignty, at least its Westphalian and international legal components (on which his work focused, as he saw them as related to distinct aspects of the location of authority within the international realm), has always been subject to incursions. As such, it is best understood as a state of "organized hypocrisy" (an institution whose resilience stems in no small part from its ability to absorb such violations).

While Krasner supported this thesis with wide-ranging historical examples, because he saw compromise as an endemic feature of the system, the issue of measuring sovereign change was of less interest than simply showing that sovereign boundaries have never been as impermeable as has often been assumed. In other words, as David Lake has observed, Krasner provided "no metric for aggregating deviance into patterns" (Lake 2003: 310). In contrast, virtually every other contributor to the "new sovereignty" debate has emphasized coming to terms with how the role of sovereignty within the contemporary international system varies.

Along these lines, a number of scholars conceptualized sovereignty as a game comprising foundational features and a host of specific practices or applications. Although the former were considered to be quite static, the latter were subject to ongoing modification and change. An important early example of such a framework for analyzing sovereign change is Robert Jackson's work on decolonization. Jackson emphasized the difference between sovereignty's constitutive rules (which "define the game") and its instrumental aspects ("precepts, maxims, stratagems, and tactics which are derived from experience and contribute to winning play"), and focused on the ties between the end of colonialism and the emergence of new sovereignty norms (which hinged on the rise of the principle of negative sovereignty that granted weak states unprecedented levels of juridical independence) (1990: 34–35). Subsequently, Janice Thomson argued that sovereignty was best understood as "the recognition by internal and external actors that the state has the exclusive authority to intervene coercively in activities within its territory" (Thomson 1995: 224). Following Jackson's lead, Thomson too highlighted the difference between its constitutive and functional aspects and defined the first as residing in the privileged position of the state within the sovereign system, while the second involved "the precise range of activities over which states can legitimately exercise their authority (extensiveness)" (p. 224). Sharing Krasner's skepticism about sovereign change, Thomson then argued that indications of such a development within the current international order were primarily limited to the latter of these two categories (pp. 224–25). More recently, Georg Sorenson has echoed these claims in an article that argued that the constitutive rules of sovereignty (the constitutional independence of states) are a robust feature of the contemporary international system, but its "regulative rules" had changed substantially over time "in order to adapt to new challenges mainly stimulated by changes in substantial statehood" (Sorenson 1999: 604).

Those working out of the critical and constructivist strands of the anarchy debate also moved to develop a framework for specifying how sovereignty's role in international politics changes. The most frequently cited example of such an effort was forwarded in a volume coedited by Thomas Biersteker and Cynthia Weber. In this work, the two scholars argued that sovereignty could be defined as "a political entity's externally recognized right to exercise final authority over its affairs," and emphasized the distinction between sovereign recognition and the components that make up the sovereign state (territory, population, and authority).[3] However, they also found that the main analytical task confronting those seeking to come to terms with how international politics is organized was to examine "the variety of ways in which states are constantly negotiating their sovereignty" (Biersteker and Weber 1996: 11).[4]

Although differences over the scope of recent systemic shifts in sovereignty's role in international politics first raised in the early 1990s still persist (and, indeed constitute one of the main ongoing points of discussion in the "new sovereignty" debate), it is also clear that a general consensus on three broad conceptual issues has recently emerged among the contributors to this literature.[5] First, usage of the term "sovereignty" has varied a great deal according to specific circumstances and references, and much of the misunderstanding about the concept stems directly from this. Second, sovereignty's role in international politics has always been defined in relationship to other norms, institutions, or processes. Third, such a role is more fluid and malleable than was conventionally acknowledged by most students of international relations.

Moving Forward: Disaggregating Sovereign Rights, Identifying New Challenges to the Lines They Create

These areas of agreement constitute a new point of departure for studying sovereignty's role in international politics. However, the "new sovereignty" debate is not without a number of flaws. First, while participants in the debate have tended to correctly assert that sovereignty's role in international politics hinges more upon how state authority is defined within the system than on the extent to which individual states exert actual control over their sovereign territory, they have failed to specify the different types of rights that constitute sovereignty. In other words, despite a wave of "basket" approaches to sovereignty in international studies, to a remarkable extent those describing sovereignty have consistently overlooked the diverse set of rights and obligations that make up its role in international relations.

Dissatisfied with such a failing, the core of my framework for examining sovereignty involves more specifically conceptualizing the variety of ways sovereign rights are organized within international politics. I agree with the consensus in the literature that sovereignty consists of mutually recognized rights and obligations possessed by states as members of the contemporary international system. However, I also argue that sovereignty contains four relatively distinct bundles, or nodes, of rights. Each state's sovereign rights encompass exclusive possession of a specified territory, jurisdiction over a defined population, political authority to govern within its own domain without foreign interference, and the ability to regulate economic activity within its territorial boundaries. As central as each of these components is the structure of the contemporary international system, their precise role is continually evolving, and often the subject of system-level change and reinterpretation. Moreover, a limited, yet significant, systemic shift has taken place since the late 1960s in international politics in the specific way each of these components of the norm has been substantiated and interpreted.

Territorial Sovereignty

The first face of sovereignty is the principle that the spatial extent of each sovereign entity, or state, is limited, and by extension, within a system of sovereign states all space is divided into discrete political units. Or, as the political geographer Peter Taylor (1989: 145) succinctly wrote, "Sovereignty must be bounded: a world of sovereign states is a world divided by boundaries." In other words, all sovereign territory is, in theory, defined by clear physical boundaries (even if the exact location of such lines is often a matter of dispute), and it is the right of each sovereign entity to delineate, demarcate, and defend such lines.

Within the current international arena, this facet of sovereignty stands out as its most static feature. States are still defined mainly by their spatial domains, and as such, each state continues to be recognized as having the right to secure its territorial boundaries through the use of border controls and military force. In addition, in contrast to each of the other aspects of sovereignty, no alternative organizing concept, or institution, has emerged to challenge its place in the international system. In other words, the territorial divide between states endures, and local differences within the system over territory remain pronounced. Nonetheless, three subtle, yet arguably systemic, shifts in how territorial sovereignty has been realized and substantiated have unfolded over the course of the post–World War II era (and picked up speed during the last three decades).

First, during this period, the way territorial boundaries were being secured changed as the system-wide level of violent conflict over such lines decreased. The most prominent component of this development was a decline in the percentage of territorial changes within the international system precipitated by violence. A 1992 survey of the Correlates of War (COW) dataset demonstrated that before World War II, military force played a role in approximately 33 percent of territorial changes; yet since then, only 16 percent of such shifts were preceded by armed conflict (Goertz and Diehl 1992: 51). Moreover, this trend of demilitarizing the transfer of territory was even more pronounced when states, or sovereign actors, were "on both sides" of exchanges (p. 43). Of the 160 instances of such "homeland transfers" during the period covered by the initial COW dataset, during the first half of the last century approximately 60 percent followed military conflict; in contrast, from 1950 through 1980 less than 30 percent were triggered by military conflict (p. 87). In addition, according to my own coding of the most recent update of the initial COW data, which covers the years 1981–2000, only 15 percent of the interstate homeland transfers that took place followed military conflict. While states continued to fight over territory, the extent to which land changed hands as a result of such conflicts dropped off quite steeply over the last few decades.

Second, during this period a tendency developed within the system toward the use of multilateral dispute mechanisms, most importantly the International Court of Justice (ICJ), to resolve outstanding boundary disputes and territorial conflicts. For example, during the first three decades of its existence (1946–75), the ICJ settled only a handful of such contentious cases (out of the total of just over forty brought before it during this period) involving borders (two maritime, two land). During the following twenty years (1976–95), over 30 percent of the court's expanded docket involved adjudicating the location of territorial boundaries, and since 1995 eight additional territorial cases (as of the end of 2003) ("International"; Prescott 1996). Moreover, as Beth Simmons recently observed, apart from such official cases, there is a host of instances where states "have seriously considered territorial arbitration, only to rule it out as a solution to territorial disputes," or have turned to one or another "quasi-judicial body" to resolve outstanding boundary claims (Simmons 2002: 830).

Alongside these behavioral shifts, a norm against the use of armed conflict for the purposes of territorial aggrandizement has arguably gained a foothold within the international system, and has been inscribed in a growing list of international legal agreements. This norm entailed a "growing respect for the proscription that force should not be used to alter interstate boundaries" (Zacher 2001: 215), and also encompassed a broad acceptance of the principle of *uti possidetis, ita possideatis* ("as you possess, so you may possess"), or respect for the status quo of established territorial boundaries. The former norm was articulated in the United Nations (UN) Charter's prohibition against the unprovoked use of military force by any member state against another's territory. The latter principle became the guiding tenet in a series of ICJ decisions on border disputes.

Jurisdictional Sovereignty

The second aspect of sovereignty is jurisdiction, each state's right to rule over the people residing within its boundaries and ensure that they remain an indivisible part of the polity. The central tenet of this component is that at the international level, people are divided into distinct groups defined by the spatial limits of individual sovereign states. Thus, both the territorial and jurisdictional facets of sovereignty involve the division of rights through the imposition of sovereign lines. However, territorial issues primarily involve how states determine the location of their shared borders. The object of such interaction is the division of a tangible material resource: land (or sea). In contrast, jurisdictional sovereignty involves the partition of a more intangible asset: population. In short, it consists of the relationship between any given state and the people residing within it, and the extent to which the state's reign over its people (not how it chooses to rule, but the very right to rule itself) is viewed as legitimate by both the domestic and international community.

As the difference between territorial and jurisdictional sovereignty is a subtle, yet crucial, element of my framework, it is worthwhile to briefly elaborate on the distinctions between the two. On the one hand, territorial sovereignty involves the boundaries of already existing states, something that at its core hinges on the demarcation of each state's spatial limits, and that is often intensely disputed. When territorial conflicts occur, jurisdictional questions may arise, but most such confrontations are over sparsely populated areas. On the other hand, jurisdictional sovereignty essentially involves how people are placed within an individual state's territory. This facet of sovereignty then revolves around the question of belonging and the principles that hold sovereign states together. Thus, where territorial sovereignty *sometimes* involves questions of national unity, jurisdictional sovereignty is always about this potentially explosive concern.

To clarify the distinction, consider for example the differences within China's stance on border relations (an issue of territorial sovereignty) and in its approach to Taiwan, Tibet, and Hong Kong (issues of jurisdictional claims). As Chapter 3 will show, the Chinese handling of the former largely hinges on reaching understandings via interactions between China and its neighbors over the location of specific stretches of territorial boundaries. In contrast, the jurisdictional dispute involving Taiwan, Tibet, and Hong Kong is primarily between Beijing and those claiming to represent the peoples residing in those territories.[6] What is at stake in Taiwan and Tibet, and to a lesser extent in Hong Kong, is the right to rule those regions, and this is a jurisdictional issue (albeit one rooted in competing conceptions of where the territorial boundary between China and the rest of the international system should be located).

As with territorial sovereignty, jurisdictional sovereignty's basic role in the current international system is quite durable. However, here too, new systemic trends have emerged that are reshaping where the lines it creates are being drawn and raising new questions about the meaning of such divisions. Specifically, two shifts have taken place.

First, over the last fifty years, the number of states recognized as possessing the right to jurisdictional sovereignty, and by extension the people affected by the distribution of such claims, grew dramatically. This occurred in two waves. The first began in the 1950s and reached its peak during the following decade. For example, when it was established in 1945, the United Nations had only fifty-one sovereign members, but by 1962 this number had more than doubled (to 110), a surge marked by the addition of sixteen states in 1955, and another seventeen in 1960 ("Growth"). This development made the sovereign state global in its reach. However, as this expansion came at the expense of the colonial system, it actually had little impact on the sovereign jurisdiction of already independent states (at least within their own boundaries). In contrast, the second wave of additions to the system came via the break-up of existing states (most significantly the Soviet Union) following the end of the Cold War. During the first four years of the last decade, the UN admitted over twenty new members, with a significant number of these being former republics of the Soviet Union.

Alongside the expansion of the right of jurisdictional sovereignty to new states and peoples, there was a second systemic shift. Roxanne Doty, in citing Anthony Smith's work on nationalism, captured the main aspects of this development when she noted that "in contemporary times, the assertion of sovereignty by a state involves implicit claims to represent an identifiable presence. While 'the people' have not always served as the foundation for state sovereignty, it is generally recognized that 'today no state possesses legitimacy that does not claim to represent the will of the nation'" (Doty 1996: 122). Doty implies this development had modified the scope of states' sovereign rights: jurisdiction was now tied to legitimate representation.

This abstract point is supported by the fact that over the course of the last century there was a trend toward grounding states' jurisdictional sovereignty in the principle of self-determination. The origins of this norm, which places states' jurisdictional rights in the hands of "the people," can be traced back to the early 1900s. However, the principle of self-determination did not mature until after World War II. During this period, the newly formed UN actively promoted the extension of the right to self-determination to colonized peoples as a means to further their struggles for independence and self-rule. Article I of the UN Charter directly endorsed the abstract idea of "self-determination of peoples." This notion was subsequently elaborated upon by the UN General Assembly in a pair of influential resolutions. The first, UN General Assembly Resolution 1514, adopted in 1960, emphasized that all peoples "have the right to self-determination; by virtue of that right they freely determine their political status and freely pursue economic and social development." However, it also quickly placed a restraint on this principle by noting that "any attempt aimed at the partial or total disruption of the national unity and the territorial integrity of a country is incompatible with the purposes and principles of the United Nations." In contrast, the second resolution, UN General Assembly Resolution 2625, passed in 1970, interpreted self-determination more expansively by reaffirming its legitimacy without directly referring to the struggle against colonialism.

In the post–Cold War period, the emphasis on preserving states' rights has been challenged by the popular acceptance of the idea that self-determination now means "every distinctive or national group has the right to independence" (Carley 1996: 4). This stage in the development of the norm has been marked by the rise of the still contested principle that "particular sections of the state's population, within a particular part of that state's territory, could unilaterally create an independent state of their own, which would then be recognized on the basis that self-determination has occurred" (Thomas Musgrave quoted in Kovacs 2003: 434).

Although such trends suggest that a radical reinterpretation of the balance between self-determination and jurisdictional sovereignty was well underway in the early 1990s, this development was ambiguous and contested. In short, what self-determination is, what rights it entails, and under what circumstances it should be applied in the international community, remain hotly contested issues. However, the combination of system-wide recognition of new states in accord with the norm (especially during the 1990s), and the forwarding of more extensive interpretations of this right in international law, have elevated its status within the international arena, and in the process further problematized jurisdictional sovereignty's status within the international system.

Sovereign Authority

Sovereign authority consists of the differentiation between each sovereign state's inside (domestic polity) and outside (the international system, community, or society). Accordingly, each state has the right to govern as it sees fit, and interference by any external entity in the internal affairs of a sovereign state is illegitimate. This doctrine extends the distinction between sovereign states beyond territorial lines and jurisdictional boundaries to the more abstract terrain of political authority. The focal point of such a right is that international recognition of a state as sovereign extends it a high degree of insularity in the way it administers and governs the spatial domain over which it rules. The nature of such authority is obviously dependent upon the lines drawn by territorial sovereignty, and in practice at times overlaps with jurisdictional issues; but its main referent is the state's exclusive right to rule, rather than its territorial reach or to whom its reign rightfully applies.

This facet of sovereignty was significantly affected by the rise of the international human rights system following World War II through the announcement of the Universal Declaration of Human Rights (UDHR). As with the two aspects of sovereignty already discussed, this development, which consisted of three broad trends, became especially pronounced in the early 1970s.

First, in the early 1970s there was a marked increase in the administrative reach of the international human rights regime. In the late 1960s the UN Charter–based and treaty-based aspects of this system began to play a more influential role in international politics. The growth in the former occurred through an expanded mandate for the UN Commission on Human Rights (UN CHR) to monitor and investigate human rights violations. The UN CHR began to assert this right in the late 1970s by issuing yearly reports on violations and subsequently establishing a web of country-specific and thematic mechanisms for tracking violations. By the end of the 1990s, over thirty such groups had been created (Sikkink and Schmitz 2002: 527). The parallel growth of the treaty-based system occurred via the writing of the International Covenants on Civil and Political Rights (ICCPR) and Economic, Social, and Cultural Rights

(ICESCR) in 1966. These keystone agreements were then complemented by four other major treaties: the Convention on Racial Discrimination, Convention on Women, Convention on Torture, and Convention on Children. Together, these treaties placed extensive reporting obligations on all participating states. As such, they "transformed many of the principles of the UDHR into binding treaties" (Doyle and Gardner 2003: 2).

As the human rights regime was becoming more substantial, a second trend also began to take shape: the formation of international nongovernmental organizations (INGOs) designed to monitor and report on human rights conditions in the international system. While there were few such INGOs in the early 1970s, there were over 300 by the end of the 1990s. At the same time, the membership and resources at their disposal also grew dramatically during this period. An example of the growing reach of these organizations is Amnesty International (AI), which was founded in 1961, but as of 1975 only had 70,000 members. By 1990 this number had mushroomed to 700,000, and exceeded one million in 1992 ("AI's"). On the financial side, Human Rights Watch, which was established in 1978, had an operating budget of over U.S.$17 million in 2001 ("Human Rights Watch").

As these developments unfolded, a broad set of human rights norms also began to take shape and gain acceptance within the international system. Although these norms are the subject of great debate, it is still possible to identify two of their central characteristics.[7] First, all individuals are entitled to the protection of the basic human rights set forth in the International Bill of Human Rights and other human rights treaties. Second, the international community has the right to oversee, or supervise, the human rights conditions within all states, and, in cases of grievous human rights violations, to intervene.

Although significant questions persist about the extent to which these norms and institutions have affected human rights conditions within any given state, their very existence challenges sovereign authority's core prohibition against foreign interference in a state's domestic domain. In contrast to this principle, the rise of the international human rights system implies that respect for, and adherence to, basic human rights standards at the very least "prescribe and proscribe" all states' activities, and may even constitute new terms for membership in the international community, without regard for the prerogatives that each state has conventionally enjoyed via the principle of non-intervention.[8] In other words, it raises questions about the location of the line between states' internal affairs and those of the international system.[9]

Economic Sovereignty

Economic sovereignty is the state's right to regulate economic activity within the boundaries specified by the territorial component of the norm. Mirroring the main features of each of the other aspects of sovereignty, this principle consists of the dual tenets that no state controls all economic activity within the system of sovereign states, and that once recognized as sovereign, a state is invested with permanent rights over its own economic system. In other words, it involves the system-wide allocation of authority to regulate economic affairs, not the degree to which individual economies are in practice insulated from one another, or the degree of actual control over economic flows between states.

The merits of isolating the economic facet of sovereignty in this way should be readily apparent when viewed against the backdrop of the preceding pages. First, although the division of economic rights is contingent on the spatial divides created by territorial sovereignty, a change in the distribution of economic rights in the international system does not necessarily have any direct effect on the location of such lines. Second, while it is possible to envision an intertwining of jurisdictional and economic issues,[10] it is also clear that economic sovereignty need not relate in any way to the jurisdictional node of rights. Finally, although there is some conceptual overlap between the economic and authority facets of the norm, their functional, or practical, differences are still quite pronounced. Whereas the former revolves around the distribution of political rights in the contemporary international system, the latter encompasses the conceptually and empirically distinct sphere of economic rights. Thus, the issue at stake here has less to do with the type of interdependence briefly touched upon in Krasner's influential four-fold categorization of sovereignty, and more to do with the distinction between the internal and international (or external) within the economic realm. Moreover, although such a line has never been particularly well defined, and is never likely to entirely disappear, over the past fifty years, but especially since the early 1970s, it has become increasingly indistinct via the mutually reinforcing consolidation of two new systemic trends.

To begin with, the three main multilateral economic institutions (the IMF [International Monetary Fund], World Bank, and GATT/WTO) created during this period have established a pervasive, and since the early 1970s, increasingly intrusive presence within the international system. For example, it was at this juncture that the IMF began to place extensive conditionality measures upon states that turned to it for loans to resolve outstanding debts. At roughly the same time, the World Bank started to broaden its mandate by instituting loan programs to member states, designed to "achieve both a long-term macroeconomic stabilization and structural transformation of [their] econom[ies] by addressing the fundamental causes of [their] economic cris[es]" (Tsai 2000:

1321). Finally, during this period the GATT/WTO developed sweeping authority to monitor and influence trade relations between its member states. Moreover, this authority has rapidly expanded over the last two decades. For example, prior to the Tokyo Round negotiations in the 1970s, GATT rules were largely limited to an attempt to lower tariff-related barriers to international trade, meaning that the organization's oversight largely stopped at the border of each state's domestic economy. However, during the 1980s and 1990s, the GATT's mandate spread to include a host of what had previously been understood as internal political issues, including technical standards and non-tariff measures. This process culminated in the 1995 establishment of the WTO, which expanded both the content of the multilateral trading regime and its ability to enforce its new mandate.

Alongside these institutional structures, a broad set of ideas also began to take shape about the international economy and each state's place within it. Although the link between the main multilateral economic organizations and such norms is even more tenuous than is the case within the international human rights system, and even more contentious, it is still possible to identify three central aspects of these ideas. First, the process of "the widening, deepening and speeding up of global interconnectedness" is a powerful, even dominant, feature of the contemporary international economic system.[11] Second, in a general sense, the health and success of any state's economy is dependent on accepting the reality of such a trend, and strategically integrating the national economy into a changing system. Finally, the main multilateral economic institutions play a key role in monitoring the exchanges within the new international economy and have the right to regulate various aspects of each of their member states' economic activities.

Obviously, ideas about the preeminence of international forces in determining economic outcomes within sovereign states date back to earlier debates about the relationship between politics and markets. In addition, the post–World War II international economic organizations were preceded by earlier structures designed to regulate economic flows between sovereign states. In this sense, there is little "new" in the way these institutions and ideas challenge sovereignty's role in international politics. However, it is also clear that the growing influence of these institutions (especially the GATT/WTO) over the last few decades, paired with the consolidation of interdependence and globalization norms, has created new points of ambiguity in the line between internal and external affairs in the contemporary international economic system. On the one hand, the norm of economic sovereignty dictates that each state has the right to regulate and govern economic activity within its own territory. In contrast, these trends raise questions about such a division and force elites within sovereign states to reconsider the location of authority over economic affairs and the distribution of rights and obligations within the contemporary international system. As a result, economic sovereignty has not been lost, but the line it imposes around each state's economic activity has become increasingly indistinct.[12]

Conclusion

Although sovereignty's role as the structural lynchpin of the contemporary international system remains largely unthreatened, in the late 1960s a series of trends began to gather momentum in ways that challenged, or at the very least raised new questions about, the impermeability of the boundaries between states established by each facet of the norm. This shift was not revolutionary, but it was substantive. In other words, it did not fulfill the expectations of those who, early in the 1990s, had predicted the "end of sovereignty," but it exceeded the claims of those who initially sought to belittle such prophecies of change. In short, during the last few decades the terrain upon which the architecture of sovereignty was being constructed shifted in meaningful and significant ways.

2

Locating and Explaining State Approaches: Defining Sovereignty after Recognition and Turning to the China Case

All states have been left with the task of determining the current and future relationship between established sovereignty norms and the recent trends within international politics that appear to challenge limited aspects of sovereignty's established role (outlined in Chapter 1). In determining the balance between "old" and "new," the behavior of individual states then either tends to reinforce the former or add strength to the latter. In other words, it is out of the intersection between systemic trends and individual state behavior that sovereignty's role in international politics is defined. Thus, it is imperative to identify just what states do to secure specific interpretations of their sovereign rights.

In considering such activity, students of international relations have generally emphasized recognition, or the process by which a political entity gains acceptance as a sovereign state by the international community.[1] This focus has shed new light on the historically varied list of attributes that have been considered essential for attaining the status of sovereign statehood. However, it has also left aside the issue of how each sovereign state then attempts to define its sovereignty *after* attaining membership in the international club of similar political actors. In light of the fact that with the demise of colonialism virtually the entire world became divided into sovereign states, most of which have shown a striking ability to maintain their sovereign status, the way in which they accomplish this goal would seem to merit closer scrutiny. Furthermore, for the purposes of this book, it is precisely this aspect of what states do vis-à-vis sovereignty that is of interest, as I am focusing on the Chinese approach to sovereignty after the PRC gained nearly universal recognition as an independent, sovereign entity—rather than on the earlier era in which many states, led by the

United States, refused to recognize the PRC's sovereignty over China.[2]

In short, another major shortcoming in the "new sovereignty" debate is its failure to examine how states' post-recognition actions construct particular interpretations of the norm. In seeking to rectify this weakness, I first accept the claim made by Biersteker and Weber (1996) that sovereignty's role in the contemporary international system is given specific meaning through the practices of states.[3] However, moving beyond their work, the first section of this chapter identifies the specific type of sovereignty-related actions states take, categorizes the way such moves vary, and outlines the competing explanations for states' sovereignty-related behavior that have been forwarded within recent international relations theory. The second section uses this framework to establish the significance of, and the conceptual and empirical foundations for, the book's focus, the Chinese approach to sovereignty.

How and Why States Construct Sovereign Boundaries

Simply noting that states articulate particular interpretations of sovereignty through their actions is tantamount to stating that sovereignty plays a foundational role in the contemporary international system; it is vague, and tells us little about what such practices actually are. Thus, for the same reasons that it was crucial to disaggregate the individual facets of sovereignty's structural role in international politics, so too it is vital to identify the most prominent conduits through which unit-level interpretations of the norm are forwarded within the international arena.

State Practices: Sovereignty Constructing Words and Actions

There are three main practices that the representatives of all states use to give substance to each facet of sovereignty's meaning. First, government officials substantiate sovereignty in their official public statements that refer to the right. The claims to sovereignty they make can be enunciated in everything from the speeches of top leaders, to comments by state department or foreign ministry spokespeople, to other official pronouncements. Such rhetoric entails assertions about what sovereignty's general role in international politics is, or should be, and explanations of why such a vision is correct. In addition, statements may concentrate on singular aspects of sovereignty and include references to the related principles, norms, and trends discussed in Chapter 1. In all cases, the intent of such statements is to form a bridge between the general structural facets of sovereignty and the way they are interpreted at a specific juncture within the international arena.

Such official claims map out sovereignty's formal parameters, but they are not the sole discursive effort undertaken within each sovereign state to obtain a specific interpretation of the norm. In addition to telling other states what sovereignty means, foreign policy elites in each state also talk to each other about how they understand the norm, what they see as its most salient aspects, and how they envision its role in the international system. Such discussions constitute a second type of sovereignty-constructing practice, mainly elite analysis of the norm. These discourses are generally less couched within the protocols of diplomatic exchanges, less driven by specific policy concerns, and, as a result, more expansive than official statements on sovereignty. It is through this practice that elites delve in much greater detail into the distinct components of sovereignty. In this way, elite analysis both supplements and informs official commentary on the norm.

Nonetheless, it is important to acknowledge two significant ambiguities related to this particular sovereignty-related practice. First, defining what constitutes "elite analysis" in any state is somewhat subjective, as the line between official and unofficial commentary can be fine, and the distinction between "elite" and "popular" views difficult to justify. However, it is still possible to identify the general sources of this particular type of discourse. It is found in editorials in influential publications, articles in foreign policy and international relations journals, discussions in academic conferences and meetings, and informal statements by members of the foreign policy and national security elite. Second, in considering such discursive efforts, I do not mean to imply that all work on sovereignty and related issues done within the boundaries of a given state represents that state's position on sovereignty; rather, my intention is to highlight that the general outline of how such research is approached will tend to reflect the most prominent concerns over the role of sovereignty within the state in which it is produced.

Although both official claims and elite analysis are discursive measures, sovereignty is not only constructed by words, it is also made through actions. Indeed, it is the broader national security and foreign policy behavior of states that lends substance to what their representatives say about sovereignty. In a narrow sense, such policies consist of the making of international legal commitments, a record of which can be found in the treaties that any given state has ratified. Thus, we can consider a state's membership in particular international organizations, its voting record in such forums, or its participation in specific multilateral treaties (and if "in," what reservations it has recorded about accession). Beyond such formal commitments, sovereignty-related behavior is also expressed in each state's record of compliance with such commitments. More broadly, it is embodied in the universe of policies states enact vis-à-vis the issues of border relations, governance (particularly in regard to the inclusion of minorities, the degree of autonomy granted to groups residing within the state, and individual rights), and regulation of economic activity.

Sovereign Variation: Boundary Reinforcement and Transgression

Identifying the centrality of such practices in the construction of sovereignty emphasizes the everyday processes by which states engage each other (and govern within their own boundaries) to establish and stabilize specific interpretations of their sovereign rights. It also raises the question of what standard should be used for gauging change in any given state's sovereignty-constructing words and actions.

The most fundamental metric for measuring change in a single state's stance on sovereignty can be conceptualized in terms of the degree to which its practices reinforce or transgress the sovereign boundaries that form the core of each component of the norm. A boundary-reinforcing position contributes to the construction of a division between internal and external affairs by emphasizing the inviolability of sovereign rights. In contrast, a boundary-transgressing policy promotes, or at least accepts, the blurring of the lines between each state's territory, people, authority, and economy. In other words, it is possible for states to substantiate interpretations of sovereignty that are absolute and unyielding, or forward acknowledgments of the possibility that sovereignty is a more malleable structure, one that can be limited, surpassed, displaced, or even erased by other factors in international politics and economics.

The distinction between these two stances is articulated via the sovereignty-constructing practices at each state's disposal. Official claims advance interpretations of sovereignty that either buttress or dilute the divisions created by each type of sovereign boundary. For example, the representatives of a state may proclaim that sending UN aid to Rwanda constitutes a humanitarian effort (boundary-transgressing), or condemn such aid as interfering in Rwanda's internal affairs (boundary-reinforcing). A state may call for international involvement in the settlement of Russia's Chechnya issue (boundary-transgressing), or contend that such a problem is Russia's internal affair (boundary-reinforcing). A state may agree to accept UN inspection crews working to verify its compliance with international agreements (boundary-transgressing), or denounce such inspections as trampling upon state sovereignty (boundary-reinforcing). A state may support conditionality for an IMF bailout of its economy (boundary-transgressing), or refuse to cooperate with the IMF on the grounds that decisions about the structure of its domestic economy should lie solely within the hands of the state's leadership (boundary-reinforcing).

Elite analysis can be categorized along very similar lines. However, due to its generally more extensive nature, it tends to address more directly the issue of sovereign change than is the case in official discourse. On one hand, analysis may describe sovereignty as an absolute right that grants the state the highest power in a given territory, asserting that such a right is a constant and unchanging aspect of international relations. On the other hand, analysis may be marked by a more flexible interpretation of the norm, one that accepts the possibility that the division between internal and external affairs may be undermined by the development of economic and political integration. The former type of analysis treats sovereignty as an essential and unbending principle of international politics. The latter explicitly, or at the very least, implicitly, accepts the possibility of sovereign change.

It is a bit more challenging to gauge the extent specific policy measures change a state's stance on sovereignty. For example, although international legal commitments can be tabulated through a review of the bilateral and multilateral agreements that a state signs, identifying the extent such treaties reinforce or transgress sovereign boundaries is more problematic; nonetheless, a close examination of such documents can still uncover substantial distinctions. On the one hand, many agreements secure sovereign boundaries. A border treaty may delineate the specific location of a previously contested territorial boundary. A UN General Assembly resolution may consolidate the rights each sovereign state has over its "people." A bilateral agreement between two states may formalize their commitment to the principle of non-interference. An economic treaty might stipulate limitations on the flow of goods, services, or capital across a state's sovereign boundaries. On the other hand, some international legal documents transgress the line between sovereign states. On one level, agreements may simply raise abstract questions about the sanctity of the prohibition against interference in each state's internal affairs by placing a particular policy issue under broad international oversight. On another level, other treaties require the submission of reports and inspections of specific aspects relating to each signatory state's domestic situation, or contain strict verification procedures and on-site investigations.

Categorizing states' more general sovereignty-related policies along these lines is even more daunting, but can also be accomplished by isolating the degree to which such actions tend to highlight and sanctify the lines that mark a state's spatial domain or de-emphasize, erode, and de-center such boundaries. The former type of action is epitomized by, but not limited to, specific acts that build up sovereign boundaries through the construction of actual physical barriers to movement across such lines, the implementation of security and surveillance mechanisms designed to police them, the consolidation of authority and control over peripheral regions and marginal peoples, and the erection of constraints on transnational economic, political, and social activity. The latter type of practice is once again best understood as a process of delegitimizing sover-eign-centric claims to power and authority. Such policies may dilute territorial distinctions, undermine or hollow out the scope and extent of states' sovereign rule through recognizing other non-territorially defined sites of authority and political organization, or cede regulative capacity to institutions outside of the state's reach.

Explaining Change: Interest-Based and Ideational Arguments

Articulating general guidelines for coding sovereignty-related practices establishes a set of standards for measuring variation in any individual state's approach to sovereignty. It also raises the obvious question of why variation in a state's sovereignty-related practices does (or does not) occur. Although they have not framed their analysis in terms of such practices, contributors to the "new sovereignty" debate have forwarded competing explanations for such behavior. Generally, they are divided over the extent to which variation in sov-ereignty is attributed to changes in how elites rationally calculate their interests vis-à-vis new material pressures and institutional frameworks, and over the degree to which the broader ideational context within which decisions are made, and state identities are shaped, are seen as playing an important role in this process.

Rationalist explanations posit that any observed variation in sovereignty is primarily the product of measurable shifts in the manner leaders of sovereign states attempt to realize fairly static interests. In other words, sovereignty is best seen as an institution, one whose malleability is, as is the case with similar con-structs, contingent upon the costs and benefits that accrue to those agents who participate in its development, evolution, and maintenance. Thus, when the leaders of states (especially those with the ability to influence the behavior of other actors) are confronted with clearly defined material incentives for chang-ing sovereignty's role in international politics (or, for that matter, maintaining such a position), they will act accordingly. Moreover, recent changes in the costs and benefits structure within the international arena have resulted in the emer-gence of new pressures on states that have led to a limited re-articulation of such a role.

This type of argument was given its clearest voice in the distinct, yet, at least in terms of explaining sovereign change, complementary work of Stephen Krasner and Robert Keohane. Krasner has argued that power and interests fre-quently override, if not rewrite, sovereignty's role in international politics. He claimed that sovereignty established rules or norms regarding "appropriate" behavior in the international arena, but concluded that such guidelines were frequently trumped by a "logic of consequences" that pushed leaders to either violate various components of other's sovereignty, or compromise on certain aspects of their own (Krasner 1999: 6–7). The mechanisms or modalities through which sovereignty is violated may vary, but the underlying causes of such encroachments have remained fairly consistent. Leaders use sovereignty when it suits their larger interests, and disregard it when such interests change due to new incentives (an opportunity to benefit from participation in an international convention or contract) or lack of choice (as the subject of international coercion or imposition).

Keohane's analysis pays less attention to power politics, but similarly emphasizes interest calculations and their impact on how states articulate their position on sovereignty. He develops this argument by identifying what he sees as the distinction between sovereignty's "formal" and "operational" role in international politics. For Keohane, the latter of these two facets of the norm could be limited and constrained, especially under the conditions of complex interdependence (Keohane 1993: 91). The cause of flexibility was the increasingly dense body of international institutions and agreements in the contemporary international system, especially in the "zone of peace" in western Europe.[4] Within their framework, "Sovereignty is less a territorially defined barrier than a bargaining resource for a politics characterized by complex transnational networks" (Keohane 1995: 177). In short, in such a context, states may be willing to "pool" their sovereignty (Keohane 2002: 748).[5]

In contrast to these two variants of the rationalist thesis about sovereign change, a diverse group of scholars has maintained that sovereignty creates distinct state identities in the international system, and changes in its role are intimately tied to the ideational forces that make basic distinctions between states meaningful. More specifically, as a result of the increasing salience of new boundary-transgressing normative structures and transnational identity constructs, sovereignty's established role is being redefined and reshaped within the current international arena. This claim has been forwarded in two parallel, yet conceptually distinct, arguments that emerged out of the broader international relations theory literature.

The radical strand of the ideational argument was articulated by a handful of theorists sharply critical of what they saw as the limitations inherent in positivist explanations of sovereignty. In their accounts, sovereignty is a powerful political discourse that disciplines (and is in turn sustained by) the divisions it creates between self and other. Shifts in the meaning of this divide are then attributed to the consolidation of alternative discursive practices that displace, erode, and challenge the dichotomy it creates between domestic and international politics (Ashley 1988; Campbell 1992; Walker 1993).

Other scholars have articulated an explanation of the evolution of sovereignty's role in international politics that also highlights the importance of ideas, but does so within the framework of more conventional, positivist sensibilities. This variant of the ideational argument hinges on the claim that sovereignty's foundational role in international politics was created and sustained through processes of social interaction between the actors (states) within the system (even as the structure of the system shaped both their interests and identities). John Ruggie, an early proponent of this proposition, argued that the bundle of rights historically granted to states by their sovereign status had varied with shifting material conditions, the matrix of social interaction, and social epistemes themselves (Ruggie 1993: 169). Moreover, "the domain of social epistemes, the mental equipment by means of which people re-imagined their collective existence, played a critical role." Furthermore, Ruggie noted that such forces appeared to once again be in flux today, thus increasing the probability of a commensurate shift in the way international politics is organized (p. 171).

A similar argument features prominently in the work of Alexander Wendt. In his influential 1992 article on anarchy, Wendt claimed that sovereignty existed "only in virtue of certain intersubjective understandings and expectations," and was contingent on the ongoing practices of the political entities that it constituted and that tend to have a "vested interest in reproducing it" (Wendt 1992: 412–13). As he later noted, states maintain sovereignty's conventional role in the Lockean anarchic culture of the contemporary international system, not simply out of concern about external coercion, or even consistent calculations of rational interests, but rather because of shared normative values with which they identify (Wendt 1999: 289).

In underscoring sovereignty's continuity within the international system, Wendt did not intend to preclude consideration of sovereign change. Indeed, it was an interest in the prospect of such change and its structural implications that motivated much of his, and other constructivists', analysis of the norm. Not surprisingly, Wendt attributed change mainly to the emergence of new norms within the contemporary international system. For example, he concluded that sovereign change might be produced by "growing 'dynamic density' of interaction among states in a world of new communications technology, nuclear weapons, other externalities, and so on" (Wendt 1992: 416). But he argued that this dynamic was rooted in the deeper process of learning new social norms (p. 417). In 1996 he, along with Daniel Friedheim, elaborated on this claim by focusing on the informal empire that the Soviet Union established in East Germany during the Cold War and noting, "sovereignty is not the only principle constituting state actors" (Wendt and Friedheim 1996: 248). Wendt and Friedheim contended that while the hierarchical relationship between the Soviet Union and East Germany was integrally linked to the unequal power

distribution between the two states, "shared beliefs" between elites on both sides
of this relationship played a foundational role in transforming the meaning of
sovereignty in their dealings with each other.

In outlining the differences between ideational arguments and rationalist
accounts of sovereignty, I do not mean to overstate the extent to which contributors to each side of this debate have forwarded mutually exclusive explanations of sovereign change. Indeed, as I have shown, the scholars who have
articulated rationalist explanations of sovereignty have acknowledged the
importance of ideas and norms, and postmodernists and constructivists have
made similar concessions in regard to the role of interests and material power.
However, the varying emphasis on one or the other set of factors is quite pronounced and constitutes a clear divide between the two camps. In short, rationalists maintain that sovereignty's relatively constant position in international
politics is largely because of the status quo interests that are served by such continuity. Change will only occur when its material benefits outweigh its costs.
The ideational argument counters that sovereign boundaries are maintained
largely because of the central role they play in framing how "we" define our-
selves. Yet, since sovereignty is largely an empty vessel (it is meaningful only with
reference to related legitimatizing principles), and dominant understandings of
what ideational substance has filled such a container have historically varied, so
too has sovereignty's role in international politics (Reus-Smit 2001: 520).

The China Case

Determining the relative strength of these competing causal claims (and the
degree to which sovereign change is taking place across the international system itself) can only be accomplished with reference to the words states use and
the actions they take to interpret sovereignty's place within their foreign relations. Yet, to date there has been very little consideration of such behavior within the "new sovereignty" debate. Indeed, the absence of such empirical studies
constitutes yet another major failing of this literature. Fully rectifying this weakness would entail a system-wide survey of state practices; the scope of such a
task extends well beyond this book. However, short of such a global study,
insight may be gained into both the extent of change and its causes through
focusing on particularly crucial cases in the contemporary international system.
This section discusses first why China is such a critical case and highlights the
merits of reexamining the Chinese stance on sovereignty for students of
Chinese foreign policy and national security making. It then outlines how the
conceptual framework developed in the preceding section was utilized to guide
analysis of the Chinese position on sovereignty. It also explains the rationale
behind the selection of specific issue areas for this study, and develops sketches

of the main features of China's stance on each aspect of sovereignty through the mid-1970s.

Why China? The Value of Studying the Chinese Approach to Sovereignty

The limited existing literature on the Chinese approach to sovereignty suggests several reasons why China is a particularly crucial case in determining the scope of, and causes for, changes in sovereignty's role in international politics. At the same time, a close review of the shortcomings of the literature also reveals the need for a theoretically sophisticated, and empirically grounded, reexamination of the Chinese stance. Thus, as mentioned in the Introduction, new research on China's position on sovereignty promises to address crucial issues of debate in international studies and the field of Chinese studies.

The Relevance of China to the "New Sovereignty" Debate

The importance of the Chinese case for the "new sovereignty" debate begins with the fact that China is a major player within the contemporary international arena. Its sheer size, its emergence as an influential global economic force, the enigmatic power of its modernizing military, its status as a nuclear weapons state, and its permanent seat in the UN Security Council all make it a crucial case for any survey of emerging trends in the international system. In the aftermath of the demise of the Soviet Union there is no other state, with the exception of the United States, that has an equivalent voice on such a broad array of crucial issues. Thus, regardless of whether or not the Chinese economy continues to grow, or China becomes a more status quo or revisionist power, its influence in international politics will still be felt, and must be taken into consideration by anyone with an interest in how the system evolves.[6] Yet, surprisingly, China's position on sovereignty has been largely absent from all of the major theoretical and empirical studies of the norm.[7]

Beyond this foundational issue, students of Chinese foreign policy and national security have offered three observations about China's approach to sovereignty that speak directly to each of the main points of contestation within the "new sovereignty" debate, thus underlining the significance of the Chinese case. First is the claim that China's position on sovereignty has been relatively static and unyielding since the founding of the People's Republic of China (PRC). This claim was a hallmark of the few studies of the issue by China scholars in the 1970s (Cohen 1973; Kim 1979: 465; Ogden 1977: 335). More recently, it has become so widely accepted that it passes for conventional wisdom in the field of China studies. However, it contradicts the emerging consensus among students of international politics that sovereignty's general role in the international system is variable, and more pointedly has shifted in significant ways over the course of the post–World War II era. Such generalizations thus raise a pair of questions. Have the China experts overstated the consistency of the Chinese position? Or have the international relations theorists overestimated the extent to which sovereign change is taking place in international politics? Determining the extent of this discrepancy therefore stands to contribute to ongoing efforts within the "new sovereignty" debate to identify just how much the norm's role is, or is not, changing.

Second, China experts have argued that while Chinese leaders and policy makers use sovereignty in a utilitarian fashion, they also view it as having an inherent, almost self-referential value. Analysts of Chinese foreign policy frequently posit that this attachment was created by the collective memory of historical transgressions against China during the "century of humiliation" that lasted from the first Opium War through the establishment of the PRC. For example, in one of the most comprehensive treatments of the Chinese position written in the 1970s, Suzanne Ogden (1977: 335–56) stressed the blending of historical factors and self-interested considerations in determining Chinese behavior. In addition, in his sweeping study of China's early involvement with the UN, Samuel Kim argued that the Chinese emphasis on sovereignty during its exclusion from the UN was in large part influenced by China's "historical grievances" against the West and Japan, and reflected "a measure of the immense weight" of such memories. But, at the same time, sovereignty was useful as a "legal shield" for China. As such, the ongoing support for a static interpretation of sovereignty in China was both "self-serving and self-limiting" (Kim 1979: 414–15). A similar refrain was prominent in commentary on China written in the 1990s (Jian 1996: 39; Yuan 1998a: 295). This aspect of sovereignty has been largely overlooked by both rationalist and ideationalist arguments within the "new sovereignty" debate. The possibility that it plays an important role in China's stance on the norm raises questions about the emphasis on interests in rationalist arguments about sovereignty and the social learning that is central to ideational explanations of sovereign change.

Third, cutting against the grain of conventional wisdom in China-watching circles about the continuities in the Chinese position, a handful of analysts have argued that, despite the constraint of history, the Chinese position on sovereignty has actually shifted over the course of the last twenty years. However, these scholars have also made contrasting explanations for such a development. For example, Ren Yue (1996), a professor in Hong Kong's Lingnan University, in a short piece on the widening gap between the principle and practice of Chinese sovereignty and the emergence of greater flexibility on some sovereignty-related issues, argued that this trend was largely contingent on the rational calculation of interests by Chinese elites. While Samuel Kim did not discount the influence of such pragmatic calculations, his most recent work on sovereignty placed even greater emphasis on two additional factors: first, as Chinese interests changed during the 1980s and 1990s due to "growing involvement with and dependence upon the capitalist world system," sovereignty increasingly took a back seat to other concerns (Kim 1991: 17); and second, as sovereignty's role in the international arena was rapidly being transformed by a host of functional and normative forces, the Chinese attachment to an unyielding interpretation of sovereignty was increasingly challenged by potentially transformative international trends (Kim 1994a, 1994b). Kim noted that although "state sovereignty is the most basic and deeply internalized principle of Chinese foreign policy," it is also in tension with "competing international norms that may place contradictory constraints and pressures on state behavior" (Kim 1998: 21). Ann Kent (1999), utilizing the spiral model of norms diffusion (Risse and Sikkink 1999) to guide her research, published a comprehensive survey of China's involvement in the international human rights system that argued that changes in the Chinese position on sovereignty during the 1980s and 1990s were the result of adaptations by the Chinese leadership to shifting domestic and international pressure, forces that represented the initial stages of the diffusion of new norms in the Chinese foreign policy community. However, Kent concluded that the internalization of such transformative norms was quite limited. More recently, Chih-yu Shih (2003), a professor at Taiwan University, expanding on his earlier work on the role of identity in Chinese foreign policy making, argued that the evolving Chinese approach to sovereignty has grown out of the shifting intersection between Confucian culture, modernist discourses on politics, and the pressures of globalizing/transnational discursive practices.

In all, the work of these four scholars suggests that China has been exposed to the full set of variables emphasized by the competing explanations of sovereign continuity and change developed in the "new sovereignty" debate. At the same time, their work shows there is little consensus among China experts on the causes of Chinese sovereignty-related behavior. This lack of consensus constitutes the final compelling reason for treating China as a crucial case.

The Value of a Reconsideration of the Chinese Approach for China Studies

The potential benefits of analyzing the Chinese position on sovereignty are not limited to testing the claims made within the "new sovereignty" debate. Significant new insights into Chinese foreign policy and national security making can also be gained from a new study of China's sovereignty-related behavior. These begin with clarifying sovereignty's role in China's foreign relations and extend to broader issues relating to its evolving relationship with the rest of the international system.

Reexamining the Chinese stance in the context of the "new sovereignty" debate will address three endemic weaknesses of the existing literature on Chinese sovereignty. First, the work gives little consideration to the more sophisticated conceptual distinctions that international relations theorists placed at the center of discussions about sovereignty during the 1990s. Consequently, it is extremely difficult to determine what various analysts of Chinese foreign policy are referring to when they use the term "sovereignty." Second, the literature relies on scattered citations of selected statements by Chinese leaders and references to China's apparent reluctance to participate in certain international organizations. Thus, even if one overlooks the pervasive conceptual confusion in the literature, the absence of empirical evidence still precludes an objective evaluation of the validity of the arguments being made. Finally, the literature does not explore the tensions and ambiguity in the Chinese stance.

In short, the literature on Chinese sovereignty lacks the conceptual refinement to capture each aspect of the Chinese stance, is weakly argued, and makes only limited use of the available empirical data on Chinese practices. Thus it leaves unanswered a number of questions about the Chinese position on sovereignty. Is it possible to identify a single Chinese position on sovereignty? Had the Chinese approach to sovereignty shifted in a significant way during the reform era? To the extent that China had maintained an unvarying stance, what factors contributed to this? Was continuity primarily a product of historical influences, or was it more the result of the usefulness of a conventional interpretation of sovereignty for PRC leaders? If change had taken place, how extensive was it, was it simply instrumental, or did it reflect deeper normative changes in the Chinese worldview?

The answers to these questions obviously speak to broader debates about the nature of China's integration with the international political and economic community over the last twenty years. Gauging the extent of change in the Chinese position will provide a crucial yardstick for measuring how far China has been integrated into the international system during this period. In addition, new research that locates the causes of Chinese sovereignty-related behavior will speak to the issue of the extent to which China is being "socialized" into the international community through adaptation and learning.[8] More broadly, by placing the sovereignty issue at its core, such research will shed light on how and why new interpretations have emerged (and are being contested) in China about the location of the boundaries between the PRC and the rest of the international system.

Applying the Research Framework to China and
Chinese Behavior Through the Start of the
Reform Era

My study of the evolution of the Chinese position on sovereignty over the course of the last twenty years involved two initial steps. First, the foreign policy and national security issue areas in China most directly related to each of the four components of the norm had to be selected. Second, the main characteristics of Chinese practices in each of these issue areas during the first three decades following the establishment of the PRC had to be identified in order to establish clear benchmarks against which to compare subsequent practices.

Territorial Sovereignty: Expansive Claims, Contested Boundaries

The literature on sovereignty identifies the process of boundary formation, delimitation, and defense as one of the key facets in each state's attempts to define sovereignty's role in international politics. China possesses expansive continental boundaries and vast maritime borders. Therefore, it was natural to select China's approach to border relations as the issue area to examine in order to locate the Chinese stance on territorial sovereignty. However, the sheer length and diversity of China's territorial boundaries makes it difficult to thoroughly survey all facets of its handling of boundary-related issues. Therefore, the initial question of case selection I faced was which subset of border relations merited attention (and which could be left aside).

Most scholars have resolved this question by focusing on specific episodes of territorial conflict, or on the evolution of particular bilateral border relations. While this has resulted in detailed descriptions and analyses of individual aspects of Chinese behavior, it has not led to a comprehensive survey of China's overall stance on territorial sovereignty. To move beyond this limitation, but avoid the danger of attempting to cover too much ground, I used two specific criteria for developing a broad, yet manageable, perspective on the Chinese position. First, since China's borders reach across land and sea, I determined that it was essential to study both maritime and continental boundaries. Second, although China shares boundaries with a host of countries, it has only a handful of neighbors capable of matching its ability to defend its boundaries. Asymmetries exist even in these relations, but they are distinct from, and more central to, the Chinese approach to territory than is the case with China's relations with its weaker neighbors. Thus, I chose to focus on these major border dyads. More specifically, in examining China's land boundaries, I selected the segments of the border between China and the Soviet Union (now Russia, Tajikistan, Kyrgyzstan, and Kazakhstan), India, and Vietnam.[9] Looking at China's sea boundary, I focused on the maritime border between China and Vietnam (in both the Beibu Gulf and South China Sea).[10] To complement these country-specific studies, I also considered how China handled territorial issues within relevant regional multilateral forums.

Through the late 1970s, China's approach to these lines was defined by recurring tensions, armed skirmishes, and threats of even more extensive confrontation. While Beijing was able to employ diplomacy soon after the founding of the PRC to secure the location of most of the boundaries China shared with its smaller neighbors, the defining feature of China's border relations with the Soviet Union, India, and Vietnam was the pairing of a readiness to use military force and combative rhetoric. Thus, at the start of the reform era, China was embroiled in long-standing military standoffs over territorial issues with each of its main neighbors, and in each of the cases considered in this book, segments of the border had been the site of fighting.

The earliest of these flare-ups occurred in 1962 when China and India engaged in a short but violent war over the location of each of the three sections of the border (the western and central segments played a peripheral role in the conflict; the eastern one was, and still is, at its core).[11] Much of the secondary literature suggests India precipitated this conflict, but at its height China threatened to move military forces well into territory that had been controlled by India prior to the hostilities. However, Beijing then withdrew its troops to a point twenty miles north of the 1959 line of actual control (LAC) in all three sections of the border (Lu 1986; Whiting 1975). Even before the 1962 border war with India, China articulated a position on the territorial issues at stake in this region. For example, a 1960 Chinese Foreign Ministry statement argued that "the two countries have never formally delimited this boundary," and that the dispute between the two was over claims to 90,000 square kilometers of territory in the eastern, 33,000 in the western, and 2,000 in the central sectors (*Documents* 1960). This stance was the basis for Chinese claims in the border region through the start of the reform era.

Seven years after the Sino-Indian border war the Sino-Soviet boundary was the site of conflict when Zhenbao Island, in the Wusuli (Ussuri) River segment of the border, became the focal point of military clashes between the two powers. In this case it appears that China initiated combat, even though it subsequently moved to prevent the spread of war (Segal 1985). Although the conflict was indeed contained, during the 1970s additional high-profile incidents of military incursions by both the Chinese and Soviets took place in both the western and eastern sectors of the border.

The territory in question in this dispute is vast. This was made apparent by an official statement issued by the Chinese Foreign Ministry against the back-

drop of the 1969 conflict, which contended that China had lost over one million square kilometers of territory through the unequal treaties Russia imposed
upon the Qing dynasty from 1840 to 1881. Although China did not demand the
return of these lands, it did object to what it considered as Soviet violations of
these agreements, and did call for a return of territories that had been transferred through later Soviet encroachments (Cohen and Chiu 1974: 452–62).

Alongside these conflicts, tensions along the Sino-Vietnamese border escalated in the 1970s in unison with the deterioration of diplomatic relations
between China and its neighbor to the south. Sino-Vietnamese differences over
the land boundary were quite limited, but those over oceanic territory were
more extensive and coalesced around a dispute over the location of the border
in the Beibu (Tonkin) Gulf and ownership of two pairs of island chains in the
South China Sea. As for the former maritime region, the PRC stated that the
boundary had never been delineated, and suggested that it was willing to negotiate an agreement with the Vietnamese (Austin 1998). These differences did not
result in armed combat, but in 1974 the Xisha (Paracel) Islands, located in the
northwestern part of the South China Sea, were the site of conflict between
China and the Republic of Vietnam (South Vietnam). Paralleling such developments, the Nansha (Spratly) Island chain in the southern edge of the South
China Sea was the destination of survey, reconnaissance, and military teams during the 1970s, and an armed skirmish between the two sides took place in 1976
(although this flare-up was quite circumscribed in comparison to the contemporary clash in the Xisha region).

China had initially laid claim to both sets of islands soon after the establishment of the PRC, and again asserted its rights to the islands (and surrounding
ocean) in a 1958 declaration (Austin 1998: 44–54). Beijing subsequently developed this position in the 1970s in its stance on the UN's evolving system for
administering the world's oceans and through condemnations of perceived
Vietnamese aggression against China.

In each of these cases, Chinese positioning was in part a product of strategic
considerations and broader issues of national security. However, it was also
grounded by vivid memories of the vast extent of past Chinese empires and the
territorial losses China suffered during the "century of humiliation." For example, well before the establishment of the PRC, the leaders of both the
Guomindang (KMT) and Chinese Communist Party (CCP) denounced the
ceding of Chinese territory to foreign countries and asserted China's right to
reclaim all such lands. Indeed, Sun Yat-sen saw Chinese territory as "very large,
extending northward to the north of the Amur, southward to the south of the
Himalayas, eastward to the China Sea, westward to the T'sung Lin" (cited in
Kim 1979: 42). In a 1936 conversation with Edgar Snow, Mao Zedong asserted,

"It is the immediate task of China to regain all our lost territories, not merely to defend our sovereignty below the Great Wall" (cited in Kim 1979: 44). Later, in 1964, Mao told a group of Japanese reporters, "About 100 years ago the area to the east of Baikal became Russian territory, since then Vladivostok, Khaborovsk, Kamchatka, and other areas have been Soviet territory. We have not yet presented our account for this list" (cited in Cohen and Chiu 1974: 447).

In sum, the Chinese approach to territorial sovereignty was unfailingly boundary-reinforcing, in that it was designed to secure a clearly defined and impregnable line between China and the Soviet Union, India, and Vietnam, but it was also expansive in the sense that China's territorial claims could only be realized by the forfeiture of lands under the control of other states. This confrontational stance on territorial sovereignty was not unusual when viewed in a comparative perspective, for territory has been a consistent source of conflict in international politics. Although China may have been more inclined to use force in attempting to settle territorial disputes than other states, it was by no means an outlier in the international system on this score. Nonetheless, as Chapter 1 argued, the frequency of military combat over boundaries steadily declined since World War II, and very few actors successfully pursued expansive territorial claims during this period. The question taken up in the following chapter is to what extent, and for what reasons, the Chinese position on territorial sovereignty changed during the reform era.

Jurisdictional Sovereignty: Unifying China

The central aspect of this component of sovereignty is the relationship between the state and the "peoples" residing within its territorial boundaries. Once again, the fact that Beijing's jurisdiction extends over a vast, diverse population underscores the importance of jurisdictional questions to China, but also precludes the examination of all aspects of this subject in a single book. Indeed, virtually all scholarship on the jurisdiction of the modern Chinese state has focused solely on the relationship between Beijing and individual minority groups within China. This has resulted in remarkably rich descriptions and explanations of Chinese behavior in specific settings, but done little to forward a systematic perspective on the Chinese stance on this facet of sovereignty. Therefore, as with territorial sovereignty, it was essential to construct a framework for analysis that would capture the issues most central to the Chinese position on jurisdictional sovereignty, but also place manageable limits on the scope of the empirical research to be carried out.

I accomplished this goal by using three selection criteria. First, as the book focuses on describing and explaining emerging patterns in China's relationship with the rest of the international system, only jurisdictional issues that had a sig-

nificant international strategic component for Beijing were considered. I isolated cases in which any change in the jurisdictional status quo would have a pronounced security benefit or cost for China. This narrowed the field of cases
under consideration to groups residing in border and frontier regions. Second,
from this set of strategically important cases, I chose cases in which preliminary
evidence suggested the existence of both domestic and international contestation of Beijing's jurisdictional rights, as well as sustained Chinese awareness of,
and reticence about, such pressures. Finally, within this group, I selected cases
that captured a representative spectrum of the challenges to Chinese jurisdictional rights. These criteria led me to focus on two specific areas, Taiwan and
Tibet and, as a secondary case, on Hong Kong.[12]

During the first three decades following the establishment of the PRC, the
defining feature of the Chinese position on all three of these regions was a consistent insistence on their status as a part of China. In short, for Beijing, although
both the island and port city remained outside of PRC administration, and the
"rooftop of the world" was the site of persistent opposition to Chinese rule,
there was no question that Taiwan, Hong Kong, and Tibet all belonged to the
PRC and the people residing in each area were subjects of Chinese jurisdictional sovereignty. While Chinese leaders and policy makers employed distinct
policies to secure such rights in the three regions, in each case the anchor for
Chinese positioning was the use of force—or at least the threat of force—paired
with bellicose rhetoric (augmented by very limited attempts to negotiate with
Beijing's opponents).

Taiwan is the most prominent of the three cases considered in this book,
since it has been well beyond Beijing's grasp ever since the KMT retreated to
the island in the late 1940s. Not surprisingly, the CCP leadership that had
gained control over the rest of China strongly objected to this and reserved the
right to use military force to return Taiwan to the mainland, while also maintaining a strong military presence in Fujian Province to support such statements.
This policy did not result in any major combat across the strait through the late
1970s, although limited armed confrontations over the Jinmen (Quemoy) and
Mazu (Matsu) Islands did take place in 1954–55 and 1958 (Roy 2003: 118–23;
Segal 1985: 114–40).

In the prelude to the first of these military engagements, an authoritative
Renmin Ribao editorial effectively captured the adamancy of the Chinese position on Taiwan: "The Chinese people once more declare to the whole world
that Taiwan is China's territory and they are determined to liberate it. The great
Chinese people can never tolerate any encroachment on the territorial integrity and sovereignty of their country. Anyone bent on such encroachment will
reap his due desserts" (quoted in Stolper 1985: 35).

Beijing frequently issued such claims and planned for a military solution of the Taiwan issue, but nevertheless through the early 1970s it was far from successful in convincing the government in Taiwan, or the international community, to accept its jurisdiction over the island. However, starting in 1971, this situation underwent a dramatic change. First, the UN General Assembly adopted Resolution 2758, which formalized the PRC's place within the UN system by stripping China's rights within the organization away from the Republic of China (ROC), or the KMT-led government of Taiwan. In doing so, the resolution amounted to an unprecedented international legal codification of the PRC's claim to Taiwan. It was followed by a wave of bilateral endorsements of Beijing's position on the island's status as a part of China. The most important of these agreements was the Sino-U.S. communiqué released in conjunction with President Richard Nixon's historic 1972 visit to China. In this document, Beijing first listed each of the main components of its claim to the island. Following this, in a passage whose precise meaning is still the subject of debate, the United States declared it "acknowledges that all Chinese on either side of the Taiwan Strait maintain there is but one China and that Taiwan is a part of China. The United States government does not challenge that position."[13]

As important as these developments were for Beijing, in the mid-1970s Chinese leaders had failed to make significant progress on bringing Taiwan under their control. In comparison, after 1949, and especially after the quelling of the 1959 uprising against Chinese rule, Chinese sovereignty over Tibet was relatively secure. However, at the same time, throughout this period, opposition to Chinese rule over Tibet persisted in the form of sporadic armed resistance within the region, and the perpetuation of broadly critical views of China's claims within the international realm. As a result, the Chinese approach to Tibet during the first thirty years of the PRC was consistently designed to silence the regime's critics (through the use of force) and bolster China's claims to the region through the enactment of a highly static set of policy and discursive practices.

There were three main components to the Chinese strategy of securing Tibet's status as a part of China. First, and most fundamentally, the Chinese simply moved to establish control over the region. The People's Liberation Army (PLA) spearheaded this effort. Indeed, "liberating" Tibet was designated as one of the major tasks for the army in the early 1950s. The rationale (and the required Tibetan response to it) was given in one of the first main policy statements on Tibet issued in November of that year: "All the religious bodies and people of Tibet should immediately unite to give the PLA every possible assistance, so that the imperialist influence may be driven out and allow the national regional autonomy in Tibet to be realized . . . so that a new Tibet within the new China can be built up with their help" (quoted in Shakya 1999: 46). Second, on the heels of early military successes (the PLA quickly established control over Tibet soon after the campaign to liberate the region was announced), Beijing acted to establish a legal framework for incorporating Tibet into China, and forwarded discursive positions to justify and legitimize such a move. The most important component of this move was the signing of the Seventeen Point Agreement in 1951. Third, within the framework of this agreement, the Chinese then enacted policies to strengthen the Tibetan economy and accommodate the obvious differences between Tibet and the rest of China. While this last line produced a host of changes within Tibet, it gave rise to intense controversy within China and ultimately collapsed under the weight of continued Tibetan opposition to Chinese rule and factional infighting in both Tibet and Beijing. Following the 1959 uprising in Lhasa, and the flight of the Dalai Lama to India, Chinese policy turned away from the relative moderation of the early 1950s and became more radical, with an emphasis first on ideological issues, and then on using the PLA to reestablish order in the region.

In comparison to these two cases, the Chinese stance on Hong Kong was significantly more moderate. Although Beijing insisted that the treaties the Qing dynasty had signed with the British to cede China's control over the region were illegitimate, following the establishment of the PRC, it made no substantive move to undermine British authority there. Instead, Beijing preferred to use more indirect measures to influence political affairs within Hong Kong (such as threatening to withhold its water supply, or allowing population flows from the mainland into the region) (Tucker 1994: 208–16).

In all three of these cases, Chinese behavior was driven by strategic considerations. Chinese leaders could ill afford to cede any of the PRC's jurisdictional claims to Taiwan, Tibet, or Hong Kong since that would jeopardize China's security. The loss of Tibet would have exposed China's southern flank to expanded Indian and Soviet influences. Taiwan provided the KMT with a base for continuing opposition to the CCP, and an opening for American military forces along China's coast. British control of Hong Kong posed a similar strategic threat, but at the same time the port city's unique status also provided Beijing with a valuable outlet for Chinese goods, and economic interests played a crucial role in moderating the Chinese approach.

Beyond strategic concerns, the Chinese position was also grounded in a deeply entrenched, and historically conditioned, belief in the legitimacy of China's claims. This view encompassed an unfailing commitment to create a unified Chinese state (that included all three regions), and a narrow and restrictive three-fold interpretation of the links between state sovereignty and self-determination norms. First, Beijing recognized the rights to self-determination of those residing within such regions through assurances and guarantees that minority groups, and special regions such as Hong Kong and Taiwan, would be granted autonomy within the Chinese state. Second, Beijing viewed the protection of such rights as only possible through the realization of national self-determination for the entire Chinese people, rather than from any subset of peoples within the Chinese state. Third, Beijing believed that only through holding onto Tibet, and bringing Taiwan and Hong Kong back to China, would the CCP's mission of unifying the country, and thus fully realizing Chinese sovereignty, be completed and the "humiliation" the Chinese had suffered as a result of the historical loss of these regions be erased.

Such a stance, and the causes underlying it, were not unusual in the international system at the end of the 1970s. Many states faced similar challenges to their national unity, and few responded by giving in to such pressures. However, the extent to which the PRC's jurisdictional claims were either under threat (Tibet), or simply unrealized (Taiwan, Hong Kong), was exceptional, and China's intransigence seemed to leave little room for compromises or breakthroughs. Instead, each appeared likely to drag China into prolonged conflict. Chapter 4 examines these conflicts during the reform era.

Sovereign Authority: Guarding against Interference

The lines between states' internal affairs and those of the international system constitute the main aspects of the authority component of sovereignty. The international human rights system poses more of a challenge to this division than any other trend in international politics. It is also obvious that controversies surrounding Beijing's participation in the international human rights system have been a prominent theme in China's foreign relations over the last few decades. Indeed, a handful of experts on Chinese foreign policy have suggested that a key aspect of China's tenuous involvement in the system is its conception of sovereign rights. Some have argued that the Chinese position on sovereignty and human rights has been unyielding (Nathan and Ross 1997: 182–85), others that Beijing's inflexibility on the principle of sovereignty must be viewed alongside its more pragmatic human rights policies (Kim 1999: 80–81), and still others that more extensive change has taken place (Zhang Yongjin 1998: 177–93). Yet, the references to sovereignty in all this work were vague and based on scant empirical evidence; it was seen as important, but largely left unexamined. This made the decision to focus my examination of the Chinese stance on sovereign authority upon the issue of human rights easy.

The nub of the Chinese position on sovereign authority can be found in Mao Zedong's famous 1949 proclamation that the Chinese people had stood up and would no longer tolerate external interference in China's internal affairs.

Mao was determined to establish firm sovereign boundaries between China and the international system. Later, in the 1950s, this approach to sovereign authority was underscored by several speeches Zhou Enlai made on the importance of the Five Principles of Peaceful Coexistence for guiding international relations. These statements were made against the backdrop of rising tensions over the status of Taiwan, and their intended audience varied, but they all emphasized that the principles of sovereignty and non-interference were the foundation stones for a stable international environment.

During the same time period, Chinese legal scholars spelled out the Chinese position on sovereign authority in greater detail. Although these scholars were divided in their understanding of international law, they were unified in their support of an unyielding interpretation of the rights sovereignty granted to all members of the international system. For example, in 1959, Yu Fan noted in a *Renmin Ribao* editorial:

> According to the principle of sovereignty, a state has the power, in accordance with its own will, to decide its own form of state, political system, and social economic system, and intervention by other states in those matters is absolutely not permissible. What particularly should be carried out, and what should be reformed in internal affairs are matters concerning a state's own affairs. Intervention by other states in those matters is absolutely not permissible. (Quoted in Cohen and Chiu 1974: 395)

This conception of an almost absolute division between internal and external affairs extended to more specific positions on the international human rights system. In 1960, the influential legal scholar Kong Meng argued that the international human rights regime must be circumscribed in order to ensure that all states maintain authority over their internal affairs. Kong noted that the intent of placing the issue of human rights within the UN Charter "was not to have an international organization bypass states and guarantee the human rights of the citizens of various states; if it were, it would be an intervention in the internal affairs of a state" (quoted in ibid.: 98). In addition, Chinese jurists expressed grave concerns over the dangers that an extension of the human rights regime posed for China. Thus, a scholar argued, "In international relations, imperialism frequently uses the pretext of 'protecting human rights' to intervene in the internal affairs of socialist countries. . . . In fact, they try to use the pretense of protecting 'human rights' to slander socialist countries, and thus pave a legal way for intervention" (quoted in ibid.: 607).

After the mid-1960s, very little was published in China on international law or human rights issues. When legal scholars returned to these concerns after the Cultural Revolution, they once again attempted to establish impregnable sovereign boundaries between China and the international system. As part of this effort, Chinese academics directly questioned the legitimacy of the international human rights system, arguing that the key to realizing human rights in contemporary international politics was the end of colonization. Accordingly, China was cautious about committing itself to the international human rights regime. Even after the return of its seat in the UN, throughout the 1970s it refused to participate in the UN CHR and other human rights organizations. Furthermore, in the late 1970s China had signed none of the nineteen major multilateral human rights treaties in existence at the time (Kim 1979: 485).

This stance, of course, drew upon the language of Maoist ideology. However, at a more fundamental level, it was a product of the legacy of the indignities China had suffered during the "century of humiliation." Identifying with this historical experience, and with the protracted struggle of previous Chinese leaders to gain sovereignty and independence, Beijing was convinced that it was necessary to guard against any perceived encroachment on contemporary China's affairs. Thus, while human rights might be of benefit for those still fighting for national liberation from colonialism, there was no place for such a system on Chinese soil.

Through the end of the 1970s, there was little question in China about the permeability of the boundary between China and the international community; the Chinese state had absolute sovereign authority; and there was no room for international oversight over any aspect of its internal affairs. Although the human rights system at this time did not have the nearly universal acceptance it now enjoys, the virulence with which the Chinese attacked the legitimacy of the system, and studiously avoided making any commitments to the extant multilateral human rights treaties, set China apart from most other sovereign states in the late 1970s. Moreover, the system-wide level of involvement in, and support for, the main multilateral human rights forums rose over the following decades. Chapter 5 examines the extent to which China joined this movement and outlines the causes of Chinese behavior in this area.

Economic Sovereignty: Self-reliance and Isolation

Economic sovereignty is the state's right to regulate economic activity within the boundaries specified by the territorial component of the norm. Although the line created by such a norm has always been less distinct than those drawn by each of the other components of sovereignty, over the past fifty years, but especially since the early 1970s, that line has become increasingly blurred by the strengthening of multilateral economic organizations and the increasing prominence of globalization norms. On the institutional side, the GATT/WTO played the leading role in this development, while ideas about the necessity of economic integration and opening markets have been the most prominent ideational features of this turn.

Over the last few years, analyses of specific aspects of China's involvement with the WTO, other multilateral economic organizations, and more broadly the issue of globalization, have shed new light on the changes in Chinese views on these issues (Deckers 2004; Feeney 1998; Garrett 2001; Kho 1998; Kim 2002; Lardy 2002; Liang Wei 2002; Moore 2000; Panitchpakdi and Clifford 2002; Pearson 1999, 2001; Petras 2000; Theirs 2002). In general, the contributors to this literature have contended that interaction with international economic institutions has already changed important aspects of the Chinese interpretation of China's foreign economic relations. However, this work has failed to consider the implications of such developments for how Beijing defines Chinese sovereignty. This failure echoes the confusion in academic analysis of the main multilateral economic organizations, especially the WTO, on the extent to which these institutions challenge sovereignty's role in international politics.[14] In short, both literatures suggest that participation in the WTO and debates over the nature of globalization constitute key points of orientation in individual states' attempts to navigate the terms of their economic sovereignty. Thus, both of these issues, complemented by a limited consideration of China's involvement in the World Bank and IMF, were selected as the key policy areas included in my examination of the Chinese stance on economic sovereignty.

Chinese sensitivity to the potential intrusiveness of both multilateral economic organizations and economic integration was writ large in Mao's policies of self-reliance and economic independence. To accomplish such goals, the Ministry of Foreign Trade was formed in 1952 and given expanded administrative capacity in 1956 (Cheng 1991: 43, 52). Alongside the trade ministry, a few foreign trade corporations were set up to oversee specific aspects of the economic relationship between China and the rest of the world (Lardy 1992: 17). After initial inquiries in 1950 about the prospects for China's participation in the IMF and World Bank, the PRC settled into a period of "protracted noninvolvement" with the major international economic institutions (Jacobson and Oksenberg 1990: 60).

Despite important shifts in the direction and level of foreign trade and investment during the first two decades of the PRC, this insular system for dealing with China's foreign economic relations remained relatively unchanged. Throughout this period, but especially after relations with the Soviet Union began to deteriorate in the late 1950s, Mao Zedong consistently emphasized the need for economic self-reliance, and attempted to limit China's dependence on external sources of capital and technology. Although his policies never fully cut the Chinese economy off from the outside world, by the late 1960s they had created a high degree of insularity and had firmly established central government control and authority over all of China's foreign economic relations.

The insistence on reinforcing China's economic boundaries was overdetermined by a combination of external and internal influences. During most of this period, the American-led economic embargo against China, and America's opposition to Beijing's participation in the main multilateral economic institutions, meant that following the collapse of the Sino-Soviet relationship China's leaders had few economic options at their disposal. In Maoist ideology, which dominated elite thinking on economic issues and drew upon images of past violations of China's economic rights, such a situation demanded a singular and defiant response.

As powerful as the drive to isolate the Chinese economy was, by the mid-1970s Chinese leaders had started to engage in a heated debate over the proper interpretation of Mao's policy of economic self-reliance. At this juncture, the externally imposed isolation of the 1960s had already begun to erode in response to improved Sino-U.S. relations and Beijing's return to the UN. At the same time, positioning to succeed Mao gained momentum as his health began to deteriorate. "Radical" supporters of the Maoist line argued that the only way to protect economic sovereignty was to strictly limit China's involvement in an international economic system dominated by expansionist imperial powers and structural inequalities.

In contrast, "reformers," led by Deng Xiaoping, maintained that securing China's economic sovereignty could only be achieved through increasing levels of foreign trade and investment in China. The core of this position was contained in Deng's 1974 speech to the United Nations General Assembly. Deng emphasized that "self-reliance in no way means 'self-seclusion' and rejection of foreign aid. We have always considered it beneficial and necessary for the development of the national economy that countries should carry on economic and technical exchanges on the basis of respect for state sovereignty, equality and mutual benefit, and the exchange of needed goods to make up for each other's deficiencies" (quoted in *Peking Review*, Apr. 19, 1974).

Both sides in this exchange forwarded strikingly boundary-reinforcing rhetoric about economic sovereignty. The crux of their disagreement, while virulent and divisive, was limited to how China, and other states, should go about securing economic rights. Thus, while the more extreme interpretation of self-reliance was quickly silenced following Mao's death in the fall of 1976 and the subsequent purge of the Gang of Four, the theme of economic independence and self-reliance remained prevalent in Chinese claims and analysis at this time. The policy complement to such rhetoric included an incremental increase in the level of China's foreign trade and investment and a limited reconsideration of China's non-involvement with the main international economic organizations.[15]

In sum, the outlines of the Chinese position on economic sovereignty remained largely unchanged through the end of 1978. Beijing maintained tight controls over virtually every aspect of China's foreign trade and investment. In addition, commentary on economic issues continued to emphasize the themes of economic self-reliance and independence. While overt criticism of the international economy was less extensive and pointed at this time (in contrast with the height of the Cultural Revolution), it had not yet been replaced by a more active endorsement of the existing system or the institutions that governed it.

While many other states pursued economic insulation during this period, the degree of Chinese autonomy in the mid-1970s was extreme and left the Chinese economy more isolated from the international system, and further outside the reach of the international organizations that had been created to regulate its workings, than virtually any other major state. This enabled China to maintain unusually sharp sovereign boundaries between itself and the international economic system, but as we have seen, it also was the source of increasing debate within China as a new generation of leaders and scholars began to consider if this position had weakened (rather than strengthened) China. Chapter 6 takes up this issue, and focuses on how Chinese policy during the 1980s and 1990s moved away from such an unyielding position.

Conclusion

The PRC was clearly attached to a boundary-reinforcing approach to securing sovereignty. This generates the book's central puzzle: how would China's integration in, and interdependence with, the increasingly densely layered international political and economic system during the subsequent two decades affect such a stance?

The following chapters answer this question by analyzing China's sovereignty-related words and actions in each of the four issue areas introduced in this chapter. In a preview of their content, here it is possible to outline the main contours of the overall shift in Chinese practices during the 1980s and 1990s.

China's leaders' commentary on sovereignty jumped during this period as is shown in Figure 2.1, which is based on a content analysis of the annual rate at which official sovereignty claims appeared in *Beijing Review* and *Zhongguo Waijiao Gailan*.[16]

As Figure 2.1 shows, Chinese leaders issued far more sovereignty claims in the 1990s than in the 1980s. Moreover, as discussed in the following chapters, despite significant variation over time in the aspects of sovereignty that such claims referred to, virtually all of them promoted a boundary-reinforcing interpretation of sovereignty.

Echoing such a trend, foreign policy analysts in China paid increasing levels

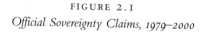

FIGURE 2.1

Official Sovereignty Claims, 1979–2000

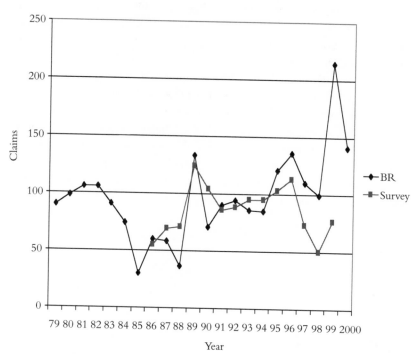

of attention to sovereignty in their work, with a pronounced rise in writing on sovereignty occurring in the 1990s. In addition, and more importantly, during the last fifteen years significant differences emerged among Chinese foreign policy analysts over sovereignty's role in international politics and the extent to which it was changing.

A quiet yet heated debate developed within China since the early 1990s over how much sovereign boundaries system-wide were being transformed, and the impact such a development would have on China's foreign relations and security policies. While this debate was discernible in the written materials I studied, it was even more pronounced in the interview data. Well over half of those interviewed in 1997–98—fifty-seven interviewees—accepted at least a limited change in sovereignty's role in international relations during the contemporary period, while thirty-four interviewees rejected the possibility of such change, staunchly promoting a boundary-reinforcing interpretation of the norm.

Chinese actions reflected these discursive trends. To begin with Beijing's involvement in multilateral organizations steadily rose from the early 1980s to the late 1990s. While Chinese leaders obviously attempted to use such involvement to reinforce China's sovereign boundaries, it led to an increasing level of ambiguity in the Chinese stance on sovereignty. However, a close inspection of this development shows that even more than with China's other practices, it was almost exclusively linked to sovereign authority and economic sovereignty (and largely absent from Chinese actions vis-à-vis the territorial and jurisdictional components of the norm).

In sum, during the 1980s the Chinese approach to sovereignty was relatively constant and boundary-reinforcing, but placed a greater emphasis on cooperation and compromise than had been the case during the first thirty years of the PRC. In contrast, during the 1990s, the Chinese position shifted. Policies preserved a static interpretation of territorial sovereignty, promoted an unyielding and increasingly combative stance on jurisdictional sovereignty, and permitted a transgression of the lines created by the economic and authority components of the sovereignty norm. The rest of the book describes and explains the nature of this development.

3

Territorial Sovereignty: De-emphasizing Lost Territory and Securing New Borders

Before the reform era, the Chinese discourse on territorial sovereignty emphasized the vast territory China had "lost" during the "century of humiliation" and the frequency with which the PRC's territorial boundaries were encroached upon by the Soviet Union, India, and Vietnam. In addition, Beijing showed a repeated willingness to use military force in conjunction with such rhetoric (even when clashes along China's border raised questions about the possibility of major military conflict). In contrast, in the 1980s and 1990s China's stance on territorial sovereignty and border relations, while anchored by relatively static interests, was defined by a pronounced move away from abrasive language and large-scale military encounters. Although this shift was less extensive, and more cautious, than that which I will show took place during this period vis-à-vis each of the other facets of sovereignty, it encompassed a turn toward relatively peaceful, cooperative discourse and policies that were designed to cement the status quo along each of China's main contested international boundaries.

This new pattern developed over the course of two phases. The first lasted from the late 1970s through 1988, and the second from the spring of 1989 through the first years of Hu Jintao's leadership (and continues to unfold). Throughout both phases, Beijing maintained the right to use force to resolve outstanding disputes over territorial sovereignty, and worked to develop the military capabilities to support such a discursive stance. However, during the former period, despite limited indications of a new, less confrontational approach to territorial sovereignty, continuities in Chinese territorial practices (in relationship to the stance China had taken on border relations during the preceding decades) outweighed such new developments. In contrast, over the last decade, the Chinese position on territorial sovereignty and border relations underwent a significant shift. In short, by the end of the 1990s the Chinese remained intent upon securing boundary-reinforcing interpretations of China's territorial sovereignty, but exhibited an unprecedented level of flexibility in the words and actions taken to realize this goal.

This chapter analyzes this shift and seeks to explain the factors that account for the relative moderation of China's stance on outstanding territorial claims in the 1980s, and for its willingness to seek legal resolutions of such disputes in the 1990s. The initial turn grew out of the demand for a more stable regional security environment created by Deng Xiaoping's reform and opening policy. Then, beginning in the late 1980s, China's dramatically improved strategic position (by virtue of changes in Moscow's role within the region) provided Beijing with an opportunity to reorient its stance on large stretches of China's contested boundaries. Chinese leaders' restrained response to this development reflected a realistic assessment of the limits of Chinese military capabilities, and more importantly the premium Deng, and the rest of the Chinese leadership, placed on securing stable relations with each of China's neighbors (even at the expense of outstanding territorial claims) at the start of the 1990s. Such caution was then girded in the mid-1990s by rising concerns with building up China's image as a "good neighbor" in the Asian region. Although each of these factors tended to push Chinese territorial practices in the direction of compromise, such influences were consistently offset by the prominence in the Chinese foreign policy and national security making community of memories of the contraction of Chinese territory during the "century of humiliation." Indeed, recitations of the territorial losses China suffered during this historical period constitute the grounding point for most of the Chinese analysis of border relations published over the last two decades. The demand for a return of such "lost territories" was carefully kept out of China's official territorial claims, but this refrain nonetheless created an unyielding determination in Beijing to avoid even the appearance of being weak on territorial sovereignty, or of giving away too much ground in border negotiations. In other words, the evolution of the Chinese position on territorial sovereignty was, and still is, the product of the intersection between ongoing interest-based calculations and ideational factors.

Phase I: Territorial Practices in the 1980s—Easing Tensions, Bolstering Claims

From 1979 through 1988, the Chinese approach to territorial sovereignty was characterized by a cautious attempt to concurrently de-escalate conflict along each of the PRC's main borders and maintain China's preexisting stance on the location of those borders. Chinese policy makers shifted their tactical approach to border relations, but maintained strategic goals and territorial claims that were consistent with earlier positioning. This approach resulted in a reduction in tensions in border relations with the Soviet Union, India, and Vietnam, but did not produce any substantive steps toward resolving the fundamental differences China had with each of these states over territorial boundaries.

In terms of discursive practices, this development involved a lessening of the hyper-vigilance on territorial issues that had been so prominent during the preceding decades. Thus, the intense sensitivity to encroachments upon China's territory was less pronounced in official statements than it had been in the past. Condemnations of neighboring states' territorial agendas were also toned down, and by the end of this phase the more expansive aspects of China's own territorial agenda were largely silenced.

While it is only possible to trace the details of this change with reference to the specifics of each of China's main border dyads, a general indication of its extent can be derived from a return to the content analysis of the official sovereignty claims published in *Beijing Review* introduced in Chapter 2, and by isolating those statements that referred directly to the territorial facet of the norm.[1] Such a study reveals that from 1979 through 1988, there was a steady decline in the number of official statements on border-related issues. Moreover, further analysis discovered that this drop was largely the product of a reduction in the number of statements issued on China's continental boundaries.[2] (See Figure 3.1.)

This silence on territorial issues was even more pervasive in unofficial analysis of border relations. During this period the major foreign policy journals contained only one article that examined the general role of geopolitical boundaries in international relations, and this focused more on U.S. security strategy than on territorial sovereignty (Xi Runchang 1985). In addition, surprisingly little analysis of more specific bilateral territorial concerns appeared in these publications. In fact, during the 1980s there were only scattered references to any aspect of territorial sovereignty and border relations. In contrast, Chinese scholars had produced extensive commentaries on China's border relations during previous decades. This relative decline constitutes an important new wrinkle in the Chinese approach to territorial sovereignty. However, the scope of this change was limited by the tendency in unofficial commentary to stress reinforcing the lines between China and its neighbors.

This limited reorientation was also evident in China's diplomatic and security policies. Although China did not become embroiled in any major military dispute during the 1980s, armed border skirmishes (with both India and Vietnam) were relatively common through 1987. Moreover, toward the end of

FIGURE 3.1

Territorial Claims in BR, 1979–88

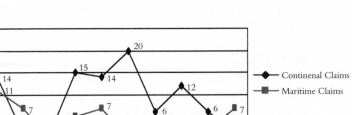

the decade, Chinese military planners noted that it was imperative for Beijing to shift its defense strategy "from fighting an overall war into that of dealing with incidents which happen because of territorial issues, and fighting local wars" (Goodwin 1989: 188). In addition, Chinese policy makers took only the most tentative steps toward negotiating settlements of all three of the main unresolved territorial disputes. Instead, from the early 1980s through 1988, Beijing's policy consisted of attempts to probe the intentions and capabilities of each of its major neighbors. In all such cases, the foundation for Chinese initiatives was an unrelenting effort to ensure that China's principled position on outstanding territorial disputes was taken as the starting point for negotiations.

The Sino-Soviet Boundary from 1979 to 1988: Easing Lingering Tensions

During the 1980s, Chinese leaders de-emphasized the territorial differences between China and the Soviet Union as they reexamined the Sino-Soviet relationship. Throughout this period, there was little Chinese commentary on the northern border, and diplomatic positioning was cautious. While a significant gap remained between the leaders of both states over the location of crucial segments of the boundary (especially in the Wusuli, or Ussuri, River segment), and the extensive Soviet and Chinese military presence along the border continued, the two sides refrained from direct military engagement. In contrast to the previous decade, during the 1980s Beijing did not publicly report any new Soviet incursions into Chinese territory. At the same time, both sides, but especially the Soviets, tentatively explored the possibility of reaching a negotiated settlement of outstanding territorial issues.

The starting point for this halting dialogue was the dual Chinese decision in April of 1979 to publicly decline renewal of the long-dormant 1950 Sino-Soviet Defense Treaty, while also calling for a new round of discussions with Moscow.

The first meeting between the two sides was held in the fall of 1979, but produced little more than acrimony, and further meetings were canceled following the Soviet invasion of Afghanistan (which the Chinese denounced). Thus, it was not until 1982, when the Soviets extended an olive branch to the Chinese (in Leonid Brezhnev's 1982 Tashkent speech), and China agreed to a new round of negotiations on normalization, that the two sides were able to begin to "mend fences" (Wishnick 2001: 75). Indeed, it was soon after this statement was issued that border trade was re-opened in sections of the eastern boundary for the first time since the 1969 conflict. In addition, Chinese and Soviet negotiators met to discuss normalizing relations and reducing the number of Soviet troops and missiles deployed in the border region. However, in the early 1980s the Chinese remained apprehensive about Soviet intentions. Thus, Beijing took the opportunity presented by the Tashkent speech to emphasize what it saw as three fundamental obstacles to improving bilateral relations—the Soviet invasion of Afghanistan, Moscow's support for Vietnam's intervention in Cambodia, and Soviet troop levels along China's northern border and in Mongolia—rather than embrace a new era of Sino-Soviet cooperation.

In accord with such concerns, Beijing consistently worked to bolster China's capabilities to defend both the eastern and western sections of the Sino-Soviet boundary. At the start of the reform era in 1978–79, there was a spike in military activity in the region. At this time the Chinese were reported to have established a northern command center to oversee defense in conjunction with concerns over Moscow's close relationship with Vietnam, and the short, but intense, armed conflict between China and Vietnam (Segal 1985: 219).

Accompanying this armed standoff, in the early 1980s the major Chinese foreign policy journals contained a significant amount of anti-Soviet commentary (which occasionally touched on Moscow's intrusions into Chinese territory). Yet, during this period only one article (in 1981) on the boundary issue was published. In it, Li Huichuan articulated a position almost identical to the one staked out in Beijing's official commentary—the only difference being Li's even more combative and dismissive attitude toward the Soviet position on the border, and blunt skepticism of Moscow's disingenuous offer to negotiate a settlement of its territorial differences with Beijing. The article warned that the biggest obstacle to the resolution of the Sino-Soviet border dispute was "the Soviet Union's military threat to China, and its hegemonic policies toward China" (Li Huichuan 1981: 18).

This critical analysis was followed in 1983 in a *Beijing Review* translation of a piece that originally appeared in *Shijie Zhishi* (World Affairs). The article not only constitutes one of the most expansive commentaries my research uncovered of the Sino-Soviet border issued during the 1980s, it also demonstrates the underlying continuities in the Chinese position on the Soviet border. The article faithfully replicated the three claims staked out by the 1969 statement introduced in Chapter 2. First, it reiterated the issue of the vast expanse of territory lost: "Tsarist Russia annexed 1.5 million square kilometers of Chinese territory through a series of unequal treaties imposed on China" ("A Reply" 1983). Second, it contended that all the border treaties signed between Russia and China after 1840 were unequal and unilaterally imposed on China. Third, it emphasized the reasonableness of the Chinese position on the border and Beijing's willingness to negotiate with the Soviets.

Despite combative commentary such as this, the mid-1980s saw a gradual thawing of Sino-Soviet relations as reflected in the dearth of subsequent critical commentary in Chinese publications and a gradual modification of Chinese defense policies. On the first front, after 1981 no article dedicated to Sino-Soviet border relations appeared in any of the three major foreign policy journals (a silence that was replicated in *Beijing Review* after 1983). On the second front, Beijing began to implement defensive policies that maintained, but did not significantly expand, its military presence along the Sino-Soviet border. In 1986 the Soviets had deployed fifty-three military divisions in border regions, while the Chinese maintained sixty-eight (whereas in 1969 the Soviets had between twenty-eight and thirty-four and the Chinese thirty-four) (Shichor 2004: 134).

It was the Soviets, led by Mikhail Gorbachev, who took the initiative in the mid-1980s toward moving China and the Soviet Union closer to a negotiated settlement of the border issue. Gorbachev made the first move in this direction in 1986 in a speech in the far eastern Soviet port city of Vladivostok. At this time, the Soviet leader committed to reducing the Soviet presence in Afghanistan and cutting Soviet forces in both the Sino-Soviet border region and Mongolia. He pledged Moscow would accept the main navigational channel, or thalweg, as the principle for locating the river boundary between China and the Soviet Union ("Text" 1986).

Following this remarkable statement, relations between the two countries edged toward a renaissance. The first tangible result of improved relations was the February 1987 announcement that accompanied the end of the first round of border talks held between the two sides since before the start of the Afghan war. The statement read, in part, that China and the Soviet Union had "agreed to review their entire boundary line, starting with the eastern section" ("Sino-Soviet" 1987).

Although no specific agreement came out of these talks, this statement, coupled with Gorbachev's additional assurances of Moscow's commitment to reduce border troops and accept the thalweg principle, meant that the Chinese had attained significant concessions from the Soviets. In the wake of these developments, boundary talks were held again in August of 1987. The following year, a group was formed to examine border demarcation, marking the first time since the 1969 confrontation that such specific discussions took place between the two sides. In addition, Moscow made a number of moves to draw down the Soviet troop presence in Asia. While this de-escalation of forces was most pronounced in Afghanistan, for the Chinese it was the 1988 moves by the Soviets (and Vietnam) to end the occupation of Cambodia that were an even more significant signal of the changing nature of Soviet policy (Wishnick 2001: 102).

As promising as these developments were for the prospects of ensuring security along the main segments of China's northern frontier, China remained concerned in the late 1980s about the Sino-Soviet border. For example, around this time several articles on Sino-Soviet border relations were published in the specialized journals of the Chinese Academy of Social Science's (CASS) Research Center for the Study of Borderland History and Geography Institute (RBHG), an academic organization (led by the influential Xinjiang expert, Ma Dazheng) that was charged with analyzing the historical development of China's border regions. In light of its mission, RBHG articles tended to avoid any specific reference to the current situation in the border region. However, the analysis published by RBHG is still of interest as it highlights just how deeply embedded such historical concerns were in Chinese thinking about the Sino-Soviet boundary in the 1980s.

Nonetheless, in 1988 momentum began to build for a Sino-Soviet summit. As we will examine in greater detail in the following section of this chapter, when this high-level meeting finally took place in the spring of 1989 it established the foundation for more peaceful Sino-Soviet (after 1991, Russian and Central Asian) border relations during the following decade.

In sum, during the 1980s Chinese leaders kept a watchful eye on the maturing Sino-Soviet relationship, quietly pushing for a settlement of the outstanding territorial disputes between the two states on terms consistent with the Chinese interpretation of the territorial status quo. The expansive territorial claims China had made prior to the start of the decade largely fell by the wayside, and armed skirmishes ended even in the most contested sections of the border. They were replaced by closed negotiations and a minimum of public statements.

These developments support the argument that Chinese policy makers viewed territorial sovereignty along the Sino-Soviet border through the prism of strategic power concerns. This is most evident in the fact that territorial issues were not heavily emphasized in the preconditions Deng set for a Sino-Soviet summit. In this case, boundaries were simply one issue to be dealt with in reference to broader national interests. Nonetheless, the repetition of vast territorial claims in the trickle of analysis that was published during the 1980s can also be seen as indication of the persistence in Beijing of historically framed under-standings of the scope of Chinese territory.

The Sino-Indian Boundary from 1979 to 1988: An Uneasy Truce

During this phase, the military standoff between China and India in the bor-der region continued, and in 1986 threatened to degenerate into a prolonged and direct military clash. Nevertheless, actual military conflict between the two sides was in the end limited. Rather, it was threats, tensions, and the mainte-nance of the ability to defend territory under Chinese control that defined Beijing's position over the course of the 1980s. Throughout this period, Chinese officials continued to issue statements sharply critical of what they categorized as Indian incursions into Chinese territory, and repeatedly threatened reprisals. In addition, a slow stream of scholarly analysis provided rhetorical support for this abrasive commentary, and in the process ensured that the claims China had previously articulated continued to define the basic parameters of the Chinese position on the border. Moreover, although boundary talks were renewed in 1981, and held on a fairly regular basis through 1987, they failed to produce any major breakthroughs.

The beginning of this phase in Sino-Indian border relations was marked by Deng Xiaoping's 1980 statement that implied Beijing would accept the status quo in the border region (and acquiesce to India's control over territory that China claimed in the eastern sector as long as India recognized Chinese sover-eignty over the Askai Chin section of the region in the west). According to a Xinhua report on Deng's comments, the Chinese leader emphasized, "China has never asked for the return of all the territory illegally incorporated into India by the old colonialists" (quoted in Garver 2001a: 101).

This statement was followed in December of 1981 by the first round of sub-stantive border talks between the two sides since the 1962 war. However, these negotiations failed to produce even a limited agreement between Beijing and New Delhi. On the contrary, even as talks were moving forward, Indian leaders rejected the idea of Deng's "package" settlement. On the heels of this public repudiation of the Chinese initiative, additional rounds of talks were held, but not surprisingly failed to bridge the gap between the two sides.

During this period, the underlying continuities in the Chinese interpretation of the nature of Sino-Indian border relations were pronounced. This can be seen in a 1982 article that appeared in one of the first issues of *Guoji Wenti Yanjiu* pub-lished since the start of the Cultural Revolution. In it, the influential internation-al law scholar Chen Tiqian reiterated the claim that the Sino-Indian boundary had never been delineated, but observed that over the course of history both sides had accepted a traditional borderline. Chen also conceded that since disagreements over the location of this boundary remained, it was necessary for China to enter into negotiations with India "in order to prevent the occurrence of another dispute" (Chen Tiqian 1982: 11–12). Yet, Chen protested that India had not accepted this position, pushed claims for territory north of what the Chinese viewed as the illegal McMahon line in the eastern sector, and demanded a withdrawal of PLA forces from territory under China's control. In response to such demands, Chen stridently asserted, "this is definitely not an issue of an unclear border, but rather one of an ideology of expansion and aggression" (p. 13).

In the fall of 1985, when the sixth round of boundary talks was convened, the Chinese pushed this more assertive claim by redefining the terms of Deng's 1980 "package" offer through emphasizing Beijing's claim to territory in the eastern sector of the boundary (Ganguly 1989: 1129; Garver 2001a: 104). The rationale behind this was explained in 1986 in another *Guoji Wenti Yanjiu* article that emphatically rejected the entire Indian position on the border. In it, Jing Hui (1986) objected to each of the agreements that India had used to support its claims about the location of the Sino-Indian border, and denied the relevance of the Simla Convention and the McMahon line to the contemporary border disputes. In addition, Jing repeated the same territorial claims against India that were made in earlier articles and Foreign Ministry statements.[3]

Such confrontational analysis set the stage for a short-lived military confrontation between China and India in 1986 and 1987. During this period the Chinese repeatedly charged India with troop incursions and the occupation of new territory in the eastern sector of the border. Against this backdrop, the seventh round of border talks was held in July of 1986, but proved to be futile (Ganguly 1989: 1130; Garver 2001a: 104–5). In fact, mutual recriminations intensified as Beijing reacted against (and New Delhi defended) India's consideration of granting statehood to the Arunachal Pradesh (a significant portion of which falls within territory the Chinese claimed in the eastern sector).[4] Despite warnings from Beijing, the Indian parliament granted the Arunachal Pradesh region the status of full statehood in December 1986. China's official response to this move was dismissive and combative. The Foreign Ministry attacked the decision for "grossly violating China's sovereignty and territorial integrity" ("Chinese Foreign Ministry Spokesman" 1987).

In the following months, reports of troop buildups and border clashes appeared frequently in the Indian press. Moreover, in early spring, India carried out a war game modeled on a border war with China that included the large-scale mobilization of Indian troops (Garver 2001a: 97). Although China initially issued no official comments on the specifics of these developments, in April the Foreign Ministry again charged India with forcibly occupying territory in the eastern sector of the boundary region. Furthermore, in May, a Chinese

Foreign Ministry spokesman warned, "China cannot remain in a state of iner-
tia, faced with the recent happenings along the Sino-Indian border" ("Foreign
Ministry Spokesman" 1987). In addition, Beijing reportedly placed the PLA on
high alert, and rotated over 20,000 additional infantry, accompanied by
advanced weapon systems, into Tibet (Garver 2001a: 97).

In short, the stage for a new war appeared to be set. However, by late spring
tension between the two sides had lessened, and Beijing issued several conciliatory statements on the boundary issue ("China Urges Tranquility" 1987; "Sino-
Indian Cooperation" 1987). Subsequently, the eighth round of border talks
between the two sides was held in November of 1987. Although these negotiations followed in the path of previous meetings in failing to make any appreciable progress, the fact that they were held at all was significant. Moreover, they
occurred against the backdrop of a burst of diplomatic activity that eventually
paved the way for Rajiv Gandhi's 1988 visit to China and the opening of a new
chapter in Sino-Indian relations.

After this spike in tensions, and the calm that followed, discussion of the
Sino-Indian boundary in official sources became rare. However, scholarly analysis critical of Indian encroachments on Chinese territory continued to find a
home in China's elite foreign policy journals. For example, Jing Hui (1988) published a second piece on the Sino-Indian border in *Guoji Wenti Yanjiu*. This article differed subtly from Jing's earlier work in that it dealt exclusively on the eastern segment of the boundary. However, Jing still strenuously objected to the
Indian occupation of Chinese territory.

In short, during the 1980s the continuities in Chinese practices on this section of the southern frontier outweighed the superficial changes that had begun
to unfold. Beijing did tentatively move to settle the dispute with India through
Deng's renewal of a "package" deal that had not been on the negotiating table
since the 1962 war. The impetus behind this initiative has been discussed in John
Garver's book on Sino-Indian relations. Although strategic considerations
involved in the expansion of Soviet influence in South Asia were important, the
more fundamental issue was the Chinese leader's effort to create a more secure
regional environment for economic modernization and development (Garver
2001a: 102). Reaching a deal with India on the border would have significantly contributed to this aspiration. However, Deng's initiative was also grounded
in relatively static, and historically conditioned, positions on the scope of territory Beijing was willing to concede. Thus, the Sino-Indian border remained the
site of combative posturing designed to inscribe a relatively rigid and unyielding interpretation of the location and meaning of the limits of China's territorial sovereignty.

*Sino-Vietnamese Border, 1979–88: From War on
Land to Conflict at Sea*

The Chinese stance on the limits of China's territorial sovereignty vis-à-vis Vietnam also remained fundamentally unchanged during the 1980s. However, over the course of this phase Beijing's territorial focus shifted from the Sino-Vietnamese land border to the disputed maritime territory between the two states. In addition, the level of direct military engagements between the two sides declined after the 1979 border war.

It was this short, but costly, conflict that marked the start of the reform era in Sino-Vietnamese border relations, when Beijing engineered a large expedition into Vietnamese territory (reportedly sending 80,000 troops, with an even larger support group held in reserve) in the winter of 1979. By most accounts this sortie was a failure, with China suffering up to 20,000 casualties (Segal 1985: 219), and was followed by a hasty withdrawal of troops in March. In the aftermath of the incursion, Beijing and Hanoi entered into limited negotiations over the status of the border and general bilateral relations. However, agreement on the location of the land boundary between the two states proved to be elusive. As a result, defensive claims about border incursions and reports of military conflicts remained common features of Sino-Vietnamese border relations even after the end of direct combat.[5]

Several scholars have argued that the frequency with which such charges were leveled is more a reflection of the ups and (mostly) downs in Sino-Vietnamese relations than of any underlying differences on the boundary itself.[6] That the disputed territory along the land border was minuscule lends credence to such an argument.[7] Such a view is bolstered by the absence of defensive rhetoric about this segment of the Sino-Vietnamese boundary in the major foreign policy journals during the 1980s. The only unofficial analysis of the land boundary I was able to discover in these journals appeared in articles on changes in the two countries' bilateral relations. References in these articles were limited to brief observations about the ongoing boundary negotiations. Only one article ("Zhong-Yue" 1981) directly referred to the land dispute. Published when Sino-Vietnamese relations were at a particularly low point, this article reported in detail the history of Chinese assistance to Vietnam and the subsequent Vietnamese betrayal of Chinese trust through siding with the Soviets and launching attacks on both China's land and sea territories.

This relative silence on the land boundary between China and Vietnam was offset by the increasingly volatile relationship that emerged during the 1980s over the maritime border in the Beibu Gulf and the South China Sea. Tensions in these areas began to heat up in the late 1970s. For example, on the heels of the border war (which was largely fought on land), Han Nianlong, a leading Chinese official, outlined a long list of Vietnamese violations of China's borders, and in doing so emphasized both land and maritime boundaries ("The Truth" 1979).[8] In an even more significant indication of the shifting Chinese focus within Sino-Vietnamese border relations, Xinhua released an authoritative editorial reiterating Chinese claims to the Xisha and Nansha islands ("Xisha" 1979). Moreover, the following year, the Chinese Foreign Ministry issued a definitive statement that left no doubt about the intransigence of the Chinese claim to this maritime region. This document sought to explode "the Vietnamese authorities' fabrications" and prove "China's indisputable sovereignty over the Xisha and Nansha Islands" ("China's Indisputable Sovereignty" 1980).

Following this elevated level of interest in maritime issues in the early 1980s, Beijing de-emphasized the conflict here during the course of most of the rest of the decade (see Figure 3.1). During this period the Chinese continued to lay claim to both the Beibu Gulf and the South China Sea, but opted not to explicitly draw attention to Sino-Vietnamese differences over ownership of both maritime regions. Nonetheless, offsetting this relative silence, China started an ambitious program to modernize and strengthen its maritime military capabilities.[9]

By the late 1980s, the dispute between the two sides again moved into the foreground as Beijing and Hanoi attempted to cement their maritime territorial claims, especially in the vicinity of the Nansha Island chain. In the spring of 1987 Beijing dispatched an unprecedented naval force to this region (Austin 1998: 82–83), and in March 1988 a brief military skirmish with Vietnamese forces erupted when China sent a "survey" team to the islands. In the midst of this flare-up, the Chinese issued yet more official statements asserting their sovereign rights over the region.

This clash marked the end of the initial phase of Sino-Vietnamese border relations during the reform era. It gave China a foothold in the southern sector of the South China Sea and confirmed that this oceanic territory would be the main site of contention between the two sides. In both the land and the sea dispute, it is apparent that the ebb and flow of hostilities was in large part a function of the overall Sino-Vietnamese relationship, and at least initially grew out of underlying Chinese concerns with preventing the expansion of Soviet influence along its southern flank. However, the fact that armed confrontation between the two states occurred in the late 1980s, soon after the discovery of reportedly vast oil reserves in the disputed region and in the face of steadily improving bilateral relations between Beijing and Hanoi, indicates the influence of broader economic motives in this conflict. Moreover, the intensity and frequency with which Chinese rhetoric emphasized China's long record of control over the disputed territory in justifying Beijing's contemporary claims to the South China Sea also suggest that collective memory of the historic reach of Chinese territory within policy making circles in Beijing also played a prominent role in framing Chinese positioning.

In sum, setting aside the prominent exception of the flare-up of the South China Sea dispute early in 1988, by the end of the 1980s Chinese policy makers had moved away from the relatively routine use of force to secure the boundaries of China's territorial sovereignty. Although there were still underlying differences with each of China's main neighbors, border skirmishes were the exception, rather than the rule, and limited progress had been made in dealing with even the most intractable disputes. In each case, this turn drew upon the broad shift in Chinese foreign and domestic policy that Deng Xiaoping had instituted in the early 1980s, and developed in line with the overall evolution of bilateral relations with each neighboring state. However, as the following decade revealed, Chinese leaders' and policy makers' flexibility and willingness to negotiate was still constrained by their tenacious maintenance of historically framed conceptions of the legitimate scope of China's territorial sovereignty.

Phase II, 1989–Present: Stabilizing Land Boundaries, and Maritime Aspirations

As is the case with so many facets of Chinese politics, the late 1980s marked a significant turning point in China's approach to territorial sovereignty. The trend toward de-emphasizing territorial disputes that began in the early 1980s gathered momentum as Beijing achieved breakthroughs with each of its main neighbors. After these dramatic developments, the Chinese approach to territorial sovereignty came to be defined by practices designed to stabilize each of China's contested continental border regions through quiet diplomacy (and, in some cases, fairly extensive Chinese compromises on the division of disputed land), accompanied by the enhancement of military capabilities (especially in the South China Sea) as part of a drive to cement China's ocean claims.

Evidence of this trend within the official Chinese discourse is presented in Figure 3.2, which traces the annual total of territorial references that appeared in *Beijing Review* from 1989 to 2000. The most striking aspect of Figure 3.2 is that no claims were issued in 1989, and during the five successive years only eleven territorial claims were reported. When compared with the overall rise in sovereignty claims issued during this period (as shown in Figure 2.1), such a drop meant that the percentage of territorial claims contracted sharply compared to other statements related to sovereignty. In addition, when read in conjunction with Figure 3.1, Figure 3.2 also shows that whereas during the 1980s Chinese statements on territorial sovereignty generally referred to continental

FIGURE 3.2

Territorial Claims in BR, 1989–2000

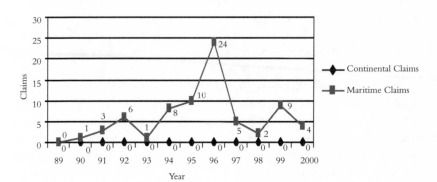

boundaries, in the 1990s maritime issues dominated the official discourse. Regardless of the geographic referent of such statements, Chinese claims uniformly promoted a boundary-reinforcing interpretation of territorial sovereignty (even as they minimized expansive territorial claims and endorsed the progress being made within each facet of China's border relations through negotiations).

Unofficial analysis tended to follow in the footsteps of official commentary in two significant ways. First, the discussion of territorial issues in the major foreign policy journals was very limited, and this near silence was broken mainly with reference to maritime concerns. For example, between 1987 and 1997 the more specialized RBHG journals contained at least seventeen articles directly related to the Beibu Gulf, the South China Sea, or the Nansha/Xisha Islands. Second, analysis tended to downplay past territorial grievances (although the litany of historical losses China had suffered was a standard feature in most articles on specific border issues), and focused instead on recent progress toward resolving China's outstanding border disputes (and the contribution Beijing had made to regional peace and stability through its restraint in handling such issues).

Over the course of the last decade, China lent substance to such cooperative rhetoric through engaging in wide-ranging border negotiations with each of its main neighbors. Although most of these negotiations were initially bilateral, in the mid-1990s they were complemented by multilateral talks (at least in regard to the South China Sea and China's border's with Russia and the Central Asian republics). Thus, while the Chinese military remained staunchly committed to defending China's frontiers and continued to develop new force projection capabilities to lay claim to contested territory (especially in the South China

Sea), compromise was the defining feature of Chinese territorial practices during this phase.[10]

The rapid change in China's strategic position vis-à-vis the Soviet Union, and by extension the rest of the region, dating to the late 1980s, provided the initial impetus for the start of this new phase in the Chinese stance on territorial sovereignty. This shift gave Beijing an unprecedented opportunity to develop a new approach to border relations. However, beyond such a change in the regional landscape, three specific factors played particularly prominent roles in determining the extent of change in the Chinese position. First, in the initial post-Tiananmen period, territorial issues were de-emphasized in concert with Deng's directive to place a premium on stability and securing good relations within the Asian region (a move that was at least in part intended to offset international pressure against China). Second, later in the decade, the emergence of new concerns about projecting a moderate, responsible image in the region once again served to moderate Chinese practices (to placate regional concerns about the potentially de-stabilizing effects of the "rise of China"). Third, at both junctures the collective memory of past territorial losses significantly limited China's flexibility in words and actions. In short, the shift in Chinese practices during this phase was the product of Chinese leaders' rational assessment of their strategic interests in the region, but was also influenced by underlying conceptions of the legitimacy of Chinese claims.

The Sino-Soviet (Russian and Central Asian) Boundary
after 1988: Cooperative Border Relations

During the late 1980s, and throughout the following decade, Beijing and Moscow repeatedly found common ground upon which to build a relatively stable bilateral relationship. The boundary disputes that had long been a source of tension between the two states were largely resolved. By the end of the 1990s the location of both the eastern and western segments of the Sino-Russian border had been agreed upon in principle and, for the most part, demarcated on the ground. Of course, it is also the case that after 1991, the length of the western part of the Sino-Soviet boundary was drastically reduced with the establishment of the three Central Asian republics (Tajikistan, Kyrgyzstan, and Kazakhstan) following the collapse of the Soviet Union. However, in general, the Chinese were also able to quickly stabilize relations with these new states, eventually reaching agreements on territorial issues with each one.

The first step in the direction of stabilizing China's northern frontier took place against the backdrop of the 1989 Tiananmen protests, when the Chinese and Soviets utilized the May Deng-Gorbachev summit to formally mark the start of a new era in Sino-Soviet relations. The joint communiqué that celebrat-

ed this historic meeting was a clear expression of intent to reach a new agreement on handling territorial issues. It publicly committed both sides to continue negotiations on both the eastern and western sectors of the border. In addition, both sides agreed "to take measures to cut down the military forces in the
areas along the Sino-Soviet boundary to a minimum level commensurate with
the normal, good-neighborly relations between the two countries and work for
increased trust and continuous tranquility along the border areas" ("Sino-Soviet
Joint Communiqué" 1989). Although the Chinese did not provide details of the
cuts they would make on their side of the border, Gorbachev, at the end of his
visit to China, made specific pledges for troop reductions in the "Soviet Far
East" (Dobbs 1989).

Gorbachev made such concessions in order to bolster his image as a reformer
(an attempt that was belied by the Chinese crackdown on the democracy
movement in China soon after his return to Moscow), and to scale back the
overall level of Soviet militarization. The Chinese agreed to his visit, despite
misgivings about the reforms the Soviet leader was instituting at home (and
fears about their potential effect on China's own reforms), because of the flexible policies the Soviet leader had already instituted with respect to China, and
in the hope of gaining new concessions. It was a strategic move, but also one
that was influenced by the memory of the history of territorial losses to Russia.
In the official Chinese record of Deng's meeting with Gorbachev, the Chinese
leader emphasized that the "past is past," but also repeatedly called attention to
the record of Russian and Soviet encroachments on Chinese territory (Deng
Xiaoping 1994: 284–87).

Despite these historical concerns and the turmoil that engulfed both China
and Eastern Europe in the summer and fall of 1989, an experts group on the
demilitarization of the border was formed and met for the first time in
November (Chen 1989a). Moreover, in the spring of the following year, a formal agreement on border troop reduction and confidence building in the border region was signed during Li Peng's historic trip to Moscow.[11]

The next major agreement reached between the two sides came in 1991,
during the lead up to Jiang Zemin's May summit meeting with Gorbachev. At
this time a treaty was signed that established the outlines for determining the
exact location of the eastern segment of the border. The agreement ensured
that, in principle, the location of the border in the river segment of the eastern
boundary was to be based on the main navigation line (*Guowuyuan Gongbao*
[State Council Gazetteer] 1992: 105–17). In addition, it conspicuously left aside
the enormous tracts of land China had highlighted in earlier commentary as
having been lost to Russian and Soviet encroachments. In short, it essentially
formalized the de facto location of the boundary between the two states and

divided the contested territory in this region equally between the two sides (Fravel 2003: 28). The 1991 treaty basically ended the dispute over the border-line in the eastern sector. However, it was not greeted with universal acceptance on either side of the border. It created a fair amount of local opposition in Russia (Burles 1999: 43–44; Moltz 1995), and in China, where the *South China Morning Post* discussed a report for internal circulation by a Chinese scholar that criticized the treaty for giving away too much territory to the Soviets. The report claimed that China had gained 600 square kilometers of disputed islands as a result of the treaty, but failed to recover territory that belonged to China through the 1920s. In addition, it argued "that with the dissolution of the Soviet Union, China was in a stronger position than ever before to negotiate for more territory around disputed border areas" ("China: Russian" 1992).

Regardless of how authoritative this report was, or how accurate its analysis of the Sino-Soviet boundary, the airing of these grievances at such a delicate stage in Sino-Soviet relations is indicative of two important trends in China. First, historically grounded understandings of the "legitimate" scope of China's territorial sovereignty vis-à-vis the Soviets/Russians were still prominent in Chinese foreign policy making circles in the early 1990s. Second, there was significant uncertainty in China over how to handle Sino-Soviet border relations in the wake of the collapse of the Soviet Union. In short, at the end of 1991, when the Soviet Union ceased to exist, Chinese policy makers had the opportunity to forward the claims outlined in the internal publication report mentioned above. However, doing so would have increased instability in the region (which was anathema to Deng's post-1989 emphasis on promoting order both at home and abroad). It would also have undercut the overall demilitarization of the border region itself. Indeed, by the end of 1991, Moscow had largely fulfilled Gorbachev's 1989 promise to reduce the Soviet troop presence in Asia (Moltz 1995: 516). Therefore, rather than pressing the Russians for more concessions, Beijing began even more strongly to emphasize negotiations (Yuan 1998b: 10).

Accordingly, Beijing sought to quickly stabilize ties with each of its new Central Asian neighbors (and in the process, secure the new territorial status quo within the region). This policy was embodied in a series of joint communiqués announcing the establishment of diplomatic relations between China and Kazakhstan, Tajikistan, and Kyrgyzstan ("China Establishes" 1992; "China, Kazakhstan" 1992; "China, Tadzhikistan" 1992). Beijing also opened negotiations on the location of the boundary, and troop reduction in the border region, with each of the Central Asian states. In addition, it issued a pair of joint statements, one with Kazakhstan and the other with Kyrgyzstan, before the summer of 1992. Both documents pledged that each of the parties would settle their territorial differences through negotiations using the norms of international law and the existing treaties as the basis for agreement, and committed each state to developing confidence-building measures (CBMs) in the border region shared with China. Finally, in one of the first indications of the multilateral forum that was to emerge later in the decade, a joint delegation of officials from each of the Central Asian republics and Russia traveled to Beijing to reiterate their states' commitments to the early Sino-Soviet boundary agreements and to work toward the creation of a demilitarized border region (Moltz 1995: 517; Wishnick 2001: 123).

In spite of this new focus on Central Asia, Chinese leaders did not neglect the Sino-Russian relationship. In mid-December 1992 Boris Yeltsin visited China, and during this trip both sides again pledged to continue negotiations on the location of the border and agreed to extend the border troop reduction and CBMs they had signed in 1990 ("China, Russia" 1992). In yet another sign of incipient multilateralism, the agreements signed by Beijing and Moscow during the summit stressed the need for the involvement of Tajikistan, Kazakhstan, and Kyrgyzstan in the border troop reduction and boundary resolution process (Yuan 1998b: 8).[12]

After this flurry of activity, 1993 was a year of relative quiet in China's effort to further stabilize its northern boundary. However, during the following year, Beijing signed two major border treaties that gave new momentum to this process. The first of these was the April 1994 Sino-Kazakh border agreement (*Guowuyuan Gongbao* 1994: 1178–94), which reiterated the importance of using existing agreements and norms of international law to determine the location of the boundary, and largely amounted to an acceptance by both the Chinese and Kazakhstan governments of the existing boundary line. However, in accepting this line, Beijing relinquished its claim to a substantial portion of the contested territory (which amounted to a little over 2,000 square kilometers) (Fravel 2003: 38; Polat 2002: 39–41). In any case, the actual transfer of territory was minimal, and a few relatively intractable differences over the location of the boundary were left aside in the agreement. In contrast, in September, during Jiang Zemin's visit to Russia, a second Sino-Russian border agreement was signed that formalized the location of the entire, admittedly short (55 km), western sector of the two states' border (*Guowuyuan Gongbao* 1994: 1205–8). The treaty noted that the border was indicated by two existing markers, and would be jointly noted on the official maps of both countries. In addition, both sides pledged to conduct joint surveys to delineate the border (although this did not begin in earnest for a number of years). The treaty did not address the "lost territory" to which Chinese commentary had pointed in the past, but instead simply made the de facto border in the region into a de jure one.

Building upon these developments, China, the Central Asian republics, and

Russia signed a historic CBM border agreement in Shanghai in April 1996 (Yu 1996). This treaty had two-fold significance. First, it formally established a 100-kilometer buffer zone on each side of the border (which had been under discussion since the early 1990s). Within this zone, it strictly limited the military exercises that could be conducted, and spelled out the notifications procedures all sides must follow in the event of such activity, as well as the type of tanks, artillery, and aircraft that were prohibited in the border region (Yuan 1998b: 18–20).[13] Second, the agreement strengthened the institutional setting for the weak multilateral framework that started to emerge in the region following the collapse of the Soviet Union, creating a mechanism for annual rounds of high-level meetings among each of the five signatories (Yuan 2003: 129).

Later in 1996, in conjunction with Jiang Zemin's visit to Kyrgyzstan, China and this Central Asian republic signed a border treaty that in principle resolved the vast majority of territorial differences between the two states (Polat 2002: 42). With the signing of this agreement, only the Tajikistan segment of the former Sino-Soviet western border remained undefined.[14] Thus, by the mid-1990s most disputes regarding China's northern boundary had each been resolved through negotiations and agreements. Furthermore, this entire border region had been partially demilitarized.

This outcome was the product of what Herbert Ellison and Bruce Acker identified as China and Russia's shared "desire to reduce tension along the border in order to focus their attention elsewhere. Russia . . . simply [could not] afford to maintain border troops and arms at the level of the earlier Sino-Soviet confrontation. With the threat along the Russian border reduced, China [was] better able to focus its resources on economic modernization and to assert its interests in the Asia-Pacific region" (quoted in Yuan 1998a: 11; also see Zhao 2001).

Unofficial commentary published in China at this time bolsters the first part of this argument (and we will see that Chinese behavior in the South China Sea during this time lends credence to the second part). For example, articles published in 1993 in *Xiandai Guoji Guanxi* and *Guoji Wenti Yanjiu* positively assessed the situation in Central Asia and the relationship between China and each of the states in the region (Wu Luming 1993; Xu Dan 1993). In addition, articles in *Dongou Zhongya Yanjiu* celebrated the progress that had been made in relations between China, Russia, and the Central Asian states and emphasized the importance for China of maintaining stability in the region ("Zhongguo-Eluosi" 1994). This sentiment was echoed in an article in *Guoji Wenti Yanjiu* in 1996 that assessed the state of Sino-Russian relations and made many references to the border and CBM agreements the two sides had signed (and steered clear of any mention of past or present territorial differences) (Shi Ze 1996).

However, not all analysis struck the same tone. Indeed, despite the significant progress that had been made in negotiations, the memory of historical transgressions against Chinese territory remained strong in foreign policy and national security circles. For example, while noting the overall progress in relations between China and Central Asia in 1992, a *Shijie Jingji yu Zhengzhi* article (Yin Weiguo 1992) also commented on the persistence of the unresolved territorial dispute between Russia, Kazakhstan, and China. In addition, it mentioned the extensive territory China lost as a result of the unequal treaties Russia forced upon the Qing dynasty. In the same vein, a 1994 forum in one of the RBGH journals reflected upon the history of Sino-Russian relations in the eastern border region, and in so doing once again recounted the long list of unequal treaties China had been forced to sign (Lu Yiran 1994). An article in a journal on Central Asian and Eastern European studies added that although 95 percent of the eastern segment of the Sino-Russian boundary had been agreed upon, a number of significant territorial differences had not been resolved. It also charged that this situation that been aggravated by the reckless way "some forces within Russia" were obstructing the implementation of the 1991 boundary agreement (Li Jingjie 1994).

Interviews I conducted in 1997 and 1998 with well-placed foreign policy analysts in Beijing revealed an even deeper level of frustration over the state of northern border relations in the late 1990s. In particular, three junior scholars voiced dissatisfaction over the border agreement China reached with Kazakhstan in 1994 (Personal interviews, Foreign Affairs College, Mar. 29,1998; Peking University, Apr. 8, 1998; and the Chinese Institute of Contemporary International Relations [CICIR], July 4, 1997). Each of these interviewees noted there had been some criticism of this agreement in internal publications for compromising too much on the recovery of territory lost as a result of the historical, and unequal, treaties between Russia and the Qing empire in the 1800s. In addition, the interviewees reported there was concern over the likelihood that China would fail to pursue historically based territorial claims along its border with Tajikistan. A scholar from the Foreign Affairs College in Beijing stated, "some within China are critical of the 'setting aside differences, mutual development approach' to handling the northern boundary. They contend 'this approach hurts China's sovereignty, and hurts China itself.' Some even joke that the government that supports such a policy is 'guilty of selling sovereignty' (*qu mai zhuquan*)" (Personal interview, May 9, 1997).

Despite the persistence of such concerns in China, over the second half of the 1990s, Beijing continued to stabilize the security situation along its northern boundaries and did so in part through accepting a series of additional territorial concessions with each of the Central Asian republics. The first of these agreements was a supplemental boundary protocol between China and Kazakhstan that was signed in the summer of 1998 (and was ratified by the National People's Congress [NPC] in November of the same year, and by Kazakhstan early the following year). Although the agreement produced resentment in Central Asia, it actually granted the Kazakhs control over the majority of territory in the disputed border regions.[15]

In the summer of 1999 Beijing also signed a follow-up treaty with Kyrgyzstan (formalizing a deal that the two sides had agreed upon the previous summer) that addressed the outstanding territorial concerns that had been left aside in the 1996 treaty. Once again, this agreement was controversial in Central Asia. The details of the treaty were kept "secret" until the spring of 2001, but reports indicated that China again opted not to push its claims to disputed territory (with most sources agreeing that the right to 70 percent of this land was given to Kyrgyzstan) (Fravel 2003; Polat 2002: 43).

In addition, the Chinese moved to finalize border talks with Tajikistan. Here again Beijing compromised on its earlier claims to territory. Indeed, flexibility here (as measured by the percentage of territory under dispute over which Beijing eventually gained control) was even more extensive. According to reports on the terms of the summer 1999 agreement and a supplemental spring 2002 protocol, Beijing gained a small amount of territory in the Pamir Mountain region, but also ceded its historical claim to a much larger stretch of land (Fravel 2003: 29–30).

Following these agreements (which essentially put an end to the very last outstanding disputes regarding China's northern territorial boundary), China hosted the summer 2001 round of the annual five-nation meetings (which had begun in 1997). At this session, held in Shanghai, the original members of the Shanghai Five were joined by Uzbekistan in signing a joint agreement that established the Shanghai Cooperation Organization (SCO) and the Shanghai Convention on Fighting Terrorism, Separatism, and Extremism (Yuan 2003: 133). The first of these agreements created a new regional security organization, and the second officially expanded the scope of activities of this nascent institution beyond the boundary settlement and military confidence-building measures that dominated the Shanghai Five's agenda in the mid-1990s.

In his official commentary on the establishment of the SCO, Jiang Zemin celebrated the organization as "as an important practice in international relations, which initiated a new type of security conception featuring mutual trust, disarmament and cooperative security" ("Chinese President Urges" 2001). He also revealed just how the Chinese conception of the main threats to China's sovereign boundaries had changed since the early 1980s. In his statement, Jiang noted the acceleration of "economic globalization and world multi-polarization," adding that such trends had resulted in a more pacific international system, but also posed "threats" (especially in the areas of terrorism, extremism, and separatism). The SCO, he declared, was designed to meet such challenges by promoting cooperation while strictly abiding by the principles of the UN Charter ("Chinese President Urges" 2001).

Chinese commentary on the SCO closely echoed Jiang's official statement. First, it was unrelentingly positive. Indeed, days before the SCO was formed, *Guofang Bao* trumpeted the Shanghai Five as an exemplar of a "new security concept" that surpassed old Cold War thinking (Shen Yan and Yu Shuyang 2001). In addition, on the day the SCO was announced, *Jiefangjun Bao* declared the development was "testimony to the rise of China's international status (*Zhongguo guoji diwei tigao de jianzheng*)" (Wang Guifang 2001). On the other hand, analysis underscored the extent to which Chinese strategy along the northern border had changed since the early 1990s. First, Chinese analysis clearly identified Beijing's growing economic interests in the region. For example, in *Xiandai Guoji Guanxi*, Xu Tao (2002: 11–12) observed, "The opening of the western region (*xibu kaifa*) is a major developmental strategy of China." Second, there was a limited acknowledgment of how participation in multilateral organizations could be used to underscore the extent to which China had become a responsible member of international society (He Weigang 2003; Jiang Yi 2003). Third, and most prominently, scholars emphasized how the threat of "terrorism" in the region had eclipsed Chinese concerns about the defense of territory against foreign incursions. For example, a second *Xiandai Guoji Guanxi* article by Xu Tao noted how the institutionalization of the organization was related to the emergence of new challenges and issues in Central Asia. Xu particularly stressed the expansion of the original Shanghai Five's commitment for cooperating in "traditional security areas" to "nontraditional ones," including separatism (*minzu fenlie zhuyi*) and religious extremism (*zongjiao jiduan zhuyi*) (Xu Tao 2003: 10–11).[16] It was this later aspect of the SCO that led some scholars to argue that it was a unique type of multilateral institution (not only in the region, but within the international system) (He Weigang 2003: 60–61; Jiang Yi 2003: 50).

These published assessments were almost identical to the views expressed during the interviews I conducted in 2001–2. In these discussions, the lingering resentments that had found a limited voice in foreign policy journals during the 1990s were largely absent. In their place, a number of security experts emphasized just how successful China had been in quickly resolving its outstanding territorial disputes to the north. While they saw this outcome as primarily the product of a shift in the balance of power between China and Russia, they also took pains to emphasize just how flexible and compromising Beijing had been in the negotiations. Underscoring his published work on these issue, a promi-nent scholar in Shanghai suggested that the Shanghai Six "should serve as a new model for multilateralism in the Asian region," and "the forum allowed each member state to preserve its sovereignty and territorial integrity, while also reaching cooperative outcomes on pressing security issues" (Personal interview, Shanghai Academy of Social Sciences, Jan. 7, 2002). In addition to such positive assessments of the SCO, a number of scholars also placed a new emphasis on the threat of terrorism in China's northwest. Although few of those interviewed even mentioned this issue in 1997–98, they raised it again and again during the 2001–2 interviews. Moreover, while a majority of this commentary focused on the impact the war on terrorism was likely to have on Sino-U.S. relations, many of the interviewees also dwelt on China's concerns about domestic terrorism and its relationship to Beijing's support of the SCO. A senior legal scholar noted, "We respect the religious rights of the people of Xinjiang, but when there is a link between religion and crime, and terrorism is without question a crime, then we must take action to protect the interests of the Chinese people. The formation of the SCO should assist us in succeeding in this difficult task" (Personal interview, Foreign Affairs College, Dec. 25, 2001).

All this reveals that the Chinese saw the SCO as a mechanism for cement-ing the territorial status quo in the region (both in terms of walling ethnic groups within states, and securing the lines between each of the members in the face of what Beijing saw as diverse transnational threats). Moreover, while many outside analysts (McNeal 2001; Oresman 2003) raised questions about the strength and relevance of the SCO in the aftermath of the September 11 attacks on the United States and the subsequent escalation of the American military presence in Central Asia, since 2001 Chinese leaders have continued to work with the other members to strengthen the organization. For example, in June 2002, the member states met in Moscow to sign the SCO's formal charter. In August of the following year, the SCO held its first "joint antiterrorism exercis-es" in the border region between Xinjiang and Kazakhstan. The operation involved over 1,000 participants from all the member states, and in a sign of the significance attached to it, Cao Gangchuan, vice-chair of the Central Military Commission and minister of defense had "profuse praise" for the multilateral effort ("China's Defense Minister" 2003).

The pathbreaking nature of this cooperative military exercise, and the per-sistence of Chinese concerns over Xinjiang, underline just how much had changed in Beijing's approach to China's northern boundary over the course of this phase, and how much had stayed the same. During this time China was, for the first time since the 1950s, able to secure a relatively peaceful security situa-tion along this entire frontier. However, it was also during this period that those in Beijing responsible for China's foreign policy making became increasingly preoccupied with the development of new threats to Chinese sovereignty in the region (namely, the apparent rise of separatist activities in Xinjiang).

Sino-Indian Border after 1988: De-escalating
Security Concerns

When viewed alongside the wide-ranging reorientation of Beijing's handling of China's northern boundary during the 1990s, China's approach to the Sino-Indian border during this period appears quite static. Indeed, in light of the fact that throughout the 1990s the Chinese extended no offers to India comparable to Deng's early 1980s suggestion that the two sides "swap" territory in the eastern and western sectors of the border region, Beijing's stance was arguably less flexible than during the first decade of the reform era. Moreover, following India's 1998 nuclear tests (and the strain they placed on Sino-Indian relations), the prospects for an early resolution of the Sino-Indian territorial dispute appeared to become even more remote. Thus, at the turn of the century, Beijing and New Delhi were in some respects further from compromising on the location of the border than they were in the 1980s. Even within the context of the recent renaissance in Sino-Indian relations (highlighted by the June 2003 summit meeting in Beijing between the Chinese leadership and Indian prime minister Vajpayee), the two sides have still been unable to make substantive progress on resolving the border issue.

Thus, over the course of the last decade, the Sino-Indian border dispute dragged on. However, such intractability should not overshadow three significant shifts during this phase in regard to how the Chinese endeavored to substantiate their claim to territory in the contested border region. First, for the first time since the 1962 border war, and in contrast to the 1980s, neither the official or unofficial discourse in China throughout this period dwelt at length on Chinese grievances against India. Second, while China maintained a strong military commitment to defending the border region, it also de-emphasized the use of military force in resolving the dispute.[17] Third, since 1988, Beijing has worked with New Delhi to establish a new framework for talking about the border. Over the course of this phase, negotiations about the handling (if not solving) of border issues, and a series of limited CBMs, have replaced the military standoffs and rhetorical confrontations that had defined both states' approach to the border through the mid-1980s. As a result, the border region, while remaining the site of pronounced differences, also became the location of an expanding web of cooperative interactions designed to prevent a reoccurrence of military conflict.

The starting point of this new phase in Sino-Indian border relations occurred during the November 1988 visit of Indian prime minister Rajiv Gandhi to China. During this visit, the escalation of hostilities that had unfolded during the preceding two years was designated as an issue of the past; for the first time since 1962, the two countries made substantive strides toward establishing a more normal, nonconfrontational relationship. New Delhi agreed that normalization could proceed even though the border issue remained outstanding and China continued its close relationship with Pakistan. For its part, Beijing tempered its position on Kashmir (by toning down its rhetorical support for Pakistan on this issue) and made additional pledges to develop Sino-Indian ties. Both sides attempted to downplay the importance of outstanding territorial concerns. Thus, the joint press communiqué issued during the summit emphasized, "The leaders of the two countries held earnest, in-depth discussions on the Sino-Indian boundary question through peaceful and friendly consultations. They also agreed to develop their relations actively in other fields and work hard to create a favorable climate and conditions for a fair and reasonable settlement of the boundary question while seeking a mutually acceptable solution to this question" ("China, India" 1988).

The impetus behind these developments was rapidly improving Sino-Soviet relations, paired with the ongoing groundswell of opposition to Chinese rule in Tibet (Ganguly 1989: 1132). The former pushed New Delhi in the direction of rapprochement (due to concerns about the possible erosion of Soviet support for India); the latter made Beijing more receptive to such moves than it had been earlier in the decade (by virtue of an interest in garnering Indian support of the Chinese position on Tibet—which it gained during the summit). These new factors then converged with Deng's overall drive to create a stable regional environment within which China could concentrate on economic growth and development, creating the foundation for a new period in Sino-Indian relations.[18]

However, such international and domestic forces proved to be insufficient to overcome the basic differences between India and China over their territorial dispute. The main obstacle to compromise on the Chinese side was, as before, concerns about how any resolution might affect Beijing's strategic position in the border region. However, it is also apparent that within foreign policy and national security making circles, historically framed conceptions of the legitimacy of Chinese territorial claims in the region also constrained China's willingness to negotiate. For example, in his consideration of the muted debate in China at this time between moderates and hardliners over the border issue, John Garver reported that a 1989 article by Wang Hongwei, director of CASS's South Asian Studies Institute, admitted that "'a significant number of comrades believe' that China's territory south of the McMahon Line must be recovered" (Garver 2001a: 107). Further evidence of this conviction is evident in an article

in a RBHG publication by Yang Gongsu (1989a), an influential Chinese scholar with extensive experience in both Indian and Tibetan affairs, which emphasized the impact of British imperial aggression on the Sino-Indian border and
repeated the claims of lost territory in each of the border sections.

Such historically framed reticence notwithstanding, in 1989 China and India
proceeded to build upon the momentum created by the 1988 summit meeting
by establishing a new joint working group on the border, which convened for
the first time in July. Although the working group produced few substantive
results, Beijing attached great importance to it. Thus, Li Peng personally greeted the Indian delegation during its stay in Beijing. During this meeting Li not
only commented upon the progress made during the negotiations, but also
emphasized Beijing's success in curbing the "counter-revolutionary rebellion"
within China ("China Hopes" 1989). Li's post-Tiananmen refrain points to the
value Beijing placed on the convocation of the joint working group at this time,
as China attempted to cope with the international condemnation of its June
suppression of the student-led protest movement. The talks provided the
Chinese leadership with a forum to confront these pressures.

Consistent with such new strategic concerns, during the immediate post-
Tiananmen period the more hard-line voices in China on Sino-Indian border
relations fell silent (Garver 2001a: 108). Moreover, two new meetings of the
joint working group were convened in the fall of 1990 and spring of 1991
respectively. As was made evident by Li Peng's December 1991 visit to India,
Beijing renewed its commitment to cementing a more stable dynamic in the
disputed border region. In the lead-up to this trip, Li talked openly about his
interest in addressing the border issue. Xinhua noted that he told an Indian
reporter he was "satisfied" with the state of border negotiations, and was "willing to exchange views with Prime Minister Rao concerning the border issue
during my forthcoming visit. . . . So long as we adopt an attitude of mutual
understanding and mutual accommodation, and continue our unremitting
efforts there will eventually be a resolution which is satisfactory to both sides"
("Li Peng Expresses" 1991). Li also claimed that China had already significantly
reduced its forces in the border region, and that "both sides should abide by the
border lines under actual control, and should strive to ensure an environment
of peace and tranquility" (Ibid.).

Following Li's visit to India, the framework for cooperative border relations
continued to expand with a series of high-level meetings. The first of these sessions was the fourth round of joint working group talks held in February of
1992, when the two sides began to substantiate their rhetorical commitment to
defusing tensions in the border region by agreeing to an expansion of cross-
border communications mechanisms in the eastern and western sections of the

border. This was followed by prominent visits to China by the Indian president and defense minister during the summer of 1992, and complemented in 1993 with the sixth session of the joint working group.[19] As in the earlier sessions of the group, the environment in this round of talks was "candid and realistic" (Mansingh 1994: 291), and at this time the two sides came to terms on a CBM regime for the border region. The formal signing of this agreement took place during Indian prime minister Rao's September 1993 visit to Beijing.

The text of the 1993 CBM revealed a mix of remaining obstacles as well as progress that had been made in Sino-Indian border relations since 1988. On the one hand, it explicitly emphasized that the CBM did not address the underlying issue of the location of the boundary. In addition, it made no mention of specific troop numbers in the border region, or of the limits that would be placed on military deployments there.[20] On the other hand, it significantly reduced the chances of accidental conflict. It committed both sides to refrain from the use of force in the border region, to observe and respect the LAC, to establish a rudimentary system of notification of violations, to reduce (in principle) military presence, and to continue negotiations and consultations.[21]

Unofficial analysis of Sino-Indian relations published during this period reflects the promise of such developments as well as the persistence of Chinese concerns about Sino-Indian relations. For example, a thorough search of Chinese commentary revealed that in contrast to the 1980s, no scholar emphasized the loss of Chinese territory through Indian encroachment. At the same time, none openly argued for the ceding of Chinese claims in the border region, and some pointed to the obstacles (relating to Tibet, territorial concerns, and India's regional ambitions) that had to be addressed before a further improvement of bilateral relations could take place (Malik 1995: 328). Yet, rather than focusing on contentious issues, contributors to the major foreign policy journals concentrated on the importance of further developing cooperative relations with India (and in the process also indirectly revealed the underlying Chinese interest in such a development). Chinese analysts pointed to three factors that had enhanced Beijing's commitment to improving Sino-Indian relations (and by extension China's willingness to postpone pressing for a quick resolution of the territorial dispute between the two sides). First, Beijing valued India's support for China during the immediate post-Tiananmen period. Second, both India and China stood to make significant economic gains if they were able to overcome their differences on security issues. Third, China still needed to secure a stable regional environment in order to continue to focus on economic growth and development at home (see Ma Jiali 1994; Zhao and Deshinkar 1995; Cheng Ruisheng 1993a, 1993b).

In a policy move that confirmed the validity of these assessments, the first meetings of a newly established experts group on the border were held in the winter and spring of 1994. Clearly, the creation of this forum for discussing border issues indicated the two sides were attempting to resolve their territorial differences. However, it was also apparent in these meetings that there were difficulties inherent in building cooperation while fundamental differences over territory remained. The first session of the experts group was held against the backdrop of rising Chinese concerns over Indian support for Tibetan independence activities within India (Wang 1995: 553–54) and reports of limited military buildups in the border region (Barnett 1994). During the second session, the Chinese side reportedly maintained that China's force reductions should be limited to border defense forces (and not include troops stationed in Tibet), while the Indian side opposed one-to-one reductions of forces in the immediate vicinity of the border, arguing instead for proportional military reductions (Foot 1996: 64; Mansingh 1994: 291).

Despite these differences, during the eighth round meeting of the joint working group in August 1995, China and India reiterated their commitment to implementing the 1993 CBM agreement. The two sides also agreed to dismantle border posts in the Wangdong area of the eastern sector of the border and called for regular meetings of border security authorities ("Sino-Indian" 1995). Subsequently, in late November of 1996, Jiang Zemin paid a state visit to India, and although no official joint statement or communiqué was issued during his trip, it constituted a symbolic high point in Sino-Indian relations. It was marked by the announcement of a second Sino-Indian border CBM.

This CBM established more extensive guidelines for the partial demilitarization of the Sino-Indian border. Both sides again pledged not to use force in the border region and, pending a final resolution of the border dispute, to accept the LAC as constituting the status quo in the region. The agreement placed a cap on infantry combat vehicles in the border region; limited the caliber of guns and mortars that would be used within the region; specified the surface-to-surface and surface-to-air missiles that could be deployed; committed both sides to refrain from military exercises involving more than one division (15,000 troops) in close proximity to the LAC; prohibited the flight of combat aircraft in airspace within ten kilometers of the LAC; and banned the firing of weapons within two kilometers of the LAC (*Renda Gongbao* no. 3, 1997: 479–85). In short, the 1996 agreement, along with the 1993 CBM, facilitated a major reduction in tensions in the border region consistent with the ongoing overhaul of Sino-Indian relations during the first half of the 1990s.

This development elicited a wave of positive Chinese commentary. For example, in a 1996 reflection on Sino-Indian relations since 1988, Ye Zhengjia, a senior researcher at the Chinese Institute of International Studies (CIIS), concluded that neither side should view the other as a threat, or "resort to war for small pieces of territory"; instead, "for the sake of peace and development, we should turn negative factors into positive ones" (1996: 120). However, the enthusiasm that marked published analysis like this was belied in 1997 during my private interviews with Chinese experts on Indian affairs, in which the historically conditioned territorial claims Yang outlined in 1989 occupied a prominent position.

The most authoritative of the individuals interviewed, a retired Foreign Ministry official who had been personally involved with the abortive border negotiations between China and India in the 1950s, was skeptical about the prospects for Sino-Indian border talks. According to the interviewee, it was only possible to understand the contemporary Chinese stance on Sino-Indian border relations with reference to the historical losses China had suffered prior to the establishment of the PRC. He observed that from the time of the Opium wars, "China's sovereignty and territorial control were abused and oppressed, therefore China developed a very sensitive attitude toward territorial issues" (Personal interview, May 20, 1997). Moreover, he was adamant about the historical legitimacy of each of the territorial claims China had made in relation to the Sino-Indian border dispute, taking pains to point out the aggressiveness of Indian posturing in the border region. When pressed, the interviewee commented briefly that negotiations had taken place between the two sides during the 1980s and 1990s. However, his consideration of those talks was couched in terms of the magnanimity of the Chinese and the recalcitrance of the Indians. Indeed, he only grudgingly accepted the proposition that any progress at all had been made on the border issue.

The persistence of reservations of this sort among informed experts underscores the limited nature of the Sino-Indian rapprochement (even when the relationship appeared to be at its most stable). Moreover, in the spring of 1998, the foundation for a cooperative framework was shaken when India conducted a series of nuclear tests (dubbed Pokhran II), and afterward attempted to justify the tests by pointing to its concerns about the security threat China posed in South Asia. Outside analysts seem to agree that Beijing's response to these moves was more directly linked to its outrage over Indian references to the "China threat" before and after the tests were carried out than it was to the tests themselves (Garver 2001b; Yuan 2001). In short, at a time when China was feverishly working to counter charges within the region (and from the United States) about the destabilizing nature of China's economic and military rise, Indian accusations struck a particularly raw nerve in Chinese foreign policy and national security making circles, temporarily setting back Sino-Indian relations.

Two months after the tests, the Chinese ambassador to India, Zhou Gang,

warned that Indian accusations about the "China threat" had "harmed the
developing bilateral relations and endangered the future of relations between
the two countries" ("India Urged" 1998). On the heels of such criticism, Beijing
also postponed the scheduled eleventh meeting of the joint working group
(which was originally to have taken place in November 1988).[22] Consistent
with these moves, for the first time since the late 1980s, China's small community of India experts issued a series of commentary that was bluntly critical of
New Delhi. Writing in *Xiandai Guoji Guanxi*, Ma Jiali observed that the Indian
tests and New Delhi's attempt to justify them with reference to the "China
threat" had revealed India's true intentions and "seriously damaged relations
between the two countries" (1998: 22).

    This consternation (and its links to Chinese thinking about the border issue)
was given an even clearer voice in the interviews I conducted in the summer of
1998 with an expert on Sino-Indian affairs at CICIR and with another expert
at the China International Studies Center. Both interviewees took umbrage at
the Indian government, loading their discussion of the border issue with historically laden references to Beijing's commitment to protect Chinese territorial
sovereignty in disputed areas. The CICIR expert, who was a frequent participant
in the 1990s border negotiations, noted that territorial sovereignty was a major
issue in Sino-Indian relations.[23] He also expressed much frustration over the lack
of progress in the negotiations and repeatedly contrasted what he saw as the reasonableness of the Chinese position with the intractability of the Indian government and scholars. The China International Studies Center expert dwelt upon
an almost identical set of points in his interview. Again, the historical sensitivity
to territorial sovereignty was highlighted, with the interviewee noting, "China's
leaders are very sovereignty minded. They are very reluctant to give up sovereignty unless there is a big benefit in return" (Personal interview, China
International Studies Center, June 30, 1998). However, in contrast with his counterpart at CICIR, this scholar used the Sino-Indian border dispute to showcase
Chinese flexibility rather than to attack Indian aggression. For example, he
claimed that although China does not recognize the legality of the McMahon
line, it has not insisted on the traditional boundary line as the basis for settling
the border dispute. He also noted that it was essential for Beijing and New Delhi
to work out their differences in order to promote regional security.

    This final sentiment surpassed (but did not replace) Chinese reservations
about cooperating with India in 1999. For example, at this time, analysts reiterated the need to patch up the tattered Sino-Indian relationship. Thus, while
Song Dexing (1999), a scholar from Nanjing University, argued in *Shijie Jingji
yu Zhengzhi* that India had deliberately misinterpreted Chinese policy and used

the excuse of concern about the Chinese threat to Indian security following Pokhran II, he also concluded that China remained committed to improving relations with India, and contended that stabilizing Sino-Indian relations was important for the development of both regional and world peace. Cheng Ruisheng (1999: 3) added, "In the long run, prospect of Sino-Indian relations is quite good because of various common interest of both countries. The most important common interest of them is to have a peaceful environment so that both could concentrate on economic and social development."[24]

Over the course of the year, a pronounced shift in the global and regional security dynamic led to new policies consistent with such cooperative rhetoric. More specifically, over the first half of the year, India became embroiled in an escalation of long-standing tensions with Pakistan over Kashmir; Beijing, which had tended to back Pakistan in such situations in the past, was notably silent on the crisis (Garver 2002). This silence, coupled with repeated backpedaling by Indian officials on the "China threat" and mounting concerns in Beijing about the possible threat posed by U.S. hegemonism (vis-à-vis Kosovo), paved the way for the visit of Indian foreign minister Jaswant Singh to Beijing in April, and the convening of the previously postponed eleventh session of the joint working group.

Although neither of these meetings produced tangible results, they represented a significant upgrade in the overall Sino-Indian relationship, and were followed in the spring of 2000 with the establishment of yet another confidence-building forum (in the form of an institutionalized exchange between the Chinese Foreign Ministry and Indian External Affairs Ministry) for managing the Sino-Indian boundary (Frasier 2000: 13), a move that was complemented by the convocation of yet another session of the joint working group (Sidhu and Yuan 2003: 123). In the wake of these two meetings, Indian president K. R. Narayanan traveled to Beijing and, according to Indian reports, pressed for a speedy resolution of the border dispute (a proposition that was met somewhat coolly by Chinese officials who laid a heavier emphasis on simply mending fences) (Frasier 2000: 15). Nonetheless, China's newly appointed foreign minister, Tang Jiaxuan, traveled to New Delhi the next month, and in 2001 additional meetings were held.[25] Moreover, during the 2001 session of the joint working group, both sides pledged for the first time to begin exchanging maps on the border (starting with the central segment) (Sidhu and Yuan 2003: 33). This paved the way for the 2003 official state visit to China by Indian prime minister Vajpayee, during which India reiterated its recognition of Tibet's status as a part of China, and Beijing in return (albeit later in the year and in a vague fashion) for the first time moved to recognize the Indian annexation of Sikkim (which New Delhi had laid claim to in the 1970s). However, despite early media reports to the contrary, the two sides were unable to make any public announcement of a major breakthrough on the border.[26]

In sum, it is clear that since 1988 China's position on securing the mountainous southern limits of its territorial sovereignty shifted from military posturing and rhetorical positioning, to participation in frequent negotiating sessions and an incremental expansion in limited confidence-building measures. This development was largely a product of a relative convergence of interests between the two sides to cement a more predictable relationship. Bracketing territorial differences with the mechanism of CBMs and institutionalized negotiating sessions allowed this process to move forward. Chinese decision makers also utilized these developments to promote an image of China as nonaggressive and cooperative, to offset charges of an emerging "China threat" in the region. However, neither China nor India was willing, or able, to resolve their border dispute.

The intractability of their differences is located in the static strategic importance of the territory at stake. The disputed section of the western sector of the boundary includes territory that contains the only land route between Xinjiang and Tibet, and thus is one of the major logistical links for the Chinese military in western China. The fate of this territory also has obvious ties to the Indian struggle with Pakistan over Kashmir and the location of the boundary between the two states along the Siachen glacier. In addition, control of contested territory in the eastern sector is considered to be of central importance to India's security vis-à-vis China. In other words, compromise by either side would have significant costs that neither is willing to bear. However, beyond such rational calculations, the intractability of the dispute is also tied to the fact that Chinese foreign policy and national security making circles have internalized historically based interpretations of the extent of Chinese territory in the region.

The Sino-Vietnamese Border after 1988: Containing Potentially Explosive Differences at Sea

Consistent with the developments during the 1990s in Beijing's approach to the boundaries China shared with the Soviet Union (Russia and Central Asian republics) and India, since the spring of 1988 the Chinese stance on Sino-Vietnamese border relations has also incrementally changed. During this period, Chinese practices generally reduced the likelihood of overt military conflict and promoted a negotiated settlement of outstanding disputes in a manner consistent with the territorial status quo established in the region in the 1980s. However, this shift was more tentative and encompassed more diverse policy measures and discursive pronouncements than was the case with either of the border dyads discussed so far in this chapter.

The starting point of this phase was the cautious, indeed somewhat contra-dictory, Chinese response to Hanoi's moves to improve Sino-Vietnamese rela-tions in the late 1980s. On the one hand, at this time the Chinese participated in a round of unofficial exchanges designed to explore normalizing relations with Vietnam. In addition, after the spring of 1988, Chinese reports of Vietnamese incursions across the land border became increasingly rare (as did Vietnamese objections to Chinese advances) (Amer 1997: 88). Moreover, sub-stantial trade resumed across this line for the first time since the 1979 war (Gu and Womack 2000: 1042). Finally, in 1990 in a statement Li Peng made in Singapore, Beijing raised the possibility of the joint development of the Nansha Islands (Garver 1992: 1015–16; Hyer 1995: 50–51). However, on the other hand, tensions in the South China Sea remained high. In the aftermath of the spring 1988 confrontation over the Nansha Islands, the People's Liberation Navy (PLAN) reiterated the need for China to develop blue water naval capabilities (to protect Chinese claims in the region and to ensure China's role as a region-al power), and continued to pursue the restructuring program first initiated in the early 1980s to make China's navy "leaner and meaner" (You 1999: 184–85, 224).[27] Furthermore, Beijing repeatedly objected to perceived Vietnamese aggression at sea, vehemently defending China's claims to contested maritime territory (Chen 1989b).

Unofficial commentary published during this period strongly supported the official rhetoric. For example, from 1989 to 1991, three articles focusing on the maritime boundary appeared in the major international relations journals. Each of these articles insisted on the necessity of defending China's territorial rights in the South China Sea. The first began by asserting that the Xisha and Nansha Islands had belonged to China "since ancient times" and followed this with a blunt declaration of the indisputable sovereignty that contemporary China had established over these islands. The authors then protested that the Vietnamese effort to give the islands Vietnamese names was an obvious attempt to create confusion over their actual status as Chinese territory (Dai Kelai and Yu Xiangdong 1989). The second article asserted that in international law, no ter-ritorial conflict existed between Vietnam and China over the Nansha Islands, as "China's sovereignty over the Nansha islands was already decided at an earlier time to be indisputable" (Cheng Xiaoxu and Zhang Wenbin 1990: 64). This position was supported by the recitation of the litany of China's historical claims to the islands. The authors concluded that "regardless of whether the issue is examined from the perspective of discovery, private activities, government administration, or individual government's recognition, China had effective sov-ereignty over the Nansha archipelago, and this is entirely in accord with the demands of international law" (p. 66). The third article, while not focused pure-

ly on Sino-Vietnamese border relations, protested against Vietnamese territorial claims to the Xisha and Nansha islands. In addition, it specifically mentioned
the Vietnamese occupation of twenty islands, reefs, and sandbars in the region
(Chen Ning 1991).

Despite such pronounced concerns, in November of 1991 China and
Vietnam moved to formally normalize relations when the general secretary of
the Vietnamese Communist Party, Do Muoi, visited Beijing. The joint communiqué that marked this dramatic development not only laid out a general framework for enhancing bilateral ties (through a commitment to "good-neighborly
and friendly relations"), but also committed the two sides to work toward a
negotiated settlement of "boundary and other territorial issues" ("China,
Vietnam Issue" 1991). A rudimentary CBM agreement on the principles for
resolving the border dispute was also signed. This agreement, while not mentioning specific border issues, did contain assurances that both sides would work
"to make the border between the two countries one of peace and friendship,"
jointly safeguard the "security of border regions," and promote "border and
regional trade" ("China and Vietnam Sign" 1991).

In general, the same set of factors that led to the moderation of Chinese handling of Sino-Soviet and Sino-Indian border relations also played a prominent
role in bringing about the establishment of this new framework for managing
the Sino-Vietnamese boundary dispute. Here too, the historically framed conceptions of the legitimacy of Chinese territorial claims in the region outlined
above (which fueled opposition to any compromise in policy-making circles),
were offset by broader strategic considerations. More specifically, a premium was
again placed on creating a more stable regional security environment. The
Chinese were willing to put aside (if not give up) the most contentious territorial claims that had previously appeared to pose insurmountable obstacles to
improving relations with Vietnam (Chen 1994: 893–94; Dobson and Fravel
1997: 260–61; Lee 1999: 10, 92–93). This shift in priorities resulted in a relatively speedy resolution of outstanding differences over the land border (where the
disputed territory was quite small, the discourse of ownership inchoate, and the
strategic and economic value very limited). However, maritime disputes proved
to be more intractable, as the Chinese struggled to balance several factors: the
deep-seated belief in foreign policy and national security making circles in the
historical legitimacy of Chinese claims to the South China Sea; interest in garnering the economic and security benefits that would flow from establishing
control over the contested territory; and the desire to promote regional stability (made all the more salient by the fact that exploiting the reported oil reserves
in the area would require at least a modicum of cooperation from other
claimants to the disputed territory).[28]

During the early 1990s, these mixed motives led to territorial practices designed to both establish Chinese authority over contested regions and develop a cooperative framework for working with Vietnam in order to mitigate the resulting tensions. In light of the incompatibility of these two goals, it is not surprising that Chinese words and actions during this period often appeared to vacillate between "hard" and "soft" positioning (Hyer 1995).

The former, hard approach was articulated at the start of 1992, through extensive PLAN inspections in the Xisha region. Moreover, the NPC approved a resolution formalizing China's authority over the South China Sea ("Text" 1992). The resolution reiterated Beijing's claim to "undisputable sovereignty" over China's maritime possessions (which were enumerated in the text of the resolution), and authorized the Chinese military to use force in the event of any attempt by other claimants to seize that territory.[29] In addition, while China had begun to participate in annual ministerial meetings of ASEAN at this time, Chinese officials also made it clear that they did not see this multilateral forum as an appropriate venue for the discussion of China's disputed territorial claims in the region (Lee 1999: 22–26).

Yet, paralleling such "assertive" moves were softer, cooperative gestures. Thus, in February Chinese foreign minister Qian Qichen traveled to Hanoi and announced, "We have finished with a phase of confrontation and we are beginning a new phase, one which will lead to development around the region" ("Chinese Minister" 1992). In addition, the land border was reopened for the first time since 1979, and Chinese and Vietnamese "experts" held talks on outstanding border issues (Amer 2002: 9). Moreover, at the end of 1992, Li Peng visited Vietnam. According to a Xinhua report on this trip, Li spoke of the need for "seeking common ground and reserving differences," urging both sides not to let border issues "hamper the improvement and development of bilateral relations" ("China, Vietnam Agree" 1992). Underscoring Li's conciliatory words, a joint communiqué was signed that established a framework for government-level negotiations on both the land and ocean (in the Beibu Gulf) boundary disputes (*Guowuyuan Gongbao* 1992: 1439–41).

In 1993, Beijing redoubled its emphasis on cooperative measures. At the regional level, Chinese officials were actively involved in the planning for an ASEAN regional security forum (even though the Chinese continued to oppose the inclusion of the South China Sea issue on its agenda). Concurrently, the first government-level talks between China and Vietnam relating to the border were held in August of 1993.[30] In addition, in October both sides recommitted to a resolution of territorial issues according to the principles agreed to in 1991. Chinese reports on these developments explained that the two sides had identified the Beibu Gulf and the land border as two distinct concerns (conspicuously omitting any direct reference to the more contentious South China Sea). An accord signed at this meeting strengthened the nascent bilateral CBM regime established in 1991 by formally creating new working groups on the land border and the Beibu Gulf. It also observed that China and Vietnam had "created conditions and laid foundations for a fair, reasonable settlement of the existing border and territorial issues between the two countries" ("China, Vietnam Sign Accord" 1993). As Ni Xiayun (1994: 14) noted the following year, these commitments meant that "China and Vietnam have already made progress on the delineation (*hua jie*) of the land and Beibu Gulf boundary issues, but contradictions still exist over the issue of the Nansha Islands."

Consistent with this observation, the first meetings of the land and Beibu Gulf working groups were held at the start of 1994, even as both Vietnam and China aggressively maneuvered to bolster their claims to the contested regions in the South China Sea. This competition crested in the summer, when Hanoi and Beijing traded pointed accusations decrying the illegitimacy of each other's claims to the region. International press reports from this period repeatedly warned that armed conflict between the two sides seemed eminent (Shenon 1994). However, even as tensions mounted, the two joint working groups met for a second time to discuss the land border and Beibu Gulf. In addition, in late July, at the first full session of the Asian Regional Forum (ARF), China and Vietnam de-escalated the conflict when they specifically agreed for the first time to address their differences over the South China Sea through talks ("China and Vietnam Agree" 1994).[31]

Later in 1994, Jiang Zemin's official state visit to Vietnam consolidated this positive turn in Sino-Vietnamese relations. The joint communiqué that marked this trip, while not directly mentioning the South China Sea, reiterated both sides' commitment to avoid using force to settle outstanding territorial differences, and set forth Beijing and Hanoi's intent to work toward a negotiated settlement of all their outstanding border disputes (including those involving "the seas"). In addition, it noted that a new experts group would be created to discuss such issues ("Joint Communique" 1994).

In the mid-1990s, Beijing and Hanoi sought to build on this cooperative trend, and continued to inch their way toward resolving all three facets of the Sino-Vietnamese territorial dispute. Talks on the land border and Beibu Gulf intensified, with multiple sessions held in both China and Vietnam. In addition, in November of 1995 a new forum for the discussion of the South China Sea was inaugurated. In the official commentary on the inaugural meeting, the Chinese attempted both to lay claim to contested territory and to underscore their interest in negotiations. Thus, the lead Xinhua report on the meeting began with an assertion of Chinese sovereignty "over the Nansha islands and the sea waters around them," but added that the dispute over the islands should "be settled by peaceful means rather than by force or the threat of using force." It concluded that China was interested in resolving the dispute with Vietnam through negotiation and the use of international law, and, making use of the words of Deng Xiaoping, encouraged the two sides to temporarily set aside differences and "seek joint development or cooperation in various forms" ("China Has Indisputable Sovereignty" 1995). During the same month, Do Muoi paid a second official visit to Beijing, and a joint communiqué once again committed China and Vietnam to resolving their territorial disputes peacefully ("Sino-Vietnamese" 1995). The following year, despite the emergence of minor differences over the development of oil concessions in contested territory, border talks continued (even as nonconventional security concerns, such as smuggling, started to attract greater attention), and Sino-Vietnamese relations were boosted by Li Peng's June visit to Hanoi.

As promising as such developments were for an eventual peaceful resolution of China's maritime border disputes, they were offset by the ratcheting up of tensions between China and other regional claimants to the South China Sea. Most significantly, in late 1994 the Chinese began work on the construction of an outpost on Mischief Reef, an outcropping located in a region of the South China Sea claimed by the Philippines.[32] When Manila discovered this at the start of 1995, it reacted vigorously, and as the year wore on minor skirmishes took place, accompanied by strident rhetorical volleys between the two capitals. Nonetheless, as ominous as such moves were, they fell well short of the sustained border wars in which China had previously become embroiled. Even as the dispute unfolded, Beijing agreed to participate in limited talks with the Philippines (and Manila also sought a negotiated settlement).

Initially, there were two main reasons for China's restraint. First, although Manila lacked the forces to engage China, a sustained confrontation would have overtaxed the capabilities of the PLAN, despite a decade of modernization. In other words, neither side had the military wherewithal for a prolonged conflict. Second, Chinese basic strategic interests in the region had not changed. Beijing still valued regional stability over reclaiming territory (and thus was unwilling to push its military operation in the Mischief Reef area too far). As the year progressed, two additional factors that moderated Chinese behavior also became more pronounced. First, although the United States reiterated its stance of non-involvement in the dispute, it also warned that the disruption of sea lanes in the region was unacceptable ("U.S. Stresses" 1995). Second, for the first time, the Southeast Asian states made concrete moves to build on their 1992 rhetorical call for a code of conduct in the South China Sea ("ASEAN Plea" 1995).

These developments were sufficient to convince Beijing to moderate its stance on the South China Sea, while falling well short of eliciting a compromise on the territorial issues at stake. Thus, at the second full session of the ARF held at the end of July, Beijing reiterated its territorial claims in the region, but also moved to counter charges about its hegemonic intent in the area. The Chinese subsequently worked to firm up the still shaky relationship with Manila and allowed for an incremental expansion in the discussion of the South China Sea issue in the ARF ("Qian on China's Stand" 1995; Lee 1999: 36–39).

The following year witnessed a continuation of these trends, as the Chinese once more emphasized bilateral talks (now with both Vietnam and the Philippines) and again tempered their opposition to the discussion of territorial issues involving China in both ASEAN and the ARF. Yet, despite such conciliatory moves, in March 1997 Sino-Vietnamese relations were again strained following Beijing's decision to explore oil reserves in territory claimed by Hanoi. Although this controversy quickly faded when Beijing withdrew, it underscored the fact that basic differences remained between China and Vietnam over territorial issues (even as the two sides were making significant strides toward the resolution of many aspects of their disputes).

Specialists on maritime territorial issues in China interviewed at this time dwelt at length on such disagreements. For example, in May 1997 a senior scholar at CASS noted, "The influence of the past is still great. Look at our problems with the South China Sea. . . . We have proposed putting aside sovereignty, mutual development, but this has not been acknowledged" (Personal interview, June 23, 1997). The following year, a retired government official who had been part of China's delegation to the law of the sea talks at the United Nations was even more direct. He noted, "They say we are the aggressors. On the contrary, we have suffered great indignities as a result of our restraint in the region, and I don't know how much longer we can do so if provocations continue" (Personal interview, Apr. 23, 1998).

Although such warnings were historically framed, it is also telling that the greatest frustration was expressed over the lack of international recognition of China's restraint (rather than over its territorial incursions). A leitmotiv on the importance of regional stability and security (overlaying the claim to contested waters) was the most prominent feature of the 1997–98 interviews and published commentary on the South China Sea. For instance, an influential scholar of Sino-U.S. relations at Peking University noted that China had been remarkably pragmatic in dealing with the South China Sea issue. He observed that China had agreed to put aside questions of sovereignty in this region and "even in territories where there are disputes over whether it is ours or yours, we are still willing to go ahead and mutually develop such territory" (Personal interview, June 6, 1997).

While published commentary contained no hint of such resentments, it gave even greater weight to responsibility and constraint. Writing in the *Xiandai Guoji Guanxi*, Ding Kuisong (1998: 12) dissected the ARF's role in Asia, and urged those involved in the organization to recognize its value as the reflection of new post–Cold War thinking about political and security cooperation and a new means for handling political and security relations in Asia, all of which made the ARF a "security pillar" of Asia (see also He Kai 1998; and Ma Zhigang 1999).

In line with such discussions, border negotiations proceeded without inter- ruption in 1997, spurred on by yet another visit by Do Muoi to China in July. Indeed, according to Vietnamese reports of this trip, Do Muoi and Jiang Zemin reached an agreement to accelerate the pace of both the land and Beibu Gulf negotiations (Amer 2002: 21). Official Chinese accounts of the summit made no mention of this timetable, but they did celebrate the progress that had been made between the two sides ("China, Vietnam Agree" 1997).

In October of the following year, during a visit by the Vietnamese prime minister to China, a Xinhua report confirmed the Vietnamese coverage of the 1997 meeting when it acknowledged Jiang Zemin's personal involvement in the preceding year's talks and referred to the "consensus" the two sides had reached at the time to "sign the land border treaty before the year 2000, and conclude the demarcation of the Beibu Gulf by the end of this century" ("Jiang Zemin Meets" 1998). These sentiments were echoed in other official coverage of the Vietnamese prime minister's trip to China, and then reinforced in December when Hu Jintao, then China's vice president, traveled to Vietnam and again called for a quick resolution of the Sino-Vietnamese dispute.

In 1999, this flurry of diplomatic activity began to yield substantial results. The year began with the visit to China of Le Kha Phieu, general secretary of the Vietnamese Communist Party. The joint statement issued in conjunction with this trip once again promised a rapid negotiated settlement of both the land and Beibu Gulf differences, and committed both sides to a weakly word- ed CBM measure in the South China Sea, through a pact to seek a "fundamen- tal and long-term solution" of other "maritime issues" ("China and Vietnam Issue Joint Statement" 1999). Following this announcement, the pace of talks between the two sides accelerated, and by the end of the year a treaty on the land border was signed during Tang Jiaxuan's visit to Hanoi. Although details of the agreement were sparse in official Chinese statements, they called attention to the fact that it had resolved all outstanding issues regarding the land border, and emphasized that it constituted a landmark in Sino-Vietnamese relations ("China, Vietnam Sign" 1999).

China ratified the land boundary agreement in the spring of 2000. According to M. Taylor Fravel's (2003) analysis of this treaty, Beijing agreed to a 50/50 split of the very small amount of territory that had been contested. However, Ramses Amer (2002: 39) points out that the agreement was signed prior to demarcation on the ground, a task that would actually "put the treaty and its contents to the test." Thus, although the treaty brought to a close a significant and conflictual chapter in Sino-Vietnamese relations, it did not, according to reports, end ongoing difficulties with demarcating the lines it established, tensions over the location of specific border outposts, and concerns over smuggling across the border (Tonnesson 2003: 62–63).

Nevertheless, with the December 1999 land border agreement in hand, the focus of negotiations between Hanoi and Beijing quickly turned to reaching an agreement on the Beibu Gulf (and managing the still pronounced differences between the two sides in the South China Sea). In 2000, this led to yet another series of high-level meetings between Beijing and Hanoi (accompanied by more negotiating sessions by the relevant working groups) (Amer 2002: 40–41). By the end of the year, this resulted in a formal agreement on the demarcation of territory in the Beibu Gulf in accordance with the time frame the leadership of the two states had previously established, and in conjunction with Vietnamese president Tan Duc Luong's visit to Beijing ("Vietnam, China Sign Deals" 2000).

The agreement has been the source of intense controversy in Vietnam, as it appears that Hanoi accepted a line of delineation that grants Beijing territory previously claimed by Vietnam (Amer 2002: 43; Tonnesson 2003: 63). While such resentment may not be entirely unjustified, as the Chinese had successfully rebuffed Vietnamese attempts to establish a boundary based on Vietnamese control of key islands in the gulf, it must be recognized that the treaty did not impose a particularly expansive interpretation of Chinese territorial claims. In short, the treaty was the product of compromises by both sides.

In comparison, more pronounced differences remain between Vietnam and China over the location of the maritime boundary that extends through the South China Sea. As Xu Mei (2000: 12) noted in the spring of 2000, "the Nansha Islands issue is the main obstacle to further developing bilateral relations." As with the boundary dispute with India, the contested Sino-Vietnamese ocean territory has important strategic value to both sides. Its security value to Vietnam is obvious, while for Beijing maintaining claims to the South China Sea is important for providing a security buffer off China's southeastern seaboard and allowing China to have a major presence in Southeast Asia. In other words, unlike the other disputed segments of the boundary between China and Vietnam, any compromise on the South China Sea would have real costs for both sides. Such a cost extends beyond the security realm to include economic issues, such as the potential loss of possible oil reserves.

In light of these factors, it is not surprising that recent talks on the South China Sea have produced few results. Moreover, the trading of accusations between Hanoi and Beijing over violations of fishing rights and aggressive behavior in the region continues. However, even as bilateral talks stalled, the Chinese still cautiously explored the possibility of expanding involvement in ARF and ASEAN discussions of the South China Sea. The Chinese calculus is perfectly captured in a short article on the ARF in *Dongnan Ya Yanjiu* by Yu Changsen, a researcher at Zhongshan University. Yu reported that the ARF's consideration of the status of the Nansha Islands presented China with both an "opportunity" and a "challenge." The former stemmed from the fact that a multilateral resolution of the dispute would contribute to China's overall development and security strategies. The latter was related to the realization that a strengthening of regional cooperation in the South China Sea would mean China would have to accept restraints (*zhiyue*) on its behavior in the region and even make some compromises (*tuoxie*) on sovereignty-related issues (Yu Changsen 2000).[33]

In 2002 Beijing committed to a multilateral, nonbinding code of conduct for the South China Sea with ASEAN (and moved to establish a free trade zone between China and the ASEAN member states).[34] According to published reports, at China's insistence the final text of the CBM was weaker than earlier drafts, which had proscribed the building of any new structures in contested regions, but it did commit all signatories to exercise self-restraint and establish a notification procedure to be used prior to the conduct of any military exercises in the region (Pan Guan 2002a). Although Chinese officials insisted that the agreement did not mean they believe differences over territory should be settled in multilateral rather than bilateral forums, it nonetheless was a milestone in the degree of Chinese involvement in such a regional security organization (Buszynski 2003).

China's drive to stabilize the situation in the South China Sea during the last few years was informed by two major developments. First, while Washington continued to distance itself from the specifics of the conflict, it followed up on its early warnings about maintaining the integrity of sea lanes in the region with a renewed military commitment in Southeast Asia (a development further cemented in the post-9/11 strategic context of fighting terrorism). As this move appeared driven at least in part by increased concerns in the region with

Beijing's territorial ambitions in the South China Sea, it behooved Chinese leaders to allay such worries by being less aggressive. Second, Beijing also became more concerned with promoting an image of China as a responsible player (both globally and regionally), and this reinforced the trend toward moderating its behavior (if not ceding its claims) in the South China Sea. This was brought out in interviews conducted with key foreign policy and national security analysts in Beijing during the winter of 2001–2. As a CIIS scholar who had been involved in regional track two meetings on maritime issues noted, while historical influences limited Chinese flexibility on the South China Sea at the start of this decade, toward the end of the decade Chinese leaders became more confident in themselves and therefore willing to compromise on territorial issues. She observed that many Chinese foreign policy decision makers were "more interested in accumulating international prestige, being accepted as part of international society, and as a result more relaxed and not so concerned about territorial sovereignty and security" (Personal interview, Dec. 12, 2001).

In short, starting in the late 1980s, Chinese policy makers began to articulate a more flexible, less confrontational position on the continental segment of the Sino-Vietnamese boundary. Conversely, during this same period, changes in their approach to securing Chinese sovereignty over contested maritime territory were more ambiguous. Over the last fifteen years, an incongruous pairing of increasing military wherewithal and expanding participation in both bilateral and multilateral negotiations has defined Chinese maritime practices. Although this has fueled speculation in the region over China's intentions (especially since China may be using cooperative gestures to buy time for more expansive territorial claims in the future), the conservative approach Beijing has taken to each of its other territorial disputes during this period, and its recent actions in both the Beibu Gulf and South China Sea, should allay such worries. Beijing will not cede any of its maritime claims in the near future, but is also unlikely to use force to alter the territorial status quo in the region.

Conclusion: The Ongoing Construction of China's Boundaries

China's obsession with solidifying its territorial claims remained constant in each of the three main territorial disputes considered in this chapter. Changes in China's official claims were limited to the specific borders that merited attention and did not entail a shift in the direction of de-emphasizing territorial issues or allowing the transgression of China's continental and maritime boundaries. Unofficial analysis faithfully replicated the patterns in official claims and resolutely defended Beijing's position on territorial issues. In addition, while China became more enmeshed in international agreements with its neighbors, it did so exclusively to stabilize and legitimize its earlier territorial claims.

This conservatism is indicative of the relatively status quo agenda that is currently guiding Chinese behavior in the region. China's persistence stands in stark contrast to the dire warnings issued by many of those who tend to emphasize China's apparently aggressive and revisionist agenda in Asia. However, Beijing's insistence on maintaining and reinscribing conventional boundaries also reflects the strict limits on its willingness to cooperate and compromise with its continental and maritime neighbors.

4

Jurisdictional Sovereignty:
Ensuring Taiwan and Tibet
Are Part of China

At the end of the 1970s, China's leaders faced the challenge of consolidating Beijing's disputed jurisdictional claims over Taiwan and Tibet (and, to a lesser extent, Hong Kong).[1] It was at this point that China began to de-emphasize the more problematic features of its approach to territorial sovereignty. Although this shift did not result in an immediate resolution of the most volatile territorial issues confronting Beijing, over the following two decades it did lead to an unprecedented de-escalation in tensions along China's borders. The question addressed in this chapter is whether similar changes took place in the Chinese stance on jurisdictional issues.

To a certain extent, Beijing's stance mirrored its position on territorial sovereignty, as it was also anchored by a boundary-reinforcing interpretation of sovereignty. China's leaders repeatedly asserted their right to rule over all three regions and challenged the legitimacy of all claims to the contrary. Elite analysis unwaveringly followed this official discourse. Broader policy measures (including the Chinese position on negotiations with relevant parties, on economic development, and on deployment of military forces) were unfailingly designed to bolster the PRC's authority over Taiwan and Tibet (and Hong Kong).

However, despite these continuities and similarities, modest changes in the Chinese position did take place and unfolded over the course of two distinct phases. In the late 1970s through the mid-1980s (phase one), China's practices were slightly moderated. In a significant departure from the preceding period, outright criticism of China's detractors in Tibet and Taiwan was muted, and the prospect for a negotiated settlement of both issues was actively considered.

Moreover, when the British presented the Chinese with an opportunity to negotiate the return of Hong Kong to the mainland, Beijing responded with a stance that was unyielding in principle, but flexible in practice. In all three cases, this relative flexibility was followed in the late 1980s, and over the course of the last fifteen years (a period that constitutes phase two, and is ongoing), by an expansion in highly critical discursive moves, pointed diplomatic activity, and displays of China's commitment to use force. This development was first visible in China's handling of the "Tibet issue" in 1989, and gradually became more prominent in its stance on Taiwan in the early 1990s, but was less pronounced in its policy on Hong Kong throughout the decade.

In a broad sense, three forces were crucial in determining Chinese policy on jurisdictional issues during both phases: the underlying strategic value of the areas involved; the persistence of historically conditioned, sovereign-centric values within elite circles in China; and Deng Xiaoping's reform and opening line. As argued in Chapter 2, the first of these forces was an anchor for all Chinese words and actions. The second created an enduring level of concern about the possible loss of each region and a hypersensitivity to any internal or international developments that appeared to jeopardize the PRC's rule, far exceeding objective strategic calculations and infusing the Chinese position with a defensive hue. Both forces ensured a high level of continuity in the Chinese approach to jurisdictional issues; the third introduced a new set of pressures for change.

Initially, in the late 1970s, Deng's pragmatic policies created an unprecedented space for, and required the consideration of, novel solutions to the unsettled relationship between Beijing and Taiwan, Tibet, and Hong Kong. At this juncture the motivation for change was largely domestic, although international strategic considerations also played a role in promoting the shift, pushing Chinese policy in the direction of compromise (albeit within a framework of securing China's sovereign rights over all three regions). In contrast, trends inadvertently created by Deng's reform also helped trigger a convergence in the late 1980s between internal opposition (as evident in the spike in open contestation of Beijing's sovereignty claims in Tibet and Taiwan) and external pressures (via a more direct international commitment to challenging Beijing's claims that emerged late in the Cold War), which caused a pronounced and costly contraction in Chinese practices on Taiwan and Tibet. This turn was sustained in the 1990s by Chinese decision makers' unrelenting commitment to overcome continued Tibetan opposition to Chinese rule and the rise of the independence movement in Taiwan, as well as by the acceleration of external trends (including both concrete policy measures by other international actors, especially the United States, and the apparent strengthening of new self-determination norms in the international arena) that the Chinese saw as bolstering such challenges.

Whereas Chapters 5 and 6 will argue that international material and normative pushes for moderating Chinese behavior (with respect to human rights and the GATT/WTO) reoriented Beijing's words and actions in the direction of boundary transgression, in regard to jurisdictional issues they produced the opposite result (a hardening of the Chinese position).

Phase I, 1979–88: Maintaining Jurisdictional Claims in a Time of Change

Starting in the late 1970s and lasting through the mid-1980s, Beijing's approach to securing its jurisdictional claims to Taiwan, Tibet (and Hong Kong) was defined by a new, more flexible approach. An initial indicator of this change is provided in Figure 4.1, which tracks trends in the publication of jurisdictional claims in *Beijing Review* from 1979 through 1988.[2]

Few jurisdictional claims were issued from 1979 to 1981, but in 1982 and 1983 there was a surge in commentary that greatly exceeds the subsequent five-year period (Figure 4.1). When cross-referenced with Figure 2.1 (in Chapter 2), we can see that these statements accounted for over 30 percent of all sovereignty claims issued in this two-year period. However, they fell to well under 20 percent of all claims issued during the following years. The notable exception is the spike in claims in 1987. Further coding of these two clusters of statements uncovered a shift in the referent of Chinese jurisdictional commentary. During the 1982–83 plateau, all but one of the coded statements directly referred to Taiwan. In contrast, in 1987, twelve of the sixteen coded claims were made with specific reference to Tibet.

These statements (and the unofficial analysis published during this time) endorsed new compromises on Taiwan and Tibet designed to defuse the tension in both regions and facilitate the consolidation of Chinese authority over them.[3] Furthermore, criticism of Beijing's opponents in both Taipei and Dharamsala was toned down, and was replaced by a cautious endorsement of talks and negotiations. Most of the critical commentary was directed against international (especially American) interference in both regions, rather than local opposition to Beijing.

Chinese policies supported this rhetorical turn. In the late 1970s, China's leaders began to explore the possibility of improving relations across the Taiwan Strait through a process of dialogue and exchange (rather than military confrontation). In addition, they took steps to reinitiate indirect talks with the Dalai Lama for the first time since his flight to India in 1959. They also bolstered the Tibetan region's economy and loosened restrictions on cultural and religious activities there. Yet, in both cases, when such policies failed to produce concrete results, signs of a return to a more combative, confrontational approach began

FIGURE 4.1

Jurisdictional Claims in BR, 1979–88

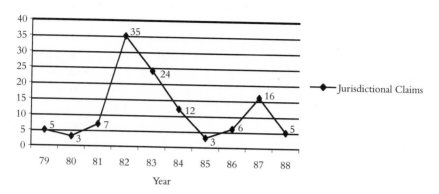

to emerge (a trend that became the defining feature of Chinese practices during the following decade).

Taiwan Policy in the Initial Reform Era: From Liberation to Unification

As had been the case ever since the KMT retreated to Taiwan, Beijing's policy on the island during the 1980s was designed to deal with both Taipei and Washington. Within this dynamic, the broad continuities and new features in the Chinese stance on Taiwan were succinctly encapsulated in the dual statements Beijing issued upon the formal establishment of normal diplomatic relations between China and the United States early in 1979. In the joint communiqué announcing this development, China's leaders were able to consolidate the PRC's jurisdictional sovereignty over Taiwan by once again gaining formal recognition from the United States of China's right to the island. However, the Chinese also showed a degree of flexibility on sovereignty by accepting an ambiguous American pledge to end arms sales to Taiwan and a marginally weaker commitment to the "one China" principle than they had previously demanded.[4] The Standing Committee's Message to Compatriots, issued alongside the joint communiqué, unequivocally stated that "Taiwan has been an inalienable part of China since ancient times." However, the message also contained a set of new limitations on the scope of jurisdictional rights China expected to have over Taiwan upon the island's return to the mainland. It promised to "take present realities into account in accomplishing the great cause of reunifying the motherland and respect the status quo on Taiwan and the opinions of people in all walks of life there and adopt reasonable policies and measures in settling the question of reunification so as not to cause the people of Taiwan any losses" ("Message" 1979).

Two years later, in September 1981, Ye Jianying, chair of the Standing Committee of the National People's Congress (NPC), issued a nine-point statement that elaborated on the policy shift that had been announced by the earlier Message to Compatriots. Ye reiterated the offer to talk with the KMT and called for the resumption of trade, communications, and travel between the two sides. In addition, in points three through six of his statement he offered to constrain core aspects of PRC administration of the island. His proposal promised Taiwan a "high degree of autonomy," maintenance of its socioeconomic system, local participation in "running the state," and, within limits, maintenance of its own currency. As conciliatory as these offers were, they were made within the context of furthering the "the great cause of national reunification" ("Chairman" 1981).

This new emphasis on cooperation and compromise can be partially explained by the changes that were taking place in China's relationship with the rest of the international system, especially the United States and the Soviet Union, during this period. On the one hand, in the late 1970s Washington and Beijing were being pushed together by shared fears of the Soviet Union, a trend that underlay the American shift in China policy but that also left China more vulnerable (due to the more immediate proximity of the Soviet threat) and thus more interested in cooperating with the United States and willing to compromise on Taiwan (see Ross 1995: 125–41). On the other hand, the deterioration of the ROC's international status during the 1970s gave Chinese leaders a new level of confidence in the strength of Beijing's position on Taiwan. The KMT's claim to represent all of China had been eviscerated, and the ROC's legitimacy on Taiwan was also increasingly challenged. The move toward normalizing diplomatic relations with Washington added momentum to this trend, and as noted above, bolstered Beijing's jurisdictional claims to the island. In this sense, the flexibility on U.S. commitments and the offer to talk with the KMT were intended as opening moves in what was expected to be the endgame of China's long, unfinished civil war (Hughes 1997).

As important as such strategic considerations were, they were not the sole impetus for the dual policy of "negotiating cooperation" with the United States and replacing liberation with reunification as the guiding principle for bringing Taiwan back to the mainland (Ross 1995). This new stance was more fundamentally tied to the rearticulation of basic policy guidelines set by the Third Plenum of the Eleventh Central Committee of the CCP in December 1978. The paramount role assigned to the task of economic development at this meeting required de-emphasizing the military and establishing a more stable economic and political environment (which we have seen led to a de-escalation of tensions within each of China's main border relations). This meant that

Chinese leaders concluded that a more flexible stance on Taiwan would facilitate cooperation with the United States, decrease the chances of military conflict across the Taiwan Strait, and in the long run likely create new economic opportunities for Beijing.[5]

In short, Chinese leaders were willing to give priority to economic issues, de-escalate cross-strait tensions, but preserved their static jurisdictional goals in regard to Taiwan. Thus, they muted their criticism of the KMT, extended offers to grant Taiwan extensive rights after reunification, and accepted limited compromises with the international system (especially the United States) on Taiwan's status. Nonetheless, they resolutely maintained China's right to use force to resolve differences with Taipei, and worked to maintain China's military preparedness through the 1980s. Moreover, especially in the early 1980s, the weakness of America's commitment to Beijing's position on Taiwan (as evident in the April 1979 passage of the Taiwan Relations Act, and the Reagan administration's position on maintaining arms sales to the island) continued to evoke Beijing's ire. Therefore, even though Taipei had rejected out of hand both of the major Chinese offers for reunification, it was the United States that was the target of most Chinese criticism during this period.[6]

Both before and after Ye issued his nine-point proposal, unofficial Chinese analysis of U.S. policy on Taiwan was sharply critical. For example, a 1981 *Guoji Wenti Yanjiu* article that stridently objected to the Taiwan Relations Act began by accusing the United States of attempting to "make Taiwan an independent political 'entity' [and grant it] . . . 'international status,'" and asked, "What right does the United States have to flagrantly interfere in the future, security, social or economic system of China's Taiwan province, which are entirely within the framework of Chinese sovereignty?" ("Chinese Journal" 1981). The remainder of the article addressed the security implications of U.S. arms sales to Taiwan, a theme that was the focal point of Chinese commentary during the first half of 1982. For example, in *Shijie Jingji yu Zhengzhi*, Zhang Ruizhuang (1982) sought to place U.S. policy in historical perspective and argued that continued arms sales violated the very principles to which the United States had already agreed in establishing relations with China.

This firestorm of commentary was largely extinguished by the issuance of a third joint Sino-U.S. communiqué in August 1982. As with the previous communiqués, this document was a study in Chinese balancing of intransigence and flexibility. Beijing had been willing to risk the overall stability of the Sino-U.S. relationship in order to force Washington to once again endorse the "one China" principle and temper its military support for Taiwan. However, the statement did not include the definitive end date for all arms sales to the island that the Chinese had been demanding. (It was also offset by what later became known as the "six assurances" that Washington reportedly made to Taipei at approximately the same time. The assurances pledged continued U.S. support of the ROC.) Furthermore, Beijing also compromised on the U.S. demand that a reduction in American military supplies to Taiwan be linked to China's commitment to peaceful unification.

With this compromise in hand, the Chinese approach to securing Beijing's jurisdictional rights over Taiwan reached a relatively stable equilibrium. Chinese officials persistently monitored Washington's relationship with Taipei, but at the same time they tended to downplay Sino-U.S. differences over this still sensitive issue. In addition, they continued to issue statements designed to enhance the prospects for negotiations with the KMT. Thus, in 1983, Deng Xiaoping (1994: 40–42) noted that "peaceful reunification has come to be common language for both the Kuomintang and the Communist Party." While he then dismissed the idea of "complete autonomy" for Taiwan, he allowed for a remarkable degree of hollowing out of China's eventual rights over the island by reiterating that Taiwan could maintain its own social system, enact its own internal policies, and enjoy a level of "autonomy" that would set it apart from all other regions.

This statement, coupled with Ye's earlier proposal, quickly achieved a reified status within the Chinese discourse on Taiwan, and became the core of the "one country, two systems" formula for the return of the island to China (a formula that also became the guiding principle for the resumption of Chinese sovereignty over Hong Kong). In accord with this rhetoric, during the mid-1980s China acquiesced to Taiwan's continued participation in the Asian Development Bank (ADB) (albeit under the name "Taipei, China") after it joined the organization, and Beijing and Taipei cooperated in resolving a hijacking case involving a China Airlines flight. Moreover, economic exchanges between the two sides of the Taiwan Strait expanded, and Taipei eased restrictions on ROC citizens traveling to the mainland (Huang and Wu 1995: 240–41).

Despite these cooperative gestures, growing dissatisfaction with the lack of progress in bringing about the return of the island began to play a more prominent role in Chinese analyses of the Taiwan issue. One facet of this turn amounted to an extension of earlier critical commentary on international interference in Taiwan (Liu Guofen 1996). However, beyond such familiar criticism, a new series of unofficial critical evaluations of developments within Taiwan— especially the emergence of the Democratic Progressive Party (DPP) as a political force on the island, and its endorsement of Taiwanese "self-determination"—began to appear. These evaluations outlined the dangers that changes in Taiwan's political climate appeared to pose for Chinese jurisdictional claims.

An early example of this sort of analysis can be found in a 1987 article in *Taiwan Wenti Yanjiu Jikan*. The author, Yang Jinlin (1987), analyzed the development of the "people's self-determination" movement in Taiwan. While charging that it was the DPP, not the KMT, that pushed the topic of self-determination onto the island's political agenda, Yang cautioned that this could jeopardize cross-strait relations and thus needed to be taken seriously. For Yang, the first step in developing a response to this threat was to demonstrate that the DPP's interpretation of self-determination was a distortion of both the principle and the broader concept of sovereignty. Yang argued, "Clearly, to abstractly [publish] articles that promote the use of the 'self-determination' concept without considering its historical preconditions, not only violates its original meaning, it also mixes up (*hunxiao*) peoples' mental horizons (*shiting*) to the point of only creating ambiguity'" (p. 21). Yang then outlined a boundary-reinforcing interpretation of the self-determination principle, claiming "international law has a clear rule, no country is permitted to engage in activities that invade or harm other countries' unity and territorial integrity; the practice of self-determination cannot harm a country's sovereignty, independence, and territorial integrity."

An article by Zhang Zhirong (1988), a Peking University professor who has written extensively on Sino-Tibetan relations, gave even more direct voice to concerns over Taiwan. Zhang followed the stages of Taiwan's independence movement through the course of contemporary history. In this survey, he noted that the most recent trend in this movement was the promotion of the idea of Taiwanese self-determination, an idea against which Zhang bitterly argued. He observed that when Americans "trumpet 'Taiwan self-determination,' in reality it is a Taiwan controlled by the United States, and self-determination under UN intervention is really self-determination under American interference" (p. 47).

Such heated commentary was a product of the evolving political situation on Taiwan. Beijing had already begun to view Taiwan's limited steps toward democratization as developing hand in hand with the maturation of a new, pro-independence Taiwanese national identity. Such a trend was anathema to China's fundamental position on Taiwan. As had been the case earlier in the decade, Chinese concern was conditioned by the belief within Beijing that any loss of China's claims to the island would greatly jeopardize the PRC's national security; but it was also embedded in an acute awareness of the unfinished project of national unification and the bitter memory of the "century of humiliation."

This later influence was clearly expressed in Chinese statements on Taiwan over the course of the decade. For example, Ye Jianying urged reunification "so as to win glory for our ancestors, bring benefit to our posterity and write a new and glorious page in the history of the Chinese nation!" Later in the 1980s, Deng Yingchao's call for talks on reunification was balanced by the warning that "anyone who persists in obstructing the country's reunification will be unworthy of both his ancestors and his descendants" ("Deng Yingchao" 1984). Two years later, commemorating the one-hundred and twentieth anniversary of the birth of Sun Yat-sen, Peng Zhen also underscored the historic sensitivities underlying Beijing's position on the island: "Whoever obstructs national reunification will be condemned by history" ("Talks" 1986).

As ominous as those warnings were, they continued to be offset through the late 1980s by limited cooperative measures (for instance, Beijing and Taipei's participation in the ADB meetings in Manila, the establishment of offices by both sides to handle cross-strait relations, and further easing of travel restrictions). In addition, Beijing repeatedly called for a negotiated settlement of outstanding differences. Thus, Zhao Ziyang quickly sent a message of condolence following the death of Chiang Ching-kuo, Taiwan's leader, in January of 1988. In his statement, Zhao emphasized Chiang's opposition to Taiwanese independence and his commitment to the "one China" principle. However, he also reiterated China's interest in "discussing affairs of state with people of all circles in Taiwan to accomplish the great cause of the reunification of the motherland and invigorate the Chinese nation" ("Zhao Ziyang" 1988). Wu Xueqian, China's foreign minister, seconded this call in a 1988 end-of-the-year statement on relations between China and Taiwan. He urged talks between the two sides and noted "once such talks are started, all existing problems can be discussed." But he also warned against the trend "towards Taiwan independence" and noted that China resolutely opposes "any opinions and deeds which would lead to Taiwan's independence and separation" ("Wu Xueqian" 1988).

Tibet Policy in the Initial Reform Era:
The Failure of Indirect Talks

During the late 1970s and most of the 1980s, Beijing's approach to Tibet closely resembled its stance on Taiwan. Here too, continuities in the promotion of the PRC's jurisdictional rights were the most prominent characteristic of Chinese practices. As with the policy on Taiwan, the Chinese claim to Tibet was seen as inviolable and this deeply held belief made compromise on basic jurisdictional issues unthinkable. However, despite this pervasive and intransigent commitment to Beijing's claim to Tibet, China's leaders in the 1970s still shifted their approach to protecting this right.

The first public hint of change was in statements by Chinese officials that welcomed the Dalai Lama's return to China, on the condition that he accept Tibet's status as a part of the PRC. During a March 1979 meeting between Deng Xiaoping and the Dalai Lama's brother, Gyalo Thondup, the possibility of the Tibetan leader's return to China was discussed, and Deng stressed that apart from independence, anything else could be considered in talks between the Dalai Lama and Beijing (Shakya 1999: 376). He also suggested that the exiled

Tibetan leader should send delegations to Tibet to discover the actual conditions in the region and thus allay his fears about Chinese rule. However, Deng also used the meeting as a platform for outlining his motivation for extending such an invitation, and to specify what would be required before any visit could take place. Deng explained that he felt a visit would help stabilize the situation in Tibet. Moreover, he contended that dialogue could only proceed if the Tibetans accepted that Tibet was a part of China (Norbu 1991: 352–53; Shakya 1999: 376). In short, although the offer to talk was a departure from the previous Chinese position, its goal of shoring up China's claim to Tibet was consistent with Beijing's existing policies.

Over the following three years (1980–82), Beijing followed up on Deng's initiative through implementing new policies within Tibet and attempting to build ties with Tibetans living outside China. The most high-profile aspect of this move was contained in Hu Yaobang's 1980 acknowledgment of persistent problems in Tibet. Hu's statement was especially significant as it was made by one of China's top political leaders, issued in conjunction with a fact-finding mission he led to Tibet, and elevated the acceptance of blame for Chinese mistakes in the region to an unprecedented level. Hu spoke of the need for reform and argued "regulations that do not suit the conditions in Tibet and are unfavourable to national unity and the development of production can be revised, modified or rejected" ("Develop" 1980). The solution proposed in Hu's statement was to allow a more thorough realization in practice of Tibet's theoretical status as an autonomous region. However, the limits on self-rule were also clearly articulated: in all cases autonomy was to be "under the unified leadership of the central people's government" (Ibid.).

An insistence on the primacy of maintaining national unity also dominated Chinese policy on contact with the Dalai Lama, even as Chinese officials initially decided to allow new Tibetan fact-finding missions into China (though the first such visit, in 1979, had led to an outpouring of public opposition to Chinese rule in Tibet). As part of this policy, in the spring and summer of 1980, two Tibetan delegations traveled to China. However, contrary to Chinese expectations, Tibetan supporters reportedly enthusiastically mobbed these missions and shouted slogans in support of the Dalai Lama when they entered into Tibetan regions. Such a public display of discontent with Chinese rule proved to be more than Beijing was willing to tolerate, and as a result two additional scheduled visits were canceled (Smith 1996: 571–72).

The halt on visits brought an end to what has been called the "fact-finding" stage in the development of a nascent discussion between Beijing and the Dalai Lama. Nonetheless, the initiative on promoting discussion with the Tibetan leader remained intact through the mid-1980s. The idea of talks was first kept

alive in Hu Yaobang's 1981 five-point statement on Tibet. In this pronounce-
ment Hu subtly increased the flexibility in the Chinese position on talks by
underscoring Beijing's willingness to redress the Dalai Lama's concerns about
conditions within Tibet. His effort to make such a concession parallels the much
more publicized one that Ye Jianying made at roughly the same time in his nine-
point proposal on Taiwan. Yet, just as Ye's statement had done, Hu's signaled the
limits to China's willingness to compromise. The invitation to the Dalai Lama
remained rooted in an assertion of Chinese jurisdictional rights over Tibet.
Thus, despite its conciliatory tone, the key point in Hu's words was not the limited flexibility it offered, but rather its insistence that the Dalai Lama "will contribute to safeguarding China's unification, to promoting unity between the
Han and Tibetan nationalities and among all nationalities in the country and to
China's modernization" ("China's Senior" 1984).[7]

In spring 1982, Hu's proposal led to a session between Beijing and a group
of Tibetan exiles with close ties to the Dalai Lama. According to Western analysis of this meeting, the Tibetans ignored the emphasis on national unity that
formed the core of Hu's 1981 statement on Tibet, and instead called for the creation of a Tibetan cultural zone within China. In addition, they pointed to the
similarities between their situation and that of Taiwan, arguing that Tibet was
deserving of more autonomy than had been offered to the island after it was
reunified with the mainland (Shakya 1999: 387; Smith 1996: 573). This argument
was not well received in China, yet Beijing continued to promote the possibility of continuing dialogue with the Tibetans.

As was the case with Beijing's Taiwan policy at the start of the reform era,
such limited flexibility was the product of two main new influences. First, the
international strategic situation facing Beijing had changed as China's relationship with both the Soviet Union and the United States evolved. In the late
1970s, both of the superpowers made new overtures to the Dalai Lama. Tsering
Shakya (1999: 376–77) has argued that the relationship between the Tibetan
leader and Moscow appeared to dramatically improve at this time. Regardless of
the accuracy of this assertion, the limited public Chinese records from this period generally show much anxiety about enhanced ties between the Soviets and
the Dalai Lama ("Banqen" 1979; "People's Daily Unmasks" 1981). Moreover, as
Beijing worried about Soviet actions, the Carter administration began to promote an initiative to strengthen Washington's relationship with the Dalai Lama
against the backdrop of the White House's uneven emphasis on human rights.[8]
The American move in support of the Tibetan spiritual leader was limited and
indirect, falling far short of the covert support that the United States had provided Tibetan rebels in the 1950s and 1960s (and also paled in comparison to
Washington's attempts to reassure Taiwan at this time). However, President

Carter's initiative did make the region more of an issue in Sino-U.S. relations than had been the case since the American rapprochement with China in the early 1970s. Since they followed Washington's drive to normalize Sino-U.S. relations, and came at a time when Beijing wished to stabilize its ties with the United States, these moves did not elicit a particularly blistering response from China. Rather, such international pressure encouraged the Chinese to work more closely with the Tibetan leader.

Beyond strategic considerations, the second factor for change was the de-emphasis on ideology and class in Chinese politics that began in the late 1970s. This generally removed the Tibet issue from the straitjacket of rigid ideological polemics, and thus made new space for a consideration of modifying Chinese practices (Shakya 1999: 371–74). It led to a greater emphasis on pragmatism and problem solving than on the issues of class and revolution that had previously stood at the core of Chinese thinking about Tibet.

Consistent with such new interests, and despite some signs of growing doubts in Beijing about the efficacy of the new Tibet initiative, during the mid-1980s Beijing continued to promote a relatively flexible approach to Tibet. The keystone of this approach was the economic "opening of Tibet," to be accomplished by developing the region's potential as a destination for international tourism and encouraging Chinese enterprises to establish operations in Tibet. In addition, the government extended tax exemptions for the region (to 1990), and approved over forty large infrastructure projects for completion in the region prior to 1985, the twentieth anniversary of the establishment of the Tibetan Autonomous Region (TAR) (Shakya 1999: 397; Smith 1996: 591). Finally, a new law on National Regional Autonomy was adopted at the June 1984 session of the NPC and went into effect in November of the same year. This law gave all autonomous regions (including Tibet) more detailed and extensive rights and privileges in the Chinese legal system, but retained the principle in Chinese law of maintaining national unity.[9]

Against this backdrop, the offer to talk with the Dalai Lama was restated by Yin Fatang, first secretary of the Tibetan regional committee of the CCP, at the Fourth Regional People's Congress. On the surface, Yin's speech reads as simply another extension of the appeal to the Tibetan leader to return to China. However, unlike earlier invitations, Yin directly criticized the Dalai Lama (a rhetorical move that had been largely missing from Chinese commentary since the late 1970s). Yin charged that the Dalai Lama's "greatest mistake is treason. He is not only carrying out traitorous activities, but also spreading erroneous remarks in foreign countries. He has done a disservice to the motherland and the people. This is very bad and he has discredited himself" ("Yin Fatang" 1984).

Despite such open questioning of the Dalai Lama's commitment to talk, in the fall of 1984 another meeting between a group of Tibetan exiles close to the Tibetan leader and Chinese officials was held in Beijing. According to recent analysis, at this session the Tibetans once again demanded greater autonomy and unification of culturally Tibetan areas within China. The Chinese predictably rejected these demands and publicly voiced their skepticism about continuing discussions with the Tibetans.

A *Beijing Review* article, indeed one that carried the main components of Hu's earlier conciliatory statement on talks with the Dalai Lama, effectively captured the main facets of the frustrated Chinese reaction to the 1984 session. Although Yang Jingren, chair of the United Front Department, was quoted in the article as welcoming the Dalai Lama's return to China, his invitation was balanced with a thinly veiled criticism of the Tibetan leader. According to *Beijing Review*, Yang noted that some of the Dalai Lama's "followers carry out activities advocating Tibetan independence," and cautioned, "It will never do for anyone to play with the idea of an independent Tibet or to restore the serf system" ("Beijing Receives" 1984).

In 1985 and 1986, the twin projects of bringing about the Dalai Lama's return to China and implementing more moderate policies in Tibet continued; but support for both within Beijing was eroding and signs of more confrontational and combative policies were mounting. This was exemplified by the dual nature of Chinese preparations for the twentieth anniversary of the establishment of the TAR. On the one hand, the anniversary was clearly seen as an opportunity to showcase the advances made in Tibet since the start of the reform era. For example, as Warren Smith has noted, every effort was made to finish the developmental projects that had been scheduled for completion prior to the holding of official festivities to mark the anniversary of the establishment of the TAR (Smith 1996: 593). In addition, new compromises on religious activity were instituted, relatively liberal regional party leadership was strengthened by the appointment of key personnel, and tourism and trade were promoted. On the other hand, the Chinese intensified security measures in the region in hope of stabilizing the situation there (Sharlo 1992).

During this period, two main factors converged to drive Chinese practices in a more defensive and confrontational direction. First, frustration with the Dalai Lama's failure to offer a substantive reply to Hu's 1981 attempt to speed up talks with the Tibetan leader had begun to mount, strengthening the hand of those who were already critical of the relatively cooperative policy line that had been implemented in the early 1980s. Second, and more importantly, the unintended consequences of China's internal reforms within Tibet began to materialize. More specifically, it was at this point that it became increasingly apparent that moderate policies had raised Tibetan expectations for more extensive liberalization without actually changing the nature of Chinese rule in Tibet, thus creating higher levels of Sino-Tibetan tensions (rather than alleviating them as was the intent of Chinese policy).

An example of such a perverse (from Beijing's perspective) trend can be found in the incomplete religious reforms that were implemented in Tibet during the first half of the 1980s. This policy, intended to placate Tibetan fears about the possible demise of Tibetan Buddhism within a Chinese state, allowed Tibet's monasteries to begin functioning once again, but did not extend religious freedoms to practice Buddhism in such institutions in accord with historical traditions. This heightened resentment of China, and at the same provided central locations for the expression of such sentiment inside Tibet.

At the same time, relatively liberal economic policies also tended to undermine, rather than bolster, Chinese rule in Tibet. These policies were clearly designed to stimulate the Tibetan economy. Economic data from the period does suggest that they resulted in modest material gains; but they also brought a flow of Chinese into the region, which again heightened, rather than placated, Tibetan fears about assimilation and cultural survival.

Finally, while promoting Tibet as an international tourist destination brought valuable foreign currency into the region, it also opened Tibet to independent observers and media. Thus, for the first time since the establishment of the PRC, there was an international audience in Tibet that could evaluate, criticize, and report on Chinese policies in the region. At the same time, news from the outside world (especially that related to the activities of the Dalai Lama) could filter into the region more freely than had previously been the case.

None of these trends boded well for the continued enactment of moderate Chinese practices on Tibet. Thus, it was not surprising that over the following years, as the Tibetan issue was further "internationalized," the original commitment to reform in Tibet, and talks with the Dalai Lama, began to collapse. Moreover, this process unfolded at a much faster rate than was the case at this time in regard to the parallel retrenchment of China's Taiwan policy.

The leading edge of this development was contained in a series of fiery official and unofficial condemnations of the Dalai Lama's expanding international itinerary, commentary that particularly objected to a perceived escalation in American support for such activity. Thus, in June of 1987 when the U.S. House of Representatives passed a resolution critical of China's rule over Tibet, the Chinese embassy in Washington complained that this "grossly violates China's sovereign rights and territorial integrity" ("China Objects" 1987). When the Dalai Lama subsequently addressed Congress, Chinese outrage was even more pronounced. This was immediately evident in the initial Xinhua response to the Dalai Lama's appearance in Washington. It chastised the United States for inter-

fering "in China's internal affairs" and allowing "the Dalai Lama to conduct
political activities aimed at advocating independence for Tibet and sabotaging
the unity of China," and rejected the Dalai Lama's statement as an attempt "to
create an independent Tibet to split the country and undermine the unity of
the various nationalities" ("Chinese Embassy" 1987).

At the same time that the Chinese were working to counter these international developments, they were confronted with a significant internal challenge:
the first of what was to be a new series of Tibetan demonstrations against
Chinese rule. Although it is beyond the scope of this chapter to examine the
immediate cause of the first protest on October 1, 1987, it is clear that the
Chinese perceived a direct link between internal dissent and international support for such activity (see Schwartz 1994). Not surprisingly, Chinese statements
repeatedly condemned these ties and increasingly treated Tibet as a region that
was in danger of being separated from China by a hostile convergence of external and internal forces.

Even as Chinese concerns over these developments mounted, Beijing con-
tinued to cautiously promote the idea of the Dalai Lama's return to China. The
Dalai Lama responded to this invitation while speaking to the European
Parliament in June of 1988. In his statement (which became known as the
Strasbourg proposal) the Tibetan leader significantly scaled back his call for
Tibetan independence and appeared to create a new opening for talks with
Beijing. However, in a signal of the climbing levels of frustration with the
Tibetan leader in Beijing, China's official commentary on the speech fixated on
the Dalai Lama's continued emphasis on Tibet's past independence and his fail-
ure to appreciate the benefits Chinese rule had brought. In the words of a
Beijing Review editorial, "The fundamental difference between the Chinese government and people on the one hand and the Dalai Lama on the other is
whether to safeguard or split the unity of the motherland" (An Zhiguo 1988).

This stance was developed in a reported contact made in 1988 by China with
the Dalai Lama's office in New Delhi. On the surface, such a move appeared to
signal that China was again endorsing the idea of dialogue with the Tibetan
leader. However, the Chinese also bracketed this proposition with a heavy emphasis on the inflexibility of the basic jurisdictional issue at stake ("China Hopes"
1988). In so doing, they highlighted the emerging gulf between the two sides.

Unofficial analysis published in China at this time elaborated on China's
reservations by forwarding particularly narrow interpretations of "autonomy"
and accentuating Chinese historically framed sensitivities to the loss of Tibet.
On the first front, in *Minzu Yanjiu*, Jin Binggao (1988: 15) declared, "Autonomous rights are rights to self-decision [making] under the leadership of a unified nation, and the conditions of the constitution, laws, and rules. This type of

national autonomy is not equal to the right of national sovereignty." On the second front, the first issue of *Zhongguo Xizang* published in 1989 elaborated on China's historical claim to Tibet. In this journal, Yang Gongsu focused on the historical framework of the current controversy over Tibetan independence. Yang asked, "Now, what is the source of the so-called Tibetan independence movement? This must be discussed from [the perspective of] the plot of the British colonialists to separate Tibet [from China] in order to attain the goal of invading China" (Yang Gongsu 1989b: 26). Yang's claim was seconded by a critical commentary written by Hua Zi (1989: 30) that also dwelt upon the historical link between imperialism and the Tibetan independence movement. However, in moving beyond Yang's article, Hua directly warned that the Dalai Lama was untrustworthy and should be held responsible for the growing unrest in Tibet.[10]

Reflection on Phase I

At the start of the reform era, Beijing's approach to both Taiwan and Tibet was characterized by flexible tactics and strategic compromises intended to bolster China's claims to both regions (and the people that resided in them). When these efforts failed to produce the outcomes the Chinese had expected, they were replaced by a return to more confrontational words and actions. The main impetus for the initial shift toward moderation came from the broad rearticulation of China's national interests in the late 1970s and early 1980s. Yet, the push for change that this development created was offset by the countervailing influences of each region's relatively static strategic value to Beijing, and the dominant role of historically conditioned sovereign-centric values within elite circles. Such factors insured that even when leaders took more flexible approaches to jurisdictional issues, they did so always within the context of buttressing (rather than undermining) Beijing's claims.

Throughout the decade, Beijing's attempt to orchestrate the resumption of Chinese sovereignty over Hong Kong was framed by the same set of influences. In other words, China's policy on Hong Kong also stood at the intersection of a historically conditioned commitment to unify China and contemporary efforts to create a stable regional environment within which to strengthen and develop the Chinese economy. Yet, as China's jurisdictional claim to the region was never seriously challenged (either by the residents of Hong Kong or by the British, who continued to administer it), the Chinese stance was less defensive and more flexible than was the case on either Taiwan or Tibet. More importantly, Beijing's abiding interest in preserving the region's economic value for China (and its acute awareness that such value could be quickly undermined by a loss of confidence among investors and the general population in Hong Kong) played an important role in moderating Chinese behavior (in a way it did not in regard to Taiwan and Tibet).

The British first broached these issues—ostensibly in order to clarify the status of commercial leases in the New Territories in 1997 (which marked the end of the ninety-nine-year period of British jurisdiction specified in the 1898 treaty that leased this land to London)—when the governor of Hong Kong, Lord MacLehose, traveled to Beijing in the spring of 1979. Although several analysts have subsequently argued that this gambit was ill conceived (Tsang 1997: 89) and caught Beijing off guard, Deng Xiaoping's response to it outlined what was to become the official Chinese stance on the region over the course of the 1980s. Deng vigorously reiterated the legitimacy of the PRC's claim to Hong Kong, but also noted that Beijing would treat Hong Kong "as a special case" (quoted in Yahuda 1996: 64). In other words, Deng was intransigent in regard to the need for, but flexible in terms of the specific content of, Hong Kong's eventual return to China.

In September of 1982, this approach was reified when Deng utilized the platform provided by Margaret Thatcher's visit to Beijing to highlight what he saw as his historical responsibility to reunify Hong Kong with China. According to his collected works, Deng (1994: 23) stated, "On the question of sovereignty, China has no room to manoeuvre." However, he also quickly balanced this declaration with an equally clear acknowledgment of the economic value of the region to China ("if prosperity is not maintained in Hong Kong, it might retard China's drive for modernization"), and an assurance that "Hong Kong's current political and economic systems and even most of its laws will be maintained" (p. 24).

During the subsequent round of Sino-British negotiations over Hong Kong, London initially dismissed Deng's call for a recognition of Chinese sovereignty, but by the summer of 1983 it had finessed this opposition in a manner the Chinese found acceptable. With such an understanding in hand, the two sides then turned to specific policy matters. At this point, the British first pushed for the maintenance of a vestigial post-1997 presence in Hong Kong. However, Chinese negotiators (on the grounds that permitting any British role would constitute an affront to Chinese sovereignty) adamantly rejected this proposition—a stand that London eventually accepted in late 1983. Beijing responded to this British concession in December with the publication of a twelve-point plan for administering Hong Kong after 1997, the core of which was a pledge not to change the region's social and economic systems for at least fifty years.

The agreements reached during this period of negotiations were then formalized in the September 1984 Sino-British Declaration on the Question of Hong Kong that laid out the main framework for the handover of the region to China and called for the establishment of a new legal system, or Basic Law, to guide Beijing's administration of Hong Kong after 1997. As James McCall Smith (2001: 108–9) has observed, the joint declaration was remarkable in that it essentially granted Hong Kong a substantial amount of what Krasner labeled international legal sovereignty, while dividing key facets of the region's Westphalian sovereignty between the local government and Beijing. Or, using the conceptual framework forwarded in this book, it placed real, largely self-imposed, constraints on how the Chinese would exercise their jurisdictional rights over Hong Kong.

In light of the ambiguities inherent in such an arrangement, defining the balance between Beijing's jurisdictional rights and Hong Kong's regional authority, and the extent to which China was complying with its commitment to preserve Hong Kong's autonomy, quickly became the central, most contentious, issue in China–Hong Kong relations both before, and after, the 1997 handover to Beijing. During the late 1980s, Beijing dealt with such questions mainly by focusing on two specific concerns. First, Chinese officials carefully monitored British efforts to introduce democratic government to the colony (which the Chinese viewed with deep suspicion and derided as a violation of the terms of the joint declaration). Second, Beijing established a mechanism for drawing up the Basic Law called for in the joint declaration. A first draft of this document was published for public comment in April of 1988, and after a contentious period of consultation and dialogue, a second revised draft was made public in February of the following year. The time allotted for public discussion of this latter draft was originally to be only a couple of months. However, this plan was quickly (if temporarily) derailed in the spring of 1989 as China's leaders struggled to deal with the student demonstrations. Their handling of the protests generated a wave of opposition to Chinese rule in Hong Kong. Thereafter, their approach to Hong Kong subtly shifted, concomitant with a more pronounced change vis-à-vis Taiwan and Tibet.

Phase II, 1989–Present: Reinforcing Jurisdictional Claims in the Face of Opposition

Beijing replaced its relatively flexible approach to jurisdictional issues during the period discussed in the preceding section with much more defensive, confrontational words and actions after 1988. Since 1989, the Chinese stance on both regions (first Tibet, and later Taiwan) has hardened.[11] It has become more emphatically boundary-reinforcing, and less compromising, than in the early reform era.

The discursive side of this development involved, on one level, a pronounced surge in official commentary on jurisdictional issues. This is illustrated in Figure

4.2, which traces the annual rate at which jurisdictional claims were made in *Beijing Review* from 1989 through 2000.

On a second level, the content of jurisdictional rhetoric also changed. To begin with, over the course of this phase, the geographic referent of most of this commentary shifted from Tibet to Taiwan. For example, an additional coding of the data presented in Figure 4.2 revealed that an unprecedented flood of Tibet-related statements constituted the 1989 flash in claims, but this was soon replaced in the 1990s by a recurring wave of references to Taiwan. Of greater significance, whereas during the 1980s the Chinese had mainly dwelt on the positive prospects for dealing with both regions (albeit while criticizing external forces they perceived to be intent on disrupting such trends), over the past fifteen years those with whom Beijing was ostensibly seeking to negotiate (the Dalai Lama and political leaders in Taiwan) were increasingly the targets of intensely negative attacks. In addition, rhetoric belabored the point that the breakup of existing states within the international system during this period (especially the Soviet Union and Yugoslavia) had no bearing on China's own disputed jurisdictional claims, and in no way changed the subordination of the right of self-determination to the sovereignty of existing states.

This contraction in the Chinese discourse on jurisdictional sovereignty unfolded in conjunction with a pronounced turn in policies away from the limited efforts Deng had initiated in the 1980s to use negotiations as a tactic for consolidating China's jurisdictional claims. While Beijing continued to espouse the idea of talks with the Dalai Lama throughout this phase, and at least through 1993 actively sought to establish a framework for cross-strait dialogue, this was eclipsed by diplomatic moves designed to undercut the rising international profile of those opposing China's claim to both Tibet and Taiwan. Moreover, Beijing repeatedly demonstrated its willingness to use blunter instruments to counter any perceived attempt to undermine China's jurisdictional rights.

These developments, when viewed in conjunction with Beijing's compromises on each of the other components of sovereignty during this period, reveal that in the 1990s a striking divergence developed in China's stance on the norm. Even as Beijing relinquished sovereign rights over other policy issues, it dramatically tightened the reins on jurisdictional concerns as it struggled to confront ongoing opposition to its claims to Tibet, Taiwan (and, in recent years, even Hong Kong).

Tibet Policy after 1988: Holding the Line
against Independence

From Beijing's perspective, the situation in Tibet was rapidly deteriorating in 1988. The Dalai Lama's effort to shift the discussion of Tibet's status to the inter-

FIGURE 4.2

Jurisdictional Claims in BR, 1989–2000

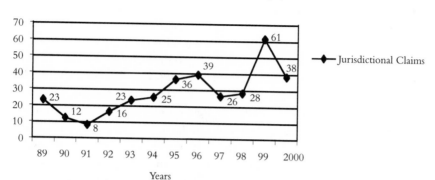

national arena had resulted in an unprecedented invitation to speak in front the U.S. Congress. At the same time, large public demonstrations against Chinese rule erupted in Lhasa. We have already seen the angry and defiant Chinese initial response to these developments. In 1989, and throughout the following decade, China continued to shore up its claim to Tibet through the suppression of dissent, attempts to stimulate the economy, and the rejection of all perceived external interference in the region.[12]

Throughout this phase, the lasting, combative shift in Chinese words and actions was a product of three main factors. First, and most fundamentally, it was simply a prolonged reaction to the initial 1987–89 demonstrations against China, and to ongoing Tibetan dissatisfaction with Beijing's rule over Tibet throughout the 1990s. In the historically framed nationalist narratives that predominate in Beijing, calls for Tibetan independence were entirely unacceptable. Thus, Beijing was determined to keep Tibet a part of China, and dissent in Tibet consistently provoked a harsh, unyielding response. A second factor accentuated sensitivity to protests: an acute awareness that the end of the Cold War had undermined China's strategic place in the international system, and, thus, seemingly made its position on Tibet more vulnerable to external, especially American, interference. In contrast to the arguments in the following chapter, here I contend that the influence of external pressure on Chinese policy was negative, in that more often than not it led to a hardening, rather than a moderation, of attitudes. A third, more abstract, international development also prompted the contraction in Chinese positioning: the apparent rise of new self-determination norms. At least with regard to Tibet, the normative changes that accompanied the end of the Cold War appear to have been read in Beijing as posing a greater threat to China than the end of the bipolar system itself. From the perspective of China's Tibet specialists, the establishment of new states in the

Baltics and Central Asia threatened to contribute to the redefinition of the relationship between sovereignty and self-determination principles in international politics and potentially posed a challenge to Chinese rule over Tibet.

The defining moment in the development of this phase occurred in March
of 1989, when Beijing declared martial law in Lhasa in a last-ditch attempt to
stem the anti-Chinese demonstrations there. Under the cover of this declaration
the Chinese quickly moved to detain all those suspected of involvement in the
protest movement and were able to efficiently curtail the public expression of
dissent. These measures were justified in Beijing's official statements with reference to the necessity of establishing order in the region and breaking the insid-
ious ties between protestors, foreign instigation, and "separatists in exile"
("Lhasa" 1989). At least at this time, the Dalai Lama himself was largely spared
from direct criticism, and invitations for him to return to China were not
entirely retracted. But this note of moderation was offset by the fact that Beijing
also adamantly rejected all international criticism of its administration of Tibet
(She Duanzhi 1989).

In the absence of the violent suppression of the Tiananmen protests in early
June, such words and actions might have been enough to mute the growing
international condemnation of the situation in Tibet. It is often forgotten that
at that time neither the region nor its exiled leader had garnered anywhere near
the level of international attention that they now attract, and that China was still
the beneficiary of a limited reserve of international goodwill generated by
Deng's earlier reforms. In addition, the apparent debate between "pragmatists"
and "hardliners" on Tibet that emerged earlier in the decade might have continued, and ended with a different outcome (Goldstein 1997: 91–92; Norbu
1991: 365–66). However, the worth of such counterfactual thinking is limited by
two factors. First, the international opposition on the Tibet issue had already
begun to take shape before June 4. For example, early in spring 1989 the UN
CHR became a significant conduit for international criticism of China's Tibet
policy (Kent 1999: 56). Second, despite evidence of factional differences in
Beijing on Tibet through early 1989, all Chinese officials shared the same basic
position: Tibet was, and must always remain, a part of China. In this sense, the
post–June 4 condemnation of Beijing was an important, but not a defining factor in reshaping Tibet policy. Rather, it simply strengthened Chinese leaders'
resolve to keep Tibet a part of China.

In the post–martial law, post-Tiananmen period, the stage for such a struggle was increasingly an international one. Thus, although the summer 1989 session of the UN's CHR subcommission did not examine the situation in Tibet
per se, it passed a resolution critical of China's human rights record (discussed
in Chapter 5) and opened the way for more extensive consideration of Tibet in

this multilateral framework. In addition, in October the Dalai Lama was award-ed the Nobel Peace Prize.

What particularly alarmed China about these events was the apparent attempt by the international community in general, and the Dalai Lama in par-ticular, to change the normative framework for jurisdictional sovereignty. This anxiety coalesced around what Chinese analysts saw as the dangers of the new attention to human rights and self-determination in international politics. In both cases, their analysis focused not just on the illegitimacy of allowing such norms to surpass sovereignty, but also on the way powerful states (especially the United States) were manipulating discussions of normative change in order to attack and criticize China.

The human rights cause was directly addressed in *Minzu Yanjiu* at the end of the year. A coauthored article first outlined the improvements that China had brought to Tibet, and then attacked the use of human rights rhetoric by Western capitalists, legislators, and Tibetans outside of China to split China, harm human rights in Tibet, and interfere in China's internal affairs (Guo Guanzhong and Zhang Guoying 1989). Similar commentary was expanded upon in the pages of *Zhongguo Xizang*. In a long article commemorating the fortieth anniversary of the UN's Declaration of Human Rights, Chen Guangguo (1989) documented the vast improvements in human rights in Tibet since the 1940s and extensive-ly criticized the historical and contemporary efforts by Western powers to use human rights to undermine Chinese sovereignty over Tibet.

In the early 1990s, scholars also repeatedly promoted a particularly conserva-tive interpretation of the relationship between self-determination, sovereignty, and China's claim to Tibet. For example, at the end of 1990, Luo Qun's article in *Zhongguo Xizang* exclusively focused on the relationship between China's right to rule Tibet and the two sets of norms. According to Luo, extending the right of self-determination to Tibet was a violation of the historical record that proved the region was a part of China, distorted the basic principle in the UN's human rights documents, and trampled on the fundamental principles of inter-national relations. Therefore, Luo (1990: 5) argued, "To promote 'Tibetan self-determination' in essence is an activity that trumpets and fans national sepa-ratists to blatantly dismember national sovereignty."

These themes were further developed in critiques of the advocacy of Tibetan self-determination that appeared in the work of Michael van Walt van Praag, a scholar of international law who had been chosen by Dharamsala to participate in talks with the Chinese (a move that Beijing rejected). One of the first of these appeared in *Zhongguo Zangxue* and challenged both the legal and historical basis of van Walt's argument. In the article, Li Zerui (1990: 16–17) argued that van Walt's promotion of an independent Tibet was "an attempt to transform the illegal British occupation of China into a legal one, it is also an attempt to recover the imperial colonists' control in the 1980s and 1990s." For these reasons, Li rejected van Walt's book with the harshest of terms, denigrating it as a manifesto on "how to invade China" (p. 21). In the following issue of the same journal, Zhang Zhirong continued the drumbeat of critical commentary against van Walt and the Dalai Lama and concluded his analysis by approvingly citing a comment attributed to Deng Xiaoping. According to Zhang (1990: 15), Deng had said, "There are some who would like (xiang) to split Tibet from China, who would like to take Tibet away, I think they don't have the ability (benshi)." Subsequently, in commenting on van Walt's appearance at the winter 1991 meeting of the UN CHR, Zhi Yun (1991) argued that the scholar had not only misinterpreted the UN Charter, but also distorted basic aspects of Lenin's work on national autonomy.

These analysts were not only working to convince supporters of the cause of Tibetan independence that such a position lacked legitimacy, they were also further entrenching within Beijing the already "sacred" status of Tibet as a part of China. In this context, any linkage made by Beijing's critics of human rights and Tibet, or self-determination and the region, was rejected out of hand, as it could only be an attempt to divide China. In other words, securing Tibet as part of China became more important to Chinese analysts and officials as questions about their right to the region increased at home and abroad. As an expert at the Chinese Institute of Contemporary International Relations (CICIR) noted later in the decade, "After some in Tibet began promoting independence, the question of Tibet become an increasingly emotional one in China" (Personal interview, May 25, 1998).

During 1991, despite the fact that martial law had been lifted in Lhasa almost a year earlier (in May of 1990), Beijing continued to closely monitor the situation in Tibet. At the same time, reports of human rights abuses in the region continued to surface in the international media and INGO reports. The pressure on Beijing on both the human rights and self-determination fronts mounted as such charges proliferated, but true to the commentary cited above, Chinese officials refused to compromise on either issue.

Initially, the promotion of human rights claims appeared to give critics of Chinese rule over Tibet the most traction. For example, in conjunction with the Dalai Lama's private meeting with President Bush in April, the U.S. Senate passed a nonbinding resolution that expressed concern about human rights conditions in Tibet but did not directly endorse Tibetan self-determination, let alone independence.[13] This meeting and the resolution constituted yet another convergence between the country the Chinese were most concerned with, the United States, and a political figure they were convinced was trying to divide

China. Beijing swiftly moved to condemn it by attacking what was denigrated as American manipulation of human rights language to unfairly criticize China's Tibet policy ("Bush" 1991).

In the face of this rhetoric and intense lobbying by the Chinese to prevent such a development, in August 1991 the Tibet issue was inserted into the UN CHR subcommission's critical review of China's suppression of the 1989 student-led demonstrations. In fact, the subcommission passed a resolution entitled "Situation in Tibet" (E/CN.4/Sub.2/1991/10). Although the text of the resolution carefully skirted the controversial issue of Tibet's political status, the line between human rights and self-determination claims was quickly blurred in the INGO's later reports to the subcommission in accord with the resolution's mandate. The memorandum China submitted to the subcommission protesting its decision anticipated this in bluntly making the case for severing the tie between human rights, self-determination, and criticism of China's position in the region (E/CN.4/1991/73: 2).

Later in the decade, the members of the coalition that had pushed through the subcommission's censure of China broke apart. In addition, China's representatives to the UN became more adept at influencing the direction of debate in the human rights bodies. As a result, China was able to stymie all later attempts in the UN CHR and subcommission to pass additional resolutions referring to the situation in Tibet.

A significant facet of this effort was China's relentless promotion of a static view of the relationship between human rights, sovereignty, and Tibet. At the start of 1992, for example, Chinese analysts published a flurry of articles explicitly designed to build a wall between the debate on human rights conditions in Tibet and any discussion of the region's political status as a part of China.[14]

The most authoritative and comprehensive articulation of this stance can be found in the September 1992 white paper on Tibet. The title of this document, "Tibet: Its Ownership and Human Rights Situation," telegraphs the main components of the Chinese argument.[15] More specifically, it meticulously outlined the history of Chinese jurisdiction over Tibet and denounced each attempt by the Dalai Lama and his international supporters to separate the region from China. In addition, it contained a long list of claims about the improved human rights situation in Tibet. It concluded that criticism of human rights conditions in Tibet could only be understood as part of a scheme to "mislead the public and create confusion in an attempt to realize their dream of dismembering China, seizing Tibet and finally subverting socialist China. Here lies the essence of the issue of so-called human rights in Tibet" ("Tibet: Its Ownership" 1992).

Although the end of the Cold War and collapse of the Soviet Union did not figure prominently in this document, an obsession with both developments constituted the main counterpart to the dominant human rights themes within the Chinese discourse on Tibet during the early 1990s. In the eyes of Chinese analysts, the collapse of the Soviet Union played a framing role in the incremental escalation of ties between the Dalai Lama and Washington at the end of the Bush administration and the start of Clinton's presidency. As a noted Tibet specialist in Beijing observed in a 1998 interview, "Yes, we placed a stronger emphasis on state sovereignty over Tibet in 1991 and 1992. The rest of the world changed at this time, and it was clear to us that the United States was starting to challenge China on Tibet to an extent that it hadn't since the end of CIA involvement in the region in the 1970s" (Personal interview, Peking University, Apr. 8, 1998).

This comment reflects the rational calculations Chinese analysts in Beijing made in the early 1990s in response to the shift in the distribution of material capabilities in the international system. However, during this period Chinese policy and rhetoric on Tibet was also strongly influenced by anxiety within Beijing over the extent to which the establishment of the Baltic and Central Asian states appeared to contribute to the redefinition of the relationship between sovereignty and self-determination principles.

One of the most direct commentaries on this threat was published at the start of 1993, when two scholars warned:

> In the last few years, with the drastic change in Eastern Europe, self-determination has been used to oppose communism and socialism, and taken on new characteristics. Under these conditions, anti-Chinese foreign forces and internal separatists have written many articles about so-called Tibetan self-determination and stated that "the realization of Tibetan self-determination is the most reasonable, ideal, and peaceful method for solving the Tibetan issue in the future." . . . Actually, this trumpeting of the theory of self-determination is a distortion and misinterpretation of the theory of self-determination, and is a deliberate misunderstanding of Tibetan history and reality. (Yang Fan and Zhi Rong 1993: 90)

The official Chinese discourse on Tibet following the publication of the white paper supported the main claims of such analysis. It was animated by an ongoing stream of criticism against international support for Tibet and the Dalai Lama's failure to accept the Chinese position on the region. In attacking both targets, official commentary placed a premium on securing China's jurisdictional claim to Tibet and discrediting any whose words or actions challenged the status quo in the region. In addition, Beijing continued to keep a close eye on the security situation in Tibet, and, in spring 1993 quickly clamped down on the first demonstration in Lhasa that had taken place since the 1989 imposition of martial law ("Xinhua Reports" 1993). Against this backdrop, the theme of promoting Tibetan regional autonomy was again given voice, but always within the boundaries of Chinese sovereignty ("'Renmin Ribao' Editorial" 1994).

The mid-1990s apotheosis of this trend can be seen in the statement Jiang Zemin issued following a national work conference on Tibet in July 1994. Jiang's assessment of the situation in Tibet first picked up on the themes of development and reform that Deng Xiaoping and Hu Yaobang had enunciated in the early 1980s. He argued that stability in Tibet was closely related to economic growth in the region and underscored Tibet's importance to China, observing that maintaining order in Tibet was "crucial to the success of reforms, development and stability throughout the country" ("Jiang Zemin on Stability" 1994). In turning to the Dalai Lama, the Chinese leader explained "the differences between us and the Dalai Lama clique are not a question of whether to believe in a religion or not, or whether to exercise autonomy or not, but an issue of safeguarding our motherland's unification and opposing secessionism." Jiang continued that the Tibetan leader was welcome to return, but warned, "nobody is permitted to pursue independence or independence in disguised forms in Tibet" (Ibid.).

Jiang's use of the derogatory term "Dalai clique" (*jituan*) brought the Chinese discourse on Tibet back to the tropes that had dominated it before the start of the Deng era. Critical views of the Tibetan leader had been percolating in academic journals since the late 1980s, and been evident in the commentary of lower-level officials as well. However, Jiang's choice of words is a striking illustration of just how frustrated Beijing had become with the Dalai Lama and the intractability of the Tibet issue, and demonstrates just how disinclined to negotiate the Chinese were in the mid-1990s.

This lack of interest in talks was not the product of confidence in the stability of China's position or of international pressure per se. Rather, it grew out of the conviction that regardless of how the Dalai Lama framed his position on Tibet, he would never accept Chinese sovereignty. Although the accuracy of this perception may be open to debate, its hegemonic status within China in the mid-1990s was supported in both elite commentary and private interview data I collected. It was coupled with a growing conviction that solving the Tibet issue might best be accomplished by waiting to see what the region would look like without the current Dalai Lama's involvement. As a well-known Chinese Tibetan specialist said, "I think in the mid-1990s we realized that it was a matter of time, so much of the independence movement depended on one individual, and people thought no one lives forever" (Personal interview, Peking University, Dec. 20, 2001).

Even as the Chinese aired their grievances with the Dalai Lama, they continued to pursue the joint policies of economic development and maintaining social stability (through preventing public protest against China) in Tibet. On the first front, the Chinese pledged to maintain a 10 percent growth rate in the region, and promised 2.38 billion yuan for sixty-two infrastructural projects in Tibet ("China's Tibet: Facts and Figures 2002"). On the second front, Beijing reportedly initiated a campaign to clamp down on the display of photographs of the Dalai Lama. In addition, INGOs and the Tibetan government in exile contended that the Chinese had increased their military presence in the region ("Striking Under Surveillance-2").

The wave of unofficial commentary that followed the work conference examined each of these developments, and in so doing expanded Jiang's pairing of a renewed commitment to economic development and a hardening of attitudes toward the Dalai Lama and his supporters. The celebratory nature of analysis of the first of these issues appeared in *Zhongguo Xizang* in January 1995 (Bengyi 1995). However, it was the highly critical commentary on the Dalai Lama published during this period that stands out.

The most striking example of such blunt criticism appeared in *Zhongguo Xizang* soon after the work conference on Tibet. At this time, an article attributed to Zhi Yun condemned the "Tibetan separatist clique" for its "violent and terrorist methods" in opposing the central government. Zhi argued that the "Dalai's" support for human rights and peace was simply a tactical move. It provided, Zhi contended, the Tibetans with rhetorical cover for their separatist aspirations. In a bold move, Zhi then discussed the potential weakening of the Tibetan independence movement in the Dalai Lama's absence (Zhi Yun 1994: 3).

As biting as such commentary was, its harshness was surpassed in the second half of 1995. The impetus for this turn was the controversy that erupted over the process of selecting and enthroning the successor to the ninth Panchen Lama, who had died in 1989. According to the Tibetan Buddhist tradition, high-level religious leaders such as the Panchen Lama can control the form of their return to this world following their deaths, through reincarnation. It is then up to religious and political figures to find such reincarnates. For Beijing, a smooth handling of this process, with references to Beijing's historical role in monitoring past searches, was a key component of the wait-and-see policy toward the Dalai Lama. As long as the Dalai Lama was outside China, and Beijing was able to control the naming of top-level lamas, it would be able to populate the upper echelons of the Tibetan leadership with figures indebted to the PRC. According to scholars with ties to the Dalai Lama, the Tibetan leader was well aware of this danger. Therefore, he took the initiative to name his own choice for a new Panchen Lama in May of 1995 before Beijing had the chance to announce its selection.

For the purposes of this book, it is unnecessary to examine the complex intrigues in Dharamsala, Beijing, and Tibet before and after this move.[16] Instead, it is sufficient to simply call attention to the extent to which it poisoned the already troubled relationship between the Dalai Lama and Beijing and deepened Chinese resentment of the Tibetan leader.

Later in the year, this resentment was given a high-level airing when top leaders in Beijing directly criticized the Dalai Lama ("Dalai" 1995; "Wu Banguo" 1995). Much of this controversy was overshadowed by the 1995–96 Taiwan Strait crisis. However, even as Beijing dueled with Taipei (and Washington) over Taiwan, the Chinese continued to implement policies to strengthen Tibet's economy, and, under the rubric of a nationwide campaign to fight crime (dubbed "strike hard"), reigned in elements of the monastic community in Tibet that had supported the Dalai Lama's selection of the reincarnate Panchen Lama ("Tibet" 1996).

Although these trends attracted little attention around the globe, this shifted in 1997 as both formal and informal developments once again began to place Tibet, and Chinese policies in the region, in a prominent international position. The first component of this turn was prompted by the Clinton White House's decision to make the Tibet issue more prominent in the American relationship with China. In July, the Clinton administration, through a statement by Madeleine Albright to congressional leaders, announced its intention to create a position within the State Department for the oversight of Tibetan affairs (Myers 1997). In addition, during his visit to the United States in October, Jiang Zemin was publicly pressed on the Tibet issue. By the end of the year the Tibet post had been established, and there was a new round of congressional criticism of China's record in Tibet (Sautman 1999; "China Slams" 1997).

The informal generation of interest in Tibet grew out of a convergence of the outreach activities of pro-Tibetan INGOs, and a surge in the pop culture status of the Dalai Lama and Tibet via the release of several high-profile Hollywood movies (Schell 2000). Interestingly, these cultural developments provoked an even stronger response from China than the formal moves of the White House (Ren Yishi 1998). They also dramatically increased the level of Chinese resentment over the Dalai Lama's positive image in the West. For example, in a 1998 interview with the author, a noted Tibet specialist observed,

> We [Chinese] simply cannot understand how you [westerners] are so supportive of this movement. I can see that your governments might have a strategic interest in supporting an independent Tibet, but I don't understand why people in the West like the Dalai Lama so much. He is nothing more than a separatist who is trying to hurt China. His talk of an independent Tibet is such an obvious distortion of international law and norms, and yet you still look up to him. This is really too much, and shows how little westerners understand about the situation in Tibet. (Personal interview, Peking University, May 4, 1998)

These sentiments also dominated a conversation about Tibet with a high-ranking, retired official who had worked for decades in Tibet, and is currently affiliated with the Academy of Military Sciences. He argued: "There is no way that we will ever permit Tibet to become independent, nor is it even worth our time to listen to the lies that the Dalai Lama is telling in India" (Personal interview, July 1, 1998).

Despite such harsh rhetoric, a slight change in the Chinese position did begin to emerge in 1998. The first indication of this change was the Chinese decision to permit a small delegation of American religious leaders to travel to Lhasa in February 1998 ("U.S. Religious Leaders" 1998). This small concession was followed in June by Jiang Zemin's response to President Clinton's mention of the Tibet issue while the American leader was in China. During a press conference that was broadcast live in China, Clinton and Jiang engaged in a remarkably frank exchange of their differences over Tibet, at the end of which the Chinese president renewed Beijing's public commitment to attempting to talk with the Dalai Lama.

Jiang's statement was remarkable for two reasons. First, the setting of a live press conference with the president of the United States meant his remarks were made on one of the most public platforms available to the Chinese president. This was a bold move, and one that differed substantially from the silence with which the Chinese leader had treated the Tibet issue during his previous trip to the United States. Second, the tone and content of Jiang's statement contrasted sharply with his address to the 1994 Tibet work conference. In addition to standard talk of economic growth and improved human rights conditions in the region, Jiang emphasized that "as long as the Dalai Lama can publicly make a statement and commitment that Tibet is an inalienable part of China, and he must also recognize Taiwan as a province of China, then the door to dialogue and negotiation is open. Actually, we have several channels of communication with the Dalai Lama. So, I hope to see positive changes (*ji ji de bian hua*)" ("Chinese, U.S. Presidents" 1998).

Although such commentary did not radically change Chinese policy on the Dalai Lama, in offering to talk (and referring publicly to the back channel communications between the two sides) while emphasizing respect for regional autonomy and religious freedom, Jiang's statement represented a partial return to the policy in place through the late 1980s. Nonetheless, in an indication of just how sensitive these issues were in China, the Clinton-Jiang exchange on Tibet (and human rights) was censored in Chinese reports of the press conference (Kolatch 1998; Sautman 1999). For example, the *Beijing Review* report on the press conference simply mentioned that Jiang and Clinton "stated their stance and views on human rights" ("Jiang and Clinton" 1998).

Recently published Western analysis of this limited initiative has contended that during the 1998 Clinton press conference, Jiang had moved the issue of talks forward before gaining consensus on this issue with other top leaders (Rabgey and Sharlho 2004). This suggests that differences within Beijing over how to handle the Tibet issue can play an important role in influencing the policy-making process toward the region. While I concur that such factors are significant, my research suggests that, as was the case at the start of this phase, it was broader international developments that more significantly constrained the Chinese. In late 1998 and the spring of 1999, the escalation of jurisdictional anxieties in Beijing was located more in the Balkans than it was in either Tibet or Dharamsala.

Although Chinese commentary published at this time refrained from directly linking Tibet and Kosovo, the charges of ethnic cleansing and human rights abuses that were at the center of NATO's justification for intervention in Yugoslavia cut close to home for the Chinese, whose policy on Tibet had already been criticized on very similar grounds throughout the preceding decade. Thus, although I discuss Chinese opposition to the Kosovo operation in more detail in the following chapter, it is important to note here that Beijing's condemnation of the U.S.-led war against Belgrade relied on precisely the same sort of terminology that had long been used to denounce external involvement in Tibet. Not only was the war condemned as a case of interference and a violation of territorial integrity, it was also attacked as illegitimate and waged under the perversely distorted banner of protecting human rights and furthering the cause of humanitarian intervention. A paper delivered by Pang Sen (2000: 5), a well-known legal scholar, at a fall 2000 meeting on humanitarian intervention at the Chinese Institute of International Studies (CIIS), highlighted the central aspects of Chinese fears over the Kosovo intervention. "Today," Pang declared, "[the] gunboat is obsolete and has been replaced by destroyers and carriers. Intervention needs a more charming camouflage. So when the holy war against the Serbs was launched, it is in the name of humanitarianism. . . . The barbarian state which refuses to surrender is dismembered."

The 2000 white paper on Tibet, while celebrating recent advances in the protection of Tibetan culture, once again placed an official stamp on such critical analysis. Indeed, it charged the Dalai Lama with "hampering the real development of Tibetan culture" ("The Development of Tibetan Culture" 2000). Yet, during the last few years it has also become possible to find a trace of creative thinking in Chinese discussions of Tibet. For example, Rabgey and Sharlho (2004) have noted apparent differences within Beijing over the degree to which time is on the Chinese side in dealing with the Tibet issue (specifically with regard to the longevity of the Dalai Lama). Some analysts have begun urging

China to drop the "wait-and-see policy" it pursued in the 1990s and talk with the Tibetan leader now (rather than dealing with the uncertainty of Sino-Tibetan relations that is likely to emerge following his death). Indeed, a few iconoclastic scholars, such as Pan Yue, have pushed for taking a "third way" (compromising) approach to Tibet (which echoes the Dalai Lama's own rhetoric).

Among the experts I spoke with in 2001 there was a general agreement that Chinese policy in Tibet had reached a dead end and that Beijing must consider new options to stabilize the situation in the region. One leading Tibet watcher argued that Chinese leaders' failure to come to terms with the central role of religion in Tibetan life continued to block the development of more successful policy making. This scholar—who had previously advocated extremely stringent measures in Tibet—stated that it was time for Beijing to reconsider its policies. But he also made it clear that, in his view, Tibet had always been, and would always remain, part of China (Personal interview, Peking University, Dec. 20, 2001).

Indirect evidence that such assessments extended to high levels within the Chinese government was apparent on a number of fronts in 2001. To begin with, throughout the year the Chinese renewed emphasis on promoting regional autonomy. For example, the year started with Jiang Zemin's endorsement of the NPC's revision of the regional autonomy law and its call to stimulate the economy in minority regions in order to "promote national solidarity" ("Jiang Zemin Signs" 2001). It ended with Li Peng addressing an NPC forum during which he declared that regional autonomy was the solution to China's ethnic problems and, turning to the main political slogan of the later Jiang period, was in line with the "three representations (*san ge daibiao*)" ("China's Li Peng" 2001).

Against the backdrop of the development of such a general line on autonomy, the Fourth Work Forum on Tibet was held in June 2001. The meeting forwarded few new initiatives on Tibet, but reiterated the importance of promoting economic development in the region and ensuring political and economic stability there. It was followed in July by carefully orchestrated observances of the fiftieth anniversary of the "peaceful liberation of Tibet." In a sign of the importance Beijing placed on this ceremony, Hu Jintao, then China's vice president, traveled to Tibet. His remarks there underscore the historical underpinnings of the Chinese stance on Tibet, and the limits on its then current policies toward the region. Hu observed that peaceful liberation had allowed the Tibetan people to "cast off the yoke of imperial aggression" and usher in "a new era in which Tibet would turn from darkness to light, from backwardness to progress, from poverty to affluence and from seclusion to openness," but warned against the "separatist and disruptive activities of the Dalai clique and anti-China forces" ("Full Text" 2001).

Despite such biting rhetoric, limited progress was made toward renewing talks with the Tibetan leader during the following two years. The first signs of this opening began to appear in the summer and fall of 2002, when Beijing permitted two delegations of prominent exiled Tibetans to return to China. While international groups supportive of the Tibetan cause reported that such visits might be "highly significant" ("Lodi" 2002), the Chinese Foreign Ministry downplayed the possibility of substantial talks by avoiding a reporter's question about them during the ministry's regularly scheduled press conference ("Foreign Ministry" 2002). An end of the year commentary posted on the official Web site of the Chinese embassy in Washington also sought to cool down speculation about both visits. The posting pointed out that the Chinese government had not recognized either of the visits as official, and also blamed the lack of progress in talks on the Dalai Lama. Moreover, it questioned his commitment to autonomy and argued that in reality he had become "a thorough chieftain of Tibetan separatism" ("Negotiations" 2002).

In light of this commentary, it is not surprising that the spring 2003 visit to China by a delegation led by Lodi Gyari did not produce any major breakthrough ("Success" 2003; "Writer" 2003). Moreover, the Dalai Lama's highly publicized trip to the United States (which included a visit with President Bush in the White House and a series of well attended public Buddhist teachings and seminars) later in the year appears to have once again hardened Chinese resolve against compromising on negotiations with the Tibetan leader. Thus, although some observers have taken note of the promise implicit in Hu Jintao's January 2004 press conference—in which Hu appeared to slightly modify the list of preconditions Beijing expected the Dalai Lama to meet before formal negotiations could begin by leaving out the necessity of recognizing Taiwan is a part of China—to date there have been no substantive results.

In fact, the gap between the two sides appears as deep (if not deeper) today as it was twenty years ago. In China, both unofficial commentary and official statements continue to label the Dalai Lama a threat to China's national unity and an obstacle to improving the situation in Tibet. On the first front, a January 2004 issue of *Zhongguo Xizang* rejected the Dalai Lama's proposal for a recognition of "greater Tibet" (*da Xizang*) as a scheme that was out of step with "history, China's present situation, and the interests of the Tibetan people" ("Ping" 2004: 2). On the second front, the May 2004 white paper on Tibet pressed the Dalai Lama to once and for all acknowledge both the benefits that Chinese-administered autonomy has brought to Tibet, and his own decreasing relevance to the region. "The destiny and future of Tibet," the white paper contended, "can no longer be decided by the Dalai Lama and his clique. Rather, it can only be decided by the whole Chinese nation, including the Tibetan people. This is an objective political fact in Tibet and cannot be denied or shaken" ("Regional" 2004).

Taiwan Policy after 1988:
Confronting New Trends

In 1989, and at the start of the 1990s, Beijing's commitment to reaching a negotiated settlement with Taipei proved to be more durable than its resolve to work with the Dalai Lama. Through 1993, the Chinese continued to build on the fragile framework for talks and exchange with Taiwan that had grown up in the 1980s. However, from the beginning of this phase, these efforts were offset by more confrontational practices that, by the mid-1990s, effectively took their place. Indeed, throughout this period Chinese rhetoric (first in unofficial publications, and later in official statements) increasingly underscored China's claim to Taiwan, and bluntly criticized any perceived attempt to prevent Taiwan's eventual reunification with China. While the Chinese stridently objected to all international (especially American) moves that appeared to bolster Taiwan's independent status, over the course of the 1990s it was the activities of Taiwan's own leaders that elicited the most acerbic criticism from Chinese analysts and officials. Harsh commentary was complemented by policies intended to isolate the island and pressure its leaders into reunifying Taiwan with China (or at least, not moving in the direction of independence). To this end, Beijing meticulously monitored Taipei's attempts to increase Taiwan's international profile (and enhance the island's ties with the United States) and repeatedly worked to stymie such efforts through an array of diplomatic measures. At the same time, Beijing increased China's military presence along the Taiwan Strait (most notably by ramping up the deployment of short-range missiles in the region).

The first indications of this shift in Beijing's approach appeared in early 1989 in a surge in analysts' attention to the changes in how Taiwan's leaders defined the island's relationship to the mainland. For example, a January 1989 *Beijing Review* editorial argued that the rise of "divisive forces" on the island was to a great extent a "result of the policy of conciliation and connivance adopted by certain policy-makers in Taiwan towards those people advocating 'the independence of Taiwan'" ("New" 1989). In addition, the KMT, still Taiwan's ruling party, was chastised for its new, flexible, and elastic policy measures for dealing with the rest of the world. Indeed, the acceleration by the KMT's new leader, Lee Teng-hui (who became Taiwan's president following Chiang Ching-kuo's death in 1988), of his predecessor's substantive diplomacy through an acceptance of dual recognition, utilization of Taiwan's economic influence, and informal diplomacy to cultivate ties with states that had already established relations with Beijing was denigrated as a blatant attempt to carve out new international space for Taiwan. In the words of another *Beijing Review* editorial, such moves were the product of "wishful thinking" and "utterly impracticable," and it was imperative for the "Taiwan authorities" to stop running "up and down the blind alley of separation" (Jing Wei 1989).

Complementing such critical commentary, the political relationship across the Taiwan Strait was temporarily strained later in the spring and summer of 1989 by the Taiwanese response to Beijing's handling of the student-led democracy movement in China. According to the *Tiananmen Papers*, even before the final decision to use force to end the demonstrations, Chinese leaders were highly critical of what they saw as Taiwan's support of the protests (Nathan and Link 2001: 346–47). Taipei's public criticism of Beijing's crackdown on the protestors confirmed these suspicions and elicited a pointed response (Lai 1989; "Taiwan's Role" 1989). Later in the year, Wang Guoxian (1989) underscored this point in a contribution to *Taiwan Yanjiu* that criticized Taiwan for using the post-Tiananmen "anti-China" trend as a ploy to increase pressure on China and press Beijing into pledging not to use force against the island.

While such verbal volleys increased tensions between Beijing and Taipei (and were a portent of the harsh rhetoric that was to flow on both sides of the strait later in the 1990s), they were insufficient to immediately undermine the cooperative framework that had been established during the preceding decade. Thus, following the historic May 1989 visit by Shirley Kuo to Beijing for the annual session of the ADB, in June 1989 direct telephone links between the two sides were established. In addition, the flow of indirect imports from China to Taiwan was facilitated by the passage of more liberal trade policies in Taipei (Zhao 1999).

During the following year, restrictions on Taiwanese investment in China were also eased, and throughout this period trade and investment across the strait mushroomed. More importantly, Beijing responded in a relatively moderate fashion to Lee Teng-hui's spring 1990 inaugural speech in which he carefully recalibrated Taiwan's position on unification. Rather than emphasizing the obstacles presented by Lee's insistence on Taiwan's distinct political status, Jiang Zemin's early June statement to a conference held in Beijing focused on Lee's recognition that Taiwan was "China's inalienable territory." Thus, he encouraged Lee to place national (Chinese) interests "above everything else, consider the realities, act on the will of the people, accept the historical responsibility and make contributions to the reunification of the motherland and the revitalization of the Chinese nation" ("Party Chief" 1990).

In 1991, Taiwan's National Unification Council parried Jiang's attempt to foster support for the realization of China's jurisdictional rights over the island with the publication of the National Unification Guidelines. This document codified much of the substance of Lee's 1990 inaugural address. While endorsing the unification of Taiwan with the mainland, it also advocated that reunification take place over three open-ended stages that placed the issue of Chinese sovereignty in the distant future. In the words of Christopher Hughes, the guidelines "neutered" Taiwan's commitment to unification (Hughes 1997). Again, the Chinese response to this stance was cool, but also quite constrained. For example, Li Peng's March report to the NPC, while chiding the Taiwanese authorities for not moving more quickly toward reunification, welcomed the publication of the guidelines. Following these guarded discursive exchanges, Taiwan's newly formed Straits Exchange Forum (SEF) sent two delegations to the mainland to meet with representatives of the semi-official organization Beijing had established, the Association for Relations across the Taiwan Strait (ARATS).

Although these visits produced few concrete results, they lent a patina of normalcy to the relationship between Taipei and Beijing by establishing an institutional mechanism for regular unofficial exchange. On the surface, they also created the impression that significant progress was being made toward a negotiated settlement of the jurisdictional standoff between the two sides. However, even as the Chinese developed such ties, they also were beginning to take a more active stance against what they perceived to be the ongoing erosion of Taiwan's commitment to the "one China" principle. Official commentary studiously avoided personally blaming Lee Teng-hui for these developments. However, unofficial analysis did not show a similar constraint. In 1991 *Taiwan Yanjiu* began to publish more extensive critical commentary on the KMT leader that strongly questioned his motives and intentions, and did so with direct reference to the basic jurisdictional issues at stake in cross-strait relations.

The best example of this trend was an article in *Taiwan Yanjiu* by Wang Kehua (1991), a researcher at CASS's Taiwan Studies Institute. In this piece Wang charged Lee with undermining China's sovereignty over the island and, more broadly, distorting sovereignty's role in international politics. Wang first attacked Lee for his collaboration with American forces that were bent on detaching Taiwan from the mainland. In particular, the CASS analyst objected to the suggestion made by James Lilley, who had just stepped down from his post as ambassador to China and was subsequently to join the Clinton administration, that China had an antiquated approach to sovereignty.

From Wang's perspective, Lilley's assertion directly led Taiwanese political leaders to suggest that in the post–Cold War period sovereignty's meaning had been tempered by the expanding influence of human rights norms and the principle of self-determination. The author argued that such a claim was of so little merit that it was hardly worth refuting. However, in defending China's rights to Taiwan, Wang also staked out a strikingly conservative interpretation of sovereignty's role in international politics, noting, "The nation and sovereignty are inseparable (*bu fenlie*), and state sovereignty is indivisible (*bu fen'ge*)" (Wang Kehua 1991: 2).

Such analysis illustrates that at this juncture a convergence of both internal and international developments pushed Beijing in the direction of a more confrontational stance on the island. On the first front, within the increasing stress on patriotism and nationalism in the post-Tiananmen period in China, securing the PRC's jurisdictional claim to Taiwan became even more salient to the Chinese leadership than before. Bereft of the mantle of ideological legitimacy the CCP had clung to prior to Tiananmen, Chinese leaders redefined themselves as defenders of the Chinese nation and the inheritors of the incomplete project of national unification. Thus, they could not but renew the call for the return of Taiwan to the mainland. As a particularly well-connected scholar at Peking University noted in 1997, "in China legitimacy has always come from unity and sovereignty, but especially after June fourth. This is why the Taiwan issue is so important, and here there is no room for compromise. It would be impossible for Jiang Zemin to give up the principle of national unity and let Taiwan become independent" (Personal interview, June 26, 1997). Yet, even as the return of Taiwan became more important to Beijing, Taiwanese politics, because of the intertwined process of democratization and the Taiwanization of national identity, were moving in the opposite direction (Hughes 1997; Rigger 1999, 2001).

On the second front, it is well known that the collapse of the Soviet Union produced a debate in Chinese foreign policy circles about the impact that the end of the bipolar distribution of power in world politics would have on China (and its claim to Taiwan). However, discussion in China was not limited to such conventional considerations. On the contrary, as previously discussed, Chinese analysts also devoted an expanding level of attention to the issue of self-determination and perceived changes in Western perceptions of sovereignty's role in international politics. In this sense, the rising misgivings in Beijing about the island were not simply the product of changing strategic calculations. Indeed, confronting perceived normative changes in the international system was perhaps of even greater concern.

The importance of such factors is particularly evident in a new strand of analysis of the situation in Taiwan that began to appear in Chinese journals at this time. For example, in *Taiwan Yanjiu Jikan*, Lin Jin (1992) meticulously traced the evolution of self-determination references in Taiwanese politics and their links to the promotion of Taiwanese independence. Throughout this critical review, Lin saw a crucial relationship between activities within Taiwan and those within the broader international community and attacked this development as a threat to sovereignty's general role in international politics.

Later in the decade, in the months preceding Lee Teng-hui's pivotal 1995 visit to the United States, Peng Xin'an, vice-director of the Xiamen Party Administration School, expanded on Lin's argument. Peng's commentary also focused on the Taiwan independence movement's apparent attempt to manipulate the principle of self-determination and transform the role of sovereignty in international politics. In rejecting this move, Peng argued that the extension of such a right to Taiwan through a referendum on independence would not only contradict established international norms and law, but would also open a Pandora's box of secessionist movements elsewhere in the world. Peng (1995: 5) warned that if the people of Taiwan have the right to vote over whether to remain a part of China, then "do other provinces, Hong Kong, Macao also have this right to secession?"

While the Chinese focused on such developments, in the United States in the fall of 1992 it was domestic political concerns that played the most prominent role in shifting a key component of America's Taiwan policy. Facing the prospect of losing his bid for reelection, President Bush announced his intention in early September to sell 150 F-16s (an advanced combat aircraft) to Taiwan (thus bolstering his support in Texas, where the planes were manufactured). Although Washington argued the sale did not violate the 1982 communiqué, it greatly expanded American military support for Taiwan. Alan Romberg (2003: 151–52) has noted that Beijing may have been somewhat placated by the relatively transparent political motives behind the sale, but, nonetheless, top Chinese officials blasted it as a violation of Chinese sovereignty. In addition, Beijing halted bilateral talks with the United States on both weapons nonproliferation (it also reportedly began arms shipments to Pakistan) and human rights (Suettinger 2003: 142). More importantly, while the Chinese did not immediately retract their offer to talk with Taipei in response to the arms deal, they did begin to more closely monitor the warming relationship between the United States and Taiwan. In addition, although there is little published data available to support the claim, some security analysts also suspect that at this time Beijing began to deploy a new generation of short-range missiles in Fujian (across the strait from Taiwan).

The U.S. arms sale also appears to have exacerbated differences in Beijing on the Taiwan issue. To a large extent, such divisions were defined by the extent to which emphasis was placed on the necessity of using non-peaceful means to bring about the return of Taiwan to China. The existence of extensive differences over this issue had been apparent in Chinese discussions about Taiwan at least since the early 1980s, but in the mid-1990s those making the harder-line argument seemed to have gained new influence. More specifically, many analysts argue that at this time, top PLA officials began to throw their weight behind a drive to take a more confrontational approach toward the island.[17]

To a certain degree, this trend may help account for Beijing's strong stance on Taiwan in the following years. However, it is important not to overstate the significance of such a development. To begin with, the military's role in formulating Taiwan policy remains quite opaque. More importantly, everyone in Beijing was operating within a common framework of promoting the return of Taiwan to China. Thus, "hawks" and "doves" alike were both categorically opposed to any challenge to this goal. Furthermore, in 1993 (and through the start of the 1995), moderate policies were still most prominent in Beijing's position on Taiwan. In other words, the Chinese continued to seek a means of avoiding confrontation across the strait (while steadfastly working toward a reunification of Taiwan with the mainland).

The best example of such a stance was the spring 1993 talks in Singapore between the heads of ARATS and SEF. These meetings between Wang Daohan and Koo Chen-fu produced limited agreements to increase economic and cultural ties between the two sides. They were followed in August by the publication of the State Council's cautiously optimistic white paper on Taiwan.

The white paper detailed the main features of Beijing's "one country, two systems" proposal, and meticulously reviewed the signs of progress and concern within cross-strait relations. With regard to the former, it reported "an atmosphere of relaxation prevails in the Taiwan Strait for the first time in the past four decades. This is auspicious to peaceful reunification." However, it also cautioned the Taiwanese authorities about their lack of sincere commitment to reunification, and noted the "shadow" that the clamor for Taiwanese independence was casting over the relationship. In addition, the paper saw an unsettling link between supporters of this movement on the island and foreign forces bent on "wounding the national feeling of the Chinese people." Indeed, by "vilely" relying on "foreign patronage," supporters of independence were working against the "fundamental interests of the entire Chinese population including Taiwan compatriots." Nonetheless, the paper concluded by restating the Chinese government's confidence in the people of Taiwan, and in China's "just cause of safeguarding its state sovereignty and territorial integrity" ("The Taiwan Question" 1993).

In the fall of 1993, Taipei challenged this moderate line on securing Beijing's jurisdictional claims with several new policies. First, the Mainland Affairs Council published its own white paper to refute each aspect of the State Council's document. In addition, following up on an announcement made earlier in the year, Taiwan moved forward with its bid (fostered by a handful of South American countries that maintained relations with the island) to reenter the UN. Complementing this drive to enhance Taiwan's international stature,

Lee Teng-hui engaged in "trip diplomacy" by expanded his international travel itinerary in 1994 to include stops in Southeast Asia and Central America for the purpose of promoting Taiwan's economic influence.

Each of these moves provoked strongly worded criticism from Beijing, the most pointed of which was directed at Lee Teng-hui and his perceived opposition to reunifying Taiwan with the mainland ("Lee Teng-hui's" 1994). Yet, even as Beijing chastised Lee, the United States was once more expanding its ties with Taiwan. Moreover, it soon became evident that the Clinton White House's 1993–94 reevaluation of the Taiwan issue posed new challenges for Beijing. Indeed, at this time America's Taiwan policy review changed the name of Taiwan's unofficial offices in Washington, allowed for expanded contact between Taiwanese and American officials, and articulated American support for Taiwan's entry into GATT (Romberg 2003: 158–60; Suettinger 2003: 206). In response to the review, Chinese vice foreign minister Liu Huaqiu protested to Stapleton Roy, the American ambassador in Beijing. In the course of his remonstrations, Liu informed Roy that the U.S. actions were an infringement on Chinese sovereignty and constituted a major retrogression of the American commitment to the "one China" principle ("Upgraded" 1994).

As ominous as such rhetoric was, a more cooperative stance on securing China's jurisdictional claims to Taiwan was once again forwarded at the start of the following year via Jiang Zemin's eight-point reiteration of the peaceful reunification policy line. Jiang's statement began by highlighting the historic underpinnings of the Chinese position on the island when it recalled the "humiliating chapter" of Japanese colonialism and the "betrayal and humiliation" of the treaty that allowed Japan to seize Taiwan in 1895. It then proceeded to a review of the progress and problems that had emerged in cross-strait relations since Deng's pledge to peacefully reunify the country.

Following this preface, the first of Jiang's eight points was in lockstep with each earlier offer made to the "Taiwan authorities." Once more, the underlying premise for cross-strait relations was that "China's sovereignty and territory must never be allowed to suffer split." However, in the rest of his talk he also forwarded new concessions by encouraging a two-staged negotiation process rather than pushing for immediate reunification. The Chinese leader argued that talks should first bring about the end of hostilities between the two sides and only then explore the basic outstanding issues in the relationship. He also reminded his listeners that China's reservation of the right to use force in Taiwan was limited to combating the "schemes of foreign forces to interfere with China's reunification and to bring about the 'independence of Taiwan'" ("President's Speech" 1995). To further mitigate this restrained threat, Jiang then highlighted the importance of building economic and cultural ties between the two sides.

This statement shows that, despite growing unease in Beijing over new developments in Taiwanese domestic politics through the start of 1995, Beijing's Taiwan policy continued to follow a relatively moderate line. However, later in the spring, there was a decisive turn toward confrontation over jurisdictional issues. At this time, Beijing first rejected Lee Teng-hui's April 8 response to Jiang's eight-point proposal (Romberg 2003: 163–64). It also reacted strongly against the May 22 announcement by the U.S. State Department that Washington would grant the Taiwanese leader a visa to attend an alumni reunion at Cornell University, his alma mater. This decision, and Lee's subsequent June visit to the United States, increased Beijing's concern about the growing international and local threats to the PRC's jurisdictional claim to Taiwan and elicited a resolute Chinese response.

The first component of this new confrontational stance was the publication of a stream of blunt criticism of Washington's decision. Stapleton Roy was again visited by the Chinese, and in an indication of the significance Beijing attached to this demarche, it was delivered by Foreign Minister Qian Qichen (who, it has been reported, was being criticized within the party for having previously taken a "soft" line on Taiwan). Qian warned Roy of the severe repercussions the U.S. visa decision would have on Sino-U.S. relations ("Chinese Foreign Minister" 1995). An abrupt downgrading of Sino-U.S. relations signaled by the suspension of talks between the PLA and the U.S. military complemented this discursive move. In addition, following Lee's speech at Cornell on June 12 (which dealt more directly with political issues and Taiwan's independent status than Washington had expected), the general bilateral relationship continued to deteriorate. This trend was accentuated when Beijing recalled Li Daoyu, the Chinese ambassador to the United States (Garver 1997: chap. 6; Suettinger 2003: 221).

While the Chinese were condemning Washington, they castigated Lee. An early indication of the level of frustration in Beijing came in the form of the postponement by Tang Shubei, vice chair of ARATS, of the second round of high-level ARATS-SEF talks that had been scheduled for later in the summer. In his statement announcing this decision, Tang referred to the link between "Lee Teng-hui and the anti-China forces in the United States," and condemned Lee's Cornell speech for "viciously attacking and blaspheming the Chinese mainland" ("Spokesman" 1995).

As biting as Tang's criticism of Lee was, it paled in comparison to the flood of bitter personal denunciations that dominated official statements on Taiwan through the summer of 1995. This invective was spearheaded by several commentaries on the Taiwanese leader that were published in July in *People's Daily* and Xinhua. Each of the commentaries challenged Lee's call for expanding Taiwan's "living space" within the international arena and endorsement of the concept of "popular sovereignty." As one editorial noted, "facts have shown that expecting a person such as Lee Teng-hui who 'doesn't know what China is' to improve and develop cross-strait relations is nothing less than climbing a tree to catch fish. All the Chinese should definitely not cherish any illusions about Lee Teng-hui" ("Fourth" 1995).

Despite this remarkable vindictiveness, to a large extent this commentary was simply an extension of the lower-profile critique of Lee that had been formulated within elite journals earlier in the decade. However, at this tenuous stage in cross-strait relations, criticism of Lee was not limited to the discursive realm. Indeed, to further underscore the unacceptability of Lee's visit, and to send a strong warning to both Taiwan and the international community, the PLA conducted missile tests in July and August off the coast of Fujian. Although Beijing insisted the exercises were a part of normal military training, top PLA leaders underscored the actual intent of the tests by issuing combative statements referring to Taiwan ("Chinese Defense Minister" 1995).[18]

After a deceptive lull in the early fall, China held a large military exercise off the Fujian coast in November, once again escalating tensions across the strait. The timing of this exercise was clearly designed to influence the outcome of the Legislative Yuan elections that were to take place in Taiwan in early December. Whether Beijing was emboldened by the subsequent electoral returns that favored candidates supporting unification with the mainland, or by the lack of clear U.S. signals to counter such moves, in March of the following year China carried out another round of military exercises and missile tests. This brought both cross-strait and Sino-U.S. relations to the very edge of outright military confrontation and elicited the deployment of two U.S. aircraft carrier groups to the region. This move constituted the apex of what has been called the "1995–1996 Taiwan Strait crisis."[19]

Against this backdrop, Lee Teng-hui prevailed in the first democratic presidential election ever held in Taiwan. In his May inaugural address, the Taiwanese leader once again steered the precarious course of forwarding his commitment to the island's independent status while attempting to avoid overtly provoking Beijing by pushing such an idea too far. The Chinese response to Lee's rhetoric was not enthusiastic, but also hinted that Beijing was ready to once again begin de-escalating cross-strait tensions. Thus, in a May news conference, Qian Qichen only tepidly criticized Lee, and encouraged the Taiwanese leader to follow up on the proposals he had made with concrete, cooperative actions ("Qian Queries" 1996).

During this initial post-crisis period, a series of factors brought about the relatively moderate turn in Beijing's approach to Taiwan. First, it quickly became obvious that Lee's political fortunes had been helped, rather than harmed, by the confrontational policies of 1995–96. Second, U.S. policies (especially the combination of warnings and assurances that came to define Washington's stance late in the crisis), while eliciting strong Chinese criticism, also pushed Beijing in the direction of moderation. Third, as the handover of Hong Kong, set for July 1, 1997, approached, maintaining stability in the region became more important for Beijing and a greater priority was thus placed on calming cross-strait relations. None of these issues was sufficient to trigger a major rethinking of China's approach to Taiwan, but in concert they were influential enough to bring about a sustained ratcheting down of the heated words and actions that had defined the Chinese stance during the preceding year.[20]

In line with this development, lower-level meetings between ARATS and SEF were held in 1997. In addition, economic and cultural ties between both sides of the strait grew. Furthermore, Chinese officials issued a string of invitations to reinitiate higher-level talks. Thus, in September of 1997 Qian Qichen declared "China is willing to increase contacts with various parties and people from all walks of life in Taiwan, except for a small number of 'Taiwan independence' supporters" ("Qian Reiterates" 1997). Expanding on this offer, at least according to reports in the Taiwan media, Chinese officials began to float subtle modifications of the "one country, two systems" formula. Ralph Clough cites Wang Daohan, a leading figure in ARATS, as proposing in June 1997 the possibility of "shared sovereignty, divided jurisdictions" (Clough 1999: 98).

In June of the following year, during President Clinton's visit to China (which, as discussed above, resulted in Jiang Zemin's unexpected statement about negotiating with the Dalai Lama), Beijing won a small diplomatic victory when the American leader told an audience in Shanghai that the United States did not support an independent Taiwan, two Chinas, or Taiwan's membership in international organizations.[21] Buoyed by this development, the Chinese moved to restart the talks that had been canceled in 1995 following Lee's trip to Cornell (Suettinger 2003: 350). A second round of the Wang-Koo talks was held in China in October. Moreover, a celebratory *Beijing Review* article published soon after the meeting announced that a new consensus had been reached between the two sides (Huang Wei 1998). However, official statements also pointed to the underlying differences that still separated the two sides ("Qian: Taiwan" 1998).

Unofficial analysis published during this period, and personal interviews with Chinese foreign policy and national security analysts in 1997 and 1998, revealed the relatively superficial and fragile nature of these cooperative developments. In fact, these sources tended to discount the prospects for dialogue, saw limited promise in the deepening economic ties between the two sides (as a potential source for eventual political reunification), and dwelt at length on the persistence of underlying tensions in cross-strait relations. In addition, ana-lysts were acutely aware of the divergence between China's own historically conditioned nationalist narratives on Taiwan and new trends on the island and in the international arena that threatened the basic story line of reunification.

Articles published in the fall of 1996 succinctly expressed the depth of Chinese unease about Taiwan. In the first of these, published in *Taiwan Yanjiu*, Liu Guofen commented on the rapid changes that had taken place in interna-tional politics in the 1990s and then observed that many Western scholars and politicians had begun to promote the idea that sovereignty had come to an end. According to Liu, it was precisely this development that gave China's opponents in the U.S. and in Taiwan the opportunity to deny Chinese sovereignty over Taiwan. Liu argued Lee Teng-hui in particular had dangerously distorted the relationship between sovereignty and democracy, and sovereignty and territori-al integrity (Liu Guofen 1996).

These sentiments were given even broader airing in the interview data. For example, a senior scholar of Sino-U.S. relations at the CICIR observed, "The Chinese are very sensitive about sovereignty. There are certain issues that we will immediately think of as sovereignty issues. The best example of this is Taiwan. When Lee Teng-hui traveled to America, we saw this as a sovereignty issue pure and simple, one that China would not accept" (Personal interview, May 14, 1997). A specialist of Sino-U.S. relations at the Foreign Affairs College echoed these sentiments when he rhetorically asked,

> Why does the issue of sovereignty remain so important to us? It is a question of national pride. Even though the politics involved are complicated, we have a need to see them in a simple light, in black and white. In this sense, we can't tolerate U.S. interference in China. It is something that the Chinese people take personally, especially when it comes to Taiwan. (Personal interview, May 27, 1998)

Despite such concerns, the interviewees were surprisingly diverse in their policy prescriptions for securing China's jurisdictional claim to Taiwan. A group of scholars at an influential think tank in Beijing were adamant in their claim that

> we are not willing to see the loss of the principle of single sovereignty—the insepa-rability of sovereignty. Since 1988 Lee Teng-hui has been talking about this, but really all he is doing is trying to split China. If any compromises are made with regard to Taiwan, they will not be made over the question of sovereignty and the one China principle, which is the key to the problem. (Personal interview, China Association for International Friendly Contact, Apr. 14, 1998)

Supporting such a claim, two researchers at CASS's Taiwan Studies Institute argued for limiting the undifferentiated application of self-determination to all counties. The two interviewees also maintained that sovereignty was a relative constant in international politics, and China's claim to Taiwan was beyond question (Personal interview, June 24, 1998).

In contrast, other scholars suggested the possibility of more extensive change in China's stance on jurisdictional claims. For example, a prominent scholar at CICIR asked, "If we gave up Taiwan, will we become a superpower? If the answer is yes, then maybe we should consider it" (Personal interview, Apr. 21, 1998). In addition, a scholar at another important security think tank emphasized the importance of sovereignty to China in terms of protecting itself, but argued that "even on Taiwan the idea of sovereignty doesn't really prevent China from coming up with [other] ways of dealing with the issue. There is now more flexibility here, maybe even a rethinking of sovereignty's role" (Personal interview, China Foundation for International and Strategic Studies, May 6, 1998).

In short, by the end of 1998, signs had emerged in Beijing that the Chinese might be willing to make more extensive concessions to resolve the "Taiwan issue." This trend mirrored the initiative Jiang had made earlier in the year to jump-start negotiations with the Dalai Lama. However, it too was derailed in 1999 by the convergence of international and local opposition to Beijing's jurisdictional aspirations for the island.

The international side of this threat initially came from Washington's promotion of missile defense as a new facet in its global security strategy. Chinese officials objected to the national component of this project and the impact it would have on all states' defensive capabilities, but it was theater missile defense (TMD) that they found most objectionable. Though the technology at the core of any TMD system was still in the early stages of development, the idea that Taiwan would be included in such a system became the subject of particularly harsh Chinese criticism in the winter and spring of 1999 ("China's Stand" 1999).

As disruptive as the TMD issue was, its influence on cross-strait relations paled in comparison to the impact of changes closer to home. Once again, Lee Teng-hui was at the center of the storm. On July 9, 1999, Lee stated "we have redefined cross-strait relations as nation-to-nation, or at least special nation-to-nation relations." He added, "under such special nation-to-nation relations, there is no longer any need to declare Taiwanese independence" ("Taiwan's Lee" 1999). Whether these remarks constituted a major departure in ROC policy is open to debate, but they nonetheless quickly became known as the "special state-to-state" formula and again fed Chinese anxieties about the state of the PRC's claim to Taiwan.

Chinese commentary critical of Lee's statement immediately honed in on his perceived attempt to erode the PRC's jurisdictional claim to the island. Such words were laden with additional significance when for the first time since the

1995–96 crisis, the leaders of the PLA played a principal role in promoting the Chinese position. For example, Chi Haotian, a leading figure in the Central Military Commission (CMC), argued that China would defend its territorial integrity and smash any attempt to divide the country ("Separatism" 1999). In addition, Zhang Wannian, also from the CMC, "warned Lee Teng-hui that he who plays with fire will get burnt. The reunification of the motherland is a historical trend and the goal of all Chinese. . . . The divisive forces are going against this historical trend. They are overrating themselves and courting their own destruction" ("Urgent" 1999).

Official statements such as these were quickly followed by yet another round of criticism of Lee in the main policy journals. This analysis even more stridently attacked Lee's formula as not only a violation of China's sovereignty, but also a distortion of the principle of sovereignty in international politics. For example, the first issue of *Taiwan Yanjiu* published after Lee's statement carried an article by Liu Wenzong (1999a) that took umbrage at the Taiwanese leader's attempt to divide sovereignty. In attacking Lee, Liu took note of the historical and legal record of Chinese sovereignty over Taiwan, and called attention to Clinton's 1998 endorsement of the "three no's," which he contended provided additional evidence that "Taiwan in no way is a 'sovereign state.' It is one hundred percent (*buzhebukou*) a part of China's territory and has no status (*zige*) with reference to our 'divisible sovereignty'" (p. 41).

Several critical commentaries in the next issue of *Taiwan Yanjiu* expanded on Liu's commentary. Pan Yu and Zhang Yonghua argued that Lee had trampled on China's national interest in a desperate attempt to split the country. Again, an unyielding belief that sovereignty's role in international politics is indivisible grounded these scholars' analysis. For them it was the "splitting (*fenlie*) of state sovereignty that was the highest principle of national interest that the two-state theory tread upon" (Pan Yu and Zhang Yonghua 1999: 38). In another article, Lai Caiqin (1999) made the case against Lee in a review of the published work of the founding father of the ROC, Sun Yat-sen. Finally, Dang Chaosheng (1999) raised questions about whether Lee's separatist activities had any support within Taiwan itself.

Liu Wenzong followed this criticism with a biting commentary on Lee published in the first 2000 issue of *Taiwan Yanjiu*. He labeled Lee's ideological development the product of an "enslaved education that reached deep into his spine (*nuhua jiaoyu shenru gusui*)" (Liu Wenzong 2000: 39). The Foreign Affairs College professor also dismissed Lee's family and philosophy as tainted by their traitorous experience of helping Japanese imperialism during the first half of the last century. Liu rhetorically asked how someone like Lee, who had identified himself as Japanese, could act as the "president of Taiwan" and be "loyal to China," and "not secretly sell out China's national interest and serve foreign [influence]" (p. 40).

Although compared to this sort of unofficial analysis the official commentary issued at the end of 1999 through the start of 2000 was conciliatory, the combative tone of Chinese publications revealed how cross-strait relations remained balanced on a precarious edge. For example, in January 2000, Jiang Zemin was quoted as warning yet again that Beijing would not "tolerate any act calculated to split China" ("The One China Principle" 2000).

The following month, during the lead-up to the second democratic presidential election in Taiwan, the State Council issued a second white paper on Taiwan that lent additional substance to Jiang's remarks, and did so with reference to the necessity of protecting China's sovereign rights. The paper warned:

> If a grave turn of events occurs leading to the separation of Taiwan from China in any name, or if Taiwan is invaded or occupied by foreign countries, or if the Taiwan authorities refuse, sine die, the peaceful settlement of cross-strait reunification through negotiations, then the Chinese government will be forced to adopt all drastic measures, including the use of force, to safeguard China's sovereignty and territorial integrity and fulfill the great cause of reunification. ("The One China Principle" 2000)

Although the white paper was obviously intended to counter Lee's "special state-to-state" statement, it was also designed to warn the United States against increasing support for Taiwan. However, ironically, as Robert Suettinger (2003: 400–405) has observed, it actually bolstered opposition to China's approach to the "Taiwan issue." In the United States it strengthened the hand of congressional supporters of the Taiwan Security Enhancement Act. In Taiwan, it arguably gave the DPP's candidate, Chen Shui-bian (an outspoken advocate of Taiwanese independence, and a political figure Beijing had long opposed), a boost in a tightly contested presidential election against the KMT's Lien Chan, whose candidacy had already been weakened by the defection of James Soong from the party (Rigger 2001: chap. 9).

China's call for reunification then suffered a serious setback in March, when, by a narrow margin, Chen was voted into office. Although he took a relatively conciliatory approach toward China during his victory speech, official Chinese commentary dismissed this gesture as hollow. Rather than offering to cooperate with Chen, Beijing cautioned that it would keep a close eye on his activities and monitor the degree to which he was willing to work with China.

Over the following months, Chinese leaders repeated these sentiments in an attempt to pressure Chen into acknowledging the "one China" principle in his inaugural address. In light of his well known preference for independence, it was not surprising he did not end up toeing this line when he was sworn into office.

However, at the same time he was careful to avoid provoking China with direct talk of Taiwanese independence (Rigger 2001: 212). While Beijing predictably found little to like in Chen's speech, and much to dislike, it also exhibited a relatively flexible approach to dealing with the "Taiwan issue" when Qian Qichen met with a visiting delegation from Taiwan in August ("Vice Premier" 2000).

During Chen's first year in office, Beijing's Taiwan policy was characterized by a steadfast refusal to deal directly with the new Taiwanese leader or other DPP representatives, limited attempts to build ties with the KMT opposition, and an ongoing buildup of a strong military presence along the Taiwan Strait. These policies initially resulted in a relative decline in cross-strait hostilities, but proved insufficient to build a lasting truce. Indeed, tensions ratcheted upward in 2001 following George W. Bush's election in the United States. More specifically, after entering the White House Bush appeared to enhance Washington's commitment to protect the island when he stated during a televised interview that the United States would to "whatever" it took to help Taiwan defend itself (Romberg 2003: 196). The Bush administration also granted Chen permission to transit through the United States before and after his trip to Central America (and allowed him to conduct extensive, albeit "private" activities during his stay) (p. 198).

These developments deepened Chinese anxieties about cross-strait relations, as was readily apparent in interviews I conducted in Beijing and Shanghai in the winter of 2001–2. Again and again, interviewees declared that China could not compromise on sovereignty over Taiwan. In addition, they argued that China had already gone to great lengths to bring Taiwan to the negotiating table. They interpreted the failure of first the KMT, and then the DPP, to respond to Beijing's offers as evidence of both parties' irresponsibility and disinterest in unifying the island with China.

Nonetheless, in private discussions, a minority of Chinese foreign policy analysts conceded that the "one country, two systems" principle was probably no longer a feasible foundation for the reunification of Taiwan with the mainland. They offered a surprising variety of alternative approaches to the Taiwan issue. A scholar at Fudan University talked about his project exploring state-local relations and suggested that this work might provide a new formula for resolving the cross-strait situation (Personal interview, Fudan University, Jan. 7, 2002). Another scholar, one with notably flexible views on sovereignty, pointed out that his newest work focused on the Taiwan issue and that he was looking for a "novel solution" to the problem. Moreover, he claimed that in both academic and policy circles, there was "more room for discussion on this issue than ever before" (Personal interview, Chinese Academy of Social Science, Dec. 28, 2001). A specialist in Sino-American relations even went so far as to criticize both Deng Xiaoping and Jiang Zemin for their handling of the Taiwan issue. He emphasized that Deng had moved aggressively and creatively on Hong Kong in the early 1980s, but subsequently both leaders "lost the opportunity on Taiwan. They failed to see changes on the island and the rest of the world and how they would affect cross-strait relations" (Personal interview, Foreign Affairs College, Dec. 30, 2001). Finally, in one of the boldest statements made during the hours of interviews conducted for this book, a young scholar observed that the Taiwan issue was increasingly becoming an obstacle to the realization of China's basic interests and participation in the international system. To get around such a dead-end, he suggested "it would be productive to move discussion of Taiwan away from sovereignty" (Personal interview, Fudan University, Jan. 6, 2002).

As fascinating as such dissenting voices are, it has to be kept in mind that in all cases criticism, and the search for new approaches, was firmly embedded in a bedrock commitment to realizing China's jurisdictional claim to Taiwan. Yet, in the summer of 2002 Chen Shui-bian rhetorically moved the island even further from the mainland when he first articulated his potential support for a referendum on Taiwan's future, and then asserted that there already was "one country on either side" (*yi bian, yi guo*) of the Taiwan Strait ("Taiwan President" 2002).

Beijing immediately rejected this assertion as "the same as, or even worse than, the state-to-state statement masterminded" by Lee Teng-hui, and warned that Chen's insistence on promoting independence "will jeopardize the well-being of Taiwan people and drag Taiwan into war" ("Xinhua, People's Daily" 2002). However, after Chen sent Mainland Affairs Council chairperson Tsai-ying Wen to Washington to explain that his remarks did not reflect a shift in policy, and after moves by Washington to show American consternation with Chen's commentary, Chinese remonstrations subsided, and it appeared that Beijing was willing to experiment with more flexible policies on Taiwan. More importantly, when Jiang Zemin visited President Bush's ranch in Crawford, Texas, both leaders called for cooperation over Taiwan. Bush, for the first time, unequivocally referred to the lack of American support for Taiwan's independence, while Jiang reportedly offered to cut the missile deployments near the strait if the United States would curtail arms sales to Taiwan (Romberg 2003: 215). Moreover, in January 2003, Beijing permitted a few commercial charter flights from Taiwan to China ("Hopes" 2003).

These measures resonated with a stream of unofficial analysis published in 2001–2 that called for China to be even more cooperative. While the majority of analysts stood firm on the question of China's absolute sovereignty over Taiwan (Yao Liming 2001), and rejected any other model for the solution of the

Taiwan issue (Li Jing 2001), Huang Jiashi and Wang Yingjin (scholars from People's University) suggested it was possible to divide functional aspects of China's claim. More specifically, Huang and Wang (2002) contended that there was a difference between China's ownership of sovereignty (*zhuquan suoyou quan*) and operationalization of sovereignty (*zhuquan xingshi quan*), with the authorities on Taiwan having a limited right to the former (also see Wang Yingjin 2003).[22] While steering clear of this core issue, other commentators were cautiously optimistic about the direction cross-strait relations were heading (Fan Xizhou 2002; Liu Guoshen 2003; Wang Jisi 2002; Yang Zejun 2001).

This optimism, however, was offset by the deep concern other scholars expressed with Chen Shui-bian's failure to abandon his advocacy of Taiwanese independence. For example, Li Jin (2001) noted that Chen had created the appearance of moderating his stance on this sensitive issue, but actually he remained committed to separating Taiwan from the mainland. In addition, Xie Yu and Liu Jiayan (2002), researchers at CASS's Taiwan Studies Institute, warned about the incipient dangers of the DPP's policy of "gradual independence" (*jianjinshi Taidu*). Moreover, Shi Yinhong (2004), a top scholar at People's University, predicted that should Chen win a second term as president of Taiwan, he would do even more to promote Taiwanese independence.

In the second half of 2003, Chinese misgivings were once again confirmed, and reinforced, by Chen's actions during the lead-up to Taiwan's March 2004 presidential election. First, he renewed his call for a referendum on Taiwan's future and reiterated many aspects of his August 2002 "*yi bian, yi guo*" statement ("President Predicts" 2003). Second, Chen stepped up his international travel. Most prominently, he made a transit stop in New York at the end of October to receive an award from the International League for Human Rights. In contrast with his 2000 stopover, Chen was permitted to meet with a large group of supporters (including members of Congress) while in the United States, and used the visit as a platform to talk about Taiwan's distinct political status. In addition, Therese Shaheen, chairwomen of the American Institute in Taiwan (AIT), America's "unofficial" embassy in Taiwan, provided Chen with added, albeit apparently impromptu, American support, when she enthusiastically declared during a toast "there is a secret guardian angel here that's really responsible for tonight, and that is President George W. Bush" (quoted in Lawrence 2003). Although Washington attempted to downplay the significance of these developments, they were generally seen in Beijing and Taipei as indications of an extension of the U.S. backing of Chen's political agenda.

Both of these policy initiatives were designed to direct voter attention to the island's tenuous political status, and appear to have played a key role in bolstering Chen's bid for reelection. Not surprisingly, they also elicited strong Chinese opposition. However, China's leaders feared that too overt an expression of their displeasure would again strengthen Chen's prospects for reelection (as was the case with Lee in 1996), and so, for the most part, official Chinese condemnations of Chen were kept to a minimum through the end of 2003.

Against the backdrop of such rising cross-strait tensions, Washington finally moved to reinforce the status quo between China and Taiwan through a combination of quiet diplomacy and public statements. Most significantly, Bush announced in a press conference during Chinese premier Wen Jiabao's December 2003 visit to the United States that "the comments and actions by the leader of Taiwan indicate that he may be willing to make decisions unilaterally to change the status quo, which we oppose" (quoted in Dinmore 2003). While this statement temporarily placated Beijing and was followed by a toning down of Chen's drive to highlight Taiwan's independent status, the president of Taiwan also made it clear that he would not halt the March referenda he had proposed earlier in the year. In response to Chen's moves, the Chinese continued to warn against the dangers inherent in the referenda plan, and, albeit in a relatively restrained fashion, against the continued promotion of Taiwan's independence (Chen Dong 2003a, 2003b; Song Linfei 2004).

In sum, over the last fifteen years, Beijing has acted to freeze the jurisdictional status quo in Tibet by pairing an economic plan designed to spur development with political policies intended to stifle dissent, and has employed a combination of carrots and sticks in an attempt to maintain its sovereign claim to Taiwan. Nonetheless, little progress was made during this phase toward shoring up Beijing's contested rights over either region. On the contrary, Chinese words and actions tended to stimulate competing jurisdictional projects in Taipei and Dharamsala (and elicit international support for both), which in turn fueled China's concerns about the threat to its claim to Taiwan and Tibet. In both cases, this dynamic created spirals of distrust and apprehension between the parties that heightened tensions and perversely undermined Beijing's drive to stabilize the situation in Tibet and realize its aspirations to reunify Taiwan with the mainland. Rather than eroding the commitment to hold onto both regions, these developments bolstered Beijing's determination to maintain an iron grip on China's jurisdictional sovereignty.

Conclusion: Will the Center Hold?

Throughout both phases discussed in this chapter, the Chinese approach to Taiwan and Tibet stood at the intersection between the historically framed

understanding of each region's strategic importance for China—which underlay Beijing's unyielding commitment to strengthen its hold over both regions
using all necessary means—and the limited incentive for employing more flexible, cooperative policies that grew out of the development of the reform and
opening line that Deng had first endorsed in the late 1970s. However, while the
latter of these two influences created a space for the consideration of novel, relatively malleable policies during the 1980s, the impetus for such innovative
approaches was extinguished in the 1990s by the rise of local challenges to
Chinese rule, paired with a shift in the global balance of power and the apparent system-wide rise of self-determination norms (both of which were also seen
as constituting threats to Beijing's position), at precisely a time when a relatively fragile Chinese government was trumpeting nationalist narratives (and the
cause of national unity). In other words, Taiwan and Tibet became more important to Beijing at precisely the time that these regions were threatening to pull
away from China.

While the same set of influences also framed the Chinese approach to Hong
Kong during the 1990s, here the challenges to Beijing's claims were quite
muted. Indeed, the key controversy in the relationship between Hong Kong and
Beijing was over the degree of autonomy the port city would have following
the July 1, 1997 resumption of Chinese sovereignty, and no actor disputed
China's basic jurisdictional claims to the region. As a result, throughout most of
this phase, the Chinese position was relatively secure. This generated a degree of
confidence in Beijing, which, coupled with clear economic incentives that
placed a premium on maintaining stability in Hong Kong, produced less confrontational practices toward Hong Kong than was the case toward either
Taiwan or Tibet. Nonetheless, Chinese words and actions consistently made
Hong Kong's sovereign status very clear: it was, and would always be, a part of
China. Moreover, when any development within Hong Kong raised even indirect questions about China's jurisdictional sovereignty over the region, Beijing
quickly moved to counter such trends and reinscribe its rule.

Both the relative flexibility of Chinese policy toward Hong Kong, and
Beijing's steadfast unwillingness to cede any ground on the basic jurisdictional
issues at stake in the region, were evident during the lead-up to the 1997 handover. For example, although the suppression of the 1989 student movement
spurred a wave of sympathy protests in Hong Kong, Chinese officials did not
directly intervene to stop them (Overholt 1991: 41–48). However, they did criticize such activity, and successfully engineered the inclusion of an antisubversion clause (Article 23) in the final draft of the Basic Law (which was adopted
by the NPC in April 1990). In addition, when the last British governor of Hong

Kong attempted to counter Beijing's policies with a drive to accelerate the democratization of Hong Kong by increasing the percentage of elected officials in the region's Legislative Council, the Chinese parried with a December 1993 announcement that the results of any forthcoming Legislative Council elections would be invalid following the 1997 resumption of Chinese sovereignty.

When the Chinese reiterated this stand following the September 1995 Legislative Council elections, it initially stoked opposition in the region. Unease in Hong Kong about Chinese intentions was then heightened by the establishment of institutional mechanisms to oversee the final stages of the handover, which appeared to grant individuals who were strongly supportive of China a leading role in this process. However, such misgivings were then assuaged by the fall 1996 selection of the at the time politically popular shipping magnate Tung Chee-hwa to serve as the first chief executive of the Hong Kong Special Administrative Region (HKSAR) (Baum 1999).

The meticulously choreographed July 1 celebration, which was marked by elaborately staged ceremonies in Beijing and Hong Kong and carefully crafted statements by China's top leaders, buoyed support for China in the region. Indeed, at this time, despite persistent, dire warnings about the impending collapse of Hong Kong, a consensus emerged that the Chinese appeared intent on complying with the terms of the 1990 Basic Law.

Confidence was reinforced by the relatively high respect Beijing showed for Hong Kong autonomy during the initial post-handover period. For example, Beijing made few changes in the Hong Kong civil service, PLA troops deployed to the HKSAR maintained a very low profile, and no effort was made to enact legislation consistent with Article 23 of the Basic Law. In addition, China's leaders stood behind local efforts to maintain the Hong Kong dollar's value in the face of intense international pressure during the 1997–98 Asian financial crisis (Baum 1999: 428–30).

Despite all this, Beijing's critics in Hong Kong continued to question China's commitment to respect the region's autonomy. Their concern sprang from a series of seemingly innocuous policies (such as the selection process for Hong Kong delegates to the NPC, and reports of moves made against the most outspoken democracy activists in Hong Kong). In contrast, in the first half of 1999 a more serious breach of the "one country, two systems" formula appeared in the "right of abode" case when the Hong Kong Court of Final Appeal ruled that all children and spouses of Hong Kong residents had the right to live in Hong Kong.

This decision immediately caused widespread consternation within Hong Kong, as it exacerbated fears that the region would be overrun with a flood of immigrants from the mainland. To address these concerns, Tung urged the court to reconsider the ruling, and in February it reversed itself. This move was popular in Hong Kong, but the court's argument for revising the verdict (that it had overstepped its bounds in attempting to interpret the Basic Law, a task that was solely the responsibility of the NPC), led to charges that the case had significantly eroded the region's autonomous status (Baum 1999; Overholt 2004).

In the aftermath of this controversy, the chorus of criticism against Beijing's Hong Kong policy grew louder (both in the HKSAR and internationally). However, even those most critical of the NPC ruling acknowledged that the Chinese leadership's handling of other potentially explosive issues within Hong Kong was relatively benign (Canning 2001; Holliday, Ma, and Yep 2002). Yet, this confidence in the "one country, two systems" approach was severely tested starting in 2002, when, against the backdrop of Tung's appointment to a second term as chief executive of the HKSAR, Beijing began to call for the implementation of the long delayed antisubversion legislation provided for in Article 23 of the Basic Law. Although such a move initially elicited little open criticism within Hong Kong, after the February 2003 first reading of the proposed bill in the Legislative Council, the issue began to generate widespread opposition. The scope of discontent in Hong Kong was then dramatically underscored on July 1, 2003, when approximately 500,000 demonstrators publicly protested against the measure (Holliday, Ma, and Yep 2004; Lague and Lawrence 2003). While leaders in Hong Kong initially downplayed the significance of this popular dissent and pledged to move forward with the proposed Article 23 initiative, within a week of the protests Tung announced he would temporarily postpone the second reading of the controversial bill (which was subsequently withdrawn) (Lague 2003).

Beijing then sought to shore up its jurisdictional claim over Hong Kong through a combination of economic incentives and political warnings, just as it had previously done with both Taiwan and Tibet. The Chinese first enacted several policies to bolster the region's faltering economy (primarily through easing trade flows between Hong Kong and the mainland), but at the same time cautioned all Hong Kong residents to remember their status as Chinese citizens and to foster patriotism (Lague 2004). While the economic stimuli were welcomed by many in Hong Kong, the warnings generated a wave of negative public opinion about China's administration of the region. Thus, a year after the initial July 1 protest, it was not surprising when a second major demonstration was held (Fong, Brown, and Pottinger 2004).

The long-term impact of this second round of protests remains unclear; but it is now obvious that, at the very least, Beijing's attempt to assert more direct influence over the region has rocked Hong Kong–China relations. As counter-productive as such policies have been, when viewed within the context of the arguments developed in this chapter, the result should also not be surprising. On the contrary, as we have seen, at least in regard to Taiwan and Tibet, China's leaders have consistently responded to direct challenges to Chinese rule with precisely the same sort of words and actions. Beijing has been unwilling to compromise when it feels its jurisdictional rights are threatened.

5

Sovereign Authority: Limiting International Oversight and Resisting Interference in Internal Affairs

The strengthening of the international human rights system over the last thirty years has raised fresh questions about the principle of non-interference in states' internal affairs. As argued in Chapter 1, the lines created by the norm of non-interference, which is at the core of sovereign authority, were undermined by an uneven, yet increasingly universal, acceptance of the right of the "international community" to supervise and monitor human rights conditions throughout the globe (and at times to intervene in the name of preventing gross violations). This development created a new system-wide sovereign authority / human rights dynamic. The representatives of each state were then left with the task of attempting to define how such a systemic trend might modify their own state's approach to this aspect of sovereignty. The positions they have articulated (through the enactment of sovereignty-related practices discussed in Chapter 2) are as diverse as the actors that developed them. Nonetheless, most states generally have begun to transgress their sovereign boundaries over the course of the last three decades.

In apparent defiance of this development, the Chinese continued to reject any perceived interference in China's internal affairs in the name of human rights during the 1980s and 1990s. However, during this period the Chinese position on sovereign authority also incrementally changed in actions (increased participation in the international human rights system) and in words (a trickle of official rhetoric and unofficial analysis that reconsidered the relationship between states' rights and human rights).

This shift developed over the course of three phases.[1] The first phase (1979–spring 1989) coincided with the opening decade of the reform era, and was characterized by a very limited modification in the Chinese position on the international human rights system. During this period, the sweeping denunciations of human rights that had been the defining feature of the Chinese stance prior to 1979 were replaced with more selective criticism and limited Chinese participation in key international human rights institutions. Such acceptance was subsequently overwhelmed by a visceral Chinese attack on the system (more specifically, the perceived American manipulation of it) during the immediate post-Tiananmen period. During this brief phase (spring 1989–summer 1991), China remained a participant in the international human rights system, but it did so in order to counter the international campaign to censure Beijing's human rights record. However, toward the end of this phase, the defensiveness and hostility of the Chinese denunciations lessened, and faint signs of a more temperate stand on human rights issues emerged.[2] This trend toward moderation became fully apparent in the fall of 1991 with the publication of the first Chinese white paper on human rights, which marked the start of the third phase in the development of the Chinese stance. Over the course of this phase (which is ongoing), China became an active member of the international human rights system, and Chinese leaders and policy analysts began to express notably pluralistic views on human rights. On balance, these practices eroded the boundary between China and the rest of the international system in regard to human rights issues.

The initial changes in Beijing's position on the sovereign authority / human rights dynamic were the product of a careful consideration of the relative costs and benefits of redefining the balance between the two components. On the one hand, denigrating the international human rights system and promoting a static interpretation of the principle of non-interference had obvious appeal to a government facing continuing international and domestic challenges to its legitimacy. Moreover, the living memory within foreign policy making circles of the so-called century of humiliation also made sovereign authority a right of intrinsic value, and this historically informed attachment tended to tilt Chinese calculations in the direction of defending sovereignty (and rejecting the human rights system). On the other hand, as the influence of this system grew within the broader international arena, and more international attention was paid to China's own checkered human rights record, the Chinese determined it was worthwhile to make very limited, strategic compromises on human rights issues (and sovereignty).

In light of the potency of the factors against change, the emergence of a new Chinese approach to human rights in the 1990s (following the initial post-Tiananmen backlash) is particularly puzzling. Why did the Chinese become more deeply involved with the international human rights system in a way that threatened to undermine the relative insulation afforded by an unambiguous promotion of the principle of non-interference? Why did some influential analysts and policy makers begin to discuss sovereign authority in new, boundary-transgressing, and at times, even transformative, terms?

On one level, the answer to these queries lies in the increased material pressure brought to bear on Beijing during this period. Following Tiananmen, the international community more than ever before (if still inconsistently) pressured China to change. This external stimulus accounts for the initial contraction in the Chinese approach to human rights in 1989, and Beijing's limited accommodations to human rights critics during the first half of the 1990s. However, on a second, more fundamental, level, over the course the decade, two new forces for change emerged. First, an increasing interest in Beijing in promoting China's role as a responsible power within the global arena, one willing to make compromises on the issue of sovereignty and cooperate with other members of the international system, created an environment in Beijing that was more conducive to compromise on the human rights front. Second, international norms on human rights and sovereign authority and on the transgression of conventional sovereign boundaries gained a foothold in China's foreign policy establishment through its long-term involvement in argumentative human rights discourses. This process, which Risse and Sikkink (1999) aptly labeled "norms diffusion," caused the Chinese to seriously engage the opinions of those outside China about human rights, and created the space within China for new debates and actions on this front.

The main models of change forwarded in the "new sovereignty" debate in international relations theory (introduced in Chapter 2) cannot adequately explain the development of the Chinese approach to the sovereign authority / human rights dynamic. At the same time, my argument differs from Ming Wan's (2001) recent rationalist explanation of the Chinese approach to human rights, and is more consistent with the work of Ann Kent (1999) and Rosemary Foot (2000) on the issue. However, it also finds a more profound change in Chinese behavior during the 1990s than either of these latter pair of scholars acknowledged, and attributes this shift (and the reticence to it within Beijing) to a broader array of forces than either they or Wan identify. Simply put, the literature is unable to explain why in some instances Chinese practices have remained the same, and why in other instances they have changed.

Phase I, 1979–89: Defending Sovereignty, Integrating with the Human Rights System

During this phase, the Chinese position on the sovereign authority / human rights dynamic was unfailingly boundary-reinforcing. However, the Chinese also incrementally recalibrated their stance on human rights in a way that suggested, albeit indirectly, a slight modification of their principled stance. This development distinguished Chinese behavior from the outright rejection of the human rights system that had previously been the defining feature of the Chinese stance, and was quite similar to the wave of adjustments Beijing made in regard to each of the other facets of sovereignty during the 1980s.

This limited change encompassed both rhetoric and policy. On the discursive front, official references to human rights became more moderate and less confrontational. The scope of this trend is illustrated in Figure 5.1, which shows that official commentary in *Beijing Review* in the early 1980s focused extensively on the issues of sovereign authority and non-interference, but then tended to de-emphasize these concerns through 1988.[3]

The sparse amount of unofficial analysis of human rights published in China during this period followed the same pattern. During the 1980s, a handful of influential scholars (mostly specialists in international legal studies), working within the constraints set by official Chinese rhetoric, cautiously endorsed the human rights system. The policy complement to such a rhetorical shift was a gradual rise in Chinese participation in the UN's charter-based human rights organs, paired with formal commitments to an expanding list of key human rights treaties.[4]

A series of Chinese moves in 1979 marked the opening of this phase. In that year, Beijing became an official observer at the UN CHR (Kent 1999: 43). In addition, during Deng Xiaoping's historic visit to the United States, the Chinese leader was reported to have responded favorably to President Carter's inquiries into several human rights–related issues (Cohen 1988: 84–85; Foot 2000: 103). These diplomatic moves were matched within China by the release of a handful of political dissidents who had been arrested in 1974 for their role in the Li Yizhi wall poster incident (Cohen 1988: 85). Although these gestures were remarkable in light of Beijing's previous stance on human rights, the subsequent silencing of the more outspoken contributors to the Democracy Wall movement later in the year (most notably through the trial of Wei Jingsheng) revealed how little the Chinese position on human rights had changed at the start of Deng's reform era.

The discursive complement to this development was a renewed consideration of human rights issues in Chinese journals.[5] The majority of articles on human rights published at this time provided rhetorical support for Beijing's official reservations about the system, and did so using Marxist terminology to attack the class biases built into it (see, for example, "Notes" 1979). However, more conciliatory analysis also began to find its way into Chinese publications. Significantly, such commentary appeared in the work of Chinese scholars before

FIGURE 5.1

Sovereign Authority Claims in BR, 1979–88

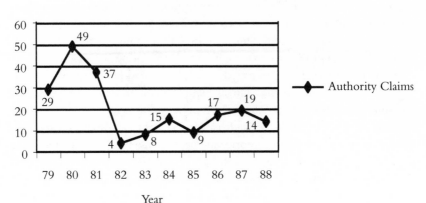

Year

surfacing in more high-profile forums (such as policy statements by top leaders or addresses to relevant multilateral forums). In other words, even at this early date, the reevaluation of human rights issues within China was not an entirely top-down operation.

An excellent early example of such a development can be found in a 1979 *Minzhu yu Fazhi* article by Liu Han and Wu Daying, which carefully steered clear of a blanket refutation of the international human rights system, and concluded that human rights were not always a tool of the bourgeoisie. However, Liu and Wu also insisted that recognizing the importance of human rights in the international system and examining China's own human rights record were not the same thing. Indeed, they explicitly warned that the calls by a small minority of "unpatriotic people" who had demanded that foreigners "'pay attention' to the so-called 'human rights' issue in China" was "totally unnecessary" (Liu and Wu 1979: 21).

In the early 1980s, this circumscribed recognition of the possible utility of participating in the international human rights system become the most predominant feature of each aspect of the Chinese position on human rights. Thus, although China remained only an observer at the UN CHR in 1980 and 1981, Chinese representatives at this time began to vote in the General Assembly (albeit, by casting abstentions) on human rights resolutions critical of a number of South American states (Kent 1999: 43). In addition, Beijing signed on to two human rights treaties. The first of these was the relatively weak (in terms of enforcement and reporting mechanisms) Convention on Women. The second, the Convention on Racial Discrimination, while also lacking teeth, placed potentially more extensive obligations on the Chinese state (in regard to the handling of Han-minority relations). Of even greater importance than the specifics of either treaty, by simply ratifying both documents Beijing increased its involvement in the burgeoning international legal system designed to protect human rights.

In 1982, this trend of expanding participation gained additional momentum when China became an official member of the UN CHR. China's participation was marked by a statement made by Gu Yijie, the head of China's delegation. Gu's comments are worth considering in detail, as they reveal how Beijing had begun to utilize human rights rhetoric as a tool to criticize China's international opponents (while attempting to forestall international inquiries into China's own human rights record). The official Chinese report on Gu's statement began by noting, "China today accused the Soviet Union and Vietnam of trampling underfoot the right of national self-determination and independence and sovereignty, violating the fundamental human rights of the Afghan and Kampuchean peoples and threatening world peace and security in their invasion and occupation of the two countries" ("China Denounces" 1982).

This guarded endorsement of the international human rights system was more broadly explored in the work of Chinese legal scholars. Most prominent was a 1982 *Beijing Review* article that accepted the idea that human rights played an important role within international politics, but paired such recognition with an insistence on the tie between human rights and sovereignty. One of the main points of the article was that the protection of human rights was not in tension with sovereign authority, but rather it was a tool to be wielded by oppressed peoples to realize their sovereign rights (Shen Baoxiang, Wang Chengquan, and Li Zerui 1982: 16).

Similar concerns were expressed by each of the main contributors to China's emerging unofficial human rights discourse. Thus, in 1984, Liu Fengmin warned that powerful states frequently used human rights language to interfere in other states' internal affairs (see Chiu 1989: 17). Yet, in their highly influential 1981 text on international law (which has long served as the introductory text to the field in Chinese universities), Wang Tieya and Wei Ming developed a more nuanced position on non-interference. They too argued that "the principle of human rights must be subordinate to the principle of state sovereignty and cannot be superior to the principle of state sovereignty" (quoted in Chiu 1989: 17). However, in a fascinating admission, Wang and Wei added that when "international crimes" had been committed, "necessary measures taken by all states and international organizations to suppress these behaviors are consistent with generally recognized principles of international law and should not be considered as intervening in the internal affairs of a state" (Ibid.).

As tentative as these arguments were (and as distinct from more expansive interpretations of the human rights system that were being articulated outside China at this time), they did open the door to the theoretical possibility of international oversight of human rights issues. The handful of additional human rights instruments Beijing signed in 1982 (the Convention Relating to the Status of Refugees, and the Protocol Relating to the Status of Refugees) and 1983 (the Convention on Genocide, and the Convention on Apartheid) sustained the guarded nature of this new Chinese commitment to the human rights system. As with the Conventions on Women and Racial Discrimination, none of these agreements required Beijing to make any real compromises in becoming a signatory; but combined, they did constitute a deepening of Chinese participation in the UN human rights treaty system.

In the mid 1980s, Beijing also began to play a more active role in the shaping of human rights discussions within the UN framework. Thus, in 1984 China participated for the first time in the UN CHR's Subcommission on the Prevention of Discrimination and Protection of Minorities. In addition, the Chinese voted in the General Assembly in favor of appointing a special rapporteur to investigate human rights conditions in Afghanistan (Kent 1999: 43). The following year, the Chinese supported a General Assembly resolution critical of Chile's human rights record (Foot 2000: 107). Beijing also favored another UN General Assembly resolution, The Indivisibility and Interdependence of Economic, Social, Cultural, Civil, and Political Rights, which reinforced the UN's commitment to human rights (Kent 1999: 44). Moreover, at the UN CHR, a member of the Chinese delegation endorsed the UN's role in attempting to prevent "mass and flagrant violations of the human rights of peoples" (while taking particular note of the abuses of the South African and Israeli governments on this score). Yet, in the same statement, the delegate warned against the manipulation of human rights principles by some states to interfere in the affairs of others.

Consistent with such a note of concern, China's representatives redoubled their efforts in 1985 to limit the consideration of their own state's human rights record within both bilateral and multilateral forums. Thus, in February 1985, when the United States issued a critical report on human rights conditions in China, a Foreign Ministry spokesperson quickly expressed his "regret" and derided the "groundless and improper comments on the domestic affairs of China" (while observing that the "rights" of everyone in China were in fact protected by the Chinese constitution) ("China Rejects" 1985). In addition, in the same year, when human rights INGOs submitted materials to the UN CHR that were critical of Beijing's policies on executions and in Tibet, the Chinese quickly rejected such actions as interfering in China's internal affairs (Cohen 1988: 92).

Despite such pronounced sensitivity to international criticism, in late 1986 Beijing enacted a series of policies that once again expanded the scope of Chinese involvement in the international human rights system. The start of this period was marked by a high-level Chinese endorsement of human rights by Wu Xueqian, China's foreign minister. In his address to the UN General Assembly in September, Wu suggested that China's stance on the ICCPR and ICESCR had shifted. The human rights covenants, Wu observed, were of "positive significance to the realization of the purpose and principle of the United Nations Charter concerning the respect of human rights" ("Wu Xueqian" 1986). Although Beijing did not follow up on this statement with any concrete moves to become a party to either document, in early December it did sign the Convention Against Torture (CAT), and before that pledged that police in China who used torture would be reeducated and, in cases where severe rights abuses had taken place, punished (Foot 2000: 103).

Unofficial analysis published at this time continued to defend Chinese sovereignty, but it also began to articulate a more positive stance on the international human rights system. For example, an article in *Beijing Review* reiterated the same claims that were featured in the 1982 piece already discussed, but added, "Human rights are part of the international moral and legal codes." The article also claimed that China supported the "international community in showing its concern about large-scale human rights violations in an appropriate manner so as to help improve and promote the human rights situations in these countries." Despite reciting the standard reservations about human rights, it added, "the People's Republic of China is steadily involving itself in the international human rights movement" (Guo Shan 1987).

This commitment gained the upper hand in 1988, as Beijing continued to steer China toward a more substantial involvement in the international human rights system. Thus, in fall 1988 a high-ranking Chinese legal official called on Beijing to do more to prevent government "infringement of human rights and dereliction of duty" ("Top" 1988). In addition, Qian Qichen, the newly appointed foreign minister, noted in an address to the General Assembly in September that even though the Universal Declaration of Human Rights (UDHR) had historical limitations, it still had "a far-reaching influence on the development of the post-war international human rights activities and played a positive role in this regard" ("China Backs" 1988). Finally, the National People's Congress (NPC) ratified the CAT that Beijing had committed to in 1986.

During this period, dissident voices on human rights issues were reaching a fever pitch in the lead-up to the 1989 student-led protest movement. These activities were harshly criticized in official Chinese commentary. Nevertheless, even as such criticism was being issued, a few scholars working within prominent think tanks and research institutes began to publish analysis that subtly pushed beyond the cautious tone and content of Beijing's formal position on human rights.

This move was particularly evident in a contribution by Xu Bing to *Faxue Yanjiu*. Xu, who had articulated a relatively moderate position on human rights at the start of the reform era, now embraced an even more expansive understanding of the principle. He argued, "I believe that the banner of human rights belongs to all humanity, and thus naturally too the Chinese people as well" (quoted in Angle and Svensson 2001: 308). Xu also found some fault with China's current human rights record and called on the government "to reaffirm human rights and correct the mistaken idea that human rights is a slogan of the bourgeoisie and not of the proletariat" (p. 317).

While such a direct statement of support for human rights (and admission of China's own shortcomings) was rare in the Chinese discourse of the late 1980s, many analysts at this time did stake out more cautious, but still accepting, positions on human rights. For example, Ma Jun (1988), a professor of international law at the Foreign Affairs College, noted, "China has no objection to the United Nations expressing concern in the proper way over consistent and large-scale human rights violations, but it opposes the interference in other countries' internal affairs under the pretext of defending human rights." In addition, in early 1989, an article dedicated to human rights appeared for the first time during the decade in one of China's major foreign policy journals. Written by a leading Chinese representative to the UN, Tian Jin, the article attempted to pair an acceptance of the human rights regime with a clear statement of its limits. Thus, Tian noted that the international protection of human rights was a positive development in international politics. However, he also warned against Western countries, especially the United States, using human rights to interfere in other countries' internal affairs. Tian (1989: 7) then went on to strenuously object to the argument made by "some in the West" who seek to "deny (*fouren*) that human rights is under the internal administration of states, and propagandize [the line] that there is only human rights and no sovereignty (*zhi you renquan, mei you zhuquan*)."

Such commentary reflects the fact that on balance in 1989, just prior to the suppression of the student-led protest movement, the Chinese position on human rights and sovereign authority had undergone a significant, if incomplete, shift. The catalyst for this change (and the framing condition for subsequent developments) can once more be found in Deng Xiaoping's repeated calls in the late 1970s to place a premium on the modernization of the Chinese economy (rather than class conflict and ideological purification). Within the context of this reform of China's basic strategic objectives, it was in the interest of policy makers to consider the potential benefits of any moves that would facilitate Chinese participation in the international system. During the 1980s, it was precisely this motive that informed the moderation in Chinese territorial practices and spurred compromises on each of China's outstanding jurisdictional issues. In regard to the issues discussed in this chapter, most relevant was the new Chinese commitment to develop a more stable, predictable legal system to regulate and govern both economic and political affairs and to create an environment conducive to rapid economic development. Indeed, as Deng himself observed in an important 1978 speech on modernizing China, it was essential to strengthen China's overall legal system and at the same time to intensify "our study of international law" (Deng Xiaoping 1995: 156). Wang Tieya and Wei Ming expanded on this statement in 1979 when they argued that allowing China to remain an outcast from the contemporary international legal system "does not fit with China's status in the world today. It is detrimental to the expansion of exchanges with other countries and to China's drive for modernization" ("'People's Daily'" 1979).

This sweeping reevaluation of China's relationship with the rest of the world, and the role of international law within the new dynamic Beijing was attempting to construct, created an opening in China for novel considerations of the international human rights system (and its relationship to the principle of sovereign authority). In the space created by this development, democracy activists in China, and international critics of Beijing, began to call attention to the shortcomings of the Chinese human rights record. Although the focus generated by both groups was uneven and incomplete (and to a certain extent simply reinforced Chinese reservations about the human rights system), it also meant that simply ignoring what was fast becoming China's "human rights issue" was not a viable policy option for Beijing. In other words, the increasing attention paid to China's human rights record reached such a level in the 1980s that it demanded a Chinese response. Beijing's reaction was designed to discredit China's critics. While the intent of such moves was clearly to limit Chinese involvement in the human rights system, they had unintended consequences. In effect, once the Chinese shifted their position from outright rejection of the human rights system to a nuanced acceptance that human rights was an integral aspect of the contemporary international legal system, China became caught up in exchanges with the proponents of the system that subtly shifted the content of Chinese practices.

However, underlying insecurities in China's foreign policy making circles about China's tenuous position in the international system—and ongoing challenges to regime survival from within, framed by references to human rights and democracy—also constrained Beijing's willingness to make any significant con-

cessions on the human rights front. Over the course of the decade, the principle of non-interference and boundary-reinforcing interpretations of state's
rights proved to be extraordinarily useful tools in Beijing's ongoing bid to fend
off criticism.

Sensitivity to interference in China's internal affairs in the name of human
rights was heightened, and resistance to change fueled, by the memory of the
"century of humiliation." This memory created a lasting animosity within
China toward the human rights system, as many Chinese perceived it a vehicle
by which powerful states (especially the United States) were attempting to push
China back into a subordinate position in international politics (just as the
unequal treaty system had done during the 1800s). In this sense, during the
1980s Beijing's human rights policies were not solely based on rational evaluations of costs and benefits. On the contrary, its policies always were shaped by
powerful collective memories of past infringements upon Chinese sovereignty.
This worldview made Chinese leaders particularly leery of ceding too much
ground on sovereignty, resulting in a high level of reserve and misgiving about
the threat posed by human rights. Such suspicions were clearly expressed in a
Peking Review article published at the end of 1979. The article noted:

> We can still remember that in the old China there was a sign bearing the words,
> "No admission for dogs and Chinese" hung on the gate of a park in Shanghai. It
> was in such a barbarian and shameless way that the foreign aggressors insulted the
> Chinese people and completely denied their human rights. . . . How can the impe-
> rialists have the effrontery to prate about the so-called human rights question in
> China? ("Notes" 1979)

Phase II, 1989–91: Reinscribing the Line between China and the Rest of the World

The trend toward partial Chinese involvement in the international human
rights system was derailed in the spring of 1989. This period was an important
turning point in Chinese handling of each of the other aspects of sovereignty,
and it was especially decisive in Beijing's stance on the sovereign authority /
human rights dynamic. Beijing's suppression of the student-led protest movement of 1989, and the wave of international condemnations it elicited, reoriented the Chinese position on human rights. Immediately following June 4, the
Chinese enacted a set of practices that directly challenged China's human rights
critics and reinforced China's sovereign boundaries.

Over the following two years, this defensive turn was the defining feature of
the Chinese stance. Official commentary on human rights during this phase was
emphatically boundary reinforcing, unfailing in its rejection of all critical
inquiries into China's human rights record, and vigorous in its erasure of the

more open statements that had begun to appear in the 1980s. The volume of such pronouncements was greatest during 1989. For example, in that year, sixty-five statements on sovereign authority appeared in *Beijing Review*, more than three times the total number of claims published in any previous year. In addition, *Beijing Review* continued to publish an elevated level of claims in 1990 and 1991. Although there was no similar outpouring of unofficial analysis at the start of this period, the slight gap that had emerged in the late 1980s between Beijing's formal position on human rights and the informal discussion of human rights in scholarly circles did disappear, replaced by a uniform, unyielding critique that initially proceeded in lockstep with the official discourse. This defiant rhetoric was complemented by a persistent policy effort to confront Beijing's new international human rights critics (in both bilateral and multilateral settings).

Chinese policy makers' primary human rights concerns initially coalesced around the new emphasis that Washington placed on this issue following the suppression of the student-led movement in China. At this time, despite divisions in the Bush administration over how to respond to the Tiananmen crackdown, the United States played a leading role in censuring China's human rights record. On June 5, Washington suspended all weapons sales to Beijing and placed a moratorium on Sino-American military exchanges (Foot 2000: 115). Later in the month it announced more extensive sanctions, and garnered broad international support for these moves (Foot 2000: 116–17; Wan 2001: 43).

These external pressures helped spark an intense debate in China over the possible necessity of fundamentally altering Beijing's basic foreign policy line away from the priorities of peace and development that Deng Xiaoping had established in the late 1970s. This debate was ultimately won by more moderate voices that argued against such a retrenchment and in favor of continued modernization and stability (Harding 1992: 235–36). However, even as Deng and other top leaders proclaimed China's ongoing commitment to these policies, official Chinese commentary pointedly rejected all international criticism of China's behavior. For instance, following the announcement of the second round of U.S. sanctions against China, Li Peng took note of the "anti-China adverse current under the banner of human rights" that had emerged since June 4 ("Li Peng" 1989).

China's representatives to the UN CHR subcommission reiterated this line in August, when they attempted to prevent the annual meeting of the organization from taking up the issue of Tiananmen. The theme of protecting sovereignty and preserving the principle of non-interference in internal affairs was a major basis of this effort (Kent 1999: 57–58). Nonetheless, the subcommission passed a relatively weak, yet still critical, and historic (it was the first time the

organization had censured a permanent member of the Security Council) resolution on China. Predictably, the Foreign Ministry responded that "quelling
the rebellion was precisely to safeguard the basic human rights and freedom of
the overwhelming majority of the people" ("'Full Text'" 1989).

Unofficial analysis produced during the initial post-Tiananmen period was
also defensive. For example, a *Beijing Review* article flatly rejected the idea of
"universal and abstract human rights" and the claim that universal human rights
"override the laws of various countries" (Yi Ding 1989: 14). Although the article acknowledged the existence of international human rights standards, it also
emphatically argued that "the theory that human rights knows no national
boundary is not only theoretically wrong, and legally groundless, but also very
harmful politically and practically. The preachers of this theory say they are
merely concerned about human rights and do not intend to interfere in other
countries' internal affairs. This runs counter to the facts" (pp. 14–15).

These practices were consistent with the behavior, and causal factors, in what
Risse and Sikkink (1999: 22–24) have categorized as the "denial" phase of the
human rights norms spiral model. The initial post-Tiananmen contraction in
China's practices was fundamentally the product of the interest of the representatives of the Chinese state to insulate themselves from international criticism
that threatened the legitimacy of Beijing's rule. It was rational for state officials
to fend off all external challenges to their handling of the student demonstrations. Or, as one international legal expert whose editorials were prominently
featured in the Chinese media following Tiananmen frankly commented during a personal interview in 1997, "You ask why we placed such emphasis on
sovereignty after Tiananmen? Because it was our aim to prevent U.S. interference in Chinese affairs" (Personal interview, Foreign Affairs College, June 17,
1997).

In short, self-preservation was clearly a prime motive behind the Chinese
retreat on human rights in 1989. However, the ferocity of the Chinese rejection
of external criticism during this period (and after) can only be fully explained
with reference to China's "century of humiliation," memories of which fed
Chinese resentment of external pressure. A prominent example of the way
Chinese leaders viewed such issues can be found in Deng Xiaoping's spring
1990 commentary on the ongoing Western-imposed sanctions China was facing. Deng noted, "I am a Chinese, and I am familiar with the history of aggression against China. When I heard that the seven Western countries, at their summit meeting, had decided to impose sanctions on China, my immediate association was to 1900, when the allied forces of the eight powers invaded China"
(Deng Xiaoping 1994: 344–45).

This vision, and the deeply held commitment to prevent a contemporary recurrence of such disgraces, multiplied the umbrage the Chinese took at international criticism of Beijing's human rights record, and led to a particularly tight embrace of sovereignty. An influential international relations scholar reflected on this period during an interview in 1998, noting that memories of China's past had ensured that "the Chinese tend to be more concerned with protecting sovereignty in calculating the relationship between national interest and sovereignty" (Personal interview, CICIR, Apr. 21, 1998). In other words, sovereignty was not simply a means to preserve the Chinese state; it was a norm that had inherent value in and of itself. It was, as many of those I interviewed observed, "a sacred right to be treasured."

Nevertheless, in the chaotic months that followed the June 4 crackdown, the Chinese did not condemn the human rights system in its entirety. Rather, a careful reading of even the bitterest editorials published during this time reveals that the chief object of Chinese ire was the perceived misuse of the system by the West. Considering how much Beijing stood to lose on the human rights front, and the weight of historical factors that tended to exacerbate Chinese sensitivities to such pressures, it is then necessary to consider why Beijing did not simply reject the regime in toto.

The answer is three-fold. First, to the extent that Deng's line on modernization and development held, Beijing could not afford to step back into the isolation of the pre-reform era. Relinquishing China's place in the human rights system through reneging on treaty commitments, or denouncing the very idea of human rights, would have threatened to isolate China and was thus rejected. Second, as we have seen, retaining membership in the main UN Charter–based bodies of the international human rights regime provided the Chinese with a high-profile platform for confronting Beijing's human rights critics. Third, during the preceding decade, China had already committed to many of the human rights system's main instruments; abandoning the reporting obligations and other responsibilities that came with them would have been a clear violation of these commitments. Although the material cost of doing so would not have been steep (as noted above, Beijing had steered clear of making any moves that placed real material constraints on its behavior), precedent for participation had clearly been established and could not easily be eradicated. Together, these factors meant that China's fight on human rights was then conducted from within, rather than outside, the international system that had evolved to monitor and supervise such issues.

During the remainder of this phase, these influences continued to shape the main contours of Beijing's struggle with China's human rights critics. However, by the end of 1989, it also became increasingly apparent that the post-Tiananmen international coalition that had condemned China was faltering.

During the fall, Japan's commitment to censuring China quickly eroded (Foot 2000: 127–28). At the same time, the Bush administration, which had initially worked to hold China accountable for Tiananmen, began to publicly equivocate on this stance (as signaled by the visits of top Bush administration officials to China and the lifting of some sanctions) (Harding 1992: 250–59). While the U.S. Congress stepped into the gap created by these conciliatory moves, especially with regard to deliberations on the renewal of China's most favored nation (MFN) status, from the start congressional efforts to criticize China's human rights record were hampered by the plethora of competing political and economic interests at play within both the House and Senate.

These developments afforded the Chinese new avenues for defending their human rights record. In the process of doing so, they continued to deploy boundary-reinforcing rhetoric and to argue the necessity of preserving China's (and other states') sovereignty. For example, even after preempting the consideration of a resolution critical of China at the February 1990 session of the UN CHR, China's representatives still condemned Beijing's critics for deliberately misinterpreting the principle of human rights (and its relationship to sovereignty's role in international politics). Or, as Fan Guoxiang, a leading member of the Chinese delegation to the UN CHR argued, "In international law, sovereignty was the most important attribute of a [s]tate, with the result that the realization and protection of human rights could not exclude the principle of sovereignty" (quoted in Foot 2000: 121). However, even as Fan issued such criticism, Beijing also pledged "the Chinese government has always abided by the principles and purposes of the UN Charter, committed itself to the respect and protection of human rights and fundamental freedoms, and [has been] actively involved in and supported the United Nations in the field of human rights" (quoted in Kent 1999: 61).

Modestly conciliatory Chinese policies in the first half of 1990 accompanied this slight rhetorical opening. During this period, the Chinese ended martial law in Beijing, released a limited number of prisoners that had been arrested in the immediate post-Tiananmen period, and signed the Convention on Children. In addition, the discussion of human rights that had dwindled to the singular refrain of defending Chinese sovereignty following Tiananmen also began to expand.

The unofficial commentary published at this time contained an extremely limited acknowledgment of the need for the protection of human rights within international politics. However, the promotion of a vigilant stance against the abuse of such a system remained the main characteristic of Chinese academic discourse. Thus, Lu Houming (1990) noted that using human rights to attack China had taught the Chinese the importance of promoting a correct interpre-

tation of the place of human rights within international politics. Lu also asserted that while human rights had become a "basic value" in the international system, such rights posed a potential danger to many states, as they had been used
to interfere in the affairs of too many countries (p. 36).

At the start of 1991, concerns such as this continued to ground the official
Chinese discussion of human rights. At this point, Beijing began to more
aggressively criticize what were characterized as the double standards of its critics' (especially America's) stance on human rights. Moreover, at the winter session of the UN CHR, Zhang Yishan, China's delegate, deployed pointed rhetoric to question the legitimacy of the UN CHR's subcommission. Zhang
objected that the subcommission had "made wanton attacks on the domestic
affairs of sovereign states," and called on the UN CHR to "seriously consider
the desirability of reaffirming the nature of the Sub-Commission's work and
mandate" (quoted in Kent 1999: 63). Nevertheless, later in the year the subcommission took up the issue of China's human rights record with specific reference to abuses reported to have occurred in Tibet (as discussed in Chapter 4).

As these international developments were unfolding, the discussion of human
rights within China began to pick up. More specifically, starting in 1991 a series
of conferences were held during which participants debated the nature of human
rights (with a focus on the principle's class characteristics), but remained particularly uniform in expressing their concern over the ongoing manipulation of the
system by powerful states (especially the United States). Thus, a report on one of
the first of these sessions complained that international forces had "used human
rights" as an excuse to "impose sanctions on China and interfere in its internal
affairs" ("Yi xiang" 1991). Subsequent meetings also heavily emphasized similar
issues. Indeed, the only limited exception to such defensive posturing was a single line published in a *Faxue Yanjiu* article on a June 1991 meeting sponsored by
CASS's Legal Studies Institute. The article took pains to point out that the conference participants felt that "sovereignty was superior to human rights, human
rights belonged to sovereignty, and sovereignty was the foundation and precon-
dition for the realization of human rights." However, it also noted that in considering the relation between the two principles, "some scholars" had pointed
out that "when a country participates in certain human rights treaties, its conduct (*xingwei*) cannot but be limited (*zhiyu*) by the treaties' provisions (*tiaokuan*)"
and these type of limitations also have an impact on the "exercise of sovereignty
(*xingshi zhuquan*)" ("Yi Makesizhuyi" 1991: 21).

Phase III, Fall 1991–Present: Transgressing Sovereign Boundaries, Expanding Involvement in the Human Rights System

At first glance, the Chinese approach to human rights during the extended post-Tiananmen phase (from the end of 1991 through the present) contains virtually no acknowledgment of the more flexible stance on human rights that was tentatively voiced by a handful of analysts prior to the publication of China's first white paper on human rights.[6] Throughout this period, rejection of international criticism of China's human rights record remained a signature feature of China's official commentary.[7] Much of the unofficial analysis published in China during this phase consisted of matching critical reflections on the international human rights system's flaws and manipulation by powerful states. At the same time, Chinese foreign policy makers implemented wave after wave of measures to prevent, rebuff, or at the very least mitigate any new criticism of China.

Yet, China's strident words and actions did not constitute the totality of its stance on human rights during this phase. Indeed, they were offset by a gradually expanding number of official endorsements of human rights and new acknowledgments of China's obligations in this area. Even before this change in Beijing's formal stance began to unfold, a few analysts had begun to counter the more unyielding positions articulated in official Chinese statements; in engaging the work of external proponents of the human rights regime, they started to reinterpret the intersection between human rights and sovereignty and the conditions under which the former may take precedent over the latter.[8] While advances in the protection of human rights within China appear to have noticeably lagged behind such discursive developments, nonetheless Beijing did implement concrete policies that lent limited substance to such words.

In this way, despite the persistence of less malleable and more defensive behavior over the course of this phase, by the latter half of the 1990s the Chinese had significantly modified their stance on human rights (and, by extension, sovereign authority). I do not contend that this development has erased China's sovereign boundaries, nor do I gauge its effect on actual human rights conditions within China (an impact that is, to say the least, open to interpretation), nor argue that the change is evolutionary, let alone one that cannot be reversed. However, it has resulted in an appreciable breaching of the previously sacrosanct line that divided China from the rest of the international system, a significant shift (especially when compared against earlier Chinese practices). Moreover, as is discussed in the Conclusion, by tentatively endorsing boundary-transgressing approaches to this facet of sovereignty, the Chinese created a widening gap between their approach to this facet of the norm and the boundary-reinforcing position they maintained on territorial, and especially, jurisdictional sovereignty.

1991–94: The Initial Extended Post-Tiananmen Phase

The publication of China's first white paper on human rights in fall 1991 marked the starting point of this process. The white paper ("Human Rights" 1991: 8) began by noting that "the Chinese Government has . . . highly praised the Universal Declaration of Human Rights, considering it the first international human rights document that has laid the foundation for the practice of human rights in the world arena." But, it also quickly added, "Despite its international aspect, the issue of human rights falls by and large within the sovereignty of each country" (p. 9). Nonetheless, in contrast to all previous official commentary, the paper also contained a detailed explanation of the efforts that China had undertaken, and progress it reportedly had made, to protect human rights. This included an accounting of China's policies on the right to subsistence, political rights, economic and cultural rights, judicial rights, the right to work, religious rights, minority rights, the right to family planning, and other rights.

Although these arguments had virtually all been made in unofficial forums during the spring and summer of 1991, their publication in such an official document represented the first time that the Chinese formally presented such specific information on human rights conditions in China to the international community. In other words, Beijing had taken a significant step toward recognizing the need to acknowledge and, at least in its official statements, follow the standards set by the international community on human rights. It tacitly conceded the crucial point that human rights conditions within China were an issue for international consideration.

Over the course of the following three years, Chinese officials attempted to shield China from direct criticism and attacked all those critical of China. However, at the same time they tried to placate China's critics by making limited concessions. Once more, such efforts unfolded in both bilateral and multilateral forums.

The most prominent bilateral battleground during this period continued to be the Sino–U.S. relationship. Each year the American State Department, as part of its annual report on human rights conditions around the globe, took issue with China's human rights record. In addition, the U.S. Congress repeatedly debated the issue of revoking China's MFN status with the United States in order to protest Beijing's behavior on the human rights front.

In each of these cases, Beijing responded with sharp criticism of the United

States for interfering in China's internal affairs. Nonetheless, it also implemented a few conciliatory measures clearly designed to diffuse American criticism.
For example, during this period Beijing released a handful of political dissidents
from prison (including Wei Jingsheng, freed in 1993). In addition, outside of the
immediate context of Sino-U.S. relations, Beijing also permitted a series of
bilateral delegations to investigate human rights conditions in China.

The first of these visits, which predated the publication of the white paper,
was in 1991, when French and Australian human rights delegations traveled to
China (Foot 2000: 136; Kent 1999: 160). A second Australian delegation visited
in 1992. By the end of 1993, delegations from the European Community,
Switzerland, Sweden, and Canada had also made the trip to China.[9] Although
all of these delegations reported that they operated within strict constraints on
their activities, and generally found Beijing's behavior to fall well short of international human rights standards, the fact that dialogue took place at all represented a significant concession on the part of the Chinese.

Chinese behavior within the UN human rights framework during this period followed a similar pattern. China's representatives to the UN CHR and its
subcommission endeavored to prevent any new measures censuring China from
reaching a vote. They were largely successful. Indeed, in the winter of 1992,
Beijing was able to easily orchestrate a non-action vote in the UN CHR (Wan
2001: 112) and to steer the subcommission away from passing any resolution
critical of China (Kent 1999: 66).

While support for China's position eroded during the following year in both
the UN CHR and the subcommission (as evident in the decline in the number of votes in favor of resolutions tabled by Beijing to preclude action against
China), the Chinese once again were able to prevent the passage in both forums
of new measures related to China (a record that remained intact in 1994 as well).
However, these victories were also accompanied by compromises that subtly
expanded China's acceptance of the human rights system. Thus, on the second
day of the World Conference on Human Rights (held in Vienna in June 1993),
Liu Huaqiu, China's vice foreign minister, warned that the imposition of "one's
own country or region's criteria on other countries or region[s] [is] tantamount
to an infringement on the sovereignty of other countries," yet concluded by
noting, "China respects and abides by the basic principles of the UN Charter
and the Universal Declaration of Human Rights" ("Proposals" 1993).[10]

This behavior was generally the product of the same factors that had framed
the Chinese position on human rights during the 1980s. On the one hand, it
remained the case that the Chinese could ill afford to simply acquiesce to this
pressure, as it would have potentially undermined the foundations of Beijing's
rule. In addition, persistent collective memories of previous incursions upon sov-

ereignty continued to heighten Chinese sensitivity to contemporary encroachments and cement attachment to a boundary-reinforcing response to such measures. Indeed, Liu Huaqiu's speech underscored this factor in noting, "As a people that used to suffer tremendously from aggression by big powers but now enjoys independence, the Chinese have come to realize fully that state sovereignty is the basis for the realization of citizens' human rights" ("Proposals" 1993).

On the other hand, although the strong American emphasis on human rights was repeatedly scorned by Beijing, it also frequently proved sufficient to elicit limited Chinese concessions. Moreover, especially after Deng's modernization and development line gained broad acceptance following the aging leader's "southern tour" at the start of 1992, the overall political climate in Beijing was more open to the prospects of adapting to international pressure. More significantly, the renewed commitment to rapid growth that came out of Deng's trip again meant that China placed a premium on attracting foreign capital and investment.

Within this environment, small compromises on human rights became more palatable. Such measures would shore up frayed bilateral relations and secure a more respectable image for China in a way that would tangibly contribute to the realization of Beijing's economic goals through reassuring potential international investors of China's growing stability. Thus, while the Chinese maintained the principle of walling China off from external human rights criticism, in practice they implemented polices that were at least partially responsive to such critiques.

Such considerations explain the limited change in Chinese policies and official rhetoric during the start of the third phase in the development of the Chinese stance on human rights, but they do not readily account for another significant shift in Chinese human rights practices that began to unfold at this juncture: the emergence in unofficial, yet influential, policy circles of notably divergent views over foundational aspects of the international human rights system.

To be sure, the institutional nexus for this development, the formation of an expanding list of human rights research institutes, was the product of Beijing's attempt to formulate a more comprehensive, defensive position on human rights that would assist it in foiling its critics on this front. Indeed, much of the analysis produced within these organizations directly contributed to this goal (see, for example, Liu Wenzong 1993; and Zhang Zhirong 1992b). However, many analysts reached well beyond such narrow parameters, and a minority of scholars began to tentatively accept the validity of ideas that had been promoted in the international sphere about the changing balance between human rights and sovereign authority.[11]

This new trend was first evident in the pages of China's major law journals from 1992 to 1994. For example, in the first issue of the 1992 volume of *Zhongguo Faxue*, an article by Xu Weidong, Shen Zhengwu, and Zheng Chengliang (1992) cautiously observed that although the Western attempt to force a single set of human rights values on others was unacceptable, and that it was imperative to recognize the centrality of sovereignty within international politics, common human rights standards did exist in the international system as well as in an extensive treaty system. Moreover, "once a state becomes a member of these international treaties, it promises to undertake (*chengnuo*) the international legal obligation to respect and realize its standards, and cannot use [its own] special standards of ideology or domestic law to undermine (*pohuai*) them" (p. 25). Subsequently, Xu Goujin (1992: 18), while defending each state's right to make its own decisions on human rights, also argued that changes in the international legal system meant that all states now had both direct (*zhijie*) obligations (not to invade others, to end colonialism, and prevent terrorism) and indirect (*jianjie*) ones (against genocide, racism, and slavery) in the sphere of human rights protection. Xu added that when a state violated such obligations, the international community had the right to act, and this could not be construed as interfering in the state's internal affairs.

The following year, Li Lin, while looking to preserve sovereignty's role in international politics, took the points raised by these scholars even further. Li (1993: 39–40) noted, "Sovereign states in the practice of their sovereignty, can join international treaties and international organizations, invite international intervention in their internal affairs, and use military means and other methods to solve internal conflicts, [and in the process] give up or compromise (*rang*) some sovereignty in order to attain even better, more effective, establishment and realization of international and domestic human rights." Moreover, in citing the work of Western scholars such as Hurst Hannum and Louis Henkin, Li (pp. 41–42) noted that the internationalization of human rights was linked to the relativization (*xiangduihua*) of sovereignty. Writing in the same journal, Li Ming (1993: 39), a legal scholar at Peking University, expanded on this argument, contending that while the UN Charter made it clear that the principle of non-interference was consistent with the protection of human rights, in regard to certain human rights problems it was still "acceptable to get rid of" such a norm (*keyi paichu bu ganshe yuanze*)."

In 1994, two additional articles also touched upon these themes. The first, by Li Buyun (1994), a scholar at CASS's Legal Studies Institute, observed that aspects of the contemporary international human rights system extended beyond domestic political concerns and ideological issues to encompass universally held "moral concepts (*daode gainian*)," and argued that monitoring human rights concerns had both "internal jurisdictional (*guonei guanxia*)" and "international jurisdictional (*guoji guanxia*)" aspects (pp. 38–39). The second, by Zhu Xiaoqing (1994), another scholar affiliated with CASS's Legal Studies Institute, attempted to detail the exact terms of the interaction that takes place between states and international organizations in the realm of human rights protection. Zhu observed the difficulties for the international protection of human rights stemming from the lack of a "unified organization that surpasses states" and "the limited scope of human rights measures," noting that international protection of human rights could be strengthened as long as the danger of using human rights to attack other countries is avoided (pp. 70–71).

1995–98: The Shadow of Tiananmen Recedes

Despite the growing openness with which such views were being articulated in unofficial circles in the mid-1990s, no explicit acknowledgment of the validity of this more malleable set of claims was forthcoming in Chinese human rights policy or official rhetoric in 1995. On the contrary, official Chinese defensiveness about human rights was reinforced at this time when Beijing's moves at the UN CHR proved insufficient to prevent the organization from tabling a China-specific resolution. Although the vote on this measure fell short, China's representative, Jin Yongjian, still warned that "Western countries have intentionally chosen the so-called question of human rights as a political weapon against China" ("U.N." 1995).

The Chinese then lent substance to this combative rhetoric by orchestrating a campaign (one that garnered the support of many of the member states) to restructure the UN CHR's subcommission so as to prevent future criticism of China (Kent 1999: 74) and by promoting the idea that in both the subcommission and the UN CHR, dialogue, conducted with respect for each member state's sovereign rights, should take the place of confrontation (Foot 2000: 191). Or, as an informed Chinese observer noted during a 1997 interview, "In the UN CHR China will use sovereignty to fight accusations made against it. This is not using sovereignty as a weapon; it is China wanting to deal with problems of international and public condemnation" (Personal interview, Beijing Foreign Language Studies University, Apr. 29, 1997).

These moves weakened both organizations' ability to pressure China (and, for that matter, other states accused of violating human rights standards). Yet, at the same time the Chinese were attempting to dismantle the UN CHR and subcommission, or at the very least reorient their activities, they also implemented policies of limited cooperation on the human rights front. The publication of a second white paper on human rights in 1995 was an early indicator of this move ("Progress" 1995). Rather than detailing past grievances (that is, historical aggression against China), the report focused on the progress China had made on human rights issues. In addition, in contrast to the 1991 document, it explicitly acknowledged China's commitment to the human rights system. However, the paper also emphasized the illegitimacy of many Western countries' attempts to pressure other states in the name of human rights. Over the course of the following three years (1996–98), the Chinese continued to promote such a two-pronged (acceptance-paired-with-criticism) approach to human rights. During this period Beijing proved increasingly adept at parrying the moves of human rights critics in both multilateral and bilateral forums. This skill, coupled with the progressive weakening of the international coalition that had previously censured China's human rights performance, gave Beijing even more leeway in its handling of human rights issues, and, arguably, resulted in a regression in human rights conditions within China. However, despite such backsliding, Beijing's human rights concessions steadily grew, elite debate about human rights and sovereignty within China broadened, and the sovereign boundary between China and the rest of the system was further redefined.

On one level, the pace of these developments was again tied to the waxing and waning of international pressure. Yet, even when attention to China's human rights record receded, the Chinese continued to implement relatively flexible policies on human rights. This new willingness to change grew out of the increasing influence of three factors that moderated historically framed Chinese reservations about human rights.[12]

First, growing concern in Beijing with the reputation that China was gaining as a "rising threat" provided additional impetus for compromise. In 1995 Chinese behavior vis-à-vis Taiwan, and to a lesser extent in the South China Sea, gave Beijing's critics powerful examples of China's growing assertiveness in the region. While the Chinese were quick to belittle the "China threat theory," it was easier to put such an argument to rest through building a record of responsibility. We have already discussed how this interest played an important role in moderating the Chinese approach to territorial issues in the second half of the 1990s; it also, albeit less directly, created a new incentive for compromise on human rights.

Second, while the principle of non-interference remained the bulwark of China's stance on human rights, in practice Beijing's consistent policy of acquiescing to participation in some aspects of the system created a new standard for Chinese behavior. In other words, rather than working from a position of outright opposition to human rights, the baseline for Chinese decision making had become vocal opposition and quiet acceptance, at times accompanied by limited concessions.

Third, this development then created space for the further extension of new norms into the Chinese foreign policy community via discussions of how to navigate the terms of Chinese membership in such a system: the more open arguments about these issues that were percolating within unofficial forums began to gain some influence within policy-making circles. As a result, human rights were increasingly viewed as a legitimate political issue, one that could not be dealt with solely in a defensive fashion.

Beijing's new strategy was first evident at the 1996 and 1997 sessions of the UN CHR. During the first of these meetings, Wu Jianmin, the head of the Chinese delegation, chastised "those countries" that used the organization as a "tool to pursue their foreign policy," but also "urged the promotion of human rights through dialogue and cooperation on an equal footing" ("China Urges End" 1996). In addition, China's alternate representative, Zhang Yishan, called for a six-point reform of the organization that would strengthen its effectiveness and reduce the likelihood of its abuse by "people bent on political confrontation" ("China Offers" 1996).

Such rhetorical moves, paired with intensive lobbying within the commission, proved sufficient in 1996 to once again secure Beijing the votes it needed to prevent the tabling of a proposed resolution on human rights conditions in China. In 1997 the Chinese again effectively stymied limited efforts in the UN CHR and subcommission to take up resolutions relating to China. However, even with these victories in hand they also forwarded conciliatory policies on human rights. For example, in February 1997, against the backdrop of Deng Xiaoping's death and a high-profile visit to China by the new American secretary of state, Madeleine Albright, the Chinese Foreign Ministry stated that Beijing was "positively considering" becoming a member of the two human rights covenants ("China Considering" 1997). Later in the year, Qian Qichen endorsed this somewhat more liberal line on human rights during his address to the UN General Assembly. The Chinese foreign minister observed, "the universality of human rights should be respected, but their realization must be integrated with national conditions" ("Chinese Vice-Premier" 1997). In addition, in the lead-up to his fall visit to the United States, Jiang Zemin formally announced China's signing of the ICESCR. At this juncture, Beijing also permitted the UN's Working Group on Arbitrary Detention to travel to China (Boyer 1997).

These trends continued in 1998. In March, during a press conference at the annual NPC meetings, Qian Qichen announced Beijing's intention to sign the last of the main human rights treaties to which it had refused to become a party, the ICCPR. On the heels of this announcement, Beijing allowed the last of the main organizers of the 1989 student protests still in detention, Wang Dan, to leave China for the United States (ostensibly for medical treatment) (Wan 2001: 57). Later in the year, Mary Robinson, the UN high commissioner for human

rights, visited China for the first time, and Beijing marked this occasion by signing a Memorandum of Intent to cooperate with the UN on technical aspects
of human rights development (Foot 2000: 231–32). In October, China signed
the ICCPR, as Qian had pledged it would do. Moreover, speaking to a conference commemorating the fiftieth anniversary of the UDHR, Qian Qichen
noted, "We all recognize the universality of human rights and observe the same
international norms on human rights; we all recognize that no country's human
rights situation is perfect, and that all countries are confronted with a weighty
task of further promoting and protecting human rights" ("Qian Qichen Urges"
1998).

At the start of the following year, Beijing reaffirmed its commitments. In
January, the Chinese hosted a round of official Sino-American dialogue on
human rights. In the spring, despite mounting tensions over the U.S.-led war
against Yugoslavia, Premier Zhu Rongji noted:

> Of course, we are not free of shortcomings on the issue of human rights. It is
> impossible for China to be perfect in this regard, because China has a history of
> several thousand years of feudal society and dictatorship . . . but we are willing to
> solicit views from all sides and especially from people in all walks of life. . . . We are
> also willing to hear and listen to the views and comments from our friends from
> abroad. ("Chinese Premier's" 1999)

Zhu's admission that China was aware of international concern and interest
in human rights conditions within China had long been foreshadowed in unofficial analysis. Indeed, while much of the analysis produced in China prior to
Zhu's statement continued to promote a defensive interpretation of human
rights (see Gu Chengkai 1997; Yao Yuanliang and Xu Qiren 1997; Zhu Ruiji
1998), a growing number of scholars pushed beyond this established theme.
They had already begun to examine the still controversial issue of how new
developments in the international human rights system were influencing the
role of sovereignty in international politics.

The first facet of this development was the fact that those who had previously taken the lead in decrying the perceived manipulation of human rights by
other states had begun to grudgingly acknowledge that the international community had the right to address human rights issues. For example, Liu
Wenzong's commentary from this period continued to rail against what he
derided as the American abuse of human rights language. However, he was also
quick to acknowledge that human rights had become an important part of the
fabric of contemporary international politics. Indeed, the Foreign Affairs
College professor insisted that the Chinese "in no way oppose the principle of
universal human rights (*renquan de pubianxing*)," but resolutely oppose America
forcing its own values and human rights models onto China "in the service of

hegemony and power politics" (Liu Wenzong 1995: 49). Zhu Muzhi's critique of the same report dwelt upon similar themes, but called for "dialogue built on the foundation of equality," and underscored that China had repeatedly declared its willingness to engage in "equal dialogue regarding the human rights issue" (Zhu Muzhi 1995: 4–5). The following year, Zhu took up the same issue, and once more sharply criticized the United States for misrepresenting human rights conditions in China. Yet, at the same time, he conceded, "at present no country dares to claim that its human rights conditions are perfect, and that it is exempt from acts that violate human rights. China also leaves much to be desired in this respect" (Zhu Muzhi 1996: 18).

Of greater significance, most of those articulating this argument paired the defense of sovereignty with endorsements of the international human rights system and the need for states to cooperate to facilitate its development. For example, in 1997, Wang Meili contributed a brief piece to *Xiandai Faxue* on the domestic and international aspects of human rights that heavily emphasized the preeminence of the former, but also noted, "after a state enters into an international human rights treaty, it must strictly abide by the obligations stipulated by the treaty (*yanshou gongyue guiding de yiwu*)" and implement these treaty obligations domestically, or else "bear the cost of international responsibility (*chengdan guoji zeren*)" (Wang Meili 1997: 78). The following year, Wang (1998: 124) added that sovereignty remained the foundation of international politics and law, yet conceded it was not absolute or without limits, and that it was no longer acceptable for any country to attempt to use sovereignty as a means to circumvent international legal obligations. Zhou Qi (1999), a researcher at CASS's American Studies Institute, constructed a similar argument in a detailed overview of new developments in Western theories of human rights. While taking pains to emphasize the gap between Western and "non-Western" analysts on this issue, and arguing that "no basic change had taken place in the international system," Zhou also conceded "the principle of the international protection of human rights had limited (*xianzhi*) state sovereignty." Finally, in the Central Party School's journal Zhang Xiaoling (1998: 63) forwarded a guarded evaluation of the UDHR that clearly stated China's preference for embedding human rights protection within a sovereign framework, but also reported that the recent surge in interest in human rights in the international sphere had insured that discussion of "the relationship between sovereignty and human rights had become the order of the day (*yishi richeng*)."

Although such analysis only indirectly considered the possibility of change in the sovereign authority / human rights dynamic, other scholars directly acknowledged that a shift in international politics on this front was already well underway. An early example is an article in *Faxue Yanjiu* by Li Buyun and Wang

Xiujing that expanded on Li's earlier arguments. The authors contended that the relationship between human rights and sovereignty was more malleable than other Chinese scholars had previously argued. Li and Wang took issue with the claims that "human rights comes before sovereignty" and "sovereignty comes before human rights." Rather, they posited that the issue of human rights was normally an internal one, but under "special conditions" it was also an international one ("without borders"). Thus, they dismissed the idea of "absolute sovereignty" as an artifact of the past, one that had been replaced within "international society" by a general acceptance of the more flexible concept of "relative sovereignty" (Li and Wang 1995: 23). In 1996, Wang Shuliang (1996: 68), a researcher at the Shanghai Academy of Social Sciences, added that the development of human rights amounted to a "new challenge to sovereignty," and created new issues in international legal studies. Wang observed, "in regard to the human rights and state sovereignty relationship, simply completely affirming or negating one or the other side is difficult to clarify (nanyi chanming)." On the one hand, "sovereignty is the foundation or guarantee of human rights." On the other, "the practice of sovereignty is limited (xianzhi) by the protection of human rights." Thus, Wang noted that the protection of human rights was basically within the hands of states, but added that if a state failed in this respect it could expect to be condemned by "international society" and in this case it would be "hard to use the claim of non-interference" to fend off such criticism (p. 69).

In 1998, limited indications of an even deeper reevaluation of these issues began to appear in elite Chinese publications. In an article that subtly broadened his stance on the sovereignty issue, Li Buyun, consistent with his earlier analysis, strongly emphasized that common standards regarding human rights exist in international society. In addition, he still found fault with the argument made by "some scholars in the West" that human rights were "without borders," but he rejected the counterargument that human rights were solely a domestic issue. Under an extensive list of circumstances, Li argued, "international society could and should intervene" to prevent human rights abuses (Li Buyun 1998). Zeng Lingliang (1998) took this argument much further in the pages of Zhongguo Faxue by maintaining that after the end of the Cold War, international law had increasingly permeated into, and decreased the domain of, state authority and jurisdiction over both territory and people. While Zeng attributed changes in the former primarily to new international legal regulations related to economic concerns, he attributed shifts in the latter to "the challenge of the international protection of human rights and international humanitarian law" (p. 118). It was increasingly clear, Zeng noted, that in international law global interests (renlei de zhengti liyi) took precedence over the interests of individual sovereign states. In addition, particularly following the end of the Cold War, international humanitarian law had "restricted (*xianzhi*) state sovereignty."

Interviews I conducted in 1997 and 1998 with thirteen international law / human rights specialists (all of whom were affiliated with leading research institutes in Beijing and Shanghai) confirmed that this more flexible perspective on the human rights / sovereignty dynamic had gained wide acceptance in elite circles in China. Indeed, only a minority (four) of those interviewed insisted that the human rights system was largely static and that sovereignty placed strict restraints on its future development. A senior legal scholar succinctly summarized this position by observing, "Of course, in terms of practical actions and policies there are many issues in the field of human rights. But as for absolute respect for sovereignty, it is necessary to protect self-interest, sovereign interest. If we give up this concept, Western countries will have an excuse to interfere" (Personal interview, Foreign Affairs College, June 17, 1997).

In contrast to this view, the majority of other scholars interviewed (nine) conceded that a major change in human rights had taken place; most of these informants (five) also observed that this had affected sovereignty's role in international politics. However, the scholars in this group also had notably different assessments of how much change had taken place. For instance, a junior legal scholar argued, "In today's world with economic interdependence, cultural globalization, and even political integration, and the rise of human rights, the practice of sovereignty is rapidly changing. It is possible to say that sovereignty is becoming a hollow concept or term" (Personal interview, Peking University, Apr. 8, 1998). A senior legal scholar similarly argued that "the human rights regime has undergone a major change as individual states have come to accept obligations in terms of the protection of human rights, and the limitations such obligations place on state sovereignty. I think that these limits are increasing in international politics" (Personal interview, Peking University, June 25, 1998).

Most of these informants maintained that China was reasonably flexible on human rights for instrumental reasons. Even within the small group of scholars who argued that no change in the sovereignty / human rights dynamic had taken place, all reported that China had adjusted its human rights policies and had done so in response to foreign pressures. As a scholar who played a significant role in the framing of the first white paper on human rights observed, Beijing's stance on human rights had shifted because of "the pressing need to respond to what is said in the West about human rights. The focus there on human rights has meant China needs to present and defend our own understanding, and explain our position" (Personal interview, Beijing Academy of Social Sciences, July 3, 1997). In contrast, most of those in the camp that accepted the premise that sovereign change had already taken place in international politics argued that the shift in Chinese practices during the 1990s was also influenced by an increasing acceptance in Beijing of new concepts such as "international obligation" (*guoji yiwu*) and being a "responsible" (*fuze*) member of the international system.

1999–Present: Kosovo and Its Aftermath

The Chinese reaction to the 1999 American-led NATO operation in Yugoslavia temporarily disrupted this pattern of change, as evidenced by the spike (214 statements) in Chinese sovereignty claims issued during this year in *Beijing Review,* and the fact that this surge consisted of a flood of unrelentingly boundary-reinforcing pronouncements.[13] The use of force against Belgrade confirmed China's suspicions about how powerful states (especially the United States) could manipulate human rights norms to legitimize what China saw as self-serving, hegemonic policies. This revitalized the Chinese defense of sovereignty's foundational role in international politics. Thus, Beijing repeatedly condemned expansive interpretations of the principle of self-determination (as seen in Chapter 4) and unleashed a wave of disparaging official and unofficial commentary on "Western" human rights concepts (especially the idea that human rights could at times take precedent over sovereign authority).

Chinese unease with the Kosovo operation was first apparent in 1998, but at that time Beijing's expression of opposition to the impending conflict was relatively muted. Once the air war began in March 1999, opposition became more direct, and was replaced with outrage in May following the unintentional NATO bombing of the Chinese embassy in Belgrade. After the incident, Beijing immediately suspended human rights dialogue (as well as high-level military contacts) with the United States. In addition, large popular protests against the bombing engulfed the U.S. embassy and consulates in China. Although the authorities appear to have initially permitted and even supported these demonstrations, after a chaotic weekend of protesting, officials quickly moved to rein in such public displays. However, even after the demonstrations were contained, official Chinese rhetoric continued to condemn the war in Kosovo, and particularly objected to the Western justification of the conflict with reference to human rights norms.

During this period, the Chinese also used multilateral forums to promote their position. For example, in June, Beijing abstained (but did not veto) a key post–air campaign UN Security Council resolution on Kosovo. In explaining this vote, the Chinese conceded that since Yugoslavia did not oppose the motion, China would not stand in the way of its passage, but emphasized that China still strongly opposed "'the so-called human rights over sovereignty' theory" that served "to infringe upon the sovereignty of other states and promote hegemonism under the pretext of human rights" ("U.N. Resolution" 1999). In addition, in the fall, the new Chinese foreign minister, Tang Jiaxuan, indirectly disputed statements by UN secretary general Kofi Annan about a trend toward redefining sovereignty's role in international politics. In contrast, Tang argued that during the Kosovo conflict, powerful states had used the issue of human rights to bypass the UN and take military action against a sovereign state ("Hegemonism" 1999).

In accord with this kind of heated official rhetoric, for months after the embassy bombing condemnations of U.S. words and actions dominated the unofficial Chinese discourse on human rights. A handful of conservative international legal specialists who had promoted particularly narrow interpretations of the human rights / sovereignty dynamic throughout the 1990s now took the lead in condemning the United States. For example, in an interview in a May issue of *Beijing Review*, Zhu Muzhi charged that the bombing of the Chinese embassy was an attempt to sabotage China and increase American hegemonic power. "NATO, led by the United States," Zhu stated, "is actually carrying out hegemonism in the name of humanitarianism. . . . But hegemonism is imposing terror upon other countries, and forbids other countries to develop and grow strong. That's why it is contrary to human rights" ("NATO" 1999). Or, as he observed in a *Renmin Ribao* editorial the following year, "Putting human rights over sovereignty = hegemoniism [*sic*]" (Zhu Muzhi 2000). Liu Wenzong (1999a) made a strikingly similar argument in his school's journal. He contended that the U.S. strikes on Yugoslavia, and against the Chinese embassy in particular, had definitively proven "the so-called theory of human rights over sovereignty is actually a type of hegemony."

This defensive line of analysis was initially broadly supported by other Chinese scholars, and as such, it temporarily erased the plurality of views on human rights that had begun to be expressed prior to the UN action in Kosovo. This was clear in the wave of articles on the war published in *Shijie Jingji yu Zhengzhi* in 1999. Whereas this journal had previously been a vehicle for the airing of relatively "open" perspectives on sovereignty and human rights (and would resume playing this role the following year), such perspectives were conspicuously absent from its pages at this time.[14] Instead, contributors dwelt at length on the underlying strategic logic behind the U.S. war, its links to the expansion of American hegemony, and its implications for the balance of power in international politics. They also labored to expose the dangers posed by the West's embrace of "new interventionism" (*xin ganshe zhuyi*). Liu Nanlai (1999: 28), who had written extensively about human rights earlier in the decade, derided the war as a "flagrant trampling upon international law" and pointedly rejected the attempt to justify the conflict with reference to human rights and derided the theory that human rights took precedent over sovereignty as being simply "cooked up (*paozhi*) by Western countries to oppose international law and interfere in other countries' internal affairs." Shen Jiru (1999), a CASS analyst who had previously published favorable analyses of globalization, added that America was attempting to use similar means (the promotion of democratic and human rights values) to interfere in China's own internal affairs.

As defensive as this rhetoric was, soon after the embassy bombing it was accompanied by the publication of relatively flexible, pragmatic analysis of the human rights issue. Thus, while Beijing clamped down on dissent at home (with particular attention to silencing the Falun Gong movement), and continued to freeze human rights dialogue with the United States, it continued bilateral talks with other states in the fall of 1999. Moreover, only months after castigating the West for interfering in Kosovo, Beijing played a quiet, supportive role in facilitating humanitarian intervention in East Timor. Indeed, China supported the two major resolutions (UN SC 1264, 1272) passed by the Security Council in the fall of 1999 on the situation in East Timor.

These apparently contradictory policies (vociferous defense of Yugoslavia's sovereignty, combined with support for intervention in Indonesia) were products of the same factors that had previously influenced Chinese policy on human rights. Protecting China's sovereignty remained a paramount concern for Chinese policy makers. Thus, any development that seemed to erode the norm's role within the international arena—even one like Kosovo, which on the surface was only of peripheral concern to Beijing—was to be opposed for fear of possible harm to China. On the other hand, Beijing was again looking for ways out of its relative diplomatic isolation. Making limited compromises on the human rights front, and cooperating with the international community on resolving the East Timor issue, provided the Chinese with a relatively easy avenue to demonstrate their willingness and ability to cooperate, and thus smooth over differences in Sino-U.S. relations (especially as Beijing and Washington were moving to restart the final stages of WTO accession talks that had been stalled following Zhu's April 1999 visit to the United States, as discussed in Chapter 6). Beyond such instrumental concerns, Chinese foreign policy circles at this time basically accepted the legitimacy of human rights and humanitarian intervention; this further pushed Chinese policy in the direction of accepting incremental change.

In line with these forces, the Chinese issued a new white paper on human rights at the start of 2000. As with each of the previous human rights documents Beijing had published, the paper combined an upbeat defense of China's human rights record with a tacit acknowledgment of its expanding human rights obligations. This approach also featured prominently in China's successful bid to head off yet another American attempt (one given added substance by the direct involvement of Madeleine Albright) to introduce a resolution on China at the UN CHR. During committee deliberations, the Chinese representative rejected U.S. criticism of human rights conditions within China, and argued that "China has long been committed to the promotion and protection of human rights" ("Chinese Ambassador Refutes" 2000).

On the surface, unofficial human rights analysis published during this period appears to show just how tentative the Chinese acceptance of the human rights system (and, more broadly, a shift in state rights) continued to be following Kosovo. Analysts who warned against the potential abuse of human rights rhetoric by strong states to further hegemonic policies continued to occupy center stage, a fact that was made abundantly clear in an August 2000 international conference organized by Chinese Institute of International Studies (CIIS) (Yong Qiang 2000).[15] For example, five of the seventeen papers in the edited volume of the conference proceedings (Yang Chengxu 2001) by Chinese authors contained the term *ganshe* (interference) in their titles. Moreover, the preface to the volume (p. 1) stressed that sovereignty and human rights "complemented each other (*xiangfu xiangcheng*)."

A second meeting at CIIS, in June of 2001, also was a forum for promoting this defensive line. The session had fewer participants than the first meeting, and was held in conjunction with a regional consultation with representatives from the Canadian-government-sponsored International Conference on Intervention and State Sovereignty (ICISS). The rapporteur's report on the views of the Chinese side highlighted the intransigence of the Chinese position on human rights and highlighted three specific points. First, "the conceptualization of humanitarian intervention is a total fallacy," one that has no basis in international law, and is linked to the dangerous proposition of giving human rights precedence over sovereignty, and is applied in such an inconsistent fashion by "certain Western powers" that it obviously only really serves "their own hegemonic interests." Second, whereas humanitarian intervention is always illegitimate, humanitarian assistance is at times necessary (as long as it is carried out with respect for the principle of state sovereignty). Third, the UN must in all cases authorize any such action ("Rapporteur's Report" 2001).

While this report appears to accurately reflect the tone and tenor of Chinese positioning at the CIIS meeting, it also overlooks the fact that the scholars who made defensive claims in most other circumstances tempered them with admissions that many states had accepted self-imposed "limits" on their sovereign rights by participating in the human rights system. Indeed, at this juncture a consensus had already begun to emerge among many Chinese analysts that under very limited conditions the international community had the right to "intervene" (*ganyu*) to prevent the abuse of human rights. Thus, despite its condemnation of "interference," the preface to the volume of papers from the 2000 CIIS conference conceded that in cases of state-sponsored genocide and racial discrimination, the world community could act (Yang Chengxu 2001: 5).

More significantly, defensive analysis was far from the sole perspective on sovereignty and human rights in China following the end of the conflict in Kosovo. On the contrary, in 2000–2001, a handful of influential analysts began to forward arguments that went well beyond the official Chinese stance by enthusiastically embracing the international human rights system and contending that its rise had significantly eroded and restrained sovereignty's role in international politics.

Cheng Shuaihua (2000: 37), a scholar affiliated with Fudan University, argued in *Ouzhou* that sovereignty should be considered an "elastic" (*tanxing*) principle. "International human rights," he maintained, "have changed the practice and principle that sovereignty is not limited (*bu shou xianzhi*)." Thus, if a state "violates its international obligations," it is illegitimate for it to fall back on the claim of defending sovereignty (to avoid censure) (p. 34). In the same vein, Yu Minyou (2000: 72) observed that sovereignty should be seen as a "dynamic" (*dongtai*) concept, and contended that sovereignty had all too often been "misused" (*liyong*) by powerful states. Thus preventing such abuses, and protecting human rights, depends on the practice of sovereignty being "coordinated with the will of the people." Shi Yinhong (2000: 8), who is now at People's University, added that international norms on human rights had come to restrain and intervene in (*xianzhi yu ganyu*) sovereignty. Moreover, he contended that despite "some problems," this development constituted "an improvement in the level of morality within international politics." Even more directly, Li Zhenguang (2001: 63), a graduate student at Peking University, contended that "the norm of human rights constitutes the foundation of legitimate sovereignty in the modern era," and argued that in contemporary international politics any state possesses sovereign rights only to the extent that it guarantees its citizens their basic human rights.

At the start of 2001, despite another round of INGO reports warning of the deterioration of human rights conditions within China, Chinese diplomacy moved in the direction of these more expansive arguments. Most importantly, the NPC finally ratified the International Covenant of Economic, Social, and Cultural Rights (ICESCR) when Mary Robinson returned to Beijing in February ("China Ratifies" 2001). However, when this decision proved insufficient to dissuade the United States from once more introducing a draft resolution on China at the UN CHR, Beijing predictably denounced Washington's efforts. Moreover, in April the Chinese effectively stymied the motion with a no-action vote and then delighted in the failure of the United States to win a reelection vote in May to remain in the organization. (Washington regained its seat in the 2002 session.) Nonetheless, in a development overshadowed by the September 11 terrorist attacks, in October the two sides held their first full dialogue session since the bombing of the Chinese embassy in Belgrade. In addition, the Chinese renewed their commitment to the 2000 memorandum of understanding (MOU) on human rights the following month, when Robinson paid yet another visit to Beijing (and warned her hosts not to use the emerging U.S.-led "war on terrorism" as an excuse for disregarding human rights).

Interviews I conducted in 2001–2 showed broad-based support in foreign policy circles for the conciliatory moves Beijing had made during the previous year (amid residual concerns about protecting sovereignty, and new worries about what post-9/11 international politics would look like). On one hand, during these discussions, a small, but adamant, minority of elites continued to argue along the lines Zhang Zhirong and Liu Wenzong had forwarded at the start of the decade and Zhu Muzhi and Fan Guoxiang had promoted immediately after Kosovo. Mainly, sovereign authority was to be defended at all costs, and any slippage in this norm would benefit solely the United States.

At Qinghua University, a senior scholar argued that the U.S. position on human rights was pure hypocrisy, nothing more than a blatant attempt to pursue power politics by using an appealing pretext. This scholar rhetorically asked, "Why didn't the U.S. talk about human rights when Hitler was destroying Europe, yet [you] now talk about human rights in China? Because of its interests, the U.S. is looking to control the world, and it is using the idea of human rights over sovereignty to achieve this goal. However, China will never accept this. In order to protect our own interests we must emphasize sovereignty" (Personal interview, Dec. 26, 2001).

However, on the other hand, many interviewees acknowledged the influence of international discourses about sovereignty and human rights in their own analysis. For example, in reassessing his stance on the sovereignty / human rights dynamic, a conservative senior legal scholar insisted on the importance of sovereignty to the human rights system, but acknowledged that he had come to accept the argument made within the international community that the "practice of sovereignty may be influenced by participation in international human rights treaties" (Personal interview, CASS, Dec. 24, 2001). An influential academic at People's University added, "there is strong feeling about sovereignty in China, but there is also a recognition of how sovereignty is changing in the world community and this influence is felt [in China] through international and transnational institutions" (Personal interview, Dec. 26, 2001). In Shanghai, a professor who has played a leading role in debates about sovereignty in China observed, "Real change has taken place in world. This means we need to change our theory of sovereignty as well" (Personal interview, Fudan University, Jan. 7, 2002).

Additional unofficial analysis from the post–September 11 period revealed that this more flexible line had finally gained widespread acceptance. While Liu Wenzong (2001: 6) continued to warn of the dangers of American hegemony and argue that sovereignty must remain the foundation for international law, he also claimed that in contemporary international politics, many states (including China) had voluntarily limited the exercise of their sovereignty. Fan Guoxiang (2003) gingerly parsed the differences between "Western human rights diplomacy" (xifang renquan waijiao) and "Western human rights theory" (xifang renquan lilun), and while finding fault in the former, conceded the validity of a few points that had been made within the latter field. In addition, Liang Shoude (2002: 17), a relatively cautious scholar who had led Peking University's School for International Studies, argued that it was possible to identify three sets of rights in contemporary international politics (sovereignty, human rights, and global rights [qiuquan]), and posited that these were "indivisible, mutually dependent, universal." Although sovereignty stood "first" among these rights, its "protection" could not stand apart from the "protection of human rights" and "the strengthening of global rights."

At the same time, other analysts publicly advocated even looser interpretations of the sovereignty / human rights dynamic. For example, Zhou Yongkun (2002: 163–64) contended that contrary to conventional wisdom in China, sovereignty was derived from human rights. Moreover, the dynamic relationship between the two principles must be seen as relative. When viewed from the side of human rights, sovereignty is no more than a construct designed to assist with the protection of such rights. Yet, at the same time sovereignty itself is a "special human right" (teshu de renquan), both guaranteeing the protection of other human rights, and restricted in terms of its practice by such rights. Thus, it was imperative to realize that it was unjustified to indiscriminately abuse (lanyong) the principle of sovereignty to undermine, harm, or block the protection of other human rights.

In addition, Li Buyun and Deng Chengming (2002) emphasized the universal dimension of human rights and promoted the constitution's function of protecting basic human rights. They argued that the current Chinese constitution's stipulation regarding citizens' basic human rights should be improved because it does not recognize citizens' right to be informed of public policy (zhiqingquan), strictly restricts citizens' freedom to assembly and protest, and fails to provide the means to realize citizens' freedom to speech and publication (pp. 45–46). By making this point, the authors seem to recognize civil and political rights that Western countries have cherished as an integral part of basic human rights.

Consistent with this sentiment within the context of the relatively fluid post–September 11 world order, Beijing has continued to promote conciliatory human rights policies in both multilateral and bilateral forums. On the first front, no draft resolution regarding human rights conditions in China was introduced at the UN CHR in the spring of 2002, and China's representative, Sha Zukang (who had previously been China's top arms control negotiator), used this reprieve as a platform for promoting balanced rhetoric that both endorsed the human rights system and indirectly criticized other members of the UN CHR for imposing "double standards" when evaluating the human rights performance of developing countries ("Chinese Ambassador Urges" 2002). In addition, Beijing began to use other UN forums to counter charges leveled against China for its apparent attempt to take advantage of the U.S.-led global war against terrorism to further its own efforts to bring Xinjiang more tightly under Chinese control (in the process violating human rights in the contested region). In July 2002, China's representative to the UN Economic and Social Council argued "the strengthening of exchanges and cooperation in the field of human rights is an effective tool to combat terrorism" ("China Calls for Enhanced Exchanges" 2002). The following month, when Mary Robinson again visited China, she challenged this claim by taking Beijing to task for reports of increased rights abuses in Xinjiang; the official Chinese media ignored her criticism and instead emphasized the positive aspects of her assessment of human rights conditions within China (Foreman 2002; Shao Zhongwei 2002).

In summer 2002, this issue also was involved in stalled Sino-U.S. talks over renewing bilateral human rights dialogue. For example, when Tang Jiaxuan, the Chinese foreign minister, met with U.S. secretary of state Colin Powell during ASEAN's annual meetings in July, it was reported that their conversation revolved around promoting cooperation between Beijing and Washington on trade and fighting terrorism. However, on the heels of this meeting, Tang also announced China's intention to restart human rights dialogue with the United States (Anthony 2002). The following month, in a move that clearly gave the impression of an unspoken quid pro quo, Washington added a prominent Uyghur organization, the East Turkistan Islamic Movement (ETIM), to the U.S. list of international terrorist organizations ("China Appreciates" 2002; Foot 2003: 179–81). In the prelude to Jiang Zemin's October visit to Bush's Crawford, Texas, ranch, Beijing then released several "political prisoners" about whom the U.S. State Department had inquired earlier in 2002.

This move facilitated an American announcement that Beijing and

Washington had set a date to officially renew bilateral human rights talks. Moreover, during the press conference that followed the Crawford, Texas, Bush-Jiang meeting, the Chinese president stated that human rights were a common pursuit of mankind, contended that China's own human rights record was constantly being improved, and de-emphasized the differences between China and the United States on this issue ("Jiang, Bush" 2002). The two sides then held bilateral human rights talks in December (with the American delegation being permitted to visit Xinjiang during its stay in China). Against the backdrop of this renewed bilateral dialogue, China reportedly issued "unconditional" invitations to three sets of UN special rapporteurs on human rights (in the fields of torture, arbitrary detention, and religious freedom) to travel to China.

In light of these conciliatory moves (and with American attention turned fully toward Iraq), it came as no surprise that the United States did not introduce a draft resolution on China's human rights record at the UN CHR in spring 2003.[16] Although visits by many multilateral human rights delegations promised at the end of 2002 did not, in the end, take place in 2003, Beijing did permit the special rapporteur on education to visit China in the fall ("Education" 2003). In addition, during his visit to the United States in December (the focus of which was largely on the issue of Taiwan, as discussed in Chapter 4), Wen Jiabao reaffirmed China's commitment to the international human rights system. Moreover, in a speech at Harvard University, Wen conceded that "China's human rights record" was not "perfect" ("Chinese Premier" 2003).

Of greater significance, during 2003, the possibility of adding a clause to the Chinese constitution to guarantee "human rights" began to garner extensive attention. This development unfolded within the context of a consideration of broader constitutional reforms first proposed during the November 2002 Sixteenth Party Congress. Momentum for amending the constitution picked up in the summer and fall of 2003, when the NPC reportedly convened meetings in which "influential intellectuals" first endorsed the idea of adding human rights to the constitution, and the Standing Committee of the NPC began to draft a human rights amendment.

In the spring of 2004, the NPC's activities resulted in a proposed amendment to the Chinese constitution that stated, "the State respects and protects human rights" ("China to Write" 2004). In lauding this landmark development, Wu Bangguo, the vice-chair of the NPC Standing Committee, enthusiastically declared, "It's a consistent principle adopted by the Party and the State to respect and protect human rights. To write this principle into the Constitution will further provide a legal guarantee for its implementation," while also promoting "exchanges and cooperation with the international community in the human rights field" (Ibid.). When the NPC formally approved the amendment days after it was introduced, it was lauded in the official Chinese media as a historic turning point in the development of human rights protection within China ("Inclusion" 2004). Although international human rights NGO's have expressed skepticism that this new law is likely to improve human rights conditions within China, its promulgation should at the same time be seen as elevating Chinese involvement in the human rights system to a new level.

Conclusion

Over the course of the last two decades, in the process of engaging the international community in a series of largely defensive exchanges, the Chinese position on human rights, and by extension sovereign authority, has significantly shifted. When China's leaders moved from actively opposing the human rights system to allowing for limited involvement in it (for largely self-interested reasons), they also unintentionally set in motion processes that allowed for the introduction of new normative influences into China that eventually had a deep impact on the Chinese conceptualization of human rights (and to a lesser extent on Chinese human rights behavior).

This trend may seem to offer a glimmer of hope to China's human rights critics, since during the 1990s Chinese leaders and analysts have reconsidered the scope and legitimacy of the human rights system and incrementally accepted changes in China's sovereign authority. However, this development is part of an ongoing, and not necessarily evolutionary, process. A rejection of the human rights system and a reduction in flexibility on sovereignty is possible, which could erase the early stages of redefining the sovereign boundaries between China and the rest of the world. Furthermore, many in China's foreign policy and national security making circles remain ambivalent about China's increasing integration with international society in general, and the human rights system specifically. The U.S. war against Iraq, and the reported human rights abuses by American troops within Iraq that occurred, have strengthened such voices within China, and increased Chinese skepticism about the role of human rights within international politics. Nonetheless, the Chinese integration with the international human rights system has continued to evolve, and has already effectively altered how Chinese leaders and foreign policy analysts interpret the meaning of the authority component of the sovereignty norm. This change sharply contrasts with the way the Chinese continue to interpret the territorial and jurisdictional components of sovereignty, examined in Chapters 3 and 4, but it is far less sweeping than the changes that took place in regard to economic sovereignty, analyzed in the following chapter.

6

Economic Sovereignty: Accelerating Integration and Accumulating Obligations

The previous chapters have shown that since the late 1970s China's policy makers have made a series of contrasting adjustments in their stance on each of the aspects of sovereignty considered so far. They de-emphasized territorial concerns and endeavored to cooperatively resolve each of China's outstanding border disputes, while accepting the territorial status quo. At the same time, after a brief experiment with a more flexible stance on jurisdictional issues, they adopted intransigent practices vis-à-vis Taiwan and Tibet designed to strengthen Beijing's claim to both regions. In contrast, they accepted the legitimacy of the international human rights system and increasingly acknowledged the need for compliance with its basic principles and norms in a way that began to transgress the lines of sovereign authority that had long separated China from the rest of the international system.

As significant and far-reaching as these developments were, they pale in comparison to the sweeping changes in China's stance on economic sovereignty—the component of the norm that stipulates that each state has the right to regulate and govern economic activity within its own territorial boundaries—during the 1980s and 1990s. During this period many of the boundaries that had previously walled off the Chinese economy from the rest of the international economic system were breached. The focal points of this development were the extended negotiations that preceded China's accession to the World Trade Organization (WTO) in 2001 and, framing that process, broader debates about how deeply China should become integrated with the global economy. During the last two decades, the official Chinese discourse on economic issues moved from insisting on almost absolute barriers between China and the rest of

the world (as outlined in Chapter 2), to promoting boundary-transgressing concepts of integration and globalization. In addition, the General Agreement on
Trade and Tariffs (GATT) / WTO went from being an organization that
Beijing largely ignored to one that was courted in official statements. Although
Chinese leaders studiously avoided directly acknowledging the implications of
these developments for Chinese sovereignty, during the 1990s unofficial analysis of this trend frequently broached that sensitive topic; many scholars concluded that, at least in economic terms, sovereignty's role in the international system
had already been substantially eroded. Some even argued that the practice of
Chinese sovereignty had been significantly affected.

Beyond such discourse, Chinese leaders also adopted policies and laws
designed to facilitate China's participation in the main multilateral economic
organizations. This shift began in the late 1970s and 1980s with modest changes
in the structure of China's foreign trade and investment rules (made against the
backdrop of China's early moves toward membership in both the World Bank
and the International Monetary Fund [IMF]), and in the early 1990s it expanded to significant reductions in tariffs on a wide range of products (as part of a
renewed campaign for membership in GATT). In addition, by the end of the
1990s it included a host of broader concessions involving virtually every sector
of the Chinese economy. Significantly, these latter changes were increasingly
made to conform to GATT/WTO rules and norms. In other words, in contrast
with the human rights issues discussed in the Chapter 5—where a subtle shift
in Chinese actions occurred in the 1990s, but was always paired with defensive
rhetoric about China's priorities—in the economic realm a publicly acknowledged link was made between emerging international standards (as articulated
by the trade organization and its member states) and Chinese behavior.
Furthermore, late in the negotiations with GATT/WTO, the Chinese accepted "WTO-plus terms," which went well beyond most other member states'
obligations and significantly reduced the impermeability of China's economic
boundaries (see Lardy 2002: 9; and Qin 2003).

This pattern developed over three phases. First, from 1979 through 1989,
change was limited to a de-emphasis in Chinese claims and analysis of the need
to maintain economic self-reliance, paired with a restricted lowering of what
had previously been formidable barriers to foreign trade. The fallout generated
by Beijing's handling of the student-led demonstrations marked the start of the
second phase in the spring of 1989; however, in contrast to the pattern discussed
in Chapter 5, the Tiananmen crackdown did not cast a dark shadow over the
economic realm. In fact, even as China was building up barriers between itself
and the rest of the world on human rights issues, in its economic behavior it
increasingly acknowledged that new economic trends were eroding sovereign-

ty's role in international politics. This discursive move was paired with new policies explicitly designed to accelerate China's participation in the international
economic system and facilitate its accession to GATT. In 1994, a shift in the
Chinese discourse on the international economy, and the tabling of an unsuc-
cessful draft protocol for China's entry into GATT, marked the beginning of a
new stage. During this third phase, the boundary-transgressing trends that had
emerged in the early 1990s gathered momentum and eventually transformed
the Chinese stance on economic sovereignty.

These developments raise the question of why the Chinese were willing to
erase sovereign economic boundaries at the same time that they resisted transgressing other components of the norm. The answer to this key question lies,
first, in the fact that at least through the early 1990s, there was little divergence
in the Chinese stance on the four aspects of sovereignty. On the contrary, the
incremental changes Chinese leaders made with regard to economic sovereignty during this period were virtually identical to the cautious approach they took
on sovereign territory, authority, and jurisdiction.

In light of such similarities, it should come as no surprise that the same factors that underlay the moderation in relation to other components of the norm
during the 1980s also drove change in the economic sphere at this time. It, too,
was a product of Deng Xiaoping's rearticulation of China's basic national interests, paired with the emergence of limited international incentives for change.
However, during the 1990s, redefined international interests (particularly those
of the United States), strengthened multilateral institutions (with the consolidation of the GATT/WTO's authority), and the diffusion of new normative
influences within China (especially, ideas about the inevitability of economic
globalization) overtook this initial impulse for limited change. The combined
weight of these factors for change was much greater than those which mate-
rialized during this period in Beijing's handling of both territorial and jurisdictional issues. It also provided clearer material incentives for change—the
potential economic benefits to be garnered from economic integration—than
was the case in regard to the international human rights system (absent most
of the costs the Chinese perceived to lie in increased participation in such a
system). In other words, despite the fact that China's initial misgivings about
transgressing sovereign boundaries were quite similar (and tied to historical
concerns) across all four components of the norm, it was only with reference
to economic issues that such reservations were largely (although not completely) erased by external factors during the 1990s. Hence, the divergence in words
and actions on sovereignty.

Yet, as important as such international pressures were, they alone cannot
account for the final wave of concessions Chinese leaders made at the end of

the decade to facilitate the speedy conclusion of the negotiations with the WTO. At this stage, Chinese leaders also saw WTO membership as increasingly valuable, due to their new emphasis on consolidating reforms and demonstrating China's responsibility to the world community. In short, it was a convergence of external pressures and domestic changes that caused Chinese leaders and policy makers to reinterpret economic sovereignty.

Phase I, 1978–Spring 1989: Increasing Economic Interaction, Minimizing the Cost to Sovereign Rights

Starting in the late 1970s and throughout the 1980s, China's stance on economic sovereignty was characterized by a turn away from the confrontational rhetoric and isolationist policies that had been so prominent during the preceding decade. Thus, in the 1980s, economic sovereignty was consistently deemphasized in Chinese discourses and policies. For example, from 1982 through the end of 1988, *Beijing Review* published no economic sovereignty claims.[1] In addition, during this period the main outlets for unofficial analysis of foreign economic relations also contained virtually no direct references to economic sovereignty, and started to move consideration of the implications of economic interdependence for China beyond the Maoist orthodoxy of the previous decade.[2] At the same time, the Chinese enacted policies that increased the flexibility of the line between China's economy and the rest of the international system, particularly through a reevaluation of Beijing's relationship with the major international economic organizations. However, toward the end of the decade, even as Beijing took significant steps toward making China a member of GATT, Chinese leaders and analysts continued to express reservations about the extent to which China could (and should) accept the trade organization's right to oversee specific aspects of China's foreign economic relations. Indeed, they gave no indication China would be willing to change its trade regime in order to facilitate accession to GATT. In this sense, while China welcomed trade and investment, and wanted to participate in the main international economic organizations, the foundation of the Chinese interpretation of economic sovereignty remained largely unchanged during the 1980s.

As in each of the cases analyzed in the preceding chapters, Deng Xiaoping's endorsement of a new, more pragmatic approach to handling China's relationship with the rest of the world played a pivotal role in this development. In this case, his expansion upon earlier pronouncements on the necessity of "opening" China to foreign technology, trade, and investment provided the official rationale for a more flexible stance on economic issues. In Deng's influential opinion, China simply could no longer afford to follow a policy of autarky, since that hampered the development of the economy and jeopardized Beijing's ability to defend the very economic rights that self-reliance was supposed to secure. As he told a group of scientists in March of 1978, developing China's technological capabilities would require independence and self-reliance, but "independence does not mean shutting the door on the world, nor does self-reliance mean blind opposition to everything foreign" (Deng Xiaoping 1995: 103). Deng made his position even clearer in an October interview with a group of German reporters, when he warned, "China cannot develop by closing its door, sticking to the beaten path and being self-complacent" (p. 143).

In line with this official commentary, Chinese policy makers rapidly reorganized each aspect of China's foreign economic relations to facilitate the increases in trade, investment, and technology demanded by Deng's call for opening. In regard to trade, the first major step was taken in 1979 with the establishment of provincial- and local-level trading corporations, and was followed by the granting of trading rights to national production ministries in 1980. To complement this change, the import and export licensing system was also revised. In addition, the existing Customs Bureau was replaced with the General Administration of Customs. Furthermore, the central foreign trade regime itself was reorganized beginning in 1979, followed by the creation of the Ministry of Foreign Economic Relations and Trade (MOFERT) in 1982. To top off these developments, the National People's Congress (NPC) also passed landmark legislation in 1979 creating the joint venture system of investment in China and establishing the initial legal framework for special economic zones (Cheng 1991: 43, 52; Horsley 1984: 7).

This new official rhetoric and institutional reform affected all aspects of China's foreign economic relations. The previous structure for regulating this activity had been designed to create virtually impenetrable walls between China and the rest of the world. In contrast, the new framework, although built around the conviction that Beijing maintained the right to restrict and control economic flows across China's boundaries, removed many barriers. Although this change was intended to be limited to restructuring the way Beijing administered economic exchanges with the rest of the world, it still opened new spaces within which leaders, policy makers, and scholars began to reconsider how they defined China's economic sovereignty.

Such an incremental shift was initially evident in Beijing's drive in 1979 and 1980 to make China a member of the IMF and the World Bank. From the start, the issue of how to guard China's economic rights was prominent in official deliberations between Beijing and the two organizations. Thus, the initial January 1979 Chinese report outlining the benefits and costs of membership in both organizations expressed particular concern about the requirement that China submit secret economic data to, and accommodate visits to China by,

IMF and World Bank officials (Jacobson and Oksenberg 1990: 69–70). Indeed, China's reservations about reporting obligations were raised in a February 1979 interview between Deng and the head of Japan's Kyodo News Service. Deng strongly endorsed China's decision to become a member of the IMF. However, when pressed about whether China was "ready to make public economic statistics as required by the IMF for accession to the world monetary body," he elliptically replied that foreign governments already had information on the Chinese economy that was "not far wrong" ("Deng on China's Intention" 1979). This assertion implied that China should not be expected to supply additional information to the outside world and underscored just how closely Deng continued to guard China's economic sovereignty.

Despite such concerns, initial contacts between Beijing and both the IMF and World Bank continued to expand and led to several private missions and public statements. In the spring of 1980 this process accelerated when two high-level delegations went to China to discuss the terms of Beijing's participation in both organizations. Talks with the first delegation revolved around the issue of "the rights and obligations" Chinese participation in the IMF would entail. On one level, delineating China's responsibilities was simply a matter of determining how much China could expect to draw from the IMF's resources and how large its quota in the fund would be. However, reaching agreement on these numbers required an unprecedented sharing of economic data by China and thus extended negotiations to the still sensitive issue of the scope of China's economic rights. In a highly pragmatic move, Chinese officials opted not to interpret IMF requests for information as an infringement on China's sovereignty, and later cooperated with IMF officials in this area. Thus, talks quickly moved forward and China formally entered the IMF on April 17, 1980 (although the size of China's quota had yet to be decided). Meetings with the second mission, led by Robert McNamara, took place against the backdrop of the successful completion of IMF talks, and focused on setting the terms for China's admission to the World Bank. Talks reportedly hinged on Chinese concerns about the bank's contacts with Taiwan and questions of how quickly Beijing would be able to draw on the bank's resources. One month later, these negotiations led to the bank's announcement of China's membership.[3]

With membership secured, China became an active participant in both organizations. In the World Bank there was unprecedented cooperation between bank officials and Chinese policy makers in producing an exhaustive report on the Chinese economy (see "Borrow" 1991). In addition, despite a retrenchment in the Chinese economy in late 1980 through 1982, Beijing requested several loans from the bank for development projects. By 1989 Beijing had been granted over fifty loans totaling over U.S.$5 billion from the bank's

International Bank for Reconstruction and Development (IBRD), and twenty-eight loans for U.S.$3.3 billion from its International Development Association (Boughton 2001: 980). In the IMF, the Chinese first negotiated a rapid increase in Beijing's quota in the fund (from the U.S.$550 million that it was allocated upon resuming China's seat to nearly U.S.$2 billion by the end of 1980), and then made several withdrawals from the organization's funds in 1981 (drawing over U.S.$1 billion, which it repaid by 1984) in order to help stabilize its rapidly growing economy (p. 979; Feeney 1989: 242–44).

In contrast, China's overtures to GATT were slow in coming and much less substantial. Initial formal contacts did not take place until the spring of 1980, when China resumed its seat on the UN's Interim Commission for the International Trade Organization. Although this move was generally seen as indicative of a growing Chinese interest in playing a more active role in the trade organization, it was only followed by cautious measures, designed more to provide China with additional information about GATT than to facilitate full participation in it. In 1981 China became an observer in the Multifiber Arrangement (MFA), a regime that regulated textile trade (which is particularly important to the Chinese economy). The following year Beijing attained full observer status in GATT, and its officials attended the pivotal 1982 meetings of the contracting parties ("China Calls" 1982). However, it was not until the end of 1983 that Beijing moved to make a more formal commitment to the trade organization by applying for full membership in the MFA and subsequently signing the related Arrangement Regarding International Trade in Textiles ("China Admitted" 1983; see also Feeney 1984; and Jacobson and Oksenberg 1990: chap. 4).

Such hesitancy was largely a product of a cautious review of the costs and benefits of joining the trade organization. As with the World Bank and IMF decisions, these calculations involved two levels of concerns. On one level, Chinese officials were simply attempting to determine the material gains and losses that Beijing could expect from membership. As Robert E. Herzstein (1986) and William R. Feeney (1989) pointed out in the 1980s, the Chinese saw participation in GATT as having a number of potential benefits. It would ensure that China had "most favored nation" status with each of the organization's member states and guarantee that its exports would be given preferential treatment by a select group of industrial countries. Moreover, it would provide Beijing with additional information about the world trading system and perhaps help to legitimize "the decisions of the reformist political leadership" while also providing "valuable trade and investment assurances to the international business and banking community" (Feeney 1989: 256). However, participation in GATT would not endow China with immediate capital for major development projects or funds to cover imbalances in its international accounts. In other words, the rewards of GATT membership were more diffused and abstract than those China enjoyed as a member of the IMF and World Bank.

More importantly, on a second level, that of sovereign rights, the price of admission to GATT was significantly higher than for IMF and World Bank membership. Jacobson and Oksenberg suggested as much in their comprehensive review of China's early negotiations with the trade organization. In 1990, they astutely observed that acceding to the GATT would require China to open its markets, liberalize its trading system, and "submit its trade regime to international scrutiny and surveillance" (Jacobson and Oksenberg 1990: 83). Agreeing to any one of these would entail a much larger adjustment in how the Chinese interpreted the scope of their country's economic sovereignty than did the relatively limited reporting obligations of the IMF and World Bank. Or, as Feeney (1989: 256) argued, GATT membership would "reduce China's control and flexibility in planning and managing its economy and foreign trade."

These factors explain much of Beijing's cautious approach toward the trade organization during the first half of the 1980s. While the benefits of membership were readily apparent, the costs of joining were potentially much more far-reaching than was the case with the World Bank or IMF. Membership in GATT was desirable, but only so far as it was seen as assisting with the modernization of China's economy and securing its economic sovereignty.

This theme was written into virtually all facets of the official discourse on China's foreign economic relations. Thus, opening was universally viewed as a way to strengthen (rather than weaken) China's economic sovereignty. The core argument for opening was that it would allow China to reap the benefits of more trade and investment without sacrificing its economic independence. Even the most enthusiastic supporters of Deng's economic liberalization policies repeatedly emphasized this point. For example, in the fall of 1981, Zhao Ziyang declared to the North-South Summit on economic relations that expanding cooperation between the two regions must "respect the sovereignty of developing countries and not interfere in their internal affairs or control their economic lifelines" ("For" 1981). The following year, in his address to the Twelfth Party Congress, Deng Xiaoping underscored this theme by bracketing his comments on "opening" with strong warnings about the need to maintain China's independence. The basic stand of the Chinese people, he maintained, was "independence and self-reliance." Hence they would always cherish their "national self-respect and pride" (Deng Xiaoping 1994: 14–15).

Unofficial analysis of economic issues published during this period tended to focus on similar issues. However, while virtually all analysts agreed with the outlines of the "opening" program, many expressed doubts about its speed and direction. In contrast to the confidence expressed in China's official claims about the limited impact that interdependence and "opening" would have on China, several Chinese scholars argued that economic interdependence was a threat.

Apprehension about these issues was poignantly expressed in a 1983 article in *Shijie Jingji yu Zhengzhi* that reviewed the main points of debate in China over the "new international economic order." The article observed that all participants in this debate agreed that "there had been an obvious deepening in economic interdependence (*jingji shang xianghu yilai*) between the developed and developing countries. This is an undeniable fact" ("Guanyu" 1983: 12). However, it also argued that there were extensive differences among Chinese scholars over the meaning and implications of such a trend. For example, the article noted that in considering the international division of labor, some contended that the dependence of the developed nations on the developing was "parasitic" (*jishengxing*). Others reportedly asserted that the relationship between developed and developing countries was more aptly described as one of exploiter and exploited, or that between a rider and his steed. Yet another group saw the issue of interdependence as integrally linked to developing countries' struggle for political independence, and warned that a lack of vigilance would lead states to fall back into subservience in the name of economic development. In addition, other scholars were reported to have claimed that interdependence in reality involved a deepening of the mutual dependence of both developing and developed countries. Moreover, some scholars were said to believe that economic interdependence did not amount to dependency. Thus, "a sovereign state that makes appropriate use of foreign capital and technology will not become dependent" (Ibid.).

Commensurate with the more liberal, or moderate, of these assessments, in the mid-1980s the Chinese began to stress the role that GATT membership might play in facilitating increased participation in the international economic system. Indeed, at the start of 1984, an unprecedented conference on GATT attended by a high-level trade organization official was held in Beijing. Against the backdrop of this meeting, the first extensive analysis of GATT began to appear in Chinese journals.

Analysis from this period paid particular attention to the rights and obligations that GATT membership entailed. For example, an article by Xue Rongjiu (1984: 14) observed that the strengthening of GATT regulations and non-tariff trade barriers during the Tokyo Round "demanded that participating member states, before the agreement went into effect, guarantee that [their] country's law, rules, and administrative procedures comply with it (*yu qi yizhi*). In other words, countries participating in the agreement need to promise to reform legislation that conflicts with the treaty's rules and administrative structure." Xue added, "China is a centrally planned economy; [its] use of tariffs, setting of exchange rates, internal market prices, credit, the economic trade administrative system, and foreign trade policy are not compatible (*bu yizhi*) with GATT. Therefore, in order to establish formal relations with GATT, to gain the largest benefits from GATT, systematic and comprehensive research on the above issues should be conducted" (p. 17). Although Xue then stopped well short of committing Beijing to such changes (and thus limiting China's economic rights), even the suggestion of such a possibility marked an important turning point in the unofficial discourse on GATT.

The policy counterpoint to such rhetoric was located in Beijing's continued efforts to restructure China's foreign trade and investment regime in a manner that would facilitate expansion in both. In addition, in the fall of 1984 the Chinese applied for observer status in GATT ("China to Attend" 1984). The primary motive for this step was the same one that had pushed the Chinese in this direction earlier in the decade: broader participation in the trade organization offered Beijing more opportunities to protect its fledgling foreign trade regime. Chinese statements issued in the MFA condemning changes in U.S. policies on textile tariffs reveal that Beijing had begun to use the limited platform within the trade organization that it had already managed to attain. However, as Jacobson and Oksenberg (1990: 88) have pointed out, moving ahead with observer status in 1984 did not solely stem from Beijing's growing interest in protecting Chinese trade. It was also related to the fact that GATT members were moving forward with a new round of talks that would likely have a profound effect on the structure of the trade organization itself, and Beijing's growing realization that it could benefit from being part of such a process.

Against this backdrop, the director-general of GATT, Arthur Dunkel, traveled to Beijing in January 1986. In conjunction with this visit, Zhao Ziyang announced China's "hope" for the speedy resumption of China's GATT status (Xinhua Jan. 10, 1986, in LexisNexis). This statement also contained one of the first official acknowledgments that it might be necessary to make changes in the Chinese economy if China was to resume its seat in the organization. Zhao claimed that "China's economic reforms will reduce differences between China and most other GATT members in prices, currency values and foreign trade systems and practices" (Ibid.). The following day, Wu Xueqian reiterated Zhao's comments by asserting that Beijing was "now keen to resume its membership, which was in line with its policy of opening to the rest of the world" (Xinhua, Jan. 11, 1986). Later in the year, Beijing followed up by sending a petition to the trade organization asking to resume China's position in GATT ("China Applies" 1986).

Paralleling these developments, China's involvement with both the IMF and World Bank also expanded in the mid-1980s. Acute balance-of-payment concerns that threatened the Chinese economy at this point led Chinese officials to again turn to the fund for assistance (with Beijing reaching agreement with the fund in November of 1986 on the terms for a twelve-month standby arrangement) (Feeney 1989: 244). At the same time, the World Bank began a second, collaborative study of the Chinese economy (pp. 247–48) and continued to provide the Chinese with extensive loans, with just over U.S.$1 billion disbursed in both 1985 and 1986 (Jacobson and Oksenberg 1990: 114–21).

In 1987, the Chinese followed up on their earlier expression of serious interest in GATT membership by submitting a memorandum to the trade organization on China's foreign trade regime ("China's Status" 1987). This document was the starting point of China's negotiations with GATT, and its submission led to the establishment of China's GATT Working Party (hereafter referred to as Working Party) in May 1987. Negotiations in the Working Party were initially limited to information-gathering through confidential written exchanges between China and GATT members. However, beginning in February 1988, this correspondence was supplanted by a series of initial meetings. The early sessions were primarily "educational," but China's representatives also used Working Party sessions to publicize their own interpretation of the growing relationship between China and GATT.

Concurrently, unofficial analysis published in China contained increasingly extensive discussions of the trade organization and the implications that membership in it would have for China. This analysis also started to explore the possibility that China might have to make deep changes in its trade regime in order to reduce the inconsistencies between GATT's rules and Chinese practices. As such, it indirectly stretched the Chinese definition of economic sovereignty.

This trend was particularly apparent in Xue Rongjiu's (1988) reappraisal of GATT. As in 1984, Xue again found significant gaps between China's trade system and GATT rules, but he also argued that China should accelerate reforms, not only to improve the administrative structure of its foreign trading system, but also to increase the compatibility between China and GATT. Xue advocated making three changes in China's trading system. First, China should reform its trade system "according to the basic principles of GATT demands" (although such demands should not be the "sole goal of reform") (Xue Rongjiu 1988: 19). Second, China should reduce its tariffs, reform the tariff system, coordinate currency policies, reform export subsidies, create an authoritative system of information on foreign trade, and establish a flexible system of trade administration. Third, in addressing legal issues, China should address the questions of mutual non-adaptability, retroactivity, and safeguards, and make corresponding changes in domestic law and bilateral trade agreements (pp. 19–20).[4]

Before the clampdown on the student-led protest movement in the spring of 1989, Chinese officials struggled to realize these goals through developing China's relationship with each of the three main multilateral economic organizations. For example, Chinese borrowing from the World Bank steadily rose from 1986 through 1989, with over sixty projects approved by the summer of 1989 (Jacobson and Oksenberg 1990: 117). In addition, training programs, as well as regular meetings between Chinese policy makers and bank officials, became increasingly routine. This trend was highlighted by high-profile contacts between top-level Chinese and bank leaders, events that elicited glowing assessments of the bank's positive role in the world economy ("Li Peng Lauds" 1988). As these ties were growing, Beijing also turned to the IMF for assistance in attempting to rein in the surging inflation that had engulfed China in the late 1980s. Even as the violent endgame of the Tiananmen demonstrations was beginning to unfold, the managing director of the IMF, Michel Camdessus, traveled to Beijing to consult with Chinese leaders about inflation, and during his visit balanced expressions of concern with a relatively optimistic assessment of the overall state of the Chinese economy ("IMF" 1989).

In sum, by the spring of 1989, the reforms that Deng Xiaoping had begun in the late 1970s had grown to the point that China's economy was more "open" to the outside world than it had been for decades. Commensurate with this development, China's leaders worked to increase Beijing's involvement in each of the major multilateral economic organizations and began to incrementally modify their stance on which economic issues fell under the rubric of sovereignty. By the end of 1988, this trend had so matured that some within China were beginning to advocate deep changes in the structure of China's foreign economic relations in order to make China more compatible with GATT rules. However, even at this date, underlying concerns about the inequity of the international economy, and the necessity of retaining a degree of independence and self-reliance within such a system, continued to anchor Chinese discursive and policy practices. In this sense, the Chinese stance on economic sovereignty remained tethered to Deng's initial pairing of "opening" and "self-reliance."

Phase II, 1989–93: Weathering the Storm, Shifting Practices

As I have argued, 1989 was a crucial turning point in the development of the Chinese approach to sovereignty. It was during this year that the shift in Chinese positioning on territorial issues involving the Soviet Union and India began to take shape. It was also in this year that leaders and policy makers reacted to a convergence of local and international challenges to China's claim to Tibet and

Taiwan, making a decisive move away from the more moderate stance on jurisdictional sovereignty of the 1980s. The year 1989 also witnessed a call to reinforce China's sovereign boundaries against human rights critics. In contrast, no
major contraction in the Chinese stance on economic sovereignty took place
during the summer and fall of 1989.

Even during the height of Chinese isolation in the second half of 1989, official commentary on economic issues showed a caution and reserve that contrasted sharply with rhetoric on sovereign authority and jurisdictional sovereignty.[5] More interestingly, despite a small surge in defensive commentary at this
time, in 1990 analysts began to expand on the initial considerations of sovereign
change that had begun to appear in the late 1980s. In addition, while official
GATT negotiations were temporarily shelved in the summer of 1989, Chinese
officials continued to expand the list of changes they were willing to make in
order to facilitate the resumption of Beijing's membership. At the same time
(between 1989 and 1992), Beijing finished repaying the IMF for the first tranche
drawing China had made in 1986 ("China: Transactions" 2004). Moreover,
despite a temporary halt in new lending following Tiananmen (for example, no
IBRD loans were made during the 1990 fiscal year), the World Bank continued
to disperse funds to China that had already been allocated (Feeney 1994:
232–35).

The initial resilience of this pragmatic approach to economic issues was
largely a product of two factors. First, the broad consensus that had emerged
among Chinese leaders and policy makers over the course of the 1980s about
the necessity of reforming China's foreign economic relations was not fundamentally shaken. Thus, even in the summer and fall of 1989, debate about
"opening" centered on how much it should be throttled back, not whether it
should be abandoned. Second, by 1989, economic reforms had already led to a
shallow integration between China and the rest of the international system;
abruptly ending this would have been exceedingly difficult and unpalatable to
a government that was already reeling. Indeed, the loss of domestic legitimacy
Beijing suffered as a result of the clampdown on dissent in the spring of 1989
made economic growth an even higher priority for officials who were search-
ing for ways to regain support in China. Thus, interest in maintaining ties with
the world economy and attaining GATT membership grew.

These influences were especially evident in the statements issued by Deng
Xiaoping in the immediate aftermath of Tiananmen. For example, in his earliest official post–June 4 statement (issued to top military leaders in Beijing on
June 9), Deng reiterated the ongoing value of economic opening. He rhetorically asked, "How could we have achieved the success we have today without
the reform and opening policy?" and then observed, "The question before us

now is not whether the policies of reform and opening are right or whether they should be implemented but how to carry them out, what to open and what to close" (Deng Xiaoping 1994: 298–99). Days later, he told the party leadership that while China should take care to maintain its "independence," it should also "carry out reform and opening to the outside world with greater daring" in order to "satisfy the people" (pp. 302–3). Indeed, Deng insisted that by absorbing more foreign capital, China would "benefit" and its economy would be "invigorated"; therefore it was imperative to "do some things to demonstrate that our policies of reform and opening to the outside world will not change but will be further implemented" (p. 303).

Deng's emphasis on continuity is particularly interesting because it was made in the face of impending economic sanctions (as discussed in Chapter 5). By mid-June, the Bush administration had called on the main international economic organizations to freeze all loans to China and had halted all public, official high-level exchanges with China. At the end of the month, the European Community quickly followed with its own sanctions, and in July the Group of Seven (G-7) meetings in Paris provided the developed countries with a forum to coordinate such activities (Feeney 1994: 232–33, 239–40).

Chinese officials responded to these moves with a stream of denunciations. However, in each case, this was balanced with assurances that the "opening" policy would continue. For example, a *Renmin Ribao* editorial published in response to the G-7 sanctions chastised the group for grossly interfering in China's internal affairs and violating international norms, but added that the Chinese people "will never change their basic state policy of reform and opening to the outside world despite the unfriendly actions of certain countries" ("People's Daily Says" 1989). Days later, Liu Xiangdong, director of the Department of Policies and Structural Reform under MOFERT, expanded on the content of this editorial in an interview with a *Beijing Review* reporter. Liu rejected sanctions as an attempt to "put pressure on our country and interfere in our internal affairs." However, he also promised that "after the counter-revolutionary rebellion is put down, China will open its doors wider to the outside world and will enjoy a more favourable environment for developing Sino-foreign economic relations and trade" ("China's Foreign" 1989).

When top Chinese leaders addressed these issues later in the year, they also worked to balance expressions of indignation with lengthy assurances to the international community that China still welcomed foreign investment and trade. Thus, when Jiang Zemin spoke during ceremonies commemorating the fortieth anniversary of the founding of the PRC, he argued, "in unswervingly following the policy of opening to the outside world, we must firmly safeguard the sovereignty, national independence and dignity of socialist China" ("Jiang

Zemin: Struggle" 1989). Subsequently, when Deng spoke to former U.S. president Richard Nixon in September, he warned, "Don't ever expect China to beg the United States to lift the sanctions. If they lasted a hundred years, the Chinese would not do that." However, he also stated, "I can assure you that no one can stop China's reform and opening to the outside world. Why? For the simple reason that without those policies we could not continue to make progress and our economy would go downhill" (Deng Xiaoping 1994: 321–22).

In other words, the Chinese resented the attempt by the outside world to shut China's economic doors and were convinced that this violated Chinese sovereignty, but they were also emphatically determined not to fall back on an isolationist interpretation of sovereign economic rights. Therefore, during this period, Beijing continued to praise GATT and even expanded its rhetorical commitment to rejoin the organization.

Thus, although negotiations with GATT slowed to a crawl in 1989, Chinese officials responded with repeated indications of interest in becoming a member in the trade organization. For example, China's observer at GATT responded to the postponement of the July Working Party meeting in a particularly muted fashion. Rather than condemning the delay, this official simply repeated that China was still "prepared to begin substantive discussions on China's rights and obligations" in GATT ("China Prepared" 1989). When the postponed meeting was finally held later in the year (albeit simply to "exchange views" among the involved parties), China's representatives took advantage of the platform it provided to forward a positive, if somewhat vague, assessment of the trade organization and China's interest in joining it. The head of the Chinese delegation argued that allowing China into GATT would be "conducive to the deepening of the reform in China and opening to the outside world and to the expansion of economic and trade relations between China and other countries" ("GATT Discusses" 1989).

The limited commentary on GATT that was published in 1989 echoed the cautious content of this type of official rhetoric. The main intent of this analysis was to portray the Chinese position as flexible despite the unreasonable demands being placed upon China in the negotiations. This trend was particularly evident in an article by Chen Dezhao (1989) that acknowledged the main reason for the delay in reentering GATT was the Chinese economy itself, but also argued that many of the contracting parties were making unfair demands on China during the negotiations. In this vein, Chen emphasized that China had repeatedly pledged to continue to reform its economic system and reduce state planning in China's foreign economic relations. However, he also objected to the attempt to force China to include in its GATT protocol a schedule for future reforms. Nonetheless, as Liu Guangxi, a prominent member of

China's GATT negotiating team, observed soon after Chen's article was published, "with the deepening of reform and opening, rapid development of economic trade, and increased foreign exchange, China's ability to assume suitable obligations in the multilateral trade system will also increase" (Liu Guangxi 1989: 43).

In 1990, Beijing accelerated the "opening" that Liu had embraced through devaluing China's currency, the renminbi, by 30 percent in a bid to cut export subsidies (Lardy 1992: 51–52; Zhang Yongjin 1998: 235). In addition, although the World Bank did not issue any new IBRD loans to Beijing during this fiscal year, its commitments to China grew in December of 1990, and in the following year it rapidly expanded its loans (Lardy 1992: 51–52). At the same time, the Asian Development Bank (ADB) resumed granting loans to China (with the total during 1991 and 1992 double that in 1986–89) (Feeney 1994: 240). Moreover, China's leaders started to carve out a more positive assessment of China's position within the international economic system. They described membership in GATT as desirable, but only on terms that acknowledged the uniqueness of China.

An initial survey of unofficial analysis published during this period reveals that most of this work simply mirrored these official moves. For example, commentary on the international economic system largely dwelt on north-south inequalities and China's capacity to withstand sanctions and grow its economy (see, for example, Liu Xin 1990; and Zhou Ying 1990). Discussion of GATT continued to revolve around the benefits China would gain from membership, and its limited ability to comply with GATT's rules. In addition, analysts began to consider the implications of the Uruguay Round talks for China and other developing countries. In touching upon these issues in a 1991 *Guoji Maoyi Wenti* article, Wang Yi revealed just how persistent sovereignty concerns were in the Chinese discourse on GATT. Wang warned that these negotiations, especially as they related to textiles and clothing, must "fully respect each state's sovereignty, laws, development policy goals, and be in accord with each country's development level" (Wang Yi 1991: 34). But, Wang also added, "China's political economic environment is increasing the depth of reform and opening, and creating even more beneficial conditions for China's entry into the multilateral trade system." For these reasons, Wang was confident that China would move toward fuller participation in the multilateral trading system.

Upon closer inspection, it is also apparent that alongside such orthodox analysis, other scholars were beginning to push well beyond the limits established by the official discourse on economic issues. Some analysts even began to give more extensive consideration to new ideas and trends within the international economic system. In so doing, they raised profound questions about the sanctity of each state's sovereign economic boundaries.

Two articles published in *Shijie Jingji yu Zhengzhi* in 1990 exemplified this trend. The first, written by Shen Jiru, focused on China's involvement in regional economic organizations and considered how such participation affected Chinese sovereignty. Shen acknowledged that China (and other states) had voluntarily "transferred (*zhuanrang*) a part of their sovereignty" when they became involved with economic institutions, but insisted that "this is in essence different from unilateral and pressured ceding (*gerang*) [of sovereignty]" (Shen Jiru 1990: 3). Furthermore, "in order to attain a type of interest, China, within the scope of the 'social functions of the nation' (*guojia de shehui zhineng*), had already placed limits on certain aspects of the practice of Chinese sovereignty, even to the extent of transferring a part of sovereignty" (Ibid.). In the second article, Xiao Qinfu dealt even more directly and expansively with these issues, asserting that internationalization had begun to erode aspects of state sovereignty (*zhuquan de qinshi*). Xiao declared that economic internationalization had "ruthlessly eroded sovereignty" and this had already had a "deep impact" on both the "world economy" and "international politics"; indeed, it produced a "revolutionary change" in international politics that extended to changes in the "concept of sovereignty, its scope, practice and guarantees" (Xiao Qinfu 1990: 25).

To be clear, this assessment of the current impact of economic forces on sovereignty's role in international politics constituted at best a marginal voice within the Chinese discussion of economic issues. Many articles written in 1991 countered Shen and Xiao's claims with assertions about the static nature of sovereignty (and the need to ensure that continuity was never challenged by new economic trends) (Gao Zhan 1991; Yang Xiyu 1991). However, the former set of analysis represents the leading edge within elite circles of the diffusion of ideas about economic integration and globalization that had already gained currency outside of China. These ideas shifted the discussion of foreign economic issues away from a universal insistence upon maintaining sovereignty toward a broader consideration of sovereign change.

This expanding discourse may not have had a direct impact on Chinese positioning in the main multilateral economic institutions, as the primary motivations for Chinese compromise—the substantive economic gains that might accrue from integrating with these organizations—remained largely the same in the 1990s as they had been during the preceding decade. But it did provide new rhetorical space for compromise in the negotiations with GATT on issues that previously would have been considered sacrosanct under the rubric of protecting Chinese economic sovereignty.

In accord with this trend, Chinese officials made a series of moves to promote negotiations with GATT. Beijing again devalued the renminbi and eliminated even more export subsidies (Zhang Yongjin 1998: 235). Over the course of the year, it also took part in bilateral talks with the United States regarding a host of specific economic issues tangentially related to GATT (Liang Wei 2002: 694–95). In addition, Fan Guoxiang, a senior Chinese representative to GATT (who, as discussed in Chapter 5, also participated in China's human rights delegations), delivered a detailed statement on the state of China's economic reforms to the annual meeting of the contracting parties. While Fan refrained from acknowledging that China had instituted new policies for the express purpose of resuming its position in GATT, he did take pains to underscore just how much closer to GATT's basic rules China had moved. Moreover, in emphasizing both tariff reductions and other administrative changes, Fan revealed that Beijing was beginning to consider the implications of GATT membership for China's economic system and the practice of Chinese economic sovereignty ("Statement" 1991).

Although Fan's analysis of change in China's foreign trade system was largely consistent with the cautious tone of previous statements from the leadership, at this time other officials began to acknowledge that such changes had been made at least in part to facilitate participation in the trade organization. In selectively emphasizing this intent, Beijing was implicitly beginning to accept a self-imposed limitation on China's economic sovereignty in a manner that was remarkably consistent with the analysis Shen Jiru had published the previous year.

The initial outlines of this subtle shift in Chinese rhetoric were visible in claims issued by senior officials in the winter of 1991–92, during a period that overlapped Deng Xiaoping's final high-level push for the opening policy via his famous "southern tour."[6] Wu Yi, then a vice minister of MOFERT, made one of the earliest such statements. She noted that reforms had made "China's foreign trade system more compatible with the international trade norms and rules, thus facilitating China's participation in international cooperation and labour division" (quoted in Zhang Yongjin 1998: 235). Li Lanqing, the head of MOFERT, followed Wu's comments with the argument that reforms instituted in 1991 "brought China's trade institutions further in line with the accepted international regimes" (Ibid.). Subsequently, in the days prior to the tenth meeting of the Working Party (which ended what had essentially been a two-year hiatus in its activities), Tong Zhiguang, yet another ranking MOFERT official, told Xinhua that China would be submitting an additional report to the Working Party. Moreover, this report would outline "China's obligation to ensuring transparency in foreign trade policies, its commitment to market access, substantial tariff reductions and its plan to eliminate more products from the country's import license coverage" ("China Seeks" 1992).

Following the publication of such conciliatory statements, Beijing viewed the February meeting of the Working Party as a major step forward in its negotiations with GATT. Chinese officials sought to build on the apparent progress during the spring through pledging to make additional changes to China's trade regime. According to an article in *China Daily* published soon after the session, "China is reforming its foreign trade system in a determined effort to comply with rules of the GATT" ("Trade" 1992). It observed that in pursuing this goal, China had already agreed to "drastically reducing product from the country's import license coverage, abolishing all import regulatory duties, formulation of foreign trade and anti-dumping laws, continuing to publicize its classified documents on foreign trade, and phasing out the policy of import substitution" (Ibid.). Moreover, Li Lanqing endorsed this expanded list of commitments in a *Renmin Ribao* interview published later in March. Li argued, "To meet the requirements of GATT, China has carried out a series of economic structural reforms since 1988. . . . Our current foreign trade system on the whole meets the requirements of GATT. For those gaps, we will carry on reforms to make the system more suitable to the requirements stipulated by GATT" ("Expanding" 1992).

Such assertions became increasingly common as negotiations moved forward later in the year. After Washington applied pressure (by threatening to impose a 301 trade action), Beijing signed a memorandum of understanding (MOU) with the United States in October that promised to further open China's trade regime. Although this agreement was reached outside of the GATT framework, it helped create new momentum in the negotiations. Indeed, against the backdrop of the signing of the MOU, two more Working Party meetings were held. In addition, Jin Yongjian, China's observer at the 1992 session of the contracting parties, subtly expanded on Fan Guoxiang's 1991 statement by formally reiterating China's commitment to the trade organization. Jin observed:

> China has continued to reform the foreign trade system by substantially enhancing its transparency and taking important trade liberalizing measures such as elimination of import regulatory taxes, reduction of tariffs on hundreds of items, and removal of a good number of products subject to import licenses. All these demonstrate China's willingness to abide by international economic and trade rules and disciplines and to make contributions to the strengthening of the multilateral trading system. ("Statement" 1992)

During this period, Chinese officials repeatedly expressed optimism about the prospects for a quick end to the negotiations. Such expectations notwithstanding, differences remained between China and the contracting members (especially the United States) over the nature of China's draft protocol and the specific obligations that China would incur from membership (Feeney 1994: 244–45). At the start of 1993 these issues featured prominently in a senior Chinese trade official's review of negotiations with GATT. The review was long and revealing. It noted that progress in talks was in part contingent on "how China will unify its foreign trade regimes, enhance the visibility of its foreign trade policies and distribute them to traders, to what extent will China reduce its tariff levels, how will China be treated in GATT, and how China will implement GATT rules on non-tariff protective measures" ("Optimistic" 1993). These concerns touched on virtually every aspect of China's foreign economic relations, and demonstrate the extent to which the Chinese had rearticulated what would previously have been considered issues of Chinese sovereignty into questions of negotiation.

Unofficial analysis of GATT published during 1993 offered specific policy guidelines on what China should do to resume its place in the trade organization, while allowing Chinese interest in economic growth to be realized (even if it meant further sacrificing certain aspects of China's economic rights). While conspicuously avoiding any direct acknowledgment that such moves would attenuate China's sovereign economic rights, in pushing for changes for the purpose of resuming China's seat in the trade organization such analysis began to stretch the Chinese discourse on economic issues in this direction.

Commentary on the international economic system published at this time directly addressed this controversial issue. On the one hand, articles that repeated familiar, defensive generalizations about both economic integration and interdependence continued to dominate the major foreign policy journals at this time (Qin Liufang 1993; Zhao Huaipu and Lu Yang 1993). On the other hand, this type of analysis was increasingly complemented by commentary that explored the implications of such trends for sovereignty's conventional role in international politics. Moreover, an increasingly vocal minority of elites began to acknowledge that the traditional concept of sovereignty was coming under attack within the international system.

This trend was led by Yu Qixiang (1993), who published an analysis in *Shijie Jingji yu Zhengzhi* that began with a simple recounting of the differences among scholars in China and the international community over the relationship between economic internationalization and state sovereignty. Generally, Yu found that scholars were divided into three groups over this issue: the first maintained that economic internationalization would not limit sovereignty; the second argued that internationalization limited sovereignty; and the third claimed that internationalization strengthened sovereignty. In order to determine which of these three positions was most accurate, Yu devised a strategy to examine the inseparability (*bu fenshan*), non-sharability (*bu fenxiang*), and non-transferability (*bu zhuanrang*) of traditional sovereignty, and the extent to which each had remained constant during the contemporary period. Overall, Yu found that each of these traits of the norm had been challenged by developments in the international political economy, and observed, "some countries, including China, in order to open, and attract foreign capital, to strengthen their own economy, in suitable regions within their own country, like China's South China Sea region, or Shanghai's Pudong, have given up a part of national territory to lease for the use of the development of foreign capital. This type of practical activity knocks apart the concept that sovereignty can't be shared" (Yu Qixiang 1993: 29). All of which meant, "as economic integration deepens and interdependence between states rises, state sovereignty is not any single country's own affair, but a right of all countries to coordinate and cooperatively resolve their own affairs, especially [when it comes to] economic rights" (p. 30).

Commensurate with such analysis, throughout 1993 Chinese officials continued to break down barriers between China and the global economy. While World Bank loans continued to flow into China at historic rates and Beijing worked to consolidate its relationship with the IMF, it was in China's concerted effort to jump-start the negotiations with GATT that this drive was most evident. During this period Beijing again reduced tariff rates on a wide variety of products, and began to take more aggressive measures to address the issue of non-tariff barriers to trade. In addition, it participated in a series of Working Party meetings over the course of 1993, and at the last of these sessions submitted a revised memorandum on trade that was accepted by the forum and moved talks into a new phase (Liang Wei 2002: 696). From this point on, discussion hinged on issues involving China's draft protocol, a document that the contracting members increasingly demanded address both tariffs and "domestic" issues such as transparency. As Stephen Kho (1998: 43) has observed, it was the United States (through a five-point plan outlining the steps Beijing needed to take before China became a participant in GATT) that played the leading role in making these demands in both the Working Party and in bilateral sessions with China. Although talks between Beijing and Washington broke down in the fall of 1993 over these issues, Chinese officials continued to express optimism about the prospects for China's return to GATT, and to expand upon the list of changes they had made to the Chinese economy in accordance with this goal.

Phase III, 1994–Present: Redefining Economic Sovereignty— New Ideas and New Commitments

In 1994, and throughout the rest of the 1990s, the Chinese began to more deeply alter their approach to economic sovereignty. During this phase (which is ongoing), Chinese official claims and unofficial analysis repeatedly acknowledged the transgression of economic boundaries by transnational forces.[7] Beijing's policies also directly accepted the authority of the main international economic organizations over extensive facets of the Chinese economy.

Throughout this phase, the core motivation behind Chinese changes continued to be a commitment to strengthening China's economy. In other words, fairly static interests in improving China's position in the international economic system remained the most prominent factor in leading to compromise. However, at the same time, the two external factors that had previously pushed Chinese practices forward became even more influential (especially in relationship to the accelerated set of talks between Beijing and the GATT/WTO).

First, the trade organization's contracting members (with the United States again taking the lead) imposed additional demands on China. At the same time, the trade organization itself became a more powerful and intrusive institution with the establishment of the WTO in 1995. Second, concepts of economic globalization and integration made increasing inroads into Chinese elite circles, as evident in the approving unofficial publications and official statements on these ideas that appeared during this period (even as a significant minority of scholars vehemently rejected globalization as a pretext for the expansion of U.S. hegemony).

These external material and normative pressures led to a broad-based questioning among officials and analysts of the ability and wisdom of preserving a narrow interpretation of sovereign economic rights. At the end of the decade they were paired with the top leadership's growing commitment to bolster reforms via entry in the WTO and a more general concern with using membership in the trade organization to secure a responsible image for China. Combined, these influences proved sufficient to transform the Chinese stance on economic sovereignty.

This development was first apparent in the more open stance Chinese analysts took on new boundary-transgressing trends and ideas in the international economy. Indeed, in 1994, contributors to *Shijie Jingji yu Zhengzhi* broadly agreed for the first time with Western analysis that such tendencies were increasingly transforming sovereignty's economic face, even as they grappled with the implications of this development for developing countries. For example, in analyzing patterns of regional economic integration in the developing world, Yu Qunzhi (1994: 18) commented, "The deepening of economic integration increasingly surpasses states' regulation, and requires that member states sacrifice a part of their state sovereignty." However, Yu also cautioned that historical experience had made developing countries especially protective of their sovereign rights, and this tendency would pose an obstacle to the development of deep integration among such countries.

Yu Qixiang and Jiang Yi expanded upon this commentary in a July 1994 issue of *Shijie Jingji yu Zhengzhi* by directly discussing the challenges such developments posed to sovereignty. Yu and Jiang noted that as globalization progressed, it would be essential to redefine conventional concepts of national interests. Moreover, as economic interdependence increased, nation-states would still be the dominant form of political organization in international politics, but "the nation-state and the concept of sovereignty will be somewhat eroded (*danhua*)" (Yu and Jiang 1994: 33). This trend was the result of the development of the world economy and, therefore, the "weakening of each country's economic decision-making power (*jingji zizhuquan*) was an unavoidable trend" (Ibid.).

Throughout 1994, contributors to *Guoji Maoyi Wenti* avoided directly addressing such a controversial issue, but continued to give extensive consideration to GATT. As seen in the preceding section, the trade journal had previously focused on describing GATT's main features and proposing ways to increase the compatibility between China and the trade organization. In 1994, analysis increasingly turned to the impact membership would have on specific industries and policies in China. Articles published in the journal at this time covered a variety of topics ranging from the difficulties that would emerge in protecting China's infant industries after resumption, to comments on China's developing-country status, to detailed descriptions of how GATT competition would influence China's transportation sector. In contrast with the content of earlier analysis, this wave of articles took as given (rather than as an issue to be negotiated and contested) GATT's authority over various economic activities, as well as the necessity for China to surrender the ability to enact extensive tariff and non-tariff barriers to foreign trade and investment upon joining GATT. Thus, for the first time, analysis was mainly preoccupied with proposing policy options that would allow China to effectively cope with the obligations of membership in the trade organization, rather than mapping out just what rights China should retain after membership was resumed. In this sense, analysts had again subtly shifted the terms of the Chinese discourse on GATT away from the divisive issue of protecting Chinese sovereignty and toward the more pragmatic concern of maximizing economic benefits within the constraining framework of the trade organization.

During this period, the major foreign policy journals did not devote nearly the same level of attention to GATT. However, articles in both *Shijie Jingji yu Zhengzhi* and the *Guoji Wenti Yanjiu* did emphasize the necessity of making extensive concessions if China was to regain its seat. In the former publication, Ren Quan repeated the claim that China was seeking to recover its legal status in GATT and should be treated the same as other developing countries. However, Ren (1994a) also suggested that membership in GATT would require China to take on extensive obligations that could not be deferred by developing-country status alone. Ren also listed reforms China should institute to facilitate a speedy end to the negotiations. Strikingly, Ren (1994b) advocated a thorough overhaul of virtually every aspect of China's foreign economic relations in order to conform to GATT rules. Wei Min's contribution to the latter publication steered clear of committing China to such broad changes, but also advocated a quick conclusion to the negotiations. In particular, Wei urged China to find a way to resume its seat in GATT prior to the establishment of the WTO at the start of 1995. As Wei noted, the WTO's rules and regulations were more rigorous than GATT's, and thus joining the trade organization after the WTO was founded would place more demands on Beijing (Wei Min 1994).

Cognizant of such an impending institutional change, Beijing took steps in 1994 to make China a founding member of the WTO (through securing a seat in GATT before it was replaced). Thus, Chinese officials again acted to liberalize China's foreign trade regime to make it more compatible with the trade organization's rules and norms (Liang Wei 2002: 698). In May, this process was accelerated by the visit of GATT secretary general Peter Sutherland to China, during which he expressed guarded optimism about the prospects for Chinese membership. His comments led Li Lanqing to assert that the Chinese government now realized that "it has to practice trade in accordance with international rules" ("Chinese Vice-Premier Meets" 1994). Moreover, in support of this rhetorical commitment, a comprehensive new foreign trade law was sent to the NPC Standing Committee. As Stephen Kho (1998: 46) has remarked, the timing of the announcement of this legislation, and its content (which mirrored the 1992 MOU on trade), were clearly intended as yet another indication of Chinese willingness to increase compatibility with GATT.

Despite such efforts, through the summer of 1994 little progress was made in either bilateral talks or in the Working Party. In both forums, the contracting parties, especially the United States, continued to express skepticism about Chinese willingness to abide by GATT's rules and regulations. At this juncture Washington formalized its opposition to China's joining GATT as a "developing country" and again pressed Beijing to make a host of additional reforms before rejoining the organization (Liang Wei 2002: 698). In response, Chinese officials increasingly began to pepper their commentary on GATT with expressions of frustration over what they viewed as the unrealistic demands being placed on China. For example, in the lead-up to the July meeting of the Working Party, Wu Yi cautioned a U.S. trade representative that "China will not restore its GATT contracting status at any cost" ("China Not to Trade" 1994). Significantly, this critical commentary was directed solely against the obstacles being placed in China's path to GATT, not the trade organization itself. Thus, even as policy makers grew increasingly desperate about the dimming prospects for an early resolution of the negotiations, they never questioned the legitimacy of GATT as an institution or the necessity to take on extensive "obligations" once becoming a member.

Evidence of such a trend can be found in the December submission of a draft protocol for Chinese membership at the final session of the GATT Working Party. Although this document failed to bring China and the contracting parties together (the draft report of the Working Party issued at this time outlined a host of outstanding concerns), its release still represented another significant step in the rearticulation of the Chinese stance on economic sovereignty. It moved Chinese commitments to the trade organization toward a concrete list of legal obligations. In addition, the expansive content of the protocol stood in stark contrast to China's initial 1987 memorandum informing GATT of Beijing's interest in resuming membership in the trade organization. Whereas the earlier document consisted of a skeletal description of China's foreign trade regime, the protocol committed China to making sweeping changes in virtually every aspect of its foreign economic relations (see Kho 1998: 48–49).

Despite the tabling of this document, there was no last-minute breakthrough in the negotiations, and China failed to enter GATT. In the aftermath of this failure, Chinese rhetoric on the trade organization reverted to denunciations of U.S. obstructionism and its influence not only on China but also on the very institution of GATT.[8] Yet, as heated as such criticism was, it never rose to the level of undermining Beijing's commitment to joining GATT and opening China's economy. In other words, at the start of 1995 the Chinese continued to want into both the global economy and the trade organization. Thus, even during the lull in negotiations after the establishment of the WTO, Chinese analysts continued to examine "Western" concepts of economic integration and their implications for sovereignty's role in international politics. On the one hand, many scholars still maintained that neither globalization nor integration had an extensive effect on sovereignty (Wu Xingzou 1995). On the other hand, expanding on earlier commentary on economic integration, a growing number of analysts acknowledged the impact of such trends on the structure of international politics.

This was particularly evident in a pair of 1995 contributions to *Shijie Jingji yu Zhengzhi*. In one of these, Liu Jingpo (1995: 52) agreed with Western scholars that the emergence of transnational economic flows in the international economy meant "some of the contents of traditional sovereignty have changed to a certain degree, and have been pounded (*chongji*) and influenced." However, Liu added that such compromise "is not handed over on a silver platter, but rather is [based on] the foundational premise of the realization of the state's highest interest. It is enacted through a certain degree of administration by international organizations, and does not negate the free practice of state sovereignty" (Ibid.). In the same vein, Ding Zhigang's (1995: 60) review of research by Western scholars on "integration" contended that "the common wish of developing countries is still to attain national independence and unrestricted sovereignty," but acknowledged that economic integration made it increasingly necessary to "give up (*rangdu*) some state sovereignty in order to protect the highest national interest."

Later in the year, in the pages of *Guoji Maoyi Wenti*, Zhao Weitian applied these arguments to the issue of WTO membership. Zhao (1995: 20) argued, "All international treaties bring both benefit and harm to their member states. If one wishes to gain the benefits of these agreements" it is necessary "to take on their obligations and respect their principles, even to the extent of limiting one's own freedom and sovereignty." Therefore, to the extent that China could gain from membership in the WTO, it should be willing to make sacrifices.

In line with such an assessment of the necessity of compromise, but absent a direct acknowledgment of the impact of cooperation on Chinese sovereignty, China's leaders continued to expand their involvement in the main multilateral economic organizations in 1995. To begin with, Beijing's ties with the World Bank remained robust throughout this period (for example, China again secured extensive loans). In addition, consultations with the IMF regarding China's external debt and currency policies were regularly held. More significantly, in the spring the Chinese also took steps to initiate talks with the newly formed WTO.

Initially, the Chinese turn to the WTO was limited to a renewed Sino-American dialogue on trade issues (including China's long-standing position that it be granted developing-country status in the trade organization) (Liang Wei 2002: 706). However, during the summer of 1995 Chinese officials also engaged in informal talks at the WTO's headquarters in Geneva (and officially applied for observer status in the trade organization). In the fall this process picked up speed when the chair of the informal Working Party visited China and there was a new round of high-level calls by both U.S. trade officials and top Chinese leaders to start negotiations between China and WTO. While in

New York in October, Jiang Zemin informed his American audience, "China's early entry into the WTO will be conducive to Sino-U.S. trade and China will work toward this end" ("China's Entry" 1995). The following month at the Asian-Pacific Economic Cooperation (APEC) meeting in Japan, the Chinese leader followed this declaration with an announcement of China's intention to implement a 30 percent tariff reduction on thousands of products during 1996.

In response, the United States issued a "secret" five-point road map that out-lined the main conditions that Washington sought to attach to Chinese mem-bership in the WTO ("Barshefsky" 1995). With this proposal, the United States, and by extension the rest of the trade organization's contracting members, had raised the bar for Chinese accession. In other words, China was once again being asked to demonstrate its willingness to increase the compatibility between its economic system and the trade organization, and to negotiate on issues that had previously been considered solely within the confines of Chinese econom-ic sovereignty. As Chapter 4 demonstrated, it was precisely at this point that U.S. initiatives vis-à-vis Taiwan were bluntly rejected as interference in, and encroachment on, China's jurisdictional sovereignty. In contrast, true to the pat-tern that emerged during the first half of the 1990s, Beijing's response to the new American WTO demands was less confrontational. As a result, in the win-ter of 1995–96 the gap between the Chinese stances on jurisdictional and eco-nomic sovereignty once again grew.

During this period official Chinese commentary continued to laud the role of the trade organization in the contemporary international economic system. Moreover, the discussion of economic integration and globalization that had gained increasing prominence in unofficial analysis in the early 1990s also began to find a place in the official Chinese discourse. For example, in the fall of 1996, Qian Qichen even included a brief reference to the "tide of globalization" in his annual statement to the UN General Assembly. Yuan Shaofu, a lower-rank-ing Chinese official, added to Qian's comments in a subsequent address to the Second Committee of the General Assembly. Yuan declared, "the globalization and liberalization of the world economy is a contest in economic power and technical capabilities, which has created opportunities for economic growth and development and at the same time presented serious challenges to the weak economies that find themselves in a disadvantageous position in the contest" ("China Urges Creation" 1996).

Although each of these references was quite cryptic, and bracketed by reminders of the inequalities globalization created, their importance should not be overlooked for two reasons. First, they represented a convergence between the unofficial and official discourse on the international economy. Indeed, in 1996, contributors to the major foreign policy journals had begun to replace the far-reaching commentary of the preceding years with much more conservative estimates of the impact of integration and globalization on the international political system. In other words, just as China's top officials were beginning to emphasize boundary-transgressing ideas in their public statements, analysts were starting to express new reservations about such trends. Second, despite the reserved way Qian and others addressed the idea of globalization and integration, by allowing such terminology into major foreign policy addresses, China's leaders were at least tacitly acknowledging the potential power of such forces in the contemporary international system. This acknowledgment implied that China's economy could only be strengthened by greater opening and participation in an increasingly complex international economic system. In other words, as Qian Qichen himself remarked at the UN General Assembly, "only by enhancing international exchanges and cooperation on the basis of equality and mutual benefit, can we jointly cope with new problems arising in the course of world economic advance and achieve sustained common development and prosperity" ("Chinese Vice Premier Addresses" 1996).

Such pragmatic assessments of the state of the international economy framed Chinese interactions with all three of the main multilateral economic organizations through the second half of 1996. Once more, Beijing continued to garner the support of the World Bank and extend upon its multi-year record as its largest borrower. In addition, at the end of the year, Beijing signed new agreements with the IMF that obligated it to abide by the fund's guidelines on exchange rate regulations ("People's Republic of China" 1996). Moreover, on the WTO negotiations front, Chinese officials also implemented several additional policies to gain international support.

At the start of the following year, the Chinese followed up on these measures by offering a revised draft protocol for accession. At the time, *Inside U.S. Trade* ("China Protocol" 1997) argued that this document was little more than a reproduction of China's last-minute 1994 offer to GATT; however, as the first comprehensive bid of the post-WTO period, it was still significant and revealed an abiding interest in the trade organization. Generally speaking, the draft protocol stated that China's trade regime should be applied uniformly, Beijing should publicize China's trade rules, and it would accept judicial review. However, substantial differences remained between Beijing and the contracting parties (with the United States again taking the lead in highlighting the discrepancies) over the specific measures China would take before and after accession.

In the following months, rhetorical sparring between U.S. and Chinese trade representatives escalated, and more detailed negotiations were held. In addition, Chinese trade officials continued to insist that they were willing to further liberalize China's trade policies in line with WTO norms. A June Xinhua news release carried a telling comment by Wang Zixian, a researcher at the Ministry of Foreign Trade and Economic Cooperation (MOFTEC), who stated that China would continue to institute reforms in accordance with "prevailing international economic practice" ("China to Reform" 1997). Moreover, in citing a previous comment by Long Yongtu (one of the leaders of China's WTO negotiations), Wang provided one of the first public revelations of the extent to which economic reformers within China viewed the WTO accession process as a vehicle for advancing their agenda for the Chinese economy. Wang noted, "China's 10–year long strenuous process of applying to integrate with the world free trade family has helped establish a market mechanism in the Chinese economy. Old-time convoluted government meddling has been cleared out of businesses" (Ibid.).

Despite such rhetoric, and a stated Chinese interest in reaching a deal with the United States in time for the October 1997 summit between Jiang and Clinton in Washington, no new agreements were reached at this time. In response to this failure, in late November the Chinese pledged to make additional tariff cuts and then forwarded another round of proposals to both the Working Party and the United States. In commenting on the tariff reductions, MOFTEC officials indicated many enterprises were beginning to express concerns about their ability to survive "constant and extensive lowering of tariffs" ("Lower" 1997). However, they argued that lower tariffs would increase competitiveness in the "worldwide trend toward free trade and globalization," and "create a better environment for China's entry into the WTO" (Ibid.).

Even as such moves were being made, the financial crisis that had started in the summer with the rapid devaluation of the Thai baht rapidly spread to Indonesia, and then South Korea, and began to threaten the economic stability of the entire Asian region. This crisis occupied a central role in Chinese foreign economic policy making as 1997 drew to an end. Throughout this period, China's leaders repeatedly proclaimed that China would play a positive role in containing the crisis through resisting pressure to devalue the renminbi.

This approach was widely lauded by China's neighbors and strengthened China's relationship with each of its main counterparts at the WTO negotiating table. Thus, while the crisis may have created new doubts among some Chinese officials and analysts about opening the Chinese economy too far and too fast in order to facilitate accession, it also provided China's trade representatives with a new way of spotlighting their interest in the trade organization. Long Yongtu observed that China's currency resolve should "help the international community to increase their awareness of China's attitude and image in international trade and economic affairs. In this sense, it will contribute to the process of negotiations on China's accession to the WTO" ("Currency" 1998).

In the spring and summer of 1998, this hope proved to be misplaced as the contracting parties, and especially the United States, once again argued that China had failed to comprehensively demonstrate an ability to abide by WTO norms. Although both sides later promised to step up negotiations in the lead-up to President Clinton's late June visit to China, high-level bilateral meetings produced little more than agreement that more talks were needed. Thus, it was not surprising that no new deals on accession were announced during Clinton's stay in China. Indeed, through the remainder of the year, both China and the United States publicly downgraded the WTO issue (even as Washington privately continued to urge the Chinese to move negotiations forward through a pair of letters from Clinton to Jiang outlining American support for a speedy conclusion of the negotiations) (Fewsmith 1999).

The relatively quiet Clinton initiative eventually led to another round of intense negotiating sessions, and by the end of 1999 the two sides had finally come to an agreement on the basic terms of China's accession to the WTO. However, before turning to the specifics of the endgame of China's accession process, it is worth noting that during this period Chinese analysts were beginning to express some misgivings about the trade organization, and were also reconsidering the pros and cons of economic globalization and integration for sovereignty's role in international politics.

Unofficial discussion of these trends in the major foreign policy journals increasingly revolved around how trade and financial integration could leave developing countries open to intense international pressure and in even greater need of protecting their sovereign economic rights. Zhou Rongguo (1997) wrote cautiously about the complex balance of opportunities and challenges China faced at the end of the 1990s due to global and regional economic integration. He Fang (1997) argued that integration and globalization called for a strengthening, rather than weakening, of the role of the state in foreign economic relations. Wang Hexing (1998) expanded on He's warning, and contended that the Asian financial crisis had illustrated how international organizations under the control of developed Western states had exploited and even "interfered" in the economic affairs of developing countries. In Shijie Jingji yu Zhengzhi, Tang Renwu seconded Wang's and He's cautions in an article on the "myth of integration." Tang (1998: 15) acknowledged that "the process of economic integration must encompass a softening, giving up and evolution of a part of state sovereignty," but added that integration had to be voluntary to be legitimate and noted that Western developed countries often "used the pretext of 'economic integration' to attain the political goal of interfering in other countries internal affairs."

In 1998, contributors to Guoji Maoyi indirectly acknowledged such warnings, but continued to promote China's accession to the WTO. Consistent with the claims previously made in *Guoji Maoyi Wenti*, membership was still seen as entailing a complex mix of costs and benefits that would allow for a strengthening of the Chinese economy in an increasingly competitive international economic arena. However, in an argument that was later featured prominently in official rhetoric on the trade organization, analysts also held that membership would provide China with a more active role in framing the rules that would regulate the international economic system (Yi Xiaozhun 1998). In addition, in a particularly defensive article that dismissed what were described as myths in China about the WTO, Zhang Hanlin (1998: 32) took pains to point out that membership would not entail a "compromise on economic sovereignty" since accession was voluntary. Furthermore, participation in the WTO would not lead to a sacrificing of the national interests of member states, but rather to the construction of a more long-lasting, stable, and scientific political and legal system.

Although such critical appraisals suggest there was a substantial contraction in Chinese approaches to economic sovereignty in 1997–98, the interview data collected during this period do not support such a conclusion. To a remarkable degree the diverse group of experts on the international political economy I interviewed agreed that sovereign change was extensive and inevitable. This sentiment was given its clearest voice by a senior scholar in Shanghai, who claimed, "With changes in the actual international economic conditions, the practice of sovereignty changes. This means that we need to be more selective in approaching the sovereignty issue. Each country needs to pick, to make choices—selective choices—in terms of how they are going to express their sovereignty" (Personal interview, Fudan University, May 18, 1997). Or, as a scholar affiliated with People's University noted:

> I see that the development of economic internationalization is a positive trend; it will influence the practice of sovereignty in regard to economic issues, which in turn influences the legal system and society. For China, this does not mean that direct intervention in Chinese affairs is acceptable, but it does limit China's ability to be independent, and creates a new level of interdependency between China and other countries. (Personal interview, Apr. 17, 1998)

The interviewees also strongly supported China's WTO bid, and approvingly framed China's efforts to join in terms of a rearticulation of Chinese economic sovereignty. They argued that WTO norms limited the economic policies of member states. Furthermore, most of them went beyond simply reporting on general trends in the international economic system, pointing out that China had specifically adapted its own practice of sovereignty as part of its drive for GATT/WTO membership.

Some scholars also noted that during the WTO negotiations China had placed limited restrictions (*zhiyu*) on its sovereignty. The most commonly cited proof of such a move was the reduction of tariff levels to meet GATT norms for developing countries. Those interviewed also referred to broader changes in the foreign trade system as indicative of Chinese flexibility on economic sovereignty. As observed by a noted expert on Sino-U.S. relations, "WTO talks have forced us to think about sovereignty. We have had to consider how much we should give up after joining. We want the economic benefits of being in; we also know that we must give up on some things to get these benefits. This is the vital issue facing us: how much more we can give up?" (Personal interview, CICIR, May 14, 1997).

As discussed above, in 1999, even more than in previous years, the Chinese calculus on these issues played out within the framework of talks with the United States about the WTO. At the start of the year, both Washington and Beijing renewed their effort to reach an agreement on Chinese membership in the WTO. As a result, in February and March both the United States and China issued public statements expressing optimism about the prospects for making significant progress in bilateral negotiations in the lead-up to Zhu Rongji's April visit to the United States. Although the United States then downplayed such a possibility, in a press conference held against the backdrop of the spring meeting of the NPC, Zhu Rongji informed reporters, "now is the time," and added, "China is prepared to make the biggest concessions within its abilities. . . . I am very hopeful that we will be able to reach an agreement" ("Premier Zhu" 1999).

Despite pronounced tensions in the Sino-U.S. relationship over the expanding conflict in Yugoslavia, Zhu followed up on this rhetoric in Washington in early April with a new offer on accession that largely met the terms the United States had previously articulated. Nonetheless, due to the Clinton administration's reluctance to accept Zhu's offer, and the American decision to publicize the concessions Zhu had made, the Chinese premier returned to Beijing with China's cards out in the open and without a final deal on the WTO on the table.[9] This caused China's own trade representatives to backtrack and unleashed a wave of criticism within China against Zhu. In addition, Beijing was reportedly faced with opposition to the WTO drive from the interior provinces and from industrial sectors likely to bear the highest economic costs of membership (Lam 1999).

Following the NATO bombing of the Chinese embassy in Belgrade in early May, the current against WTO concessions grew even more pronounced as the United States was repeatedly denounced. Unofficial analysis published in the major foreign policy journals at this time gave full airing to such resentment and anger. More specifically, as discussed in Chapters 4 and 5, analysts focused on

American hegemonism, a concern that also colored discussion of what had previously been generally accepted as the relatively benign (indeed, progressive)
trends of economic globalization and integration. Zou Jiayi (1999: 9) argued
that the Asian financial crisis and Kosovo served as a warning to take even
greater care to protect domestic markets and tightly "grasp economic decision-
making power (*zizhuquan*)." More specifically, Zou recommended that China
take a more active role in protecting its basic interests in the accession process,
thus avoiding "paying an unnecessary price" (p. 10). In addition, Xiao Gang cautioned that globalization was an uneven process that was primarily beneficial to
Western capitalist countries, and that those states were attempting to harness the
process to secure benefits. Xiao directly criticized America and the other
Western states for placing unreasonable obstacles in China's path to the WTO,
arguing that if the Western position on China's WTO membership was accepted, China would be attacked, its security undermined, and its politics rocked; it
could even face "national separation." According to Xiao, "This is precisely the
real goal of the group under Western control (*xifang guojia tongzhi jituan*)" (Xiao
Gang 1999: 32).

   As critical as such commentary was, other analysts continued to promote
more positive interpretations of globalization and advocate additional compromises in order to facilitate Chinese participation in the international economic
system. For example, in the same issue of *Shijie Jingji yu Zhengzhi* where NATO
and the West were attacked for trampling on international law, Cheng Yan (1999:
65) argued that economic globalization had "weakened the property of sovereignty (*zhuquan shuxing de ruohua*)." For Cheng, this trend required a realization
that states compromised on sovereignty in order to gain national interest and
aid; without getting beyond "outdated concepts it would be impossible to benefit from globalization" (p. 66).

   By the end of the year, it was this more flexible analysis that appears to have
informed Chinese decision making on the WTO. Thus, although American
expectations were quite low when talks resumed in late September, over the following two months China and the United States finally reached bilateral agreement on the terms of China's entry into the WTO. President Clinton reportedly sparked this turn of events in mid-October by telephoning Jiang Zemin to
encourage the Chinese to return to the WTO negotiating table.[10] Although
China did not officially acknowledge this contact, Jiang repeatedly endorsed
China's WTO bid during a tour of Europe just a few days after it was reported
to have occurred. In addition, back in China, U.S. Treasury secretary Lawrence
Summers met with Zhu Rongji in an attempt to bridge the differences
between the two sides. Following this high-profile meeting, and a last round of
negotiations, on November 15 China and the United States signed an agree-

ment on Chinese accession to the WTO ("Press" 1999).

By signing the agreement, the Chinese cleared the main remaining hurdle to China's involvement in the trade organization and opened the way to more thoroughly integrating the Chinese and global economic systems. To be clear, it was a bilateral understanding, and did not directly commit China to the trade organization itself. However, in formally meeting outstanding U.S. demands, it did decisively move China's involvement with the WTO beyond the realm of pledges toward a more legally binding position, and formally committed China to implement policy measures that would significantly limit its economic rights.

The agreement touched upon virtually every aspect of the Chinese economy. It charged Beijing with making sweeping new reductions of tariff and non-tariff barriers to foreign trade and accepting a review mechanism for monitoring compliance. It also outlined restrictions on Chinese exports to the United States involving product-specific safeguards, and bound China to accept the WTO's dispute-settlement procedures following accession ("Clinton" 1999).

Following this rapid turn of events, Beijing continued to navigate the terms of its relationship with each of the main multilateral economic institutions. At the start of 2000 the Chinese signed an MOU with the IMF to establish a Joint China-IMF Training Program ("IMF" 2000). At the same time, although World Bank loans to China failed to reach the levels seen in the mid-1990s, ties between the World Bank and China continued to grow. Moreover, the focus of China's negotiations with the WTO shifted away from Washington toward the trade organization itself.

During 2000 and 2001, the Working Party became the primary site of negotiations as China made its final drive for membership in the WTO. However, before substantive progress could be made, questions had to be addressed regarding pending U.S. congressional votes on granting China permanent normal trading relations (PNTR) status, as well as European concerns over securing a China-EU agreement. These issues dominated the initial post–Sino-U.S. agreement meeting of the Working Party. In May, Beijing came to initial terms with the EU, and Jiang used the forum provided by this milestone to again emphasize Chinese responsibility and call for U.S. congressional approval of PNTR ("China, EU" 2000). When the U.S. House of Representatives subsequently passed PNTR legislation in May, it appeared that an accession protocol in the Working Party would soon follow. Yet, during the summer, disagreements between Mexico and China on membership became more pronounced, and the U.S. Senate postponed voting on China's PNTR status as questions arose about the level of support for passage of such legislation.

As these events unfolded, discussion in the Working Party increasingly turned to the specific terms of China's accession protocol and the report on China that the Working Party itself would issue to the WTO. Intense debates and negotiations took place over the nature of China's review mechanism, the type of judicial review process that would be established, and what safeguards China and the member states would accept. While the Chinese had tentatively agreed to accept forms of all three of these commitments in the 1997 draft protocol, reaching agreement on the specifics proved to be daunting.

In the fall of 2000 additional meetings of the Working Party were convened and these sessions were again marked by friction between China and the member states. The Chinese vigorously defended their position, but also made limited new concessions. On the heels of such developments, Jiang Zemin highlighted the issue of economic globalization in his address to the annual APEC meeting. The Chinese president lauded this trend as bringing "new opportunities for various countries and regions," but also warned against its abuse by "a few countries." To prevent abuse, Jiang called for the establishment of "effective rules" to regulate economic activity and close the gaps between the north and the south ("Jiang Zemin" 2000).

Such rhetorical posturing produced few substantive results in the spring of 2001, as China and the contracting parties continued to quibble over a wide range of issues. However, in the summer, the United States and the EU reached agreements with China on several issues. In addition, drafts of each of the key accession documents were forwarded to the WTO. This was followed by the conclusion of China's last set of bilateral negotiations (with Mexico), and the final meeting of the Working Party in September. China then signed its membership protocol and annex in November, and became a full member of the WTO a month later.

As part of this package China committed to establish a uniform and transparent trade regime and establish a judicial review process. Beijing also pledged to eradicate all special trading rights "in conformity with the WTO agreement," liberalize trading rights "consistent with the WTO agreement," and end state trading within China. Consistent with the bilateral agreement reached with the United States in 1999, the average tariff rate was to be cut below 10 percent by 2005, and reduced to even lower levels on agricultural products. In addition, remaining nontariff barriers were to come down, and China's import and export licensing system would be brought into compliance with the WTO. Price controls on all but a few products (specified in the annex to the protocol) were to be replaced by "market forces," while subsidies, taxes, technical barriers to trade, sanitary and phytosanitary measures, and dumping regulations would all be adjusted to meet WTO rules. Beyond such reforms, Beijing also accepted the insertion of the hotly debated product-specific safeguard mechanism in the protocol. It also agreed to a rigorous transitional review mechanism (TRM) that would evaluate the terms of Chinese compliance with the protocol nine times during the first ten years after accession.[11]

At the end of 2001, Jiang Zemin explained why China had agreed to take on such extensive commitments in a way that closely linked globalization with Chinese membership in the WTO. Jiang suggested that nonparticipation in the WTO was simply not an option, and that compromise was the only way for China to grow stronger. For example, on the day of the submission of the protocol, the Chinese president observed to an audience in Guangdong, "during the process of economic globalization, the economic and technical cooperation of a country with other parts of the world can be expanded advantageously only after the country establishes an economic and trade administrative system adaptable to internationally accepted norms and in line with the country's actual conditions" ("Chinese President on China's" 2001).

Unofficial analysis published between the signing of the Sino-U.S. bilateral agreement and Chinese accession to the WTO dwelt at length on these themes. Analysts tended to emphasize the benefits of membership, but also outlined the potential costs (Li Cong 2000; Zhang Songtao 2001; Zheng Bingwen 2000). In addition, most scholars avoided touching upon the controversial issue of the extent China's sovereign rights would be limited following accession. However, a handful of analysts did breach this sensitive topic (mostly in discussing the WTO's dispute resolution mechanism), and those who did so widely concurred that membership did place limits on Chinese sovereignty (but since these restrictions were voluntary, they were acceptable) (Li Cong 2000; Zhang Naigen 2001).

Broader commentary on the international economic system, especially on the issue of globalization, was more wide-ranging as scholars articulated strikingly divergent opinions on how much economic sovereignty's role in international politics had been transformed. On one side, a small group of "sovereignty hawks" took a more critical stance on globalization than the one Jiang had adopted to justify China's accession to the WTO. One of the most direct statements of this position was articulated by Sun Jianzhong, a professor affiliated with a PLA-run university, in *Taipingyang Xuebao*. Sun (2000) argued that it was essential for developing countries to jealously guard their sovereign rights in an era of economic globalization. For Sun, it was natural for developed countries to promote the erosion of sovereignty's role in international politics, as that suited the new national interests of such states. However, he also warned that developing states did not share such interests and should not be taken in by stories of globalization and integration. In light of such dangers, Sun urged developing countries to secure their independence and territorial integrity and to protect their political status and ability to choose their own economic and political systems (see also Sun Jian 2000; and Yu Xiaofeng and Jia Yajun 2000).[12]

In contrast with Sun's dire warnings, the majority of scholars took a more flexible line on sovereignty, one that viewed globalization as inevitably having a profound impact on the norm and requiring all states (especially developing ones) to make new choices about the scope of their sovereign rights. For example, three issues after Sun's article appeared in *Taipingyang Xuebao*, Yu Zhengliang (2000), a leading scholar then at Fudan University, argued that in the context of globalization it was essential to develop a "levels-of-analysis" approach to sovereignty. Within such an approach, it would be possible to reach a new, more flexible understanding of sovereignty's role in international politics. Yu argued that China had already moved in this direction and had reaped the rewards of such a move.

In interviews I conducted in the winter of 2001–2, analysts more directly acknowledged a broad diminution in economic sovereignty within the international system due to globalization and integration. Even more strikingly, with a few notable exceptions, all of the individuals interviewed agreed that China had shown flexibility on sovereignty in dealing with the WTO. Running against the tide, one prominent international legal scholar argued that participation in the trade organization (and other multilateral institutions) had no impact on sovereignty (Personal interview, CASS, Dec. 24, 2001). However, each of the other forty-plus interviewees claimed that China had taken on extensive international obligations that constrained its economic sovereignty. One young scholar at Peking University, who had become renowned for his expertise on the WTO in the late 1990s, summarized this position during his interview. He noted that, at the end of the decade, Chinese approaches to sovereignty had changed in two ways. First, a broad consensus had emerged in elite circles that globalization was inevitable and that it was better to ride such a wave than to be caught under it. Most elites agreed that this would require a new interpretation of Chinese sovereignty, one that was amenable to more extensive transgressions of China's boundaries. Second, with membership in the trade organization, China had no choice but to abide by WTO norms (Personal interview, Dec. 20, 2001).

This sentiment dominated unofficial commentary on the WTO published during the initial post-accession period, with repeated emphasis on the importance of accession in what was seen as a rising tide of economic globalization within the international economic system. Most analysts saw these trends as both inevitable and positive, calling on China's leaders to wholeheartedly embrace them. For example, in *Dangdai Faxue*, Xia Yi observed that any state that accepted the WTO dispute mechanism had to relinquish (*fangqi*) certain aspects of its own sovereign rights, while also agreeing to regulate all economic activity in accord with the rules and norms of the WTO. Xia even protested that any attempt to diminish this aspect of WTO's power by placing sovereign rights above all else would be sure to damage both the WTO and the overall international economic system (Xia 2002: 38). Jin Xiaochen (2003: 92) took this point even further by contending that in the area of economic activity, globalization had already led states to "give up" or accept "constraints" upon their sovereignty. It was essential (*you biyao*) for the WTO's dispute mechanism to become more powerful and intrusive. In contrast, other analysts staked out a more critical stance on these issues and balanced their support for China's joining the WTO with warnings about the ongoing need to protect Chinese sovereignty in the wake of such a momentous development (Du Xinli 2003; Jiang Changbin 2002). In addition, a handful of commentators forwarded much blunter refutations of the WTO accession deal (Yang Hongmei and Zhou Jianming 2003; Yang Fang 2003; Zuo Dapei 2003).

This type of criticism of globalization was especially pointed. However, such voices were marginal within the unofficial Chinese discourse. Indeed, during this period the majority of analysts continued to stress globalization's benefits. Many writers even acknowledged that it had already significantly diminished the sovereign authority of all states (including China) to govern economic activity.

This sentiment was aptly captured by a 2002 article by Zu Qiang that appeared in *Shijie Jingji yu Zhengzhi Luntan*. Zu argued that globalization was a "double-edged sword" (*shuang ren jian*). It allowed for greater flows of capital and labor between states, thus presenting developing countries with a "historic opportunity," but it also "challenged" their "economic sovereignty," increased north-south tensions, and created new concerns about economic security (Zu Qiang 2002: 8).

Beyond such cautious commentary, a handful of scholars continued to promote a broader interpretation of how such developments were changing the face of international politics. For example, in early 2002, Liu Li, an assistant researcher at the Central Party School, contended that economic globalization had significantly eroded all states' sovereign economic rights, which demanded a "new understanding of sovereignty" (*xin zhuquan guan*) that acknowledged the differences between facets of the norm that are exclusive and those that can be shared (Liu Li 2002).

As commentators contemplated these issues within China, substantiating Beijing's position within the WTO became a focus of Chinese foreign economic relations following the 2001 accession.[13] This task encompassed two distinct components. First, the Chinese, as members of the WTO, had to articulate their stance on the complex trade issues being negotiated within the Doha Round, and weigh in on trade disputes within the organization. Second, as China's protocol laid out steps that Beijing was required to take following accession, policy makers in Beijing faced the challenge of implementing policies that lived up to such commitments. During the initial post-accession period, Chinese behavior with regard to both of these issues was of concern to the contracting parties. On the first front, there was worry that China might act as a revisionist power within the trade organization by actively seeking to revamp its rules and norms. On the second front, the question of China's ability to comply with the commitments it had made loomed large.

Chinese behavior in 2002–3 somewhat relieved such concerns. At Geneva, China maintained a relatively low profile, with the exception of vocally parrying all Taiwanese attempts to raise their status within the organization. In short, Chinese representatives have worked to familiarize themselves with the WTO's complex rules and procedures (Pearson 2002). Moreover, Beijing has made only very selective use of the trade organization's dispute mechanism (to date only joining in with complaints raised by other member states, such as the one by Japan and EU against U.S. steel tariffs, rather than initiating complaints on its own).

Chinese compliance efforts have largely followed the same pattern. Most observers agree that Beijing has (with some important exceptions) moved in the direction of living up to the commitments it made in the accession protocol. Indeed, during 2002 Beijing reportedly made substantial progress on reducing tariffs, standardizing economic rules and regulations, and developing "capacity-building" procedures (training officials in WTO standards) (Kapp 2002). Moreover, China's top leaders repeatedly underscored their commitment to such a process ("NPC" 2002).

In 2003, Beijing continued to implement laws and issue statements to demonstrate its ongoing resolve to comply with its WTO commitments. A particularly high-profile aspect of this activity was the open discussion of amending China's foreign trade law to bring it more in line with the trade organization's norms and rules (a measure that was finally taken in spring 2004). However, such measures were offset by increasingly divisive wrangling between China and the other contracting parties over the TRM process, and a surge in international criticism of Beijing's record in adhering to the schedule it had agreed to for dismantling a wide range of both tariff and nontariff trade barriers.

Because of such irritants, doubts within the WTO over China's post-accession compliance record became more pronounced. For example, the 2003 TRM review noted seemingly troubling trends in Beijing's compliance record (Wilder 2003). Chinese officials bristled at such criticism, and underscored the difficulties Beijing had faced since joining the WTO. However, at the same time (and consistent with previous interactions with the trade organization), Chinese leaders pledged to work toward reducing such frictions. Indeed, in a spring 2004 speech, Long Yongtu promoted this theme with specific reference to Beijing's increasingly responsible role in international politics fueled by Chinese confidence in, and integration with, the global economy ("Official" 2004). In short, despite growing questions about China's role within the WTO, Beijing remains deeply involved with the trade organization, and has (for the most part) worked to comply with the obligations it accepted in its push for membership.

Conclusion

The pattern of Chinese involvement with GATT/WTO during the last two decades initially grew out of a shallow set of adaptations. However, during the 1990s it was increasingly driven by a combination of sustained external pressure for change, the strengthening of the structure of the main international economic organizations (especially GATT's replacement by the WTO), and the widespread embrace in China of norms of economic globalization and integration. These forces led to the making of a series of final concessions on WTO membership that proved sufficient to allow China to reach a bilateral agreement with the United States. In 1999, this agreement, and China's subsequent 2001 accession to the WTO, constituted a major milestone in the evolution of the Chinese position on economic sovereignty.

Conclusion: Intransigence and Change—
The Chinese Battle to Secure Sovereignty
in a Changing World

Sovereignty, and the extent to which it creates impermeable walls between any given state and other actors in the international system, lies at the core of contemporary China's evolving relationship with the rest of the world. The system-wide interpretations of the main components of sovereignty moved in the direction of boundary transgression starting in the 1970s, and at the time Beijing's stance on the norm was clearly out of step with such developments. However, China's position on sovereignty changed over the course of the 1980s and 1990s. While China's leaders were quite successful at promoting their interests in both integrating and unifying in the 1980s through enacting relatively congruous policies vis-à-vis each component of sovereignty, during the post-Tiananmen period Chinese words and actions on separate aspects of the norm diverged.

This final chapter addresses two issues raised by this trend (and the causes underlying it). First, it reconsiders the evolution of China's increasingly divergent approach to sovereignty with reference to the main points of contention within the "new sovereignty" debate. Second, it examines how Beijing's partial compromises on certain components of sovereignty, and refusal to make any concessions on other facets, have created new, mounting difficulties for those who govern China. Although most of these challenges lack the weight to fundamentally alter the dual approach of integrating while unifying, the ongoing, and escalating, conflict across the Taiwan Strait increasingly has the potential to upset such a balancing act.

The Chinese Approach to Sovereignty
and the "New Sovereignty" Debate

Although contributors to the "new sovereignty" debate now generally agree that sovereignty's role in the international system is more variable than it was once conventionally understood to be, they remain divided over two significant facets of the issue of sovereign change. First, they continue to differ over how extensive current change within contemporary international politics may be (Hall 1999; Krasner 2001a, 2001b; Lake 2003; Steven Smith 2001). Second, they do not agree on why states shift or do not shift their position on sovereignty over time (Keohane 1995; Krasner 1999; Wendt 1999). Chapter 2 laid out the reasons why China is a crucial case for this literature; in this section I outline the implications of the recent development of the Chinese approach to sovereignty for both of these points of contention within the "new sovereignty" debate, and in so doing substantiate the claim made in the introduction of this book that China's stance is now quite consistent with broader trends in international politics.

Limited Sovereign Change

Beijing's insistence on maintaining sovereignty's role as an anchor of China's foreign relations reveals the inaccuracy of the prediction about the incipient demise of the norm that many students of international politics made over the course of the 1990s. Indeed, the Chinese case shows that sovereignty's role within the international arena remained quite robust during this period. However, the ongoing rearticulation of the Chinese stance on sovereignty during the reform era also belies the argument that the norm's role in international politics is static. In addition, it contradicts the conventional wisdom in the work of Chinese foreign policy specialists that China's position is fixed and unyielding. On the contrary, the Chinese approach to sovereignty during the reform era was quite malleable, and the changes that occurred generally contributed to the strengthening of the systemic trends in regard to each of the specific components of the norm outlined in Chapter 1.

During this period the general role of territorial sovereignty within the international system was relatively consistent as the vast majority of states continued to be delimited by clearly defined, demarcated, and defended boundaries, and differences between many neighboring states over the specific location of their shared boundaries remained a persistent source of tension within international politics. However, alongside such continuities, there was a systemic turn away from the use of military force to secure contested territory and a concomitant rise in the use of international legal and political forums to mediate disputes.

During the 1980s and 1990s the Chinese approach to territorial sovereignty clearly paralleled this general shift in the broader international arena. Chapter 3 showed that Beijing's stance remained steadfastly boundary-reinforcing, but the way China's leaders went about attempting to achieve this goal changed considerably. In the 1990s the Chinese relinquished the majority of the expansive territorial claims they had previously made against their main continental neighbors, and, as a result, they were able to successfully conclude talks on the location of virtually all of China's contested land borders. In the one significant case where agreement proved to be elusive, Chinese diplomats worked with their Indian counterparts to greatly reduce tensions in the border region. At sea, the Chinese stance was less flexible, as Beijing worked to strengthen its claim to the South China Sea and escalated its political and military efforts to secure Chinese rights over this region. Yet, since the mid-1990s China's behavior has somewhat softened. Thus, although the Chinese approach to border relations through the late 1970s appeared unusually aggressive, subsequent behavior quickly converged with the more moderate stance on territory taking root within the rest of the international system.

The scope of change in system-wide interpretations of jurisdictional sovereignty during this period was quite limited as the right of sovereign states to maintain the unity of the people who resided within their territorial boundaries remained one of the core organizing tenets of international politics. However, the increasingly close pairing of this facet of sovereignty with the principle of self-determination during the post–World War II era subtly modified its meaning. Moreover, when this coupling extended beyond the colonial context and self-determination gained new prominence through the breakup of several sovereign states—most notably, the Soviet Union and Yugoslavia—following the end of the Cold War, even more fundamental questions were raised regarding the sanctity of existing jurisdictional boundaries between states.

Throughout the 1980s and 1990s China's leaders and foreign policy analysts were acutely aware of these developments in international politics. Chapter 4 demonstrated that they unrelentingly worked to insure the preeminence of jurisdictional sovereignty within the system by forcefully arguing that self-determination was a right that should only be applied to the unified peoples within already-sovereign states, and, more substantively, in their policies on Tibet, Taiwan, and Hong Kong. During the 1980s, Beijing championed the extension of the right of self-determination for colonized peoples around the world, and domestically experimented with relatively moderate policies. At the end of the 1980s and through the 1990s, the Chinese played a leading role in vocally opposing a liberal application of self-determination norms within international politics. At the same time, China's leaders took decisive steps to clamp down on dissent in Tibet, orchestrated the handover of sovereignty over Hong Kong (from the British), and took a more combative stance against Taiwan.

Such a resolutely boundary-reinforcing interpretation of jurisdictional sovereignty, combined with a determination to maintain authority over peoples and regions within the state's domain and an unwavering dedication to regaining rights over a place and population considered to lie within the scope of a state's legitimate jurisdictional rights, is relatively commonplace in international politics. The collective weight of such commitments has insured that the jurisdictional facet of sovereignty retains a relatively sacrosanct place within the system.

Thus, while the virulence with which the Chinese have maintained their right to rule over Tibet, Taiwan, and Hong Kong has been at times characterized as "antiquarian" and "Victorian," one is hard pressed to find more than a handful of states that have relinquished their jurisdictional rights when faced with similar challenges. Nonetheless, the depth of resistance to Beijing's rule, and the extensive resources at the disposal of opposition groups in all three regions (but especially, Taiwan), coupled with the crucial importance of all three areas to the central government's basic national security and economic development goals, do set China apart from most other international actors. They make China's jurisdictional struggles, particularly the conflict over Taiwan, among the most prominent and potentially destabilizing in the international system.

While jurisdictional sovereignty was the subject of intense contestation but ultimately limited change in both China and the international system during the 1980s and 1990s, during this period the face of sovereign authority underwent a substantial shift. In international politics, this development began in the late 1960s with the strengthening of the UN's Charter- and treaty-based human rights instruments, and the establishment of a growing number of INGOs dedicated to monitoring human rights conditions around the globe. It gathered momentum over the course of the 1980s and 1990s via a system-wide wave of participation in the system. For example, in 1979, only four main human rights treaties had come into effect, with 267 state ratifications of them. In contrast, in the late 1980s there were 533 parties to the then six major human rights documents. This trend accelerated in the 1990s. A report to the 2003 inter-committee meeting of the human rights treaty bodies found that over 80 percent of states had ratified at least four of the main human rights agreements (for a total of 975 of the potential 1,358 possible ratifications) (Methods 2003, also see Bayefsky 2001). As noted in Chapter 1, these developments did not result in system-wide agreement on the specific content of human rights, or the best manner to assure their protection. Moreover, it is also clear that the participation of any given state in the international human rights system should not be assumed to correlate with improvements in its human rights record. However, such caveats aside, the rise of such a regime has led to a system-wide weakening of the principle of non-interference, the central tenet of the authority component of sovereignty.

At the end of the 1970s, China, perhaps more than any other state, had expressed firm opposition to the early stages of this development. During the subsequent reform era, Chapter 5 argued, China's leaders continued to express skepticism about human rights, but also became deeply involved in the international human rights system. The first steps in this direction took place when China began to participate in the UN CHR and its subcommission, and acceded to a number of the main international human rights treaties. The official Chinese rejection of the international condemnation of Beijing's handling of the 1989 protest movement temporarily derailed this trend. However, it then expanded over the course of the 1990s with the signing of the International Covenant on Economic, Social, and Cultural Rights (ICESCR) and the International Covenant on Civil and Political Rights (ICCPR), a series of official endorsements of the system, and the emergence of increasingly direct endorsements of human rights norms within unofficial Chinese analysis. Although this record of participation has not resulted to date in a marked improvement in human rights conditions within China, it still amounts to a remarkable (if incomplete) opening of China's political system to international review, and as such it has modified the Chinese position on the inviolability of China's sovereign authority.

This record again falls well short of placing China on the margins of the international system. Indeed, the story of China's reluctant compromises on human rights and carefully orchestrated rearticulation of its position on sovereign authority could easily be retold with reference to the behavior of many other states. What sets China apart is the degree to which its behavior has been the subject of prolonged international criticism (both from other states and from human rights INGOs), and the ability that Chinese officials have shown to counter (both domestically and internationally) the charges leveled against China. In other words, while Beijing's stance on both human rights and the broader principle of sovereign authority changed during the 1980s and 1990s, the Chinese also showed they had the ability to directly influence the content of the international human rights system (especially in regard to promoting the issue of economic rights and preserving the role of the principle of non-interference within international politics). In short, as Ann Kent (1999: 244) has remarked, in the human rights arena China has been a "taker, shaper and breaker of norms."

Such influence was much less palpable in China's stance on the economic component of sovereignty. In this case, it is first evident that since the late 1960s economic sovereignty's role in international politics has been eroded by the rising prominence of the GATT, IMF, and World Bank. This trend first gathered momentum in the 1970s with the expansion of all three institutions' authority to intervene in their member states' economic affairs, and was sustained during the 1980s through their frequent utilization of this right. Membership in these organizations then became nearly universal in the 1990s (Boughton 2001; Das 2002; "IMF at a Glance"; "World Bank"). Moreover, as participation in these institutions rose, globalization and economic integration norms grew in acceptance. As a result, the lines that had previously been drawn between each sovereign state's economic affairs were in practice supplanted by an increasingly dense web of transnational economic ties and regulatory agencies.

As was the case in regard to sovereign authority, in the late 1970s the Chinese position on economic sovereignty was adamantly opposed to such trends, but here Chapter 6 illustrated that the subsequent shift in Chinese words and actions occurred at a faster rate and was more extensive. In the early 1980s Beijing quickly moved to become a member of both the IMF and World Bank. While it showed more caution in joining the GATT, by the end of the decade Beijing had also made a concerted effort to begin negotiations with this key international economic organization. In addition, throughout the 1990s when talks with GATT, then the WTO, stalled, Beijing reacted by pledging to speed China's transition toward a market-oriented economy, and explicitly promised specific changes in Chinese law in order to bring it more into line with the rules and principles of the trade organization. Against this backdrop, unofficial Chinese analysis repeatedly highlighted the speed with which economic globalization was occurring and frequently observed that this trend had already begun to undermine sovereignty's established role in the international system.

The shift in the Chinese stance on economic sovereignty in the direction of boundary transgression was very much in line with the behavior of other states. As mentioned above, during this period almost all states moved to join the three main international economic institutions. Moreover, in their bid to participate in such organizations and hasten integrating with the international economic system, most states appear to have taken on similar obligations and ceded a comparable degree of authority over economic affairs within their own boundaries.

In sum, China is much less of an outlier on sovereignty than it was portrayed to be during the late 1990s by those warning of the dangers of a "rising China." In fact, it is usual for political leaders worldwide to compromise on certain facets of sovereignty, even as they reinforce its other facets. For example, in Asia, Tokyo continues to cede significant portions of Japanese territory for use by the U.S. military but has consistently maintained its rights to relatively insignificant

offshore islands claimed by China and Russia, even though this position significantly complicates relations with these countries. Moreover, even as Jakarta
reluctantly ceded Indonesia's claims to East Timor, it has gone to great lengths
to insure and more deeply inscribe Indonesia's jurisdictional sovereignty over
Aceh and Papua. In many parts of Africa, states that have effectively ceased to
rule over much of their sovereign territory endeavor to maintain the location
of boundaries created by colonial magistrates. In Europe, Moscow has arguably
ceded much of Russia's economic sovereignty to international economic
organizations (in return for loans and restructuring programs designed to bolster the country's faltering economy), but has resolutely refused to yield on the
issue of Chechnya (and bristled at all international criticism of its handling of
the breakaway region). In South America, Peru and Ecuador have repeatedly
granted international actors extensive rights within their borders, yet until
recently were engaged in a prolonged conflict over a relatively small patch of
territory they both claimed.

Such patterns of behavior point to a pair of new conceptual considerations
for students of international politics. First, the range of sovereignty-related
words and actions underscores the value of conceptualizing the norm in terms
of distinct bundles of sovereign rights. Disaggregating sovereignty in this way is
a necessary first step in coming to terms with the complexity of the evolving
Chinese stance on sovereignty. More specifically, mirroring changes in the international arena, Beijing's interpretation of the "functional" or "regulative" rules
of all four facets of sovereignty was clearly fluid during the reform era and, in
regard to sovereign authority and economic sovereignty, such malleability
arguably extended into the realm of the norm's basic, "constuitive" features. If
an analyst frames his or her consideration of sovereignty in either narrow
(focusing solely on territorial concerns, or just economic issues) or vague
(defining the norm as merely a right in international politics) conceptual terms,
then such diversity of behavior is impossible to detect.

Second, the research findings speak directly to the tendency within much of
the "new sovereignty" literature to weight analysis in the direction of discover-
ing and proving that sovereignty's role in international politics is changing.
Admittedly, the framework for analyzing sovereignty forwarded in this book is
embedded within such a tendency, and the evidence presented here is consistent with the growing list of scholarship that argues sovereignty is not a constant in the contemporary international system. Yet, it is also clear that stasis has
been as much an aspect of the Chinese position as has change. Much of what
Chinese leaders have done to define sovereignty during the reform era has consisted of repeating existing claims and trying to maintain an unchanging interpretation of China's sovereign rights. In other words, sovereignty as something

static, which stands as an assumption within Waltz's work, and is so frequently challenged in the "new sovereignty" literature, has never achieved a "taken-for-granted" status in Chinese foreign relations. Keeping things the same took as much, and sometimes more, work than allowing them to change.

The Causes of Change

The pattern of Chinese behavior can only be explained with reference to the shifting point of intersection within China between "old" sensitivities to any perceived infringement on Chinese sovereignty, domestic political developments that reframed how China's leaders approached sovereignty-related issues, and international pressures (both material forces and normative influences) for change. Moreover, the weight of international influences was uneven across the four facets of sovereignty. This argument is consistent with the constructivist turn in international relations (in emphasizing the power of old and new ideas in international relations), but it is an integrative variant of this general approach in that its analytical scope includes a consideration of the relationship between power, interests, and ideas.

I argued in Chapter 3 that the Chinese position on territorial sovereignty during the 1980s and 1990s was grounded by all three of these variables. Throughout this period, China's leaders and policy analysts, versed in the nationalist narratives of the establishment of the PRC, shared a collective vision of the vast stretch of territory China had historically "lost" and maintained a common rhetorical commitment to overcome this "disgrace" by restoring what they viewed as the legitimate location of each of their states' contested boundaries. Nonetheless, they also tended to view border relations with reference to the existing regional balance of power that during the 1980s was not especially promising in terms of providing China with an opportunity to actually realize its claims. Moreover, following the ascendancy of Deng Xiaoping's reform and opening policy in the early 1980s, China placed a relatively high premium on maximizing regional stability (as a necessary condition for realizing such a policy line). This interest, although insufficient to erase the underlying normative drive to realize China's basic territorial aspirations, was strong enough to bring about a marked decline in hostilities within each of China's contested border regions over the course of the decade.

China's extensive territorial compromises during the 1990s were the product of a shift in the balance between these factors. Over the course of this period, the story of China's "lost" territory proved to be quite durable (with reference to both continental and maritime boundaries), and continued to frame Chinese considerations of each of China's contested border relations. However, the weight of such an ideational construct was increasingly offset by the paramount importance placed on building a more stable regional security dynamic. This interest caused Beijing to act cautiously in the early 1990s when the collapse of the Soviet Union placed China in a position to press extensive, preexisting territorial claims along its northern border. Over the course of the decade, it also prompted Beijing to partially demilitarize the Sino-Indian border. Yet, here, the relative continuity in the military balance within the border region and the strategic importance to both sides of crucial segments of the disputed land precluded a similar resolution of outstanding differences. In the South China Sea, this interest in regional stability also had a moderating effect on Chinese policy, but the strategic and economic importance of the contested territory made China's leaders even less willing to compromise and more inclined to use military force in support of Beijing's territorial claims in the region. Nonetheless, in the second half of the decade, despite an increase in the capabilities of the Chinese navy to project power in the South China Sea, concerns with preserving regional stability proved strong enough to partially efface previous Chinese reservations about allowing the dispute over this territory to be discussed in regional multilateral forums.

Chapter 4 contended that an underlying nationalist commitment to sustain (in the case of Tibet), and complete (with regard to Hong Kong and Taiwan), the project of unification, anchored China's stance on jurisdictional sovereignty. However, whereas during the early 1980s this drive was partially balanced by the new interests and strategic considerations created by Deng's reform and opening line, by the end of the decade the historically conditioned Chinese intractability on jurisdictional issues was bolstered by a convergence of a range of factors. First, during the late 1980s and early 1990s, local material challenges to Chinese jurisdictional claims in both Tibet and Taiwan intensified. In both cases, this trend directly threatened the jurisdictional status quo, and stands out as the main catalyst for the subsequent shift in Chinese behavior. Yet, it alone does not account for the sustained hardening of Beijing's stance. To fully explain this trend it is necessary to include a consideration of the impact that the end of the Cold War had on China's leaders. Simply put, Beijing viewed this event as undermining much of the strategic rationale for the United States (China's most significant bilateral partner) accepting Beijing's contested jurisdictional claims, and as such directly challenged China's right to both regions. In addition, Beijing also perceived it as spurring the development in international politics of a more permissive interpretation of the balance between states' sovereign rights and groups' rights to self-determination.

The more extensive changes in the Chinese position on the authority component of sovereignty that occurred during the 1990s grew out of a distinctly different configuration of causal factors. This being said, Chapter 5 posited that

during the 1980s the development of China's stance on the sovereign authority / human rights dynamic was largely the result of new interests overcoming
preexisting normative biases against the human rights system within the
Chinese leadership, and the abiding awareness within Beijing of the utility of
non-interference claims for the Chinese state. When Beijing was later challenged by both domestic and international critics for its human rights record
(especially in regard to the suppression of the 1989 student movement), such
criticism had the short-term effect of simply reinvigorating historically based
animosity toward the system and pushing Chinese behavior in the direction of
rejecting human rights (with particular reference to the preeminence of the
principle of non-interference).

Yet, over the course of the 1990s, external forces played a more constructive
role in reshaping the Chinese position on human rights. During this period sustained international attention to human rights conditions in China (especially,
although not consistently, from the United States) increased the instrumental
value of concessions for the Chinese, and led to policy moves designed to placate Beijing's critics. In addition, the increasing salience in Beijing of concerns
over projecting a responsible, mature image in international politics (to offset
charges that China's rise posed a threat to the system) fostered an environment
that made such moves more appealing to the Chinese leadership. Finally, and
more fundamentally, prolonged participation in the human rights system
markedly increased the extent to which China's leaders and foreign policy analysts viewed international human rights norms as legitimate. As such, it eroded
historically grounded reservations about human rights. It also reduced
entrenched reticence to any international monitoring of human rights conditions in China, and consolidated the belief that the protection of human rights
(at least in theory) was a basic responsibility of the Chinese state. In short, it
altered the foundations of Chinese thinking about human rights issues.

Chapter 6 showed that the shift in China's stance on economic sovereignty also
stands at the intersection between new interest articulation and "old" normative
structures. The policies of the early reform era that allowed for a limited loss of
authority over China's foreign economic relations were products of the ascendancy of Deng's pragmatic call to strengthen China through the selective use of foreign technology and investment. Moreover, in the post-Tiananmen period,
growth (and, by extension, continuing the process of integration) became an even
higher priority for Chinese leaders as they attempted to stabilize the shaky legitimacy of their rule through the dual strategy of cultivating nationalism and building the economy. With such priorities, interest in the potential rewards of GATT
membership grew, and policy makers sacrificed much of what they had previously contended was within the scope of China's economic sovereignty.

In the mid-1990s, this impulse for change was augmented by new instrumental and normative factors. First, GATT's contracting members repeatedly imposed increasing demands on China during the negotiations and via the publication of various "road maps" for Chinese accession. Second, the trade organization itself became more powerful and intrusive with the establishment of the WTO in 1995. Third, starting in the late 1980s, but especially in the mid-1990s, concepts of economic globalization and integration made increasing inroads in Chinese leadership circles. This process was never complete, as many Chinese analysts vehemently rejected globalization as a pretext for the expansion of U.S. hegemony. However, despite such objections, as part of their acceptance of this trend as an inevitable one within the international system, a majority of influential policy analysts reevaluated the ability and wisdom of preserving a narrow interpretation of China's sovereign economic rights. At the same time, the bid to create a responsible international image led Beijing to use pledges to participate in the trade organization as evidence of its benign international role.

Thus, in the 1980s it was primarily Deng's pragmatism that provided the underlying motive for limited changes in the Chinese stance on each aspect of sovereignty (by overcoming the reticence to change created by historical and ideological causes). Yet, over the course of the 1990s, external factors (both material forces and new normative influences) pushed newly emerging interpretations of sovereignty from the international arena into China. This calls into question basic facets of both rationalist and ideationalist explanations of sovereign change that have been forwarded within the "new sovereignty" debate.

Rationalists cannot account for the pervasive role of ideational factors in influencing the development of the Chinese stance on sovereignty. The underlying continuities in Beijing's position can only be partially explained with reference to rational calculations. On the contrary, reticence to change was to no small extent a product of entrenched, normative trends within China in regard to the necessity of overcoming the "humiliation" caused by past violations of China's sovereign rights. As such, China's leaders and policy analysts tended to view sovereignty as a principle of intrinsic value. Thus, sovereign boundaries were to be reinforced, not because of what China could gain from such moves, but rather because failing to do so would constitute a betrayal of those who had fought to protect China. This impulse made the Chinese more reticent about relinquishing sovereign rights than cost-benefit analysis alone can account for. However, despite such a pronounced proclivity, we have seen that Beijing did allow for a significant transgression of limited aspects of China's sovereign boundaries over the course of the 1990s. In these cases, the influence of external normative factors on the Chinese approach to sovereignty also extends well beyond the limited role they have been given within rationalist explanations of sovereign change.

The factors that underlay Chinese sovereignty-related behavior also expose underlying shortcomings in existing ideationalist explanations of sovereign change. First, defending sovereignty's established role in international politics had a greater utilitarian value for Beijing than is commonly acknowledged in the ideationalist strand of the "new sovereignty" debate. In short, boundary-reinforcing sovereignty-related words and actions constituted one of the most powerful tools in Beijing's foreign policy kit at times when China was under attack from external critics and internal forces bent on either regime change or radically challenging the jurisdictional claims of the PRC. Second, most of the early compromises that Chinese leaders made on sovereignty grew out of transparent calculations of the relative costs and benefits of allowing any given transgression of China's sovereign boundaries. Finally, the process of "norms diffusion" in China (which eventually played a central role in bringing about more extensive changes in the Chinese position on sovereignty) was more complex than has been accounted for in this literature. The Chinese came to terms with the meaning of international normative changes always within the framework created by preexisting domestic normative structures. As such, external norms only gained prominence through a process of active selection and reinterpretation on the part of Chinese leaders and scholars. Even as these actors began to integrate new ideas into their own consideration of sovereignty-related issues, they projected their own positions on sovereignty in international politics (and as such helped shape normative change in this arena).

The arguments made in this book are broadly compatible with recent eclectic analysis in security studies (Alagappa 2003; Suh, Katzenstein, and Carlson 2004). They also resonate with the claims made in Risse and Sikkink's (1999) "spiral model" of norms diffusion in that here too an emphasis is placed on the explanatory value of identifying separate phases, or stages, in the development of any given state's foreign relations and national security making. However, at a more fundamental level the book may be read as an attempt to show the value of combining the rationalist and ideationalist strands of the "new sovereignty" debate within an integrative constructivist framework. As such, the analytical claim about sovereign change advanced in this book is that leaders of individual states may initially become more willing to negotiate new interpretations of the norm in order to gain short-term economic or political benefits. However, such calculations normally take place within the context of preexisting concepts about the legitimate scope of the state's sovereign rights that tend to tilt behavior in the direction of boundary reinforcement. Out of incremental, self-interested changes in the direction of boundary transgression, more extensive shifts can unfold due to the inadvertent creation of new sensitivities to external pressures for change, extended involvement in new institutional structures, and the production of new normative concepts about sovereignty.

Looking Ahead: Looming Challenges
to China's Approach to Sovereignty

Beyond speaking to these broad issues of analyzing changes in sovereignty's role in international politics, the book also sheds light on the increasingly complex nature of China's relationship with the rest of the international system over the course of the 1980s and 1990s by focusing on the evolution of the Chinese stance on the norm. During this period, China's leaders were particularly adept at controlling the pace and scope of change in the Chinese position (and thus the boundaries that separated China from the rest of the world). In short, words and actions on each component of the norm were quite discrete, with little spillover from one facet of sovereignty to the other. The final question to address then is how long Beijing will be able to keep moving practices in the divergent directions that began to take shape in the 1990s. In other words, at the start of a new century, how robust is the dual project of integrating China with a changing international arena while completing the project of unifying a multi-national state built upon the remains of the Qing empire?

To date, this stance has been quite durable. In fact, such an incongruent approach to sovereignty is one of the defining characteristics of China's foreign relations during the reform era, and the main contours of such a position are largely consistent with the changes that have taken place in the international arena. As such, divergence in behavior is not inherently unstable. However, over the course of the last decade the partial concessions the Chinese made on territorial sovereignty, sovereign authority, and economic sovereignty have triggered still relatively inchoate developments (at home and abroad) that may reorient the current direction of change with regard to each of these aspects of the norm. I treat these issues in order of the degree to which they challenge China's leaders, although it is unlikely any of them will destabilize the dual project of integrating while unifying. In contrast, the increasing volatility of China's most intractable jurisdictional challenge—namely, Beijing's commitment to reunifying Taiwan with the mainland—is a much more explosive issue.

Territorial Sovereignty: Relinquished Claims, Concerned
Neighbors, and Nationalist Sentiment

On the surface, the carefully orchestrated compromises China's leaders made on territorial sovereignty during the 1990s cost them little, and the benefits garnered have arguably grown over time. However, such gains have also been partially offset by the emergence of new difficulties. First among these was the fact that despite the general improvement in the Sino-Russian relationship during the 1990s, relations within the border region itself remained quite strained.

Throughout the decade local differences over the location of the contested section of the eastern sector of boundary (agreed to in principle in the 1991 border treaty) complicated the process of actually demarcating this line and created lingering resentment on both sides of the border. More significantly, while the rise in border trade that followed the normalization of relations stimulated economic growth in the border region (especially the eastern segment), it was accompanied by a surge in illicit cross-border activity (such as smuggling and population flows) that proved to be especially hard to monitor and police. Such illegal activity tended to reinforce negative cross-border perceptions. As a result, while conventional military threats to security have become a thing of the past, managing the border during a period of relative calm has continued to be daunting.

In addition to these problems in Sino-Russian border relations, establishing control over the boundary between China and the Central Asian republics has also proven to be problematic despite the territorial agreements Beijing reached with the leaders of Kyrgyzstan, Kazakhstan, and Tajikistan since 1991. Such difficulties were compounded by the political instability in each of these states (but especially Tajikistan), and persistent differences in the region over how to contain the rise of Uyghur nationalism. In addition, the compromises that each of the Central Asian republics made on territory (in order to secure even more extensive Chinese concessions) generally were unpopular in Central Asia and strengthened, rather than lessened, concerns about China's increasingly dominant role in the region (particularly in Kazakhstan and Kyrgyzstan). The recent marked increase in Chinese trade and investment in Central Asia has arguably done little to relieve such worries and may actually reinforce misgivings about Chinese intentions. Thus, even following the formal resolution of each of China's territorial disputes with the Central Asian republics, differences over territorial sovereignty have remained pronounced.

Along China's southern frontier, the 1993 and 1996 confidence-building agreements effectively ended the likelihood of large-scale military conflict with India; however, they also raised expectations in both countries for a relatively quick resolution of the underlying territorial dispute. The failure to reach such an understanding, and India's 1998 nuclear tests, quickly revealed such sentiments to be misplaced and created a new level of frustration on both sides. Moreover, final resolution of the border dispute remains quite remote. Although the persistence of this dispute has not hobbled the overall improvement in relations between Beijing and New Delhi, the inability of both sides to address this issue at a time when the Sino-Indian relationship is stronger than it has been in decades underscores the limited potential for compromise. One can surmise that in the event of a broader break in the bilateral relationship, territory will quickly reemerge as the subject of open confrontation between the two sides.

The South China Sea continues to be the site of such conflict. Although Beijing's policies there have become more moderate (especially since the mid-1990s), concerns in Southeast Asia about China's intentions in the region remain pronounced. Many in the region have questioned the underlying motive behind such a turn, arguing that it is primarily strategic and instrumental (designed to buy time for Beijing to develop the military capabilities needed to realize relatively static territorial interests in the South China Sea), rather than a fundamental shift toward more cooperative behavior. In order to overcome such doubts, Beijing has made even more concessions (for example, signing the 2002 multilateral code of conduct confidence-building measure). However, since the Chinese leadership can ill afford to give up their claim to the region, it is unlikely they will risk making additional, extensive compromises. As a result, tensions over sovereign ownership of the South China Sea are likely to persist for the foreseeable future.

In sum, while each of China's contested border relations are significantly more stable today than at the start of the 1980s, territorial sovereignty continues to be the subject of controversy, and potentially, limited military confrontation. Moreover, Beijing is arguably in a less favorable position to make further compromises on border issues today than it was in the early 1990s. To begin with, China's outstanding border disputes are appreciably more difficult to solve than the ones that the Chinese have already resolved (in that the territory in question has greater value for each of the involved claimants). Second, as argued in Chapter 3, the concessions China has made on territory had already created some resentment among Chinese foreign policy analysts in the mid-1990s (as related in personal interviews) in regard to Beijing's failure to press for more land at a time when China's neighbors were in a comparatively weak strategic position. While interviewees placed less emphasis on this theme in 2001–2, they were quite insistent on the basic intractability of China's position on the location of the Sino-Indian border and its claim to the South China Sea (and right to the Diaoyu Islands). Thus, it is likely that significant compromises on any of these issues by Beijing would generate even more anger within this community and, more significantly, cut against the grain of popular nationalism within China. Thus, I do not anticipate that Beijing will make any major territorial concessions in the near future. On the contrary, I expect the Chinese will continue to seek to maintain the territorial status quo within each of China's outstanding territorial disputes.

Sovereign Authority: A Partially Opened Door

Beijing's limited, but expanding, participation in the international human rights system (and by extension acceptance of a partial erosion of the boundaries created by China's sovereign authority) produced fewer tangible benefits than did its moderation on territorial sovereignty. Nonetheless, during the 1990s Beijing's willingness to engage in human rights dialogue did generate short-term diplomatic gains, positive international media coverage, and arguably enhanced regime legitimacy. However, over the course of the decade, the failure to consistently follow up on progressive human rights rhetoric with measurable improvements in human rights conditions in China also began to make it harder to attain such results. Such slippage was first evident in the mid-1990s in the international arena when China's human rights critics increasingly began to denigrate its concessions on human rights as "hollow" and "superficial." By the end of the decade, human rights INGOs remained skeptical of even Beijing's most extensive commitments to participate in the human rights system. These organizations, and the international media, instead concentrated their attention on the extensive human rights violations still occurring in China. Such voices were less prominent in each of Beijing's main bilateral relations, but here too, pointed criticism of the pace of human rights reform has continued despite persistent Chinese attempts to extinguish it. As a result, human rights today remain a central, contested issue in China's relationship with the rest of the world.

The domestic costs of Chinese hypocrisy on human rights have so far been less pronounced, but could eventually be even more significant. As discussed in Chapter 5, a significant number of Chinese foreign policy analysts have recently published articles suggesting that human rights norms have gained broad acceptance within this community. In addition, a minority of these scholars have publicly called for both a strengthening of China's legal system and improvements in its human rights record. In the near term, the inclusion of a reference to the state's obligation to protect human rights in the revised constitution approved by the NPC in spring 2004 will strengthen these voices. Over a longer time it will arguably make it easier for both intellectuals and activists within China to hold Beijing accountable for future violations of human rights. In other words, it should make the Chinese state more accountable to its own people.

China's leaders could react to such international and domestic developments by retracting their earlier endorsements of human rights. Yet, this outcome is unlikely. Frustration in Beijing continues to mount and generate resentment against perceived international interference in China's internal affairs in the name of human rights. Such an environment is not conducive to more extensive Chinese human rights concessions, but it will not bring about any major, regressive shift in Chinese human rights behavior (as Beijing has already invested too much in its current involvement in the international human rights system). Internally, blatant violations of human rights through a crackdown on China's domestic human rights critics. However, there is no need for Beijing to take such a move since domestic proponents of human rights are not powerful enough to strongly promote their position in China, and human rights related issues do not yet constitute a central facet of popular dissatisfaction with Communist Party rule. Thus, over the next decade, we will likely see incremental increases in China's compliance with its international human rights commitments, coupled with limited violations of human rights where such moves are perceived as necessary for defending national security and political stability.

Economic Sovereignty: Integration as a Source of Social Instability?

The initial rearticulation of the Chinese stance on economic sovereignty, most visible in the shift in Beijing's position on the World Bank and IMF, and GATT/WTO, brought China's leaders a long list of benefits. As discussed in Chapter 6, membership in the first two organizations made China eligible for concessionary loans and assistance in the event of balance of payment or currency crises. Beijing's drive for admission to GATT was both an indication of China's overall commitment to economic opening, and a means of opening foreign markets to Chinese goods. In composite, overtures to all three organizations were part of a broader effort to strengthen the economy by making China a more appealing location for foreign capital and investment. The stellar growth of the 1980s and 1990s is ample testimony of the success of China's leaders in achieving these goals.

Nonetheless, gains were only possible as long as Beijing accepted a diminution of the scope and impermeability of China's economic sovereignty. In other words, they came at the expense of China's earlier boundary-reinforcing stance on this facet of the norm. The costs of such concessions will largely be determined by how much the Chinese economy continues to grow now that China has become a member of the WTO. If growth proves to be sustainable, and China continues to consolidate its position as a world economic power, then the sacrifices China's leaders made in the 1980 and 1990s in order to integrate China into the international economy will have relatively few disruptive short-term consequences.

Through the first half of this decade, Beijing successfully steered the Chinese economy in this direction. However, even as it accomplished this goal, questions emerged about the impact of export-led growth, symbolized by the WTO accession agreement, on Chinese society. It is increasingly apparent that although opening has fueled the overall rise of the Chinese economy, it has deepened preexisting regional inequalities in China and created a host of new challenges for the Chinese leadership. First among these has been the deepening economic divide between China's coastal regions and interior. The marked surge in incomes in major urban areas has contributed to this gap, while also rapidly widening the already vast disparity between the rising standard of living of city dwellers and the comparably stagnant standard of living of peasants. According to a recent survey conducted by a pair of Chinese journalists, conditions in the Chinese countryside have deteriorated, rather than improved, as the economy has become more open (Chen Guidi and Chun Tao 2004). Problems, however, are not limited to remote rural areas. On the contrary, increased competition in the manufacturing sector has created unprecedented pressures on inefficient state-owned enterprises, and resulted in high levels of unemployment in many cities (especially in the northern industrial belt). At the same time, those who have managed to keep their jobs have often been subjected to dangerous, deteriorating working conditions, or, in many cases, have simply not been paid. To make matters worse, official corruption (at all levels of government) now appears to be endemic in a system that retains features of both a market-oriented and a planned economy.

China's leaders, especially following Hu Jintao's rise, have responded by implementing high-profile policies to placate those who have fallen behind during the later reform era. This, alongside the selective use of force to stifle dissent, has so far stemmed the tide of social unrest created by the economic dislocations caused by opening, and allowed for the continued expansion of Deng's policy line. However, in the event of a major downturn in the global economy, it is far from clear if such stopgap measures will be sufficient to prevent widespread protest. Indeed, a sustained contraction in the world economy would both elevate societal pressures on Beijing and reduce policy makers' ability to address them. Moreover, within such an environment, China's WTO accession protocol, which has been Beijing's greatest concession on economic sovereignty to date, is likely to emerge as a target for elite and popular criticism.

As previously noted, the protocol contradicts deep-seated Chinese sensibilities about the need to maintain and protect each facet of China's sovereign rights. China's leaders, with the help of the vast majority of Chinese policy analysts, overcame such sensitivities over the course of the negotiations by methodically effacing the link between sovereignty and the WTO. As effective as this was, in a period of economic distress, disaffected opposition leaders could quickly undo such efforts by drawing attention to the parallels between the protocol and the unequal treaties that led to the historical establishment of China's treaty port system. Moreover, such views would likely find a ready audience among China's disenfranchised workers and peasants. They would be viewed all the more sympathetically because before accession there was virtually no open discussion of the potential drawbacks of WTO membership. Thus, it is possible that nationalists and leftists within China could use such arguments to effectively attack the position of the reformers in the party who were instrumental in the negotiations. In such a case, it would not be hard to imagine that the WTO deal could be openly rejected, or at the very least vilified, by a new generation of Chinese leaders.

In any case, the current leadership has staked its right to rule on the promise of ongoing growth and integration. Thus, a radical inward shift of China's economic activity is highly unlikely. Drastic change will only occur if social unrest becomes so threatening that it provokes a violent political clampdown or regime change. Neither is likely in the near future, as China's leaders have repeatedly proven themselves to be expert at maximizing the benefits of economic integration while maintaining an ironclad grip over the state. However, the new pressures outlined above will also make it especially difficult for Beijing to comply with all of its WTO commitments. Moreover, due to the extensive safety and monitoring mechanisms built into China's accession protocol, such behavior is likely to generate a firestorm of international criticism and could quite easily trigger retaliatory actions on the part of China's main trading partners. If targeted in this way, it is quite easy to predict that the Chinese would then respond with their own countermeasures. Such a dynamic would quickly produce a volatile trade war. Nonetheless, even facing such a challenge, it is unlikely that China's leaders would lead their country into a new era of economic isolationism. On the contrary, they are likely to continue economic integration in hopes of sustaining growth.

Jurisdictional Sovereignty: Maintaining Chinese Rule
over Tibet and Hong Kong, and the Rising Threat
of Conflict across the Taiwan Strait

The Chinese stance on jurisdictional sovereignty has not only remained resolutely boundary-reinforcing over the course of the last two decades, but has become even less flexible. During this period, Beijing retained control over Tibet and took over Hong Kong, but failed to make any progress in its drive to return Taiwan to the mainland. China's leaders have maintained these positions for both strategic and identity-based reasons. Quite simply, they could not afford to make any major concessions on China's claim to any of the three regions. When Beijing's jurisdictional rights over these territories were challenged, this inevitably provoked a harsh Chinese response.

Such a stance has already cost Beijing significantly in Tibet, where it has required China to maintain a strong military / security force to contain and prevent pro-independence protests, been the source of frequent international criticism (in both bilateral and multilateral forums), and led to a series of large-scale economic development projects. In recent years, these expenses have grown. While Tibet has not been the site of extensive, open, political protest since the late 1980s, it remains restive and is still the subject of intense surveillance efforts on the part of the Chinese. At the same time, Beijing continues its efforts to spur the development of the Tibetan economy through massive construction projects (such as the still unfinished Qinghai-Tibet railroad) and a wide range of economic subsidies. It has also waged an international campaign against the Dalai Lama, portraying him as a dangerous ideologue, who, before the Chinese liberation of Tibet, cruelly ruled over a backward, isolated land.

These efforts notwithstanding, the Dalai Lama's stature in the international community has actually grown over the last decade. Whereas in the late 1980s he was a religious figure who had a relatively small but devoted group of followers in the West, today he is a pop culture icon who enjoys approval ratings that rival those of even the most beloved public figures. In other words, Beijing has quite clearly been losing its war of words with the Tibetan leader, and as a result the Chinese have increasingly found themselves on the defensive within the international arena over the Tibet issue. Alongside human rights, Beijing's policies in Tibet have emerged as one of biggest liabilities in China's foreign relations. Moreover, it is hard to imagine that China's leaders and policy analysts will reverse this trend. Although the Dalai Lama's popularity outside of China may cool off, his status as a peaceful, engaging, spiritual leader has already gained broad acceptance. As a result, his calls for protecting Tibet's history, culture, and people will continue to have a strong appeal in the international community for the foreseeable future (and Beijing will have to continue to struggle to counter this trend with its own public relations efforts).

In contrast, within Tibet the dual policies of stifling dissent and spurring economic growth that Beijing implemented during the 1990s have proven to be relatively effective. While occasional anti-Chinese attacks have occurred over the past fifteen years, there have been no replays of the large public demonstrations against Chinese rule that rocked Tibet during the late 1980s. In addition, despite the controversy over the selection of the new Panchen Lama, Tibet's monasteries have largely been brought to heel. Moreover, ongoing Han migration into Tibet's cities, and the overall modernization of these urban areas, has arguably begun to erode Tibetan culture and identity in the region, and has increased the gap between Tibetans in Tibet and those living in exile. In short, today Chinese rule may still lack legitimacy within Tibet, but Beijing's control over the region has been consolidated.

As a result of these trends, China's leaders will likely continue to be willing to bear the weight of international criticism of their Tibet policies while they work to bolster Chinese jurisdictional rights over the region through continuing the initiatives of the 1990s. Therefore, although the recent renewal of contact between Beijing and Dharamsala suggests that the Chinese are once again trying to make a breakthrough on Tibet by entering into serious negotiations with the Dalai Lama, such diplomacy is unlikely to produce dramatic results. On the contrary, Beijing is more adamant now about defending China's claims to Tibet than during the previous high-water mark in relations between Beijing and Dharamsala. At the same time, the Dalai Lama can ill afford (owing to opposition within the exile community) to make additional compromises on Tibet's status. In other words, while talks will probably continue, neither side will be willing to make the type of compromises that would be necessary to bring about a major change in China's approach to securing sovereignty over Tibet.

For most of the 1990s, the prospects in Hong Kong for the type of political unrest seen in Tibet seemed quite remote. However, over the last two years it has also become apparent that Beijing is finding it increasingly difficult to govern within the confines of the Basic Law. Apparent Chinese violations of this document have led to a storm of criticism internationally as well as in Hong Kong (and in Taiwan, where a very close watch is kept on Beijing's application of the "one country, two systems" approach to the harbor city). In response, Beijing has implemented new, flexible economic measures and a flurry of pointed reminders that Hong Kong is a part of China. This approach has, for the time being, dampened political protests in Hong Kong. Thus, over the next few years there should be few major shifts in China's Hong Kong policy. Nonetheless, it is also apparent that Hong Kong–China relations have entered into a new, and possibly more volatile, stage.

Cross-strait relations have long had such an explosive potential, which has had major costs for Beijing. As Chapter 4 discussed, sustaining China's claim to Taiwan has led to the maintenance of a long-term, and growing, military presence across from the island. It has also placed the Taiwan issue at the center of much of China's foreign policy, and made it the main obstacle to developing stable relations within many of China's main bilateral relationships (especially with the United States). In addition, by the mid-1990s (if not before), Taiwan also came to occupy a central position in Chinese foreign policy analysts' thinking about sovereignty.

In the interviews I conducted in 1997–98, Taiwan was the only issue whose inclusion made a significant difference in interviewees' interpretation of the norm. As mentioned in Chapter 2, over half of the nearly 100 individuals I interviewed contended that sovereignty's role in international politics was being eroded, if not replaced, by new trends within the system. In contrast, only about 30 percent argued that no such change was taking place, and, if it was, this presented a threat to international stability, and should be stopped. Analysts from a wide range of universities and think tanks stood on both sides of this divide. In addition, there was no strong correlation between the age of interviewees and the views they expressed on sovereignty. However, when I coded each of the interviews in regard to whether individuals emphasized Taiwan, it immediately became clear that the vast majority of those who did (twenty-three of thirty-seven interviewees) had "closed" views about sovereignty.[1] In contrast, interviewees who did not dwell on Taiwan (sixty-two) strongly tended (forty-seven) to have "open" views about sovereignty. In short, those who viewed sovereignty through the lens of the "Taiwan issue" rarely expressed any flexibility on the norm and often argued strongly in defense of reinforcing the boundaries it creates within international politics.

Although I have not conducted extensive follow-up interviews to update this information, as shown in Chapter 4, today Taiwan occupies an even more central position in Beijing's calculations. Moreover, recent developments on both sides of the strait suggest that the possibility of outright military conflict is higher now than at any point since the start of the reform era. Indeed, incumbent Chen Shui-bian's narrow March 2004 election victory appreciably escalated Chinese concerns about cross-strait relations. On the one hand, Chen garnered only 0.2 percent more votes than his opposition, and both of the proposed referenda he supported failed. This outcome obtained despite the fact that the vote followed a botched assassination attempt against his life on the eve of the election, which many analysts contend helped sway the election in his favor. On the other hand, by retaining the presidency, Chen gained another four years as leader of Taiwan, strengthened the DPP's dominant role on the island, and dealt a crucial blow to the opposition. On balance, then, Chen's reelection insured that the issue of Taiwanese independence will remain a lightning rod in cross-strait relations. This point was underscored by the fact that following the election, Chen reiterated his promise to both revisit the referendum issue and consider revising Taiwan's constitution.

After the election, China's leaders issued a series of strong warnings about the overall state of cross-strait relations. First, despite a number of high-profile U.S. statements supporting the status quo in cross-strait relations (Kelly 2004), the Chinese have repeatedly criticized Washington for failing to comply with its policy commitments to Beijing. Second, although Beijing initially maintained a low profile in the aftermath of the election, it quickly upped the volume of its disapproval of Chen. Thus, just before Chen's May inauguration, Beijing issued a high-level and blunt rebuttal of his policies. Moreover, although Chen then delivered a cautiously worded inaugural address, a Taiwan Affairs Office spokesperson quickly questioned the sincerity of his words and asserted that Chen in reality continued to advocate Taiwanese independence ("Chen Shui-bian's" 2004).

Since this time the war of words across the strait has escalated, and it is now apparent that today, perhaps more than at any point over the last twenty-five years, China's leaders may be forced to choose between integrating and unifying. Although previous Chinese behavior reveals that they have gone to great lengths to avoid overt conflict over jurisdictional issues in order to attain the economic benefits that came from integration, it also suggests they will use whatever means necessary, including military force, to avoid the perceived costs of a further devolution of China's claim to Taiwan. Prior to taking such a step, they will seek to isolate the Taiwanese president internationally, circumvent his authority on the island by attempting to build ties with opposition leaders, encourage Taiwanese investment on the mainland, and continue the missile buildup near the strait. Moreover, due to the damage that it would do to the broader policy goal of growing the economy, the Chinese will not use military force in a preemptive fashion to return Taiwan to China. Nonetheless, if Chen crosses any of the redlines laid out in the 2000 white paper on Taiwan (see Chapter 5), Beijing will act.

The crux of this matter, then, now lies in Taiwan, where Chen appears to be intent on pressing for international recognition of the island's independent status. Since the spring 2004 election he has exercised caution in pursuing this goal, but the status quo in cross-strait relations nonetheless remains particularly tenuous and could easily be undone by the Taiwanese president, or damaged by an unintentional misunderstanding, or accidental military engagement between the military forces on either side of the strait. In such a context is easy to predict a jump in cross-strait hostilities. If this occurs, it could also lead to a rapid unraveling of Beijing's efforts to both integrate China with the world and unify China's jurisdictional claims. Chinese moves to return Taiwan to what those in Beijing see as its legitimate place as a part of China would disrupt integration, perhaps irreparably, and the likelihood of American involvement in such a conflict would be quite high. The impact of such a crisis would thus not only imperil China's rise in Asia, but also jeopardize the relatively stable security dynamic in the region, and have a profound impact on the broader international political and economic system.

Conclusion

What are the final implications of the pattern of Beijing's divergent sovereignty-related practices for the way we think of China's evolving relationship with the international system? Most importantly, it highlights the superficiality of the main conceptual frameworks, the containment-engagement debate and the "China threat" argument, that have been deployed in academic and policy-oriented discussions to describe China's rise in international politics.

Within this debate, China has been characterized in sharply contrasting terms. Those advocating containment have tended to portray China as a revisionist state that is only weakly constrained by the web of economic ties and institutional links with the world that have emerged during the reform era. Thus, once the Chinese are able to consolidate their economic and military power, they will overturn the existing balance of power in the international system. China is a "threat." In contrast, proponents of engagement have contended that China's economic and political commitments to the rest of the world have begun to (or will) have a transformative effect on the Chinese polity. They will rearticulate Chinese security interests, wed China to the status quo in the Asian region, and may even lead to the emergence of new forces in China that will eventually make the PRC more democratic. In other words, China is well along the way to being incorporated into the existing world order. While these characterizations may somewhat oversimplify the differences between the two positions, they do capture the main components of the sharply contrasting interpretations that both sides have forwarded about the nature of China's changing place within international politics.

The pattern of behavior analyzed in this book stretches across both arguments and reveals a China that is at all times both integrating with, and differentiating itself from, the international community in which it is now firmly embedded. For example, China's leaders remain deeply attached to the project of completing China's national unity and have adamantly resisted any moves they perceived as interfering with their task. Indeed, Chinese sensitivities on this front were so pronounced that in the early 1990s Beijing decisively repudiated what was largely a nonexistent normative shift in the international arena on the balance between sovereign rights and self-determination norms. Such a stance reveals a China that is still very much defining itself against the rest of the international community and intent on ensuring that the peoples and territories that currently lie within the scope of Beijing's sovereign rights remain there. However, at the very same time, Chinese words and actions have been powerfully shaped by external material pressures and, perhaps even more importantly, by the diffused reinterpretation in the international arena of the legitimate intersection between states' rights, individual rights, and multilateral institutions. This development suggests that a significant movement has already begun in the direction of erasing the sharp lines that once divided China and the rest of the world.

Those envisioning the dangers posed by a rising China fixate on the intransigent side of the Chinese stance and argue that it demonstrates that Beijing poses a threat to regional and world security and thus necessitates the application of more vigilance and surveillance to guard against even more aggressive Chinese actions. In contrast, advocates of engagement tend to emphasize the cooperative aspects of Chinese behavior and argue that it reveals just how successful the integration of China has been in terms of bringing Beijing into the international fold. Yet, it is precisely the juxtaposition of both behaviors, the ability to both change and stay the same, that constitutes the main story of Chinese foreign relations over the last two decades.

In sum, Beijing has been unable to ignore systemic trends in the international arena that have subtly transformed sovereignty's role in international politics. As sovereignty's rules have changed, so has the way Chinese foreign policy and national security makers interpret and use the norm. It no longer (if it ever did) provides them with an impenetrable shield (via the invocation of China's sovereign rights) with which to ward off Beijing's domestic and international critics. Instead, it is now understood as a principle that encompasses a wide range of rights and obligations, a concession that represents a striking shift in China's relationship with the rest of the international system. Yet, at the same time Beijing still places a premium on the walls sovereignty can build. In other words, "new" interpretations of sovereignty have not erased "old" ones within China, rather they have been written alongside them. Securing Chinese sovereignty then encompasses both approaches, and as a result it is marked by apparent contradictions and tensions. Balancing the demands of integration and unification has been the defining feature of Chinese foreign relations and national security policies since the early 1980s. Such a task is becoming increasingly precarious, and because of looming challenges, is likely to become even more arduous in the near future.

Notes

1. Throughout this book I use the term "Tibet" rather than "Tibetan Autonomous Region" (TAR) (the official term for the area used in Chinese statements) or "free Tibet" (the term of choice by many international nongovernmental organizations that favor Tibetan independence). While I shift to "TAR" when directly discussing issues of regional autonomy, I prefer to use the generic "Tibet" because it is the most neutral term available to describe the region. I have opted to use the terms "Taiwan" (rather than Republic of China) and "Hong Kong" (rather than Hong Kong Special Autonomous Region [HKSAR]) for similar reasons.

2. These are CASS's *Shijie Jingji yu Zhengzhi* (World Economics and Politics), CIIS's *Guoji Wenti Yanjiu* (International Studies), and CICIR's *Xiandai Guoji Guanxi* (Contemporary International Relations).

3. Follow-up interviews were conducted in Beijing and Shanghai in December 2001 and January 2002.

4. I use the term "norm" throughout this book in a way consistent with Martha Finnemore and Kathryn Sikkink's definition of it "as a standard of appropriate behavior for actors with a given identity" (1998: 891).

5. Examples of recent work in international relations theory and security studies that directly advocates the development of eclectic, or integrative, analysis include Alagappa (2003), Elman and Elman (2002), Fearon and Wendt (2002), Sil (2000), and Suh, Katzenstein, and Carlson (2004).

CHAPTER I

1. For the postmodernist argument along these lines, see Ashley (1988), Walker (1993), and Bartelson (1995). For a more conventional criticism, see Keohane (1988) and Weingast (1995). For an influential argument that stakes out a theoretical middle ground between these two approaches, see Ruggie (1983).

2. According to a 1995 count by Michael Fowler and Julie Bunck (1995: 2n12), between 1985 and 1993 the term "beyond sovereignty" was featured in five scholarly works on the norm. An exemplar of the "end of sovereignty" argument can be found in Camilleri and Falk (1992).

3. Such a definition was indebted to the writings of Hedley Bull (1977) and John Ruggie (1983).

4. Also see Reus-Smit (1999), Hall (1999), Philpott (2001), Barkin and Cronin (1994), and Osiander (2001).

5. For representative work from the first half of the 1990s that predicted the end of sovereignty, see Wriston (1992). See also Gottleib (1993), Hieberg (1994), and Ohmae (1995). For a contemporary critique of the claims made in this literature, see Krasner and Thomson (1989), and Krasner (1993). For more recent, albeit more cautiously worded, work that describes a process of substantive change in sovereignty's role in international politics, see Chayes and Chayes (1995), Held et al. (1999), Steven Smith (2001), and Lake (2003). For an updated, slightly modified, response to such arguments, see Krasner (2001b).

6. In the case of Taiwan, this is the Republic of China (ROC), and in Tibet, the Dalai Lama's government-in-exile. The referent in Hong Kong is less clear.

7. This definition of human rights norms draws upon Donnelly (1995, 1999), Risse and Sikkink (1999: 2–3), and Barkin (1998).

8. This phrasing borrows from Jepperson, Katzenstein, and Wendt (1996) and from Risse and Sikkink (1999: 8).

9. For similar arguments, see Barkin (1998), Henkin (1999), Cassel (2001), Reus-Smit (2001), Held (2002), and Doyle and Gardner (2003).

10. For example, through the question of what region or group within a sovereign state has the right to participate in an international economic organization.

11. This definition draws on the one proposed in Held et al. (1999: chap. 1).

12. Thus, for the purposes of this book it is the acknowledgment via words and actions of WTO authority (and consideration of globalization norms), rather than any single set of economic indicators (trends in foreign investment, imports/exports, or the development of bilateral economic relations), that are important, as it is through such practices that each state defines the general parameters of its sovereign economic rights (an issue of authority, rather than control over economic flows).

CHAPTER 2

1. For examples, see Thomson (1995: 219), Krasner (1999: chap. 1), and Biersteker and Weber (1996: 11). For a more detailed discussion, see James (1986), and Fowler and Bunck (1995).

2. Even today, recognition of the PRC is contested by the ROC and, to a lesser extent, the Dalai Lama. However, this contestation is limited to questioning the PRC's right to rule over specific peoples and territories; it does not extend to the issue of the PRC's status a member of the community of sovereign states.

3. My use of the term "practice" is more in line with Ruggie's (1993) depiction of the bundling (and unbundling) of territoriality than it is with Ashley and Walker's (1990) emphasis on discursive representations. In other words, the conceptual frame presented in this chapter (and thus the content of the following empirical chapters) is not about discourse alone, but rather about what states say and do.

4. In his 1995 article on sovereignty, Keohane emphasized that the pattern of complex interdependence that characterized the "zone of peace" of western Europe was sharply different from the relatively unstable situation that had emerged in other parts of the world. Indeed, in the "zone of conflict," which encompassed much of the former Soviet Union, Asia, and Africa, Keohane saw a trend toward the retention of sovereignty's traditional role in regulating interstate relations. However, he also noted that even in such regions, "global institutions" might change traditional notions of sovereignty. In other words, sovereign change in such regions would be the product of the same mechanism that had already produced new interpretations of sovereignty in the "zone of peace."

5. For similar arguments, see Chayes and Chayes (1995), and Held (2002).

6. See Segal (1999) for a dissenting opinion.

7. An exception to this trend was the inclusion of three China-focused chapters in Krasner's edited volume that explored how a variety of states approach sovereignty (2001a).

8. On this issue, see Johnston (1996), Zhang Yongjin (1998), and Kent (1999).

9. In the early 1990s there was disagreement over the appropriate romanization of the names of each of these Central Asian republic. Throughout this book, except when original sources differed, I use these now commonly accepted spellings.

10. This focus leaves aside the outstanding territorial issue between Japan and China over the Diaoyu/Senkaku Islands, and the Sino-Filipino dispute in the South China Sea. I decided not to include the former based on my understanding that the dispute between Beijing and Tokyo over this territory is minor (in terms of the extent of territory in dispute, and the level of strategic, military, and political importance attached to it) in comparison with the maritime issues at stake in the Sino-Vietnamese relationship. The latter decision was made based on the fact that the Philippines has not made as extensive claims against China, or as consistently acted in support of such a position, as Vietnam has.

11. Prior to this confrontation the two sides had attempted to work out a negotiated settlement, but made little progress.

12. China's claim to Hong Kong, unlike its claims to Tibet and Taiwan, has not been the site of similar local or international challenges. However, as Hong Kong remained outside of Chinese administration until 1997, and the nature of Chinese rule following the resumption of Chinese sovereignty has generated new contentious issues, the region is included in this study. In contrast, the issue of Mongolia was left aside because its status is relatively uncontested. Xinjiang, another candidate for inclusion in this study, was left out since there has been comparatively little international pressure on China in regard to this region.

13. There are differing interpretations of the text. For an even-handed treatment of this subject, see Ross (1995).

14. For exceptions, see Jackson (1998), and McGinnis and Movesian (2000).

15. For a more detailed description of this period, see Jacobson and Oksenberg (1990: 64–66). On the "self-reliance" debate, see Barnett (1981: 122–32).

16. Although these two publications do not contain all official policy statements made during the 1980s and 1990s, they do offer an authoritative and consistent source of foreign policy rhetoric. The sovereignty-related claims made in these publications are representative of the trends in the frequency and intensity with which such claims were made by Chinese officials.

The recording unit used in the content analysis of *Beijing Review* was the sentence.

Each sentence that included the term "sovereignty" or "(non)interference" was treated as a single claim. In addition, sentences containing the terms "choice according to national characteristics," "territorial integrity," "economic independence," or "sovereignty" were also coded as official claims. Only the claims attributed to government officials, official spokespeople, or quoted from official publications (such as Xinhua General News Agency [Xinhua] or *Renmin Ribao* [People's Daily]), were designated as official. The entire contents of each issue were coded. However, since coding was conducted of the mainland edition of *Beijing Review*, it did not include the section that was added to the North American edition in the late 1980s. In mid-2001, the format of *Beijing Review* fundamentally changed, with a decrease in direct coverage of leadership statements, Foreign Ministry press briefings, and full-text government reports. With this sharp drop in the level of overall "official statements" within the publication, I discontinued the content analysis that I had conducted for each of the preceding twenty-two years.

Zhongguo Waijiao Gailan (the name was changed to *Zhongguo Waijiao* in the mid-1990s) was first published in 1987. The same coding rules that were used to analyze *Beijing Review* were also used here. However, in this publication, which is published under the direct guidance of China's Foreign Ministry, all claims were treated as official. Each volume is divided into sections covering general developments in international relations, China's relations with different regions, and China's involvement with the UN and its related organs. The entire contents of each volume were coded, except for the final two chapters of each volume and the appendixes. Each volume covered events that took place in the year prior to its publication; thus the 1987 volume covered 1986, and so on. Therefore, Figure 2.1, which covers data from the 1987 to 2000 volumes, lists claims in the years 1986–99.

CHAPTER 3

An earlier version of this chapter was published in the *Journal of Contemporary China*. See Carlson (2003).

1. Territorial claims in *Beijing Review* were identified through separating all statements that specifically referred to any segment of China's boundaries, or infringement upon Chinese territory, from the total number of sovereignty claims coded.

2. Claims were coded as containing a land referent if specific mention was made of any segment of China's continental borders, territorial sovereignty (not specified as sea), and air space. Claims coded in the sea category contained reference to any of the following: "territorial waters," "ocean" or "maritime" boundaries, "Diaoyu Islands," "Beibu Gulf," "Xisha/Nansha Islands."

3. John Garver (2001a: 401n43) notes the authoritative nature of this article by observing that it probably served as the working paper for the negotiators who took part in the sixth round of border talks between the two sides.

4. For Chinese charges, see "Chinese News Service" (1986), and "Answers" (1986).

5. For an authoritative Chinese overview of Vietnamese provocations in the border region at this time, see the 1987 and 1988 volumes of *Zhongguo Waijiao Gailan*.

6. For an example of how such an argument was made via the 1979 war between the two countries, see Ross (1988) and Segal (1985: 215–16).

7. For example, in the mid-1990s, Yang Gongsu (1997: 347) noted that China and Vietnam agree on the location of 1,230 kilometers of the 1,300–kilometer land border,

with China's position being that only sixty-two points along the border comprising sixty-three square kilometers are in dispute.

8. In addition, Stephen Hood (1992: 123) reported that at this time Chinese and Vietnamese forces had fired on boats that crossed into each other's territory, but generally refrained from engaging each other.

9. For a detailed account of this development, see You (1999: chap. 6).

10. For a recent, official Chinese review of this policy, see "Chinese Defense White Paper" (2002: 7–8).

11. Li was the first top level Chinese official to visit the Soviet Union since the 1969 border war.

12. Shichor (2004: 153) reported that by 1992 the Russians had already cut border troops by 200,000 men and removed advanced military equipment from the border region. Moltz (1995: 519) has also noted that actual deployment of troops in the border region was probably significantly less than reported since most divisions were operating at far less than full strength.

13. The secondary literature disagrees about precisely which forces were included in this number. See Yuan (1998a: 12) and Shichor (2004: 154) for differing interpretations.

14. The lack of progress in Sino-Tajik border relations in the mid-1990s was primarily a product of the chaos in Tajikistan (which was mired in a civil war whose active phase lasted through 1997).

15. Polat (2002) and Shichor (2004) contend the China received 43 percent of this land; Fravel (2003) argues that the number is lower, at around 20 percent.

16. A pair of articles by Pan Guan (2002a, 2002b), a specialist on Central Asia affiliated with the Shanghai Academy of Social Sciences, dealt with the same issues.

17. Estimates of the extensiveness of the Chinese military presence in the border region vary. For examples of differing analyses, see Malik (1995: 320), Yuan (2001: 990), and Sidhu and Yuan (2003: 50–51).

18. As Deng noted in the published transcript of his meeting with Gandhi, "If China and India are developed we can say that we have made our contributions to mankind. It is precisely for this great goal that the Chinese government has suggested that all developing countries should improve relations and increase cooperation with each other. China and India in particular should do so" (Deng Xiaoping 1994: 275).

19. During this period there was also a noted increase in the level of informal exchanges between Indian and Chinese security analysts. See Bajpai and Coe (1995: 204–25).

20. Mansingh (1994: 291) reported that in the early 1990s India had reduced its military forces in the eastern sector by 35,000.

21. The full text is in Crepon and Sevak (1995).

22. The Chinese Foreign Ministry also criticized President Vajpayee's October 1998 meeting with the Dalai Lama. Its statement underscores the intimate role of Tibet in Sino-Indian border relations. Another example can be found in the title of Wang Hongwei's book on Sino-Indian relations, *Ximalaya Shan Qingjie*, which translates as *The Himalayan Sentiment* (Wang Hongwei 1998).

23. This interview was originally scheduled on the day after India conducted the first of its nuclear weapons tests in 1998. As the interviewee was involved with high-level meetings on China's intended response to the tests, the interview was postponed. Two weeks later, when the rescheduled interview was conducted, discussion naturally turned

to these events. The interviewee expressed anger over Indian duplicity revealed by the tests. He said that as late as November 1997 he had been involved with a delegation that had received assurances from Indian counterparts that no such tests would be conducted. However, he also acknowledged India's right to conduct such tests.

24. For additional commentary from this period on similar issues see Tang Shiping (2000), Ma Jiali (2000), Wang Hongwei (2000), and Zhang Li (2001). While none of these directly addresses the issue of territorial sovereignty, during interviews I conducted in Beijing in 2001, two top security experts argued that China's endorsement of CBMs with India demonstrated that China was now willing to compromise on certain limited facets of this foundational aspect of foreign relations. However, both interviewees also contended that a breakthrough in talks was unlikely in light of the strategic value of the territory at stake (Personal interview, Chinese Foundation for International and Strategic Studies, Dec. 28, 2001).

25. Nonetheless, India carried out an extensive military training exercise in May of 2001 that some analysts in Beijing viewed as directly related to Indian preparation for possible future conflict with China. In addition, India continued to maintain a reported force of over 200,000 troops in the border region (Sidhu and Yuan 2003: 62).

26. A new forum for the discussion of the boundary issue was created following the Vajpayee visit, but as of this writing it has failed to produce any major new initiatives on the border question.

27. PLAN chief Liu Huaqing had articulated these doctrines and policies earlier in the decade. See Cole (2003).

28. Moreover, as Eric Hyer (1995) has emphasized, the fact that Taiwan made its own claims to this territory further complicated the Chinese calculus on how to handle outstanding disputes in the region.

29. John Garver (1992: 1017) has reported that there were substantial differences between the Foreign Ministry and PLAN over the text of this document. The PLAN pushed for an inclusion of such specific referents; the Foreign Ministry was opposed (Garver 1992: 1017).

30. Amer (2002) refers to these talks as the second round of negotiations. However, official Chinese reports ("More" 1993) from this time called the 1993 meetings the "first" official round of negotiations.

31. In using this setting for repairing the strained Sino-Vietnamese relationship, Beijing tacitly acknowledged the increasing importance of multilateral institutions in addressing territorial issues.

32. Ang (2000: 206–7) has argued that this assertive move was undertaken by the PLAN without the prior consent of the central party leadership. Although such a claim is hard to disprove, it is more likely that the action was simply part of the contradictory (both conciliatory and combative) policies Beijing was pursuing in the region.

33. For more skeptical assessment of these issues, see Li Jinming (2002) and Zhao Yueliang (2002).

34. For a full text of this agreement, see "Declaration of Conduct."

CHAPTER 4

Sections in this chapter on Tibet draw on material I previously published. See Carlson (2004).

1. In line with the arguments for case selection made in Chapter 2, the focus of this chapter is on Taiwan and Tibet. Hong Kong is treated as a secondary case. Thus, I did not include Hong Kong in the content analysis of Chinese sovereignty claims, nor did I conduct the same sort of comprehensive study of unofficial Chinese analysis that was carried out in regard to Taiwan and Tibet.

2. Jurisdictional claims were selected from the total number of claims analyzed by coding all such claims for specific reference to Taiwan, Tibet, and the principle of territorial integrity. Where a sentence referred to both "sovereignty" and "territorial integrity," but did not mention Taiwan or Tibet, it was left as a general claim. Jurisdictional claims were further categorized as statements on Taiwan or Tibet based on their geographic referent. Claims that referred to the "resumption of" Chinese "sovereignty" over Hong Kong were not included in this analysis.

3. "Unofficial analysis" refers to articles published in China since the start of the reform era. A comprehensive review of this literature involved an examination of all articles that mentioned Taiwan, Tibet, or self-determination in their titles and appeared in the major international relations journals. It extended to a study of the specialized journals dealing with Taiwan, Tibet, and minority issues. These included *Minzu Yanjiu* (Minority Studies), *Zhongyang Minzu Xueyuan Xuebao* (Journal of the Central Institute for Minority Studies), *Taiwan Yanjiu* (Taiwan Studies), *Taiwan Yanjiu Jikan* (Taiwan Studies Quarterly), *Xizang Yanjiu* (Tibet Studies), *Zhongguo Zangxue* (Chinese Tibetology), and *Zhongguo Xizang* (China's Tibet).

4. For a full text of the second communiqué, see Ross (1995: 269–70).

5. For a comment on this linkage, see Deng Xiaoping (1994: 164).

6. On Taiwan's stance at this time, see Clough (1993: 11–12, 14).

7. Although Hu's statement was issued in 1981, I did not find a public acknowledgment of it in the Chinese press until 1984.

8. I would like to thank Elliot Sperling for calling my attention to this side of the new international equation on Tibet during the late 1970s.

9. For a detailed review of both of these developments, see Smith (1996: 584–95).

10. Articles attributed to Hua Zi appeared frequently in the 1990s and generally were highly critical of the Dalai Lama. The name Hua Zi is widely thought to be a pseudonym; its literal meaning is Son of China. See Smith (2003).

11. Because this change occurred at a somewhat earlier date, and more definitively in China's Tibet policy, in this section I reverse the order in which the cases are examined, with Tibet first and Taiwan second.

12. The Tibetan government in exile, INGOs, many Western states, and virtually all Western Tibet specialists have contended that during the 1990s the Chinese committed brutal human rights abuses in Tibet as part of this effort. On the following pages, I will not attempt to ascertain the validity of such charges. My analysis of Chinese policies and discursive practices on Tibet suggests the Chinese leadership has no reservations about using whatever means necessary to secure its rule over the region. However, I conducted no field research in Tibet in researching this book that would allow for a thorough verification of this observation. Instead, I focus on the way the Chinese responded to international criticism of their handling of the "Tibet issue."

13. Later the same year the House did attach a resolution to the Foreign Relations Act that characterized Tibet as an occupied country. See Smith (1996: 622–23).

14. In contrast, as the next chapter shows, from the early 1990s through the last few

years, when consideration of Tibet was removed from Chinese deliberations on these issues, analysts' stance softened considerably. For a representative sample of Tibet-related commentary issued at this time, see Duojie (1992), and Zhang Zhirong (1992a).

15. In Chinese the words *zhuquan guishu*—literally "sovereign jurisdiction" or "belonging"—are used rather than the more neutral "ownership" that appears in the title of the English-language document.

16. For a journalistic account of this controversy, see Hinton (1999).

17. For examples of this argument, see Garver (1997: chap. 5), and Suettinger (2003: 207–11), who dates the emergence of a more forceful PLA stance to 1994.

18. Chinese military analysts now largely concur that the reported deployment of short-range ballistic missiles, which some argue began in 1992, expanded at this time, with reports of approximately fifty such weapons near the strait in 1995.

19. For more on the crisis, see Garver (1997: chaps. 7–9).

20. However, even as the Chinese began to implement this stance, they also continued to gradually increase the number of short-range missiles in Fujian. The exact number deployed is exceedingly difficult to determine; the U.S. Defense Department reported that by 1999 there were between 150 to 200 missiles in the region.

21. On the Clinton statement referring to these topics (which are known as the "three no's") and how it changed American policy on Taiwan, see Romberg (2003: 180–85), and Suettinger (2003: 344–51).

22. For a criticism of this argument, see Chen Dong (2003a).

CHAPTER 5

1. These phases resemble the first three stages in the diffusion of human rights norms identified by Risse, Ropp, and Sikkink (1999). However, the specifics of Chinese behavior, and its causes, at each stage differ in substantial ways from the patterns identified in this model.

2. Rosemary Foot (2000) has also identified these two periods as distinct stages in the development of the Chinese stance on human rights.

3. These claims were extracted from all statements on sovereignty (as discussed in Chapter 2) based on the appearance of the terms "internal affairs," "interference," "non-interference," "meddling," "armed intervention," "right to choose," and "right to solve" own problem.

4. By 1989, Beijing was a signatory to seven of the core agreements that make up the human rights treaty regime (although this did not include either of the main human rights covenants).

5. The examination of the Chinese discussion of human rights in this chapter concentrates on analysis that appeared in the major Chinese international relations journals, and in the specialized law journals *Faxue Yanjiu* (Studies in Law) and *Zhongguo Faxue* (China's Legal Studies). Left aside are dissident and activist voices on human rights. This allows for a more effective tracing of the shifts in the views on human rights of those working within the foreign policy making establishment.

6. Rosemary Foot (2000) divided this period into a number of distinct phases; while I largely agree with her analysis, and use similar subheadings in the following section, there is not a sufficiently significant break in Chinese behavior (or the causal forces driving it) to emphasize such specific time frames when examining this period. On the con-

trary, from the perspective of the foundational issue of sovereign authority, the gradual expansion of cooperative measures and expansive human rights rhetoric during the 1990s is best understood as occurring within a single phase.

7. The themes of preventing interference and promoting sovereignty dominated the claims published in *Beijing Review* from 1992 to 2000.

8. This unofficial analysis appeared in publications by the expanding web of research institutes created in the 1990s for studying human rights. The first of these centers were established in 1991 in existing research institutions (such as People University's Center for Human Rights Studies, and CASS's Center for Human Rights Studies). It was not until 1993 that an independent institute devoted primarily to human rights was set up: the Chinese Society for Human Rights Studies. This organization, which dubs itself a human rights NGO (but is derided as an GONGO, or government-organized non-governmental organization, by international human rights activists), is led by former officials (such as Zhu Muzhi) who were involved in China's human rights activity in the UN.

9. This policy was suspended after 1993.

10. See Kent (1999: 170–93) for a more detailed review of the evolution of Beijing's stance on human rights over the course of the World Conference on Human Rights.

11. The analysts who began publishing articles promoting more flexible, open interpretations of human rights at this time were not marginal figures within Chinese foreign policy and decision-making circles. For example, a consistent, relatively liberal voice that emerged during the 1990s was Xia Yong, a CASS scholar who later became head of CASS's Legal Studies Institute, and is reported to now have ties with Chinese president Hu Jintao.

12. For a pointed reference to the ongoing influence of historical memory on contemporary Chinese thinking about these issues, see Sha (1995).

13. As Chapter 4 has shown, part of this surge was driven by rising concerns in Beijing about the trend toward Taiwanese independence. However, of the forty-seven claims related to sovereign authority published in *Beijing Review* in 1999, most involved criticism of the allies' supposed violation of sovereignty in the war in Yugoslavia. This total was only surpassed by the sixty-five such statements published in 1989, and the fifty in 1997.

14. Wang Yizhou, one of the main editors of the journal, was one of the first Chinese scholars to publish analysis that extensively considered the possibility of sovereign change. Other analysts informed me during interviews I conducted in 2001–2 that one of the possible reasons the journal took such a critical stance on Kosovo was to protect it from charges that it was "weak" on sovereignty. An informed source related to me that Wang had frequently been the subject of such criticism prior to the war in Kosovo.

15. The conference was funded by the Ford Foundation. As a contact subsequently related, most Chinese participants regarded the conference as an extension of the post-Kosovo battle over humanitarian intervention, and thus many of them deliberately tried to reflect and justify the official position rather than offer independent observations regarding sovereignty or human rights (confidential e-mail contact, Apr. 2004).

16. In 2004, the United States returned to its earlier policy of sponsoring draft resolutions on China in the UN CHR.

CHAPTER 6

1. Economic statements have been selected from all sovereignty claims by coding for references to "foreign trade," "opening policy," "economic affairs," and "economic sanctions." As already mentioned, when a single sentence contained references to more than one component of the norm, it was treated as a general claim rather than one that was specific to any single aspect of sovereignty. In addition, claims that referred to "choice" were coded as authority claims (unless they specifically referred to the economic terms listed above). Prior to 1982, a handful of claims referred to the new international economic order (NIEO) and the need to protect developing countries' economic sovereignty.

2. This chapter, like each of the previous chapters, treats the three main foreign policy journals published during this period as the major source of unofficial analysis in China. It also examines *Guoji Maoyi Wenti* (International Trade Journal) and *Guoji Maoyi* (International Trade).

3. This paragraph draws extensively on Jacobson and Oksenberg (1990: chap. 3).

4. Xue added that China should try to ensure that it was granted "developing-country status" in GATT. This issue was quickly becoming one of the central points of contention between China and GATT members in the negotiations, and Xue acknowledged that the opposition of the GATT member states on this point made it unlikely (*keneng xing bu da*) that China would in fact be granted such status.

5. For example, 1989 was the only year in which the content analysis of claims issued in *Beijing Review* uncovered repeated references to economic sovereignty. Furthermore, each of the twelve economic claims identified referred to how sanctions interfered in China's internal affairs.

6. This trip also led to a surge in economic growth in China, and, in 1992 and 1993, resulted in unprecedented new highs in the level of World Bank lending to Beijing, a development that saw China replace India as the largest borrower from the bank (Lardy 1992: 52).

7. Throughout this period, only a handful of sovereignty-related statements issued in *Beijing Review* fulfilled the coding requirements for economic claims. No more than two claims appeared in any given year between 1993 and 2001. This smattering of commentary was related to the issue of economic sanctions and interference in internal affairs.

8. However, a handful of the officials involved in the negotiations later acknowledged Beijing had missed an opportunity to join the organization at this time (at a much lower cost than it subsequently paid for admission to the WTO). See Liang Wei (2002: 703).

9. The American release of a statement outlining Chinese concessions at this juncture led to a flurry of conflicting reports from both Beijing and Washington over whether the document had been intended for public consumption. See Fewsmith (1999) and Liang Wei (2002: 710).

10. Both Fewsmith (1999) and Pearson (2001: 345) make this claim. Although Liang Wei's (2002: 710–11) detailed account of this period does not mention this call, it repeatedly emphasizes the role that personal involvement by Clinton, Jiang, and Zhu played in pushing the process forward.

11. See "Protocols" for a link to the WTO's full text version of this protocol.

12. Sun's call resonated with the combative analysis of China's new security strategy endorsed by Zhang Wenmu, a researcher at CICIR. In a powerful wordplay on a well-known revolutionary slogan, Zhang (2000) argued that "sovereignty comes from the bar-

rel of a gun." For a similar argument that strongly emphasized the dangers of globalization, see Tang Renwu and Hu Chunmu (2000). Perhaps the best-known anti-globalization work from this period was written by Han Deqiang (2000).

13. Arguably, accession ended the third phase in the development of the Chinese approach to economic sovereignty. However, since such a short time has passed since this event, I have opted to treat the post-accession period simply as a continuation of the stage that began in 1994 with the tabling of the first draft accession protocol.

CONCLUSION

1. The interviews were conducted in an open-ended fashion. As such, there was no single answer to a set question that led me to code a given interview as emphasizing Taiwan. Instead, where 25 percent or more of the recorded interview revolved around cross-strait relations, I categorized it as Taiwan specific.

References

"AI's First Forty Years." Amnesty International. http://web.amnesty.org/pages/aboutai-timeline-eng.

Alagappa, Muthiah. 2003. *Asian Security Order: Instrumental with Normative Contractual Features*. Stanford, CA: Stanford University Press.

Amer, Ramses. 1997. "The Territorial Disputes between China and Vietnam and Regional Stability." *Contemporary Southeast Asia* 19, 1 (June): 86–113.

————. 2002. *The Sino-Vietnamese Approach to Managing Boundary Disputes*. Durham, UK: International Boundaries Research Unit.

An Zhiguo. 1988. "The Dalai Lama's 'New Proposal.'" *Beijing Review*, Aug. 1.

Ang, Cheng Guan. 2000. "The South China Sea Dispute Revisited." *Australian Journal of International Affairs* 54, 2: 201–16.

Angle, Stephen C., and Marina Svensson, eds. 2001. *The Chinese Human Rights Reader: Documents and Commentary, 1900–2000*. Armonk, NY: M. E. Sharpe.

"Answers to Readers by Xinhua News Agency on So-called 'Arunachal Pradesh.'" 1986. Xinhua, Dec. 16.

Anthony, Ted. 2002. "Chinese Foreign Minister: Human Rights Dialogue with United States to Resume." Associated Press, July 31.

"ASEAN Plea for Peace in the Spratlys." 1995. Agence France-Presse, Mar. 18.

Ashley, Richard. 1988. "Untying the Sovereign State: A Double Reading of the Anarchy Problematique." *Millennium* 17, 2 (Summer): 227–62.

Ashely, Richard, and R. B. J. Walker. 1990. "Conclusion: Reading/Writing the Discipline: Crisis and the Question of Sovereignty in International Studies." *International Studies Quarterly* 34, 3: 367–416.

Austin, Greg. 1998. *China's Ocean Frontier: International Law, Military Force and National Development*. St. Leonards, Australia: Allen and Unwin.

Bajpai, Kanti P., and Bonnie L. Coe. 1995. "Confidence Building between India and China." In Michael Krepon and Amit Sevak, eds., *Crisis Prevention, Confidence Building and Reconciliation in South Asia*, 199–266. New York: St. Martin's Press.

Banning, Garrett. 2001. "China Faces, Debates, the Contradictions of Globalization." *Asian Survey* 41, 3: 409–27.

"Banqen Erdini Urges Dalai Lama to Return to China." 1979. Xinhua, June 22. In LexisNexis.

Barkin, Samuel J. 1998. "The Evolution and Constitution of Sovereignty and the Emergence of Human Rights Norms." *Millennium* 27, 2 (Summer): 229–52.

Barkin, Samuel J., and Bruce Cronin. 1994. "The State and the Nation: Changing Norms and Rules of Sovereignty in International Relations." *International Organization* 48, 1 (Winter): 107–30.

Barnett, A. Doak. 1981. *China's Economy in Global Perspective.* Washington, DC: Brookings Institution.

Barnett, Robert. 1994. "Army Doubles Troops in Tibetan Border Area." *South China Morning Post*, Apr. 25.

"Barshefsky Calls on China to Take Next Step on WTO Accession." 1995. *Inside U.S. Trade*, Nov. 17.

Bartelson, Jens. 1995. *A Genealogy of Sovereignty.* New York: Cambridge University Press.

Baum, Richard. 1999. "Enter the Dragon: China's Courtship of Hong Kong, 1982–1999." *Communist and Post-Communist Studies* 32: 417–36.

Bayefsky, Anne F. 2001. *The UN Human Rights Treaty System: Universality at a Crossroads.* Ardsley, NY: Transnational Publishers.

"Beijing Receives Dalai Lama's Latest Envoy." 1984. *Beijing Review*, Dec. 3.

Bengyi. 1995. "Sixty-two Aid Projects in Full Swing." *China's Tibet* (English edition) 1: 7–12.

Biersteker, Thomas J., and Cynthia Weber. 1996. "The Social Construction of State Sovereignty." In Biersteker and Weber, eds., *State Sovereignty as Social Construct*, 1–22. Cambridge, UK: Cambridge University Press.

"Borrow and Prosper, Says the World Bank." 1981. *Economist*, June 20. In LexisNexis.

Boughton, James M. 2001. *Silent Revolution: The International Monetary Fund, 1979–1989.* N.p.: International Monetary Fund.

Boyer, Jacques. 1997. "UN Mission Peeks Inside China's Gulag." Agence France-Presse, Oct. 21.

Bull, Hedley. 1977. *The Anarchical Society.* New York: Columbia University Press.

Burles, Mark. 1999. *Chinese Policy toward Russia and the Central Asian Republics.* Santa Monica, CA: RAND, Project Air Force.

"Bush-Dalai Lama Meeting Protested." 1991. *Beijing Review*, Apr. 29.

Buszynski, Leszek. 2003. "ASEAN, the Declaration of Conduct, and the South China Sea." *Contemporary Southeast Asia* 25, 3: 343–62.

Camilleri, Joseph A., and Jim Falk. 1992. *The End of Sovereignty: The Politics of a Shrinking and Fragmented World.* Brookfield, VT: Edward Elgar.

Campbell, David. 1992. *Writing Security.* Minneapolis: University of Minnesota Press.

Canning, Craig N. 2001. "Hong Kong: Still 'One Country, Two Systems'?" *Current History* (Sept.): 285–90.

Carley, Patricia. 1996. *Self-Determination: Sovereignty, Territorial Integrity, and the Right to Secession.* Report from a roundtable held in conjunction with the U.S. Department of State's policy planning staff. Herndon, VA: United States Institute of Peace.

Carlson, Allen. 2003. "Constructing the Dragon's Scales: China's Approach to Territorial

Sovereignty and Border Relations in the 1980s and 1990s." *Journal of Contemporary China* 37: 677–98.

———. 2004. *Beijing's Tibet Policy: Securing Sovereignty and Legitimacy.* East-West Center Washington, Policy Studies no. 4.

Cassel, Douglass. 2001. "A Framework of Norms: International Human-Rights Law and Sovereignty." *Harvard International Review* (Winter): 60–63.

"Chairman Ye Jianying's Elaborations on Policy Concerning Return of Taiwan to Motherland and Peaceful Reunification." 1981. *Beijing Review*, Oct. 5.

Chayes, Abraham, and Antonia Chayes. 1995. *The New Sovereignty: Compliance with International Regulatory Agreements.* Cambridge, MA: Harvard University Press.

Chen, David. 1989a. "Moscow Talks on Reducing Border Troops." *South China Morning Post*, Nov. 15.

———. 1989b. "China: Crackdown Gave Vietnam Time to Invade Spratlys." *South China Morning Post*, Sept. 29.

Chen Dezhao. 1989. "Zhongguo huifu guanmao zongxieding xiwei zhong de jige wenti" [A Few Issues of the Recovery of China's GATT Seat]. *Shijie Jingji yu Zhengzhi* 9: 58–63.

Chen Dong. 2003a. "Ye tan zhuquan lilun ji zai Taiwan wenti shang de shiyong" [Follow-Up Comments on Sovereignty Theories and Their Application to the Taiwan Issue]. *Taiwan Yanjiu Jikan* 1: 27–33.

———. 2003b. "Ping Taiwan de 'gongtou'" [Criticism of Taiwan's "Referenda"]. *Taiwan Yanjiu Jikan* 4: 28–36.

Chen Guangguo. 1989. "Shehui zhuyi de Xizang yu zangzu renmin de renquan: Jinian 'shijie renquan xuanyan' fabiao 40 zhounian" [Socialist Tibet and the Human Rights of the Tibetans: In Commemoration of the Fortieth Anniversary of the Declaration of Human Rights]. *Zhongguo Zangxue* 4.

Chen Guidi, and Chun Tao. 2004. *Zhongguo Nongmin Diaocha* [A Survey of China's Peasants]. Beijing: Renmin wenxue chubanshe.

Chen, Jie. 1994. "China's Spratly Policy: With Special Reference to the Philippines and Malaysia." *Asian Survey* 34, 10: 893–903.

Chen Ning. 1991. "Nanhai zhuquan fenzheng xingshi yu woguo de duice" [Trends in the Dispute over the Sovereignty of the Southern Sea and China's Countermeasures]. *Shijie Jingji yu Zhengzhi* 11: 41–43.

"Chen Shui-bian's May 20 Speech Foreshadows Attempt for 'Taiwan Independence.'" 2004. Xinhua, May 24.

Chen Tiqian. 1982. "Zhong-Yin bianjie wenti de falü fangmian" [The Legal Aspects of the Sino-Indian Border Issue]. *Guoji Wenti Yanjiu* 1: 11–43.

Cheng Ruisheng. 1993a. "Xin xingshi xia de Zhong-Yin guanxi" [Sino-Indian Relations Under New Conditions]. *Guoji Wenti Yanjiu* 4: 4–8.

———. 1993b. "Shifting Obstacles in Sino-Indian Relations." *Pacific Review* 6, 1: 63–69.

———. 1999. "Sino-Indian Relations after India's Nuclear Tests." Paper presented at UNESCO, LNCV & USPID Nuclearization of South Asia Conference, May 20–22, Como, Italy.

Cheng Shuaihua. 2000. "Guojia zhuquan yu guoji renquan de ruogan wenti" [Several Issues Involving International Human Rights and State Sovereignty]. *Ouzhou* 1: 31–37.

Cheng Xiaoxu, and Zhang Wenbin. 1990. "Zong guojifa kan woguo dui Nanshaqundao de zhuquan" [Looking at Chinese Sovereignty over the Nansha Islands from the

Perspective of International Law]. *Shijie Jingji yu Zhengzhi* 1: 64–68.

Cheng Yan. 1999. "Quenqiuhua yu guannian geng xin" [Economic Globalization and the Renewal of Concepts]. *Shijie Jingji yu Zhengzhi* 6: 64–68.

Cheng, Yuan. 1991. *East-West Trade: Changing Patterns in Chinese Foreign Trade Law and Institutions.* New York: Oceana.

"China Admitted into GATT Textile Arrangement." 1983. Xinhua, Dec. 15. In LexisNexis.

"China Applies to Resume Its GATT Membership." 1986. Xinhua, July 12. In LexisNexis.

"China Appreciates US Listing of ETIM as Terrorist Organization." 2002. Xinhua, Aug. 27.

"China to Attend future GATT Council Meeting." 1984. Xinhua, Nov. 8. In LexisNexis.

"China Backs U.N. Efforts to Protect Human Rights, Qian Says." 1988. Xinhua, Sept. 28.

"China Calls for Enhanced Exchanges, Cooperation in Field of Human Rights." 2002. Xinhua, July 24. In LexisNexis.

"China Calls for New International Economic Order at GATT Meeting." 1982. Xinhua, Nov. 25. In LexisNexis.

"China Considering Signing Human Rights Agreements." 1997. Associated Press, Feb. 27.

"China Denounces Soviet, Vietnamese Violation of Human Rights." 1982. Xinhua, Feb. 18. In LexisNexis.

"China Establishes Diplomatic Relations with Kirghizstan." 1992. Agence France-Presse, Jan. 6. In LexisNexis.

"China, EU Reach Agreement." 2000. *Beijing Review*, May 29.

"China Has Indisputable Sovereignty over Nansha: Official." 1995. Xinhua, Nov. 15. In LexisNexis.

"China Hopes for Continuous Improvement in Sino-Indian Relations: Li Peng." 1989. Xinhua, July 4.

"China Hopes for Direct Talks with Dalai Lama." 1988. Xinhua, Sept. 23. In LexisNexis.

"China, India Issue Joint Communiqué." 1988. Xinhua, Dec. 23. In LexisNexis.

"China, Kazakhstan Establish Diplomatic Relations." 1992. Xinhua, Jan. 4. In LexisNexis.

"China Not to Trade off State Interests for GATT Entry." 1994. Xinhua, July 19. In LexisNexis.

"China Objects to Two U.S. Amendments." 1987. *Beijing Review*, July 6.

"China Offers Views to Improve UN Human Rights Work." 1996. Xinhua, Apr. 10.

"China Prepared for Substantive Talks with GATT." 1989. Xinhua, July 5. In LexisNexis.

"China Protocol Shows Progress But Wide Gaps on Trade Rules." 1997. *Inside U.S. Trade*, Mar. 14.

"China Ratifies Convention on Human Rights." 2001. Xinhua, Feb. 28. In LexisNexis.

"China to Reform Trade Practices in WTO Bid." 1997. Xinhua, June 13. In LexisNexis.

"China Rejects U.S. Rights Report." 1985. Xinhua, Feb. 18.

"China, Russia Issue Joint Declaration." 1992. Xinhua, Dec. 18. In LexisNexis.

"China: Russian Border Deal Criticized." 1992. *South China Morning Post*, Feb. 21. In LexisNexis.

"China Seeks to Regain GATT Status (1)." 1992. Xinhua, Feb. 5. In LexisNexis.

"China Slams U.S. Decision to Appoint Tibet Affairs Official." 1997. Associated Press, Aug. 6.

"China, Tadzhikistan Establish Diplomatic Relations." 1992. Xinhua, Jan. 5. In LexisNexis.

"China: Transactions with the Fund from January 1, 1984, to March 31, 2004." International Monetary Fund. www.imf.org/external/np/tre/tad/extrans1.cfm?memberKey1=180&endDate=2004%2D06%2D30&finposition_flag=YES.

"China Urges Creation of Good Economic Environment." 1996. Xinhua, Nov. 7. In LexisNexis.

"China Urges End to Confrontation on Human Rights." 1996. Xinhua, Mar. 19.

"China Urges Tranquility on Border." 1987. *China Daily*, May 8.

"China and Vietnam Agree on Spratlys Self-Restraint." 1994. *Reuters*, July 22.

"China and Vietnam Issue Joint Statement." 1999. Xinhua, Feb. 27.

"China and Vietnam Sign Two Agreements, Leaders Hail 'New Beginning.'" 1991. Xinhua, Nov. 7.

"China, Vietnam Agree on the Need to Speed up Border Talks." 1997. Xinhua. In BBC Monitoring Service, July 15.

"China, Vietnam Agree to Avoid Conflict over Territory." 1992. Xinhua, Nov. 30.

"China, Vietnam Issue Joint Communiqué." 1991. Xinhua, Nov. 10.

"China, Vietnam Sign Accord on Territorial, Border issues." 1993. Xinhua, Oct. 19.

"China, Vietnam Sign Land Border Treaty." 1999. Xinhua, Dec. 30. In LexisNexis.

"China to Write Human Rights Protection into Constitution (more added)." 2004. Xinhua, Mar. 8.

"China's Defense Minister Praises Shanghai Organization Anti-Terror." 2003. Xinhua. In BBC World News, Aug. 15.

"China's Entry into WTO Conducive to China-U.S. Trade: Jiang." 1995. Xinhua, Oct. 23.

"China's Foreign Trade Policy Remains Unchanged." 1989. *Beijing Review*, July 26.

"China's Indisputable Sovereignty Over Nansha and Xisha Islands." 1980. *Beijing Review*, Feb. 11.

"China's Li Peng Addresses Forum on Regional National Autonomy Law." 2001. Xinhua, Dec. 6. In LexisNexis.

"China's Senior Official Reaffirms Five-point Policy toward Dalai Lama." 1984. Xinhua, Nov. 27. In LexisNexis.

"China's Stand on Non-Proliferation." 1999. *Beijing Review*, Feb. 8.

"China's Status as a Contracting Party: Memorandum on China's Foreign Trade Regime." 1987. General Agreement on Tariffs and Trade. Restricted, Feb. 18. GATT Fiche L/6125.

"China's Tibet: Facts and Figures 2002." www.china.org.cn/english/tibet-english/jjzs.htm.

"Chinese Ambassador Refutes Groundless Charges against China." 2000. Xinhua, Mar. 23. In LexisNexis.

"Chinese Ambassador Urges UNCHR to Abandon Double Standard." 2002. Xinhua, Apr. 4. In LexisNexis.

"Chinese Defense Minister on Taiwan Issue." 1995. Xinhua, Aug. 24.

"The Chinese Defense White Paper." 2002. State Council. www.china.org.cn/e-white/20021209/IV.htm#6.

"Chinese Embassy Accuses U.S. Congressional Members of Allowing Dalai Lama to

Sabotage China's Unity." 1987. Xinhua, Sept. 21. In LexisNexis.

"Chinese Foreign Minister Lodges Protest with U.S." 1995. Xinhua, May 23.

"Chinese Foreign Ministry Spokesman on Indian Granting of Statehood to 'Arunachal Pradesh.'" 1987. Xinhua, Feb. 21.

"Chinese Foreign Ministry Spokesman on Tibet Issue." 1991. Xinhua, Aug. 24. In LexisNexis.

"Chinese Journal on U.S. Relations Act." 1981. Xinhua, July 3. In LexisNexis.

"Chinese Minister Makes Historic Trip to Vietnam." 1992. *Reuters*, Feb. 12.

"Chinese News Service Answers Questions on Sino-Indian Boundary Issue." 1986. Xinhua, May 8.

"Chinese Premier Delivers Speech at Harvard University." 2003. BBC Monitoring, International Reports, Dec. 11. In LexisNexis.

"Chinese Premier's Press Conference: The Full Text." 1999. China Central TV, Mar. 15. In LexisNexis.

"Chinese President on China's WTO Entry." 2001. Xinhua, Nov. 11. In LexisNexis.

"Chinese President Urges Further Collaboration of the SCO." 2001. Xinhua, June 15.

"Chinese, U.S. Presidents Give Live News Conference." 1998. China Central TV, Beijing, June 27. In BBC Monitoring Asia Pacific.

"Chinese Vice Premier Addresses U.N. on World Economy." 1996. Xinhua, Sept. 25. In LexisNexis.

"Chinese Vice-Premier Meets GATT Chief." 1994. Xinhua, May 10. In LexisNexis.

"Chinese Vice-Premier on Human Rights." 1997. Xinhua, Sept. 24.

Chiu, Hungdah. 1989. *Chinese Attitudes toward International Law of Human Rights in the Post-Mao Era*. School of Law, University of Maryland. Occasional Papers / Reprints in Contemporary Asian Studies 5.

"Clinton Administration Fact Sheets on China Deal." 1999. *Inside U.S. Trade*, Feb. 11.

Clough, Ralph N. 1993. *Reaching Across the Taiwan Strait: People-to-People Diplomacy*. Boulder, CO: Westview.

———. 1999. *Cooperation or Conflict in the Taiwan Strait?* Lanham, MD: Rowman and Littlefield.

Cohen, Jerome Alan. 1973. *China and Intervention: Theory and Practice*. Cambridge, MA: Harvard University, Studies in East Asian Law.

Cohen, Jerome Alan, and Hungdah Chiu, eds. 1974. *People's China and International Law*, vol. 1. Princeton, NJ: Princeton University Press.

Cohen, Roberta. 1988. *People's Republic of China: The Human Rights Exception*. School of Law, University of Maryland. Occasional Papers / Reprints Series in Contemporary Asian Studies 3.

Cole, Bernard. D. 2003. "The PLA Navy and Active Defense." In Stephen J. Flanagan and Michael E. Marti, eds., *The People's Liberation Army and China in Transition*, 129–39. N.p.: National Defense University, Center for the Study of Chinese Military Affairs.

Crepon, Michael, and Amit Sevak. 1995. *Crisis Prevention, Confidence Building, and Reconciliation in South Asia*. New York: St. Martin's Press.

"Currency Stability Conducive to China's Accession to WTO." 1998. Xinhua, Mar. 9. In LexisNexis.

Dai Kelai, and Yu Xiangdong. 1989. "'Fubian Zalu' yu suowei 'Huangsha,' 'Changsha' wenti" [The Ancient "Fubian Text" and the So-Called Issue of "Huangsha" and "Changsha"]. *Guoji Wenti Yanjiu* 3: 24–29.

Dalai Lama. 1988. "Address to Members of the European Parliament." Tibetan Government in Exile, www.tibet.com/Proposal/strasbourg.html.

"Dalai Lama Is Responsible for Delaying Confirmation of Reincarnated Child for Panchen Lama." 1995. Xinhua, Nov. 12.

Dang Chaosheng. 1999. "Li Denghui zai yishi xingtai lingyu de fenlie huodong jianshi" [On Lee Teng-hui's Activities in the Ideological Sphere]. *Taiwan Yanjiu* 4: 48–52.

Das, Dilip. 2002. "Globalization: A Guide for the Concerned Policymaker." CSGR Working Paper no. 91/02. University of Warwick, Centre for the Study of Globalisation and Regionalisation.

Deckers, Wolfgang. 2004. "China, Globalization, and the World Trade Organization." *Journal of Contemporary Asia* 34: 102–20.

"Declaration of Conduct of Parties in the South China Sea." ASEAN. Available at www.aseansec.org/13163.htm.

"Deng on China's Intention to Join IMF." 1979. Xinhua, Feb. 28. In LexisNexis.

Deng Xiaoping. 1994. *Selected Works of Deng Xiaoping, Volume 3 (1982–1992)*. Beijing: Foreign Languages Press.

———. 1995. *Selected Works of Deng Xiaoping, Volume 2 (1975–1982)*, 2nd edition. Beijing: Foreign Languages Press.

"Deng Yingchao on Importance of Reunification." 1984. Xinhua, Jan. 1.

"Develop Tibetan Economy, Raise People's Living Standards, Say Party Leaders." 1980. Xinhua, May 31. In LexisNexis.

"The Development of Tibetan Culture." 2000. State Council of the PRC, www.china.org.cn/e-white/2/index.htm.

Ding Kuisong. 1998. "Dongmen diqu luntan yu Yatai anquan hezuo" [The ARF and Security Cooperation in Asia]. *Xiandai Guoji Guanxi* 7: 7–12.

Ding Zhigang. 1995. "Guoji yitihua de zhengzhi yiyi" [The Political Meaning of International Integration]. *Shijie Jingji yu Zhengzhi* 6: 59–63.

Dinmore, Guy. 2003. "Bush Sides with China over Taiwan Referendum: White House Highlights Partnership with Beijing as Premier Gets Red Carpet Welcome." 2003. *Financial Times*, Dec. 10.

Dobbs, Michael. 1989. "Gorbachev Proposes 'Border of Peace' with China." *New York Times*, May 18.

Dobson, William J., and M. Taylor Fravel. 1997. "Red Herring Hegemon: China in the South China Sea." *Current History* (Sept.): 258–63.

Documents on the Sino-Indian Boundary Question. 1960. Beijing: Foreign Languages Press.

Donnelly, Jack. 1995. "State Sovereignty and International Intervention: The Case of Human Rights." In Gene Lyons and Michael Mastanduno, eds., *Beyond Westphalia? State Sovereignty and International Intervention*, 115–47. Baltimore: John Hopkins University Press.

———. 1999. "Social Construction of International Human Rights." In Tim Dunne and Nicholas Wheeler, eds., *Human Rights in Global Politics*, 71–103. Cambridge, UK: Cambridge University Press.

Doty, Roxanne Lynne. 1996. "Sovereignty and the Nation: Constructing the Boundaries of National Identity." In Thomas J. Biersteker and Cynthia Weber, eds., *State Sovereignty as Social Construct*, 121–48. Cambridge, UK: Cambridge University Press.

Doyle, Michael W., and Anne-Marie Gardner. 2003. "Introduction: Human Rights and International Order." In Jean-Marc Coicaud, Michael Doyle, and Anne-Marie

Gardner, eds., *The Globalization of Human Rights*, 1–19. New York: United Nations University Press.

Du Xinli. 2003. "Woguo zai WTO zhong weihu guojia jingji zhuquan de falü baozhang (shang) [The Legal Safeguards for Protecting China's Economic Sovereignty within the WTO (Part 1)]. *Zhongguo Lüshi* 1: 51–73.

Duojie Caidan. 1992. "'Xizang wenti' bu shi renquan wenti er shi weihu Zhongguo zhuquan wenti" [The "Tibet Issue" Is Not a Human Rights Issue But an Issue of Protecting Chinese Sovereignty]. *Zhongguo Zangxue* 2.

"Education Right[s] Rapporteur of UN Human Rights Commission Visits China." 2003. Xinhua, Sept. 20.

Elman, Colin, and Miriam Fendius Elman. 2002. "How Not To Be Lakatos Intolerant: Appraising Progress in IR Research." *International Studies Quarterly* 46, 2 (June): 231–62.

"Expanding Foreign Trade Relations." 1992. *Beijing Review*, Mar. 9.

Fan Guoxiang. 2003. "Zenyang kan de xifang renquan sixiang" [How to Regard Western Human Rights Ideology]. *Zhongguo Dang Zheng Ganbu Luntan* 4: 59–61.

Fan Xizhou. 2002. "Xian jieduan Minjindang dalu zhengce fenxi" [An Analysis of the Recent Phase of the DPP's Mainland Policy]. *Taiwan Yanjiu Jikan* 4: 14–21.

Fearon, James, and Alexander Wendt. 2002. "Rationalism and Constructivism in International Relations Theory." In Walter Carlsnaes, Thomas Risse, and Beth Simmons, eds., *Handbook of International Relations*, 52–72. Beverly Hills: Sage.

Feeney, William R. 1984. "Chinese Policy in Multilateral Financial Institutions." In Samuel S. Kim, ed., *China and the World*, 266–93. Boulder, CO: Westview.

———. 1989. "Chinese Policy Toward Multilateral Economic Institutions." In Samuel S. Kim, ed., *China and the World*, 2nd edition, 237–64. Boulder, CO: Westview.

———. 1994. "China and the Multilateral Economic Institutions." In Samuel S. Kim, ed., *China and the World*, 3rd edition, 226–55. Boulder, CO: Westview.

———. 1998. "China and the Multilateral Economic Institutions." In Samuel Kim, ed., *China and the World*, 4th ed., 239–64. Boulder, CO: Westview.

Fewsmith, Joseph. 1999. "China and the WTO: The Politics Behind the Agreement." *National Bureau of Asian Research* 10, 5.

Finnemore, Martha, and Kathryn Sikkink. 1998. "International Norm Dynamics and Political Change." *International Organization* 4: 887–917.

Foot, Rosemary. 1996. "China-Indian Relations and the Process of Building Confidence: Implications for the Asia-Pacific." *Pacific Review* 9, 1: 58–76.

———. 2000. *Rights Beyond Borders: The Global Community and the Struggle over Human Rights in China*. Oxford: Oxford University Press.

———. 2003. "Bush, China and Human Rights." *Survival* 45, 2: 167–86.

"For a New International Economic Order." 1981. Xinhua, Nov. 2. In LexisNexis.

"Foreign Ministry Spokesman on Tensions along Sino-Indian Border." 1987. Xinhua, May 6.

"Foreign Ministry Spokesperson's Press Conference." 2002. www.fmprc.gov.cn/eng/xwfw/2510/2511/t14661.htm.

Foreman, William. 2002. "Top U.N. Human Rights Official Says China Still a 'Cause for Deep Concern.'" Associated Press, Aug. 19.

"Fourth Commentary: Lee Teng-hui Guilty of Damaging Cross-Straits Relations." 1995. Xinhua, July 26.

Fowler, Michael, and Julie Bunck. 1995. *Law, Power, and the Sovereign State*. University Park: Pennsylvania State University Press.

"Full Text of Speech by Hu Jintao at Tibet's Peaceful Liberation Anniversary Rally." 2001. Xinhua, July 19. In LexisNexis.

"'Full Text' of Statement Issued by Chinese Foreign Ministry Spokesman." 1989. Xinhua, Sept. 2. In LexisNexis.

Frasier, Mark W. 2000. "China-India Relations since Pokhran II: Assessing Sources of Conflict and Cooperation." *Access Asia Review* 3, 2 (July): 5–36.

Fravel, M. Taylor. 2003. "Closing Windows on the Frontier: Explaining China's Settlement of Territorial Disputes." Paper presented at the annual meeting of the International Studies Association, Portland, OR, Feb. 25–Mar. 1.

Ganguly, Sumit. 1989. "The Sino-Indian Border Talks, 1981–1989: The View from New Delhi." *Asian Survey* 29, 12 (Dec.): 1123–35.

Gao Zhan. 1991. "Shilun Dong-Xi jingji yitihua de san da zhangai" [A Brief Discussion of Three Large Obstacles to East-West Economic Integration]. *Shijie Jingji yu Zhengzhi* 1: 48–51.

Garver, John W. 1992. "China's Push through the South China Sea: The Interaction of Bureaucratic and National Interests." *China Quarterly* 132 (Dec.): 999–1028.

———. 1997. *Face Off: China, the United States and Taiwan's Democratization*. Seattle: University of Washington Press.

———. 2001a. *Protracted Contest: Sino-Indian Rivalry in the Twentieth Century*. Seattle: University of Washington Press.

———. 2001b. "The Restoration of Sino-Indian Comity following India's Nuclear Tests." *China Quarterly*: 865–89.

———. 2002. *The China-India-U.S. Triangle: Strategic Relations in the Post–Cold War Era*. NBR Analysis 13, 5. Seattle: National Bureau of Asian Research.

"GATT Discusses China's Request for Full Membership." 1989. Xinhua, Dec. 13. In LexisNexis.

Goertz, Gary, and Paul F. Diehl. 1992. *Territorial Changes and International Conflict*. London: Routledge.

Goldstein, Melvyn C. 1997. *The Snow Lion and the Dragon: China, Tibet, and the Dalai Lama*. Berkeley: University of California Press.

Goodwin, Paul B. 1989. "Soldiers and Statesmen: Chinese Defense and Foreign Policies in the 1990s." In Samuel Kim, ed., *China and the World*, 2nd edition, 181–203. Boulder, CO: Westview.

Gottlieb, Gideon. 1993. *Nation against the State*. New York: Council on Foreign Relations Press.

"Growth in UN Membership, 1945–2003." United Nations. www.un.org/Overview /growth.htm.

Gu Chengkai. 1997. "Lun guoji renquanfa zhong de cunzhong guojia yuanze" [A Discussion of Respect for the Principle of State Sovereignty in International Human Rights Law]. *Falü Kexue* 4: 11–15.

Gu, Xiaosong, and Brantly Womack. 2000. "Border Cooperation between China and Vietnam in the 1990s." *Asian Survey* 40, 6: 1042–58.

"Guanyu jianli guoji jingji xin zhixu wenti taolun zongshu" [Summary of a Discussion Concerning the Establishment of the NIEO]. 1983. *Shijie Jingji yu Zhengzhi* 1.

Guo Guanzhong, and Zhang Guoying. 1989. "Xizang de renquan yu zhuquan" [Tibet's

Human Rights and Sovereignty]. *Minzu Yanjiu* 5: 10–12.

Guo Shan. 1987. "China's Role in Human Rights Field." *Beijing Review*, Feb. 9.

Hall, Rodney Bruce. 1999. *National Collective Identity: Social Constructs and International Systems*. New York: Columbia University Press.

Han Deqiang. 2000. *Pengzhuang: Quanqiuhua xianjing yu Zhongguo xianshi xuanze* [Collision: The Globalization Trap and China's Real Choice]. Beijing: Jingji guanli chubanshe.

Harding, Harry. 1992. *A Fragile Relationship: The United States and China since 1972*. Washington, DC: Brookings Institution.

He Fang. 1997. "Diqu jingji yitihua yu Zhongguo" [Regional Economic Integration and China]. *Xiandai Guoji Guanxi* 4: 12–17.

He Kai. 1998. "Kaichuang Dongya hezuo xin pianzhang" [Opening Up a New Page in East Asia's Cooperation]. *Xiandai Guoji Guanxi* 2: 6–9.

He Weigang. 2003. "Guoji jizhi lilun yu Shanghai hezuo zuzhi" [The Theory of International Regimes and the Shanghai Cooperation Organization]. *Erluosi Zhongya Dongou Yanjiu* [Russian, Central Asian, and Eastern European Studies] 5: 58–64.

"Hegemonism, Power Politics Are Root Causes for Turmoil in the World." 1999. Xinhua, Sept. 29.

Heiberg, Marianne, ed. 1994. *Subduing Sovereignty*. London: Pinter.

Held, David. 2002. "Laws of States, Laws of Peoples: Three Models of Sovereignty." *Legal Theory* 8: 1–44.

Held, David, Anthony McGrew, David Goldblatt, and Jonathan Perraton. 1999. *Global Transformations: Politics, Economics and Culture*. Stanford, CA: Stanford University Press.

Henkin, Lois. 1999. "That 'S' Word: Sovereignty, and Globalization, and Human Rights, Etcetera." *Fordham Law Review* (Oct.): 1–14.

Hertzstein, Robert E. 1986. "China and the GATT: Legal and Policy Issues Raised by China's Participation in the General Agreement on Tariffs and Trade." *Law and Policy in International Business* 18, 2: 371–415.

Hinton, Isabel. 1999. *The Search for the Panchen Lama*. New York: Norton.

Holliday, Ian, Ma Ngok, and Ray Yep. 2002. "A High Degree of Autonomy? Hong Kong Special Administrative Region, 1997–2002." *Political Quarterly* 73, 4: 455–64.

————. 2004. "After 1997: The Dialectics of Hong Kong Dependence." *Journal of Contemporary Asia* 2: 254–70.

Hood, Stephen J. 1992. *Dragons Entangled: Indochina and the China-Vietnam War*. Armonk, NY: M. E. Sharpe.

"Hopes Rise for Direct Cross-Straits Flights." 2003. *China Daily*, Jan. 28.

Horsley, Jamie. 1984. "The Regulation of China's Foreign Trade." In Michael Moser, ed., *Foreign Trade, Investment and the Law in the People's Republic of China*. Oxford: Oxford University Press.

Hua Zi. 1989. "On Negotiations with the Dalai Lama." *Beijing Review*, Mar. 13.

Huang, Chi, and Samuel S. G. Wu. 1995. "Inherited Rivalry: A Chronology." In Tun-jen Cheng, Chi Huang, and Samuel S. G. Wu, eds., *Inherited Rivalry: Conflict Across the Taiwan Strait*, 227–61. Boulder, CO: Lynne Rienner.

Huang Jiashi, and Wang Yingjin. 2002. "Zhuquan goucheng yanjiu jiqi zai Taiwan wenti shang de shiyong" [A Study of the Composition of Sovereignty and its Application to the Taiwan Question]. *Taiwan Yanjiu Jikan* 2: 28–36.

Huang Wei. 1998. "A Firm Handshake Makes History." *Beijing Review*, Nov. 23.

Hughes, Christopher. 1997. *Taiwan and Chinese Nationalism: National Identity and Status in International Society*. London: Routledge.

"Human Rights in China." 1991. *Beijing Review*, Nov. 4.

"Human Rights Watch Income and Expenses." www.hrw.org/donations//finance.htm.

Hyer, Eric. 1995. "The South China Sea Disputes: Implications of China's Earlier Territorial Settlements." *Pacific Affairs* 68, 1: 34–54.

"The IMF at a Glance." International Monetary Fund. www.imf.org/external/np/exr/facts/glance.htm.

"IMF Chairman Warns against Inflation Affect on Reform." 1989. Xinhua, Apr. 12. In LexisNexis.

"IMF–People's Bank of China Sign MOU to Establish Joint Training Program." 2000. IMF News Brief no. 00/11, Feb. 21.

"Inclusion of Human Rights in Constitution Marks a Milestone in Human Rights Progress in China: Expert." 2004. Xinhua, Mar. 14.

"India Urged to Stop Slandering China." 1998. *China Daily*, July 20.

"International Court of Justice, List of Cases brought before the Court since 1946." International Court of Justice. www.icj-cij.org/icjwww/idecisions.htm.

Jackson, John H. 1998. "The Uruguay Round Results and National Sovereignty." In Jagdish Bhagwati and Mathias Hirsch, eds., *The Uruguay Round and Beyond: Essays in Honour of Arthur Dunkel*, 293–305. Ann Arbor: University of Michigan Press.

Jackson, Robert. 1990. *Quasi-States: Sovereignty, International Relations and the Third World*. New York: Cambridge University Press.

Jacobson, Harold, and Michel Oksenberg. 1990. *China's Participation in the IMF, the World Bank, and GATT*. Ann Arbor: University of Michigan Press.

James, Alan. 1986. *Sovereign Statehood: The Basis of International Society*. London: Allen and Unwin.

Jepperson, Ronald, Peter Katzenstein, and Alex Wendt. 1996. "Norms, Identity and Culture in National Security." In Peter Katzenstein, ed., *The Culture of National Security*, 33–79. New York: Columbia University Press.

Jian, Sanqing. 1996. *Foreign Policy Restructuring as Adaptive Behavior*. Lanham, MD: University Press of America.

"Jiang and Clinton Meet the Press." 1998. *Beijing Review*, July 20.

"Jiang, Bush Vow to Push Sino-US Ties Forward." 2002. Xinhua, Oct. 26. In LexisNexis.

Jiang Changbin. 2002. "Zhuquan lilun yu woguo jiaru WTO" [The Theory of Sovereignty and China's Entry into the WTO]. *Zhonggong Zhongyang Dangxiao Xuebao* 2: 67–70.

Jiang Yi. 2003. "Zhongguo de duobian waijiao yu Shanghai hezuo zuzhi [China's Multilateral Diplomacy and the Shanghai Cooperation Organization]. *Eluosi Zhongya Dongou Yanjiu* 5: 46–52.

"Jiang Zemin Meets Vietnamese Prime Minister." 1998. Xinhua, Oct. 20. In LexisNexis.

"Jiang Zemin on Stability in Tibet." 1994. Xinhua, July 26. In LexisNexis.

"Jiang Zemin Signs Order Announcing Revision of Minority Self-Rule Law." 2001. Xinhua, Mar. 1. In LexisNexis.

"Jiang Zemin: Struggle against 'Peaceful Evolution' Will Last for a Long Time." 1989. Xinhua, Sept. 29. In LexisNexis.

"Jiang Zemin: What We Need is an All-Win Globalization." 2000. *Beijing Review*, Dec. 4.

Jin Binggao. 1988. "Shilun zizhi jiguan de jianshe yu zizhiquan de xingshi" [Discussion of the Construction of Autonomous Organs and the Exercise of Autonomous Rights]. *Minzu Yanjiu* 2: 14–20.

Jin Xiaochen. 2003. "Guojia zhuquan rangdu zai WTO zhengduan jiejue jizhi zhong de fazhan" [Compromises on Sovereignty within the Development of the WTO's Dispute Settlement Mechanism]. *Zhengzhi yu Falü* 2: 92–94.

Jing Hui. 1986. "You guan Zhong-Yin bianjie zhengduan de yixie qingkuang he beijing" [Some Facts about the Situation and Background of the Sino-Indian Boundary Dispute]. *Guoji Wenti Yanjiu* 2: 1–9.

———. 1988. "Zhong-Yin dongduanjie zhenxiang" [The Real Facts of the Eastern Sector of the Chinese-Indian Border]. *Guoji Wenti Yanjiu* 1: 6–13.

Jing Wei. 1989. "Overstretched: Taiwan's 'Elastic Diplomacy.'" *Beijing Review*, Apr. 3.

Johnston, Alastair Iain. 1996. "Learning Versus Adaptation: Explaining Change in Chinese Arms Control Policy in the 1980s and 1990s." *China Journal* 35: 27–61.

"Joint Communique Issued on Jiang Zemin Visit." 1994. BBC Monitoring Service, Nov. 23.

Kapp, Bob. 2002. "WTO: Toward 'Year Two.'" *China Business Review*, Nov.–Dec.: 10.

Kelly, James. 2004. "Overview of U.S. Policy Toward Taiwan." Testimony at a hearing on Taiwan, House International Relations Committee, Apr. 21.

Kent, Ann. 1999. *China, the United Nations, and Human Rights: The Limits of Compliance.* Philadelphia: University of Pennsylvania Press.

Keohane, Robert O. 1988. "International Institutions: Two Approaches." *International Studies Quarterly* 32, 4 (Dec.): 245–53.

———. 1993. "Sovereignty, Interdependence, and International Institutions." In Linda Miller and Michael Joseph Smith, eds., *Ideas and Ideals: Essays in Honor of Stanley Hoffman*, 91–107. Boulder, CO: Westview.

———. 1995. "Hobbes's Dilemma and Institutional Change in World Politics: Sovereignty in International Society." In Hans-Henrick Holm and Georg Sorenson, eds., *Whose World Order?* 165–86. Boulder, CO: Westview.

———. 2002. "Ironies of Sovereignty: The European Union and the United States." *Journal of Common Market Studies* 40, 4: 743–65.

Kho, Stephen. 1998. *The Impact of the World Trade Organization on the Lack of Transparency in the People's Republic of China.* University of Maryland, Occasional Papers / Reprints Series in Contemporary Asian Studies 2.

Kim, Icksoo. 2002. "Accession into the WTO: External Pressure for Internal Reforms in China." *Journal of Contemporary China* 11: 433–58.

Kim, Samuel S. 1979. *China, The United Nations and World Order.* Princeton, NJ: Princeton University Press.

———. 1991. *China In and Out of the Changing World Order.* Princeton: World Order Studies Program Occasional Paper, no. 21.

———. 1994a. "China and the World in Theory and Practice." In Samuel Kim, ed., *China and the World*, 3rd edition, 3–42. Boulder, CO: Westview.

———. 1994b. "Sovereignty in the Chinese Image of World Order." In Ronald St. John Macdonald, ed., *Essays in Honour of Wang Tieya*, 425–47. Dordtrecht: Matinus Nijhoff.

———. 1998. "Chinese Foreign Policy in Theory and Practice." In Samuel Kim, ed., *China and the World*, 4th edition, 3–34. Boulder, CO: Westview.

———. 1999. "China and the United Nations." In Elizabeth Economy and Michel Oksenberg, eds., *China Joins the World: Progress and Prospects*, 42–90. New York:

Council on Foreign Relations.

Kolatch, Jonathan. 1998. "Censoring Clinton in China." *Washington Post*, July 28.

Kovacs, Maria M. 2003. "Standards of Self-Determination and Standards of Minority-Rights in the Post-Communist Era: A Historical Perspective." *Nations and Nationalism* 9, 3: 433–50.

Krasner, Stephen D. 1988. "Sovereignty: An Institutional Perspective." *Comparative Political Studies* 21, 1 (Apr.): 66–94.

———. 1993. "Economic Interdependence and Statehood." In Robert Jackson and Alan James, eds., *States in a Changing World*. Oxford: Clarendon Press.

———. 1995/96. "Compromising Westphalia." *International Security* 20, 3 (Winter): 115–51.

———. 1999. *Sovereignty: Organized Hypocrisy*. Princeton, NJ: Princeton University Press.

———. 2001a. *Problematic Sovereignty: Contested Rules and Political Possibilities*. New York: Columbia University Press.

———. 2001b. "Sovereignty." *Foreign Policy* (Jan.–Feb.): 20–29.

Krasner, Stephen D., and Janice E. Thomson. 1989. "Global Transactions and the Consolidation of Sovereignty." In Ernst-Otto Czempiel and James Rosenau, eds., *Global Changes and Theoretical Challenges*, 195–221. Lexington, MA: Lexington Books.

Lague, David. 2003. "In the Eye of the Storm." *Far Eastern Economic Review*, July 31.

———. 2004. "A Patriotic Brawl over Democracy." *Far Eastern Economic Review*, Mar. 18.

Lague, David, and Susan V. Lawrence. 2003. "Tung in Trouble." *Far Eastern Economic Review*, July 17.

Lai Caiqin. 1999. "Jing yi Sun Zhongshan yanguang toushi Li Denghui 'liangguolun' de shizhi" [On the Essence of Lee Teng-hui's "State-to-State Relations" in the View of Sun Yat-sen]. *Taiwan Yanjiu* 4: 43–47.

Lai, Shirley. 1989. "Thousands Rally Against Massacre; President Condemns Crackdown." Associated Press, June 4. In LexisNexis.

Lake, David A. 2003. "The New Sovereignty in International Relations." *International Studies Review* 5: 303–23.

Lam, Willy Wo-lap. 1999. "Zhu Deal Backlash." *South China Morning Post*, May 5.

Lardy, Nicholas. R. 1992. *Foreign Trade and Economic Reform in China, 1978–1990*. Cambridge, UK: Cambridge University Press.

———. 2002. *Integrating China into the Global Economy*. Washington, DC: Brookings Institution.

Lawrence, Susan V. 2003. "Diplomatic but Triumphal Progress." *Far Eastern Economic Review*, Nov. 13.

Lee, Lai To. 1999. *China and the South China Sea Dialogues*. Westport, CT: Praeger.

"Lee Teng-hui's Separative Words Refuted." 1994. *Beijing Review*, July 18.

"Lhasa: From Riots to Martial Law." 1989. *Beijing Review*, Mar. 27.

Li Buyun. 1994. "Renquan de liangge lilun wenti" [Two Theoretical Human Rights Issues]. *Zhongguo Faxue* 3: 38–42.

———. 1998. "Lun renquan de pupianxing he teshuxing" [A Discussion of the Universal and Special Aspects of Human Rights]. *Zhongguo Shehui Kexue Yanjiusheng Xuebao* 5: 45–48.

Li Buyun, and Deng Chengming. 2002. "Lun xianfa de renquan baozhang gongneng" [A Discussion of the Function of Constitutional Guarantees of Human Rights]. *Zhongguo Faxue* 3: 41–49.

Li Buyun, and Wang Xiujing. 1995. "Renquan guoji baohu yu Guojia Zhuquan" [The International Protection of Human Rights and State Sovereignty]. *Faxue Yanjiu* 4: 19–23.

Li Chengbin. 2001. "WTO zhengduan jiejue jizhi dui guojia zhuquan lilun de yingxiang" [The WTO's Dispute Settlement Mechanism's Impact on the Theory of State Sovereignty]. *Falu Shiyong* 9: 13–17.

Li Cong. 2000. "Duiwai kaifang yu jianshi you Zhongguo tese de shehuizhuyi: Zhongguo 'rushi' zhiji de sikao" [Opening up to the Outside World and Building the Socialist Economy with Chinese Characteristics: Reflections on China's Entry into the WTO]. *Shijie Jingji yu Zhengzhi* 6: 5–11.

Li Huichuan. 1981. "Zhong-Su bianjie tanpan de zhengjie renhe" [The Crux of the Sino-Soviet Border Question]. *Guoji Wenti Yanjiu* 10: 1–11.

Li Jin. 2001. "Dangqian liang'an guanxi de zhengjie chuxi" [An Analysis of the Crux of Current Cross-Strait Relations]. *Shijie Jingji yu Zhengzhi Luntan* 6: 62–64.

Li Jing. 2001. "Lun banglianzhi yu Zhongguo de tongyi" [On Confederation and China's Reunification]. *Taiwan Yanjiu* 3: 44–51.

Li Jingjie. 1994. "Xin shiqi Zhong-E guanxi" [Sino-Russian Relations in a New Era]. *Dongou Zhongya Yanjiu* 6: 77–80.

Li Jinming. 2002. "Nanhai zhuquan zhengduan de xianzhuang" [The Present Situation of the Sovereignty Situation over the South China Sea]. *Nanyang Wenti Yanjiu* 1: 53–65.

Li Lin. 1993. "Guoji renquan yu guojia zhuquan" [International Human Rights and State Sovereignty]. *Zhongguo Faxue* 1.

Li Ming. 1993. "'Lianheguo xianzhang' zhong de renquan yu bu ganshe neizheng wenti" [The Issue of Non-Interference in Internal Affairs in the U.N. Charter]. *Zhongguo Faxue* 3.

"Li Peng Expresses Willingness to Discuss Border Issue." 1991. Xinhua, Dec. 7. In LexisNexis.

"Li Peng Lauds China-World Bank Cooperation." 1988. Xinhua, Mar. 24. In LexisNexis.

"Li Peng Meets Foreign Minister of Sao Tome and Principe." 1989. Xinhua, June 29. In LexisNexis.

Li Zerui. 1990. "Zhiminzhuyizhe qinhua celue de zibai" [Confession of the Tactics of Aggression against China Employed by the Colonists]. *Zhongguo Zangxue* 2.

Li Zhenguang. 2001. "Renquan yu zhuquan guanxi de lishi kaocha yu sikao" [An Investigation and Reflection on the Historical Relationship between Sovereignty and Human Rights]. *Taipingyang Xuebao* 1: 62–67.

Liang Shoude. 2002. "Shilun lengzhan hou guoji zhengzhi zhong de zhuquan yu 'qiuquan'" [An Analysis of Sovereignty and "Global Rights" in Post–Cold War International Politics]. *Taipingyang Xuebao* 1: 13–23.

Liang Wei. 2002. "China's WTO Negotiation Process and Implications." *Journal of Contemporary China* 11: 683–719.

Lin Jin. 1992. "Taiwan zujue zhuzhang de Taiwan qiantu wenti" [The Advocacy of Taiwan's Self-Determination and the Future of Taiwan]. *Taiwan Yanjiu Jikan* 4: 16–27.

Liu Guangxi. 1989. "Guanmao zongxieding jinkou xukezheng shoudu xieyi yu woguo jinkou xukezheng guanli zhidu (du)" [GATT's Import Licensing Agreement and China's System of Import Licensing Administration (Cont.)]. *Guoji Maoyi Wenti* 10: 40–43.

Liu Guofen. 1996. "Dui zhuquan wenti de lishi yu xianshi zhi kaocha" [An Examination of The History and Practice of the Sovereignty Issue]. *Taiwan Yanjiu* 3: 19–25.

Liu Guoshen. 2003. "Shixi xian jieduan liang'an guanxi" [Analysis of the Recent Phase of Cross-Strait Relations]. *Taiwan Yanjiu Jikan* 2: 26–32.

Liu Han, and Wu Daying. 1979. "Shenme shi 'renquan'? Woguo de xianfa he falü weishenme buyong 'renquan' yi ci?" [What is "Human Rights"? Why China's Constitution and Law does Not Use the Term "Human Rights"]. *Minzhu yu Fazhi* 2.

Liu Jingpo. 1995. "Lun xianghu yicun tiaojianxia de guoji guanxi xin tedian" [Discussing the New Characteristics of International Relations under the Conditions of Interdependence]. *Shijie Jingji yu Zhengzhi* 4: 51–55.

Liu Li. 2002. "Jingji quanqiuhua dui guojia zhuquan de chongji yu 'xin zhuquanguan'" [Economic Globalization's Attack on State Sovereignty and the "New Sovereignty Concept"]. *Shijie Jingji yu Zhengzhi* 4: 77–81.

Liu Nanlai. 1999. "Yi Meiguo wei shou de beiyue cubao jianta guojifa" [American-Led NATO Crudely Tramples on International Law]. *Shijie Jingji yu Zhengzhi* 6: 26–28.

Liu Wenzong. 1993. "Lun Meiguo de 'renquan waijiao'" [A Discussion of American "Human Rights Diplomacy"]. *Guoji Wenti Yanjiu* 3: 28–34.

———. 1995. "Baquanzhuyi de zhuolie biaoxian: Ping Meiguo guowuyuan 'renquan baogao'" [Hegemonism's Clumsy Display: A Criticism of the U.S. State Department's "Human Rights Report"]. *Waijiao Xueyuan Xuebao* 2: 47–49.

———. 1999a. "Zong guojifa lun zhuquan bu ke fenxiang ji Taiwan de falü diwei" [Sovereignty Cannot Be Shared in the View of International Law and Taiwan's Legal Status]. *Taiwan Yanjiu* 3: 38–42.

———. 1999b. "Lun guojifa zhong de zhuquan yu renquan" [A Discussion of Sovereignty and Human Rights in International Law]. *Waijiao Xueyuan Xuebao* 3: 38–44.

———. 2000. "Beiban guojia minzu liyi de 'Taidu' zibai shu ping Li Denghui de 'Taiwan de zhuzhang'" [A Written Confession of "Taiwan Independence" that Betrays the National Interests: Comments on Lee Teng-hui's "The Position of Taiwan"]. *Taiwan Yanjiu* 1: 39–44.

———. 2001. "Principle of Sovereignty is the Foundation of International Law." Unpublished manuscript.

Liu Xin. 1990. "North-South Gap Continues to Widen." *Beijing Review*, Mar. 5.

"Lodi Gyari's Visit to China: A Significant Development." 2002. Tibet Information Network. www.tibetinfo.net/news-in-brief/nib130902.htm.

"Lower Tariffs Benefit China's Balanced Growth of Trade." 1997. Xinhua, Nov. 27. In LexisNexis.

Lu, Chih H. 1986. *The Sino-Indian Border Dispute: A Legal Study*. New York: Greenwood Press.

Lu Houming. 1990. "Renquan wenti qianyi" [A Brief Opinion on the Issue of Human Rights]. *Shijie Jingji yu Zhengzhi* 2: 32–37.

Lu Yiran. 1994. "Guanyu zaoqi Zhong-E dongduan bianjie de jige wenti" [Some Issues Concerning the Eastern Part of the Early Sino-Russian Border]. *Zhongguo Bianjiang Shidi Yanjiu* [Borderland History Report] 4.

Lun Renquan yu Zhuquan [Human Rights and Sovereign Rights]. 2001. Zhongguo Renquan Yanjiuhui. Beijing: Dangdai shijie chubanshe.

Luo Qun. 1990. "Ping 'Xizang renmin zijuequan'" [Criticism of "Tibetan People's Self-

Determination"]. *Zhongguo Xizang* 4.

Ma Jiali. 1994. "Hou lengzhan shidai Yindu de dui Hua guanxi" [India–China Relations in the Post–Cold War Era]. *Xiandai Guoji Guanxi* 3: 26–33.

———. 1998. "Yin-Ba heshiyan jiqi dui Nanya anquan taishi de yingxiang" [The Influence of the Indian and Pakistani Nuclear Tests on the State of South Asian Security]. *Xiandai Guoji Guanxi* 7: 20–23.

———. 2000. "Nuli guozhu Zhong-Yin jianshixing hezuo huoban guanxi" [Striving to Build a Constructive and Cooperative Partnership with India]. *Xiandai Guoji Guanxi* 4: 1–5.

Ma Jun. 1988. "Human Rights: China's Perspective." *Beijing Review*, Nov. 28.

Ma Zhigang. 1999. "Dongmeng xin anquan huanjing yu Zhongguo dui ying zhanlüe" [The New Security Environment of ASEAN and China's Countermeasures]. *Zhanlüe yu Guanli* 2: 43–46.

Malik, Mohan. 1995. "China-India Relations in the Post-Soviet Era: The Continuing Rivalry." *China Quarterly* 142: 317–55.

Mansingh, Surjit. 1994. "India-China Relations in the Post–Cold War Era." *Asian Survey* 34, 3 (Mar.): 285–300.

McGinnis, John, and Mark Movesian. 2000. "Commentary: The World Trade Constitution." *Harvard Law Review* (Dec.): 511–605.

McNeal, Dewardic. L. 2001. "China's Relations with Central Asian States and the Problem of Terrorism." *CRS Report for Congress*, Dec. 17.

Mei Fong, Andrew Brown, and Matt Pottinger. 2004. "Massive Protests in Hong Kong Challenges China; So Far Beijing has Failed in Efforts to Deflect City's Democratic Aspirations." *Wall Street Journal*, July 2.

"Methods of Work Relating to the State Reporting Process." 2003. Second International Committee Meeting of the Human Rights Bodies. HRI/ICM/2003/3.11 April.

"Message to Compatriots in Taiwan." 1979. *Beijing Review*, Jan. 5.

Moltz, James Clay. 1995. "Regional Tensions in the Russia-Chinese Rapprochement." *Asian Survey* 35, 6 (June): 511–27.

Moore, Thomas G. 2000. "China and Globalization." In Samuel Kim, ed., *East Asia and Globalization*, 105–33. Lanham, MD: Rowman and Littlefield.

"More on First Round of Boundary Negotiations." 1993. Xinhua, Aug. 29.

Myers, Steven Lee. 1997. "Albright to Name Special Aide on U.S. Policy toward Tibet." *New York Times*, July 30.

Nathan, Andrew, and Perry Link, eds., and Zhang Liang, compiler. 2001. *The Tiananmen Papers*. New York: Public Affairs Press.

Nathan, Andrew, and Robert S. Ross. 1997. *The Great Wall and the Empty Fortress*. New York: Norton.

"NATO Lifts Its Mask of 'Humanitarianism.'" 1999. *Beijing Review*, May 24.

"Negotiations with the 14th Dalai Lama and the Issue of Regional Autonomy." 2002. www.chinaembassy.org.in/eng/premade/48326/Tibet%20Feature.htm.

"New Trends on Taiwan." 1989. *Beijing Review*, Jan. 9.

Ni Xiayun. 1994. "Yuenan waijiao qianxi" [A Brief Analysis of Vietnam's Foreign Relations]. *Xiandai Guoji Guanxi* 6: 11–14.

Norbu, Dawa. 1991. "China's Dialogue with the Dalai Lama 1978–1990: Pre-negotiation or Dead End?" *Pacific Affairs* 3: 351–72.

"Notes on the Human Rights Question." 1979. *Peking Review*, Nov. 9.

"NPC to Continue Making Laws to Comply with WTO Rules: Li Peng." 2002. Xinhua, Mar. 9.

"Official Says China's WTO Accession Shows 'Peaceful' Development." 2004. Xinhua, Apr. 24.

Ogden, Suzanne. 1977. "The Approach of the Chinese Communists to the Study of International Law, State Sovereignty and the International System." *China Quarterly* 70: 315–37.

Ohmae, Kenichi. 1995. *The End of the Nation State: The Rise of Regional Economies.* New York: Free Press.

"The One China Principle and the Taiwan Issue." 2000. *Beijing Review*, Mar. 6.

"Optimistic of China's GATT Status Resumption." 1993. Xinhua, Jan. 31. In LexisNexis.

Oresman, Matthew. 2003. "The SCO: A New Hope or To the Graveyard of Acronyms?" Center for Strategic and International Studies: Pacific Forum, *PacNet Newsletter* 21.

Osiander, Andreas. 2001. "Sovereignty, International Relations, and the Westphalian Myth." *International Organization* 55, 2 (Spring): 251–87.

Overholt, William H. 1991. "Hong Kong and China after 1997: The Real Issues." *Proceedings of the Academy of Political Science* 38, 2: 30–53.

———. 2004. "Hong Kong at the Crossroads." Testimony to the Subcommittee on Asia and the Pacific, House Committee on International Relations, June 23.

Pan Guan. 2002a. "Xin xingshi xia de Shanghai hezuo zuzhi: Tiaozhan, jiyu he fazhan qianjing" [The Shanghai Cooperation Organization in a New Situation: Challenge, Opportunity, and Prospects for Development]. *Guoji Wenti Yanjiu* 5: 38–43.

———. 2002b. "Zhong-E guanxi de liangxing fazhan yu xin xingshi de Shanghai hezuo zuzhi" [The Benign Development of Chinese-Russian Relations and the Shanghai Cooperation Organization in a New Situation]. *Shijie Jingji Yanjiu*: 30–36.

Pan Yu, and Zhang Yonghua. 1999. "Lun 'liangguo lun' dui guojia liyi yuanze de jianta" ["State-to-State Relations" Treads on National Interests and Principles]. *Taiwan Yanjiu* 4: 38–43.

Pang Sen. 2000. "International Protection of Human Rights: Groping for the Way Ahead." Draft conference paper, Beijing, Guoji Wenti Yanjiu Suo.

Panitchpakdi, Supachai, and Mark Clifford. 2002. *China and the WTO: Changing China, Changing World Trade.* New York: Wiley.

"Party Chief Stands for One China and Two-Party Negotiation." 1990. *Beijing Review*, June 18.

Pearson, Margaret. 1999. "China's Integration into the International Trade and Investment Regime." In Elizabeth Economy and Michel Oksenberg, eds., *China Joins the World: Progress and Prospects*, 61–206. New York: Council on Foreign Relations.

———. 2001. "The Case of China's Accession to GATT/WTO." In David Lampton, ed., *The Making of Chinese Foreign and Security Policy*, 337–71. Stanford, CA: Stanford University Press.

———. 2002. "China's Multiple Personalities in Geneva: Constructing a Template for Future Research on Chinese Behavior in the WTO." Paper presented at conference in honor of Allen S. Whiting at the Fairbank Center for East Asian Research, Nov. 8–9.

Peng Xin'an. 1995. "Taiwan zijue lun de lilun tuoshi" [The Theory of Self-Determination by Tawian X-Rayed]. *Taiwan Yanjiu* 2: 1–6.

"'People's Daily' Calls for International Law Studies." 1979. Xinhua, Mar. 31. In LexisNexis.

"People's Daily Unmasks Moscow's Designs over Tibet." 1981. Xinhua, Jan. 2. In LexisNexis.

"People's Daily Says Paris Economic Summit Declaration Concerning China Groundless." 1989. Xinhua, July 17. In LexisNexis.

"People's Republic of China Accepts Article VIII Obligations." 1996. International Monetary Fund. Press release no. 96/58 Dec. 4.

Petras, James. 2000. "China in the Context of Globalization." *Journal of Contemporary Asia* 30, 1: 108–16.

Philpott, Daniel. 2001. *Revolutions in Sovereignty: How Ideas Shaped Modern International Relations.* Princeton, NJ: Princeton University Press.

"Ping Dalai Lama de 'da Zixang'" [Criticism of the Dalai Lama's "Greater Tibet"]. 2004. *Zhongguo Xizang* 1: 2–3.

Polat, Necati. 2002. *Boundary Issues in Central Asia.* Ardsley, NY: Transnational Publishers.

Prescott, Victor. 1996. "Contributions of the United Nations to Solving Boundary and Territorial Disputes, 1945–1995." *Political Geography* 15, 3/4: 287–318.

"Premier Zhu Meets the Press." 1999. *Beijing Review,* Apr. 5.

"President Predicts Cross-Strait Talks to be Resumed after Next March." 2003. Central News Agency, Aug. 13. In LexisNexis.

"President's Speech on Taiwan Reunification." 1995. BBC Summary of World Broadcasts, Jan. 31. In LexisNexis.

"Press Communique." 1999. *Beijing Review,* Nov. 22.

"The Progress of Human Rights in China." 1995. State Council. www.china.org.cn/e-white/phumanrights19/index.htm.

"Proposals for Human Rights Protection and Promotion." 1993. *Beijing Review,* June 28.

"Protocols of Accession for New Members since 1995, Including Commitments in Goods and services." 2004. World Trade Organization. www.wto.org/english/thewto_e/acc_e/completeacc_e.htm.

"Qian on China's Stand over Nansha Islands." 1995. Xinhua, July 30.

"Qian Qichen Urges Further Promotion of International Human Rights." 1998. Xinhua, Oct. 20. In LexisNexis.

"Qian Queries Lee Teng-hui's Intention to visit Mainland." 1996. Xinhua, May 21.

"Qian Reiterates 'One China' Principle." 1997. Xinhua, Sept. 29.

"Qian: Taiwan Should Face Up to the Int'l Situation." 1998. *Beijing Review,* Nov. 23.

Qin, Julia Ya. 2003. "'WTO-plus' Obligations and Their Implications for the World Trade Organization Legal System." *Journal of World Trade* 37, 3: 483–522.

Qin Liufang. 1993. "Yinianlai shijie jingji quyu jingji maoyi yitihua dongtai" [The Year's Developments in World Economic Regional Trade Integration]. *Shijie Jingji yu Zhengzhi* 8: 17–23.

Rabgey, Tashi, and Tseten Wangchuk Sharlho. 2004. *Sino-Tibetan Dialogue in the Post-Mao Era: Lessons and Prospects.* East-West Center Washington, Policy Studies.

"Rapporteur's Report." 2001. http://web.gc.cuny.edu/icissresearch/Reports/Beijing_Rapporteur_Report.html.

"Regional Ethnic Autonomy in Tibet." 2004. State Council. www.china.org.cn/e-white/20040524/index.htm.

Ren Quan. 1994a. "Guanmao xieding ji Zhongguo de diyuefang diwei" [GATT and China's Signatory Status]. *Shijie Jingji yu Zhengzhi* 2: 34–38.

————. 1994b. "'Fu guan' hou woguo ying caiqu de zongti duice" [The General Policies

China Should Enact after "Resumption"]. *Shijie Jingji yu Zhengzhi* 12: 40–44.

Ren Yishi. 1998. "Hollywood Film Lavishes Praise on a Nazi." *Beijing Review*, Mar. 16.

"'Renmin Ribao' Editorial Marks Anniversary of Minorities Autonomy Law." 1994. Xinhua, Sept. 19. In LexisNexis.

"A Reply to 'Observer' in the Soviet Weekly *New Times*." 1983. *Beijing Review*, Jan. 31.

Reus-Smit, Christian. 1999. *The Moral Purpose of the State: Culture, Social Identity, and Institutional Rationality in International Relations*. Princeton, NJ: Princeton University Press.

———. 2001. "Human Rights and the Social Construction of Sovereignty." *Review of International Studies*: 519–38.

Rigger, Shelley. 1999. "Competing Conceptions of Taiwan's Identity: The Irresolvable Conflict in Cross-Strait Relations." In Suisheng Zhao, ed., *Across the Taiwan Strait*, 229–43. New York: Routledge.

———. 2001. *From Opposition to Power: Taiwan's Democratic Progressive Party*. Boulder, CO: Lynne Rienner.

Risse, Thomas, and Kathryn Sikkink. 1999. "The Socialization of International Human Rights Norms into Domestic Practices: Introduction." In Thomas Risse, Stephen Ropp, and Katherine Sikkink, eds., *The Power of Human Rights: International Norms and Domestic Change*, 1–39. Cambridge, UK: Cambridge University Press.

Risse, Thomas, Stephen C. Ropp, and Kathryn Sikkink, eds. 1999. *The Power of Human Rights: International Norms and Domestic Change*. Cambridge, UK: Cambridge University Press

Romberg, Alan. 2003. *Rein in at the Brink of the Precipice: American Policy toward Taiwan and U.S.-PRC Relations*. Washington, DC: Henry L. Stimson Center.

Ross, Robert S. 1988. *The Indo-China Tangle: China's Vietnam Policy, 1975–1979*. New York: Columbia University Press.

———. 1995. *Negotiating Cooperation: The United States and China, 1969–1989*. Stanford, CA: Stanford University Press.

Roy, Denny. 2003. *Taiwan: A Political History*. Ithaca, NY: Cornell University Press.

Ruggie, John G. 1983. "Continuity and Transformation in the World Polity: Toward a Neorealist Synthesis." *World Politics* 35, 2 (Jan.): 261–85.

———. 1993. "Territoriality and Beyond: Problematizing Modernity in International Relations." *International Organization* 47, 1 (Winter): 139–74.

Sautman, Barry. 1999. "The Tibet Issue in Post-Summit Sino-American Relations." *Pacific Affairs* 1: 7–21.

Schell, Orville. 2000. *Virtual Tibet*. New York: Metropolitan Books.

Schwartz, Ronald. 1994. *Circle of Protest*. New York: Columbia University Press.

Segal, Gerald. 1985. *Defending China*. London: Oxford University Press.

———. 1999. "Does China Matter?" *Foreign Affairs* (Sept.–Oct.): 24–36.

"Separatism Runs against the People's Will." 1999. *Beijing Review*, Aug. 2.

Sha Yong. 1995. "Sovereignty Reigns Supreme." *Beijing Review*, Aug. 21.

Shakya, Tsering. 1999. *The Dragon in the Land of the Snows: A History of Modern Tibet since 1947*. New York: Columbia University Press.

Shao Zhongwei. 2002. "Robinson Satisfied with Human Rights Co-op." *China Daily*, Aug. 19.

Sharlho, Tseten Wangchuk. 1992. "China's Reforms in Tibet: Issues and Dilemmas." *Journal of Contemporary China* 1: 34–61.

She Duanzhi. 1989. "Human Rights Abuse or Prejudice? *Beijing Review*, Apr. 10.

Shen Baoxiang, Wang Chengquan, and Li Zerui. 1982. "On the Question of Human Rights in the International Realm." *Beijing Review* 30: 16.

Shen Jiru. 1990. "Jiushi niandai shijie jingji diqu yitihua de tiaozhan yu Zhongguo de duice" [The Challenge of Economic Regional Integration in the 1990s and China's Policies]. *Shijie Jingji yu Zhengzhi* 4: 1–7.

————. 1999. "Kesuowo wenti yinfa de ruogan sikao" [Several Considerations Initiated by the Kosovo Issue]. *Shijie Jingji yu Zhengzhi* 7: 11–16.

Shen Yan, and Yu Shuyang. 2001. "Chenqqian qihou, jiwang kailai, mulin youhao, zai chuang huihang, 'Shanghai wuguo' jiangxu xie shiji xinpian" [The Carrying on of Good-Neighbor Policy and Continuation of the Writing of a New Chapter of the "Shanghai Five" in a New Century]. *Guofang Bao* [National Defense], June 1.

Shenon, Philip. 1994. "China Sends Warships to Vietnam Oil Site." *New York Times*, July 21.

Shi Yinhong. 2000. "Lun 20 shiji guoji guifan tixi" [A Discussion of the System of International Norms in the Twentieth Century]. *Guoji Luntan* 3: 2–11.

————. 2004. "Taiwan wenti shang de yanzhong weyan he zhanlüe bixu" [Strategic Necessity and Grave Danger in the Taiwan Issue]. *Shijie Jingji yu Zhengzhi* 7: 33–38.

Shi Yun. 1984. "Guanyu Zhonghua renmin gongheguo minzu guyu zizhifa" [Concerning the PRC's National Regional Autonomy Law]. *Minzu Yanjiu* 5, 3: 1–11.

Shi Ze. 1996. "Lun xin shiqi de Zhong-E guanxi" [Sino-Russian Relations in a New Time]. *Guoji Wenti Yanjiu* 2: 1–8.

Shichor, Yitzhak. 2004. "The Great Wall of Steel: Military and Strategy in Xinjiang." In S. Fredrick Starr, ed., *Xinjiang: China's Muslim Borderland*, 120–63. Armonk, NY: M. E. Sharpe.

Shih, Chih-yu. 2003. *Navigating Sovereignty: World Politics Lost in China.* New York: Palgrave Macmillan.

Sidhu, Wangheguru Pal Singh, and Jing-dong Yuan. 2003. *China and India: Cooperation or Conflict?* Boulder, CO: Lynne Rienner.

Sikkink, Kathryn, and Hans Schmitz. 2002. "International Human Rights." Walter Carlsnaes, Thomas Risse, and Beth Simmons, eds., *Handbook of International Relations*, 517–37. Beverly Hills: Sage.

Sil, Rudra. 2000. "The Foundations of Eclecticism: The Epistemological Status of Agency, Culture, and Structure in Social Theory." *Journal of Theoretical Politics* 12, 3: 353–87.

Simmons, Beth. 2002. "Capacity, Commitment, and Compliance: International Institutions and Territorial Disputes." *Journal of Conflict Resolution* 46, 6: 829–56.

"Sino-Indian Boundary Talks Make Good Progress." 1995. Xinhua, Aug. 20.

"Sino-Indian Cooperation Urged." 1987. *China Daily*, June 17.

"Sino-Soviet Border Talks End in Moscow." 1987. Xinhua, Feb. 23.

"Sino-Soviet Joint Communiqué." 1989. Xinhua, May 18. In LexisNexis.

"Sino-Vietnamese Communiqué." 1995. Xinhua, Dec. 2.

Smith, James McCall. 2001. "One Sovereign, Two Legal Systems: China and the Problem of Commitment in Hong Kong." In Stephen Krasner, ed., *Problematic Sovereignty*, 105–41. New York: Columbia University Press.

Smith, Steven. 2001. "Globalization and the Governance of Space: A Critique of Krasner on Sovereignty." *International Relations of the Asia-Pacific* 1: 199–226.

Smith, Warren W. 1996. *Tibetan Nation: A History of Tibetan Nationalism and Sino-Tibetan Relations.* Boulder, CO: Westview.

———. 2003. "Sino-Tibetan Dialogue: Talks or Tourism?" Tibetan News Update, Aug. 2003, www.friends-of-tibet.org.nz/news/august_2003_update_20.htm.

Song Dexing. 1999. "Shixi Yindu zai Zhong-Yin bianjie wenti shang de zhanlüe gouxiang" [A Preliminary Analysis of India's Strategic Cooperation on the Sino-Indian Border Problem]. *Shijie Jingji yu Zhengzhi* 6: 73–78.

Song Linfei. 2004. "'Taidu' de benzhi shi maiguozhuyi" [The Essence of "Taiwan Independence" is Treason]. *Shijie Jingji yu Zhengzhi Luntan* 1: 69–73.

Sorenson, Georg. 1999. "Sovereignty: Change and Continuity in a Fundamental Institution." *Political Studies* 48: 590–604.

"Spokesman on Postponing of Wang-Koo Meeting." 1995. Xinhua, June 16.

"Statement by H. E. Mr. Fan Guoxiang, Ambassador, Permanent Representative (Speaking as an Observer)." 1991. General Agreement on Tariffs and Trade. GATT Fiche SR.47/ST/6, Dec. 20.

"Statement by H. E. Mr. Jin Yongjin, Ambassador, Permanent Representative of China (Speaking as an Observer)." 1992. General Agreement on Tariffs and Trade. GATT Fiche SR.48/ST/6, Dec. 23.

Stolper, Thomas E. 1985. *China, Taiwan, and the Offshore Islands: Together with an Implication for Outer Mongolia and Sino-Soviet Relations.* Armonk, NY: M. E. Sharpe.

"Striking Under Surveillance-2." Government of Tibet in Exile, www.tibet.com/Humanrights/diir94hrrpt2.html#A2.

"Success of the Second Round of Dialogue Uncertain." 2003. Tibet Information Network, June 12, 2003, www.tibetinfo.net/news-updates/2003/1206.htm.

Suettinger, Robert. 2003. *Beyond Tiananmen: The Politics of U.S.-China Relations.* Washington, DC: Brookings Institution Press.

Suh, J. J., Peter Katzenstein, and Allen Carlson, eds. 2004. *Rethinking Security in East Asia: Identity, Power and Efficiency.* Stanford, CA: Stanford University Press.

Sun Jian. 2000. "Jingji quanqiuhua yu guojia zhuquan" [Economic Globalization and State Sovereignty]. *Nanjing Zhengzhi Xueyuan Xuebao* 3: 54–57.

Sun Jianzhong. 2000. "Fazhanzhong guojia he fada guojia zai zhuqan wenti shang de butong zhanlüe yitu" [Different Strategic Intentions between Developing Countries and Developed Countries over Sovereignty Issues]. *Taipingyang Xuebao* 1: 31–39.

"Taiwan President Calls for Urgent Referendum on Island's Future." 2002. Central News Agency, Aug. 3. In BBC Worldwide Monitoring.

"The Taiwan Question and Reunification of China." 1993. State Council. www.china.org.cn/e-white/taiwan/index.htm.

"Taiwan's Lee Redefines Relations with China as Nation-to-Nation." 1999. Associated Press, July 10. In LexisNexis.

"Taiwan's Role in Beijing's Counter-revolutionary Rebellion Exposed." 1989. Xinhua, July 26. In LexisNexis.

"Talks between KMT and Communist Party Urged." 1986. Xinhua, Nov. 12.

Tang Renwu. 1998. "Quanqiu yitihua de shenhua, fazhanzhong guojia de xianjing" [The Myth of Economic Globalization Serves as a Trap for Developing Countries]. *Shijie Jingji yu Zhengzhi* 12: 14–19.

Tang Renwu, and Hu Chunmu. 2000. "Lun quanqiuhua guize de fuqiang yu ruoxing" [Discussing the Rules of Globalization: "Assist the Violent and Curb the Weak"].

Shijie Jingji yu Zhengzhi 4: 44–48.

Tang Shiping. 2000. "Zhongguo yi Yindu guanxi de boyi he Zhongguo de Nanya zhanlüe" [Sino-Indian Relations and China's South-Asia Strategy]. *Shijie Jingji yu
Zhengzhi* 9: 24–30.

Taylor, Peter. 1989. *Political Geography*. 2nd edition. Essex: Longman Scientific and
Technical.

"Text Excerpts from Gorbachev's Speech." 1986. Associated Press, July 28.

"Text of 'The Law of the People's Republic of China on Its Territorial Waters and Their
Contiguous Areas.'" 1992. Xinhua, Feb. 25.

Theirs, Paul. 2002. "Challenges for WTO Implementation: Lessons from China's Deep
Integration into an International Trade Regime." *Journal of Contemporary China* 11:
413–31.

Thomson, Janice E. 1995. "State Sovereignty in International Relations: Bridging the
Gap between Theory and Empirical Research." *International Studies Quarterly* 39:
213–33.

Tian Jin. 1989. "Guoji renquan huodong de fazhan he cunzai zhengyi de wenti" [The
Historical Development of International Human Rights Activities and Some
Controversial Issues]. *Guoji Wenti Yanjiu* 1: 4–7.

"Tibet: Its Ownership and Human Rights Situation." 1992. State Council.
www.china.org.cn/e-white/tibet/.

"Tibet: One More Year of Repression, 1996 Annual Report." 1996. Government of Tibet
in Exile, www.Tibet.com/Human Rights/Human Rights96/hr96ExSum.html.

Tonnesson, Stein. 2003. "Sino-Vietnamese Rapprochement and the South China Sea
Irritant." *Security Dialogue* 34, 1: 55–70.

"Top Procurator Calls for Protection of Human Rights." 1988. Xinhua, Sept. 7.

"Trade Reforms Follow GATT Rules." 1992. Xinhua, Mar. 1. In LexisNexis.

"The Truth about the Sino-Vietnamese Boundary Question." 1979. *Beijing Review*, May
25.

Tsai, Mary C. 2000. "Globalization and Conditionality: Two Sides of the Sovereignty
Coin." *Law and Policy in International Business* 31: 1317–29.

Tsang, Steve. 1997. *Hong Kong: An Appointment with China*. London: I. B. Tauris.

Tucker, Nancy Bernkopf. 1994. *Taiwan, Hong Kong, and the United States, 1945–1992:
Uncertain Friendships*. New York: Twayne.

"U.N. Meeting Rejects Resolution against China." 1995. Xinhua, Mar. 8. In LexisNexis.

"U.N. Resolution Fails to Fully Reflect China's Stand: Envoy." 1999. Xinhua, June 10. In
LexisNexis.

"Upgraded U.S.-Taiwan Ties Protested." 1994. *Beijing Review*, Sept. 19.

"Urgent: Chinese Military Completes Landing Exercises." 1999. Xinhua, Sept. 10. In
LexisNexis.

"U.S. Religious Leaders Visit Prison in Lhasa." 1998. *Beijing Review*, Mar. 16.

"U.S. Stresses Freedom of Navigation in South China Sea." 1995. Agence France-Presse,
May 17.

"Vice Premier Qian Qichen Meets Taiwan Visitors." 2000. Xinhua, Aug. 29. In
LexisNexis.

"Vietnam, China Sign Deals Setting Tonkin Gulf Border." 2000. Reuters, Dec. 26.

Walker, R. B. J. 1993. *Inside/Outside: International Relations as Political Theory*. Cambridge,
UK: Cambridge University Press.

Waltz, Kenneth. 1986. "Political Structures." In Robert Keohane, ed., *Neorealism and its Critics*, 70–98. New York: Columbia University Press.

Wan, Ming. 2001. *Human Rights in Chinese Foreign Relations*. Philadelphia: University of Pennsylvania Press.

Wang Guifang. 2001. "'Shanghai wuguo' jizhi: Zhongguo guoji diwei tigao de jianzheng" [The "Shanghai Five" Organization: Testimony to the Rise of China's International Status]. *Jiefangjun Bao*, June 15.

Wang Guoxian. 1989. "Taiwan dangju tuixing 'tanxing waijiao' de yitu yu houguo" ["Flexible Diplomacy" of the Taiwanese Authorities: Intention and Consequence]. *Taiwan Yanjiu* 4: 1–5.

Wang Hexing. 1998. "Zong Yazhou jinrong fengbao kan jingji quanqiuhua" [Looking at Economic Globalization from the Perspective of the Asian Financial Crisis]. *Guoji Wenti Yanjiu* 3: 33–38.

Wang Hongwei. 1998. *Ximalaya shan qingjie: Zhong-Yin guanxi yanjiu* [The Himalayan Sentiment: Studies in Sino-Indian Relations]. Beijing: Zhongguo Xizangxue chubanshe.

———. 2000. "Zai xin shiji jiaqian he shenhua Zhong-Yin guanxi de jidian jianyi" [A Few Recommendations on Strengthening and Deepening Sino-Indian Relations in the New Century]. *Nanya Yanjiu* 1: 8–14.

Wang, Hongyu. 1995. "Sino-Indian Relations: Present and Future." *Asian Survey* 35, 6 (June): 546–54.

Wang Jisi. 2002. "Dui woguo guoji huanjing he Meiguo zhanlüe zouxiang de ji dian guji" [A Few Predictions on the Direction of U.S. Strategy and China's International Environment]. *Xiandai Guoji Guanxi* 11: 1–3.

Wang Kehua. 1991. "Ping Li Jieming yu Li Denghui de 'xin zhuquanlun'" [Criticism of James Lilly and Lee Teng-hui's "New Sovereignty Concept"]. *Taiwan Yanjiu* 4: 1–5.

Wang Meili. 1997. "Renquan de guoneixing yu guojixing" [The Domestic and International Sides of Human Rights]. *Xiandai Faxue* 1: 76–79.

———. 1998. "Guojia zhuquan yuanze: Shizhong shi guojifa he guoji guanxi de jichu" [The Principle of State Sovereignty Has Always Been the Foundation Stone of International Law and International Relations]. *Xiandai Faxue* 1: 124–27.

Wang Shuliang. 1996. "Guojia zhuquan yu renquan" [State Sovereignty and Human Rights]. *Shanghai Shehui Kexueyuan Xueshu Jikan* 1: 65–72.

Wang Yi. 1991. "Wulagui huihe duobian maoyi tanban yu woguo de jiben lichang" [The Uruguay Round Multilateral Trade Talks and China's Basic Position]. *Guoji Maoyi Wenti* 6: 31–34.

Wang Yingjin. 2003. "Banglianzhi moshi yu liang'an tongyi tanxi" [An Exploration of the Model of Confederation System and the Reuniting of the Chinese Mainland and Taiwan]. *Taiwan Yanjiu Jikan* 3: 53–59.

Wei Min. 1994. "Wulagui huihe tanban jieshu ji yingxiang" [The Results and Influence of the Uruguay Round]. *Guoji Wenti Yanjiu* 2: 32–35.

Weingast, Barry. 1995. "A Rational Choice Perspective on the Role of Ideas: Shared Belief Systems and State Sovereignty in International Cooperation." *Politics and Society* 23, 4 (Dec.): 449–64.

Wendt, Alexander. 1992. "Anarchy Is What States Make of It." *International Organization* 46, 2: 391–425.

———. 1999. *Social Theory of International Politics*. Cambridge, UK: Cambridge University Press.

Wendt, Alexander, and Daniel Friedheim. 1996. "Hierarchy under Anarchy: Informal Empire and the East German State." In Thomas J. Biersteker and Cynthia Weber, *State Sovereignty as Social Construct*, 240–78. Cambridge, UK: Cambridge University Press.

Whiting, Allen S. 1975. *The Chinese Calculus of Deterrence: India and Indochina.* Ann Arbor: University of Michigan Press.

Wilder, David. 2003. "China to Receive Grudging Passing Grade on WTO as 2nd Anniversary Nears." *South China Morning Post*, Dec. 5.

Wishnick, Elizabeth. 2001. *Mending Fences: The Evolution of Moscow's China Policy from Brezhnev to Yeltsin.* Seattle: University of Washington Press.

"World Bank Historical Chronology." http://web.worldbank.org/WBSITE/EXTER-NAL/EXTABOUTUS/EXTARCHIVES/0,,contentMDK:20035653˜7EmenuPK:5 6305˜7EpagePK:36726˜7EpiPK:36092˜7EtheSitePK:29506,00.html.

Wriston, Walter. 1992. *The Twilight of Sovereignty.* New York: Scribner.

"Writer Rejects US Report on Tibet." 2003. Xinhua, June 11.

"Wu Bangguo Calls for Struggle against Dalai Clique." 1995. Xinhua, Aug. 31.

Wu Luming. 1993. "Zhongya wuguo xianzhuang" [The Current Situation in Central Asia]. *Guoji Wenti Yanjiu* 1: 23–28.

Wu Xingzou. 1995. "Guojia zhuquan minzu guojia yongheng de yuanze" [Sovereignty: The Unchanging Principle of Nation-States]. *Guoji Guanxi Xueyuan Xuebao* 4: 56–64.

"Wu Xueqian: China Upholds Respect of Human Rights." 1986. Xinhua, Sept. 24. In LexisNexis.

"Wu Xueqian: Mainland-Taiwan Relations Must be Resolved." 1988. Xinhua, Dec. 30. In LexisNexis.

Xi Runchang. 1985. "Lun Meiguo de guojia zhanlüe: 'Gao bianjiang' zhanlüe" [A Discussion of American National Strategy: The Strategy of "Surpassing Borders"]. *Shijie Jingji yu Zhengzhi* 7.

Xia Yi. 2002. "WTO zhengduan juejie jizhi guanxiaquan tantao" [An Inquiry into the Administrative Authority of the WTO's Dispute Settlement Mechanism]. *Dangdai Faxue* 1: 36–38.

Xiao Gang. 1999. "Jingji quanqiuhua de shenhua yu bu duicheng de xianghu yicun" [The Myth of Economic Globalization and Asymmetrical Interdependence]. *Shijie Jingji yu Zhengzhi* 9: 30–34.

Xiao Qinfu. 1990. "Lüelun jingji guojihua dui guojia zhuquan de qinshi" [A Brief Discussion of Economic Internationalization's Erosion of State Sovereignty]. *Shijie Jingji yu Zhengzhi* 5: 25–32.

Xie Yu, and Liu Jiayan. 2002. "Taiwan dangju 'jianjinshi Taidu' tuoshi" [Perspectives on the "Gradual Taiwan Independence" of the Taiwan Authorities]. *Taiwan Yanjiu* 3: 28–35.

"Xinhua, People's Daily Denounces Chen's Pro-independence Remarks." 2002. Xinhua, Aug. 6. In LexisNexis.

"Xinhua Reports 'Social Order' in Lhasa 'Returned to Normal.'" 1993. BBC Summary of World Broadcasts, May 28. In LexisNexis.

"Xisha and Nansha Islands Belong to China." 1979. *Beijing Review*, May 25.

Xu Dan. 1993. "Gaike kaifang de Zhongguo he Zhongya" [China and Central Asia during Reform]. *Xiandai Guoji Wenti* 9: 1–4.

Xu Guojin. 1992. "Guojia luxing guoji renquan yiwu de xiandu" [The Limits on State Performance of Human Rights Obligations]. *Zhongguo Faxue* 2.

Xu Mei. 2000. "Zhong-Yue guanxi de huiguyu zhanwang" [The Past and Future of Sino-Vietnamese Relations]. *Dongnanya Yanjiu* 2: 11–14.

Xu Tao. 2002. "Lun xin xingshi xia de Shanghai hezuo zuzhi" [A Discussion of the Shanghai Cooperation Organization in a New Situation]. *Xiandai Guoji Guanxi* 6: 6–14.

———. 2003. "Lun Shanghai hezuo zuzhi de jizhihua" [A Discussion of the Institutionalization of the Shanghai Cooperation Organization]. *Xiandai Guoji Guanxi* 6: 7–14.

Xu Weidong, Shen Zhengwu, and Zheng Chengliang. 1992. "Lun renquan de yishixing-tai biaozhun yu falü biaozhun" [A Discussion of Ideological and Legal Standards of Human Rights]. *Zhongguo Faxue* 1.

Xue Rongjiu. 1984. "Guanshui yu maoyi zongxiedingde xingzhi, zuoyong yu liyong" [The Nature, Role, and Use of GATT]. *Guoji Maoyi Wenti* 2: 13–17.

———. 1988. "Guanshui ji maoyi zong xieding yu woguo waimao tizhi gaige" [GATT and the Reform of China's Foreign Trade System]. *Guoji Maoyi Wenti* 1: 16–21.

Yahuda, Michael. 1996. *Hong Kong: China's Challenge*. London: Routledge.

Yang Chengxu, ed. 2001. *Xin Tiaozhan: Guoji Guanxi zhong de "Rendaozhuyi Ganyu"* [A New Challenge: "Humanitarian Intervention" in International Relations]. Beijing: Zhongguo qingnian chubanshe.

Yang Fan. 2003. "Cong he jiaodu lijie WTO tiaokuan?" [From What Angle to Understand the WTO Terms?] Blogchina.com. www.gjmy.com/Article/case/case_policy/200303/6681.asp.

Yang Fan, and Zhi Rong. 1993. "Lun minzu zijuequan" [Discussion of Self-determination]. *Shoudu Shifan Daxue Xuebao* 2.

Yang Gongsu. 1989a. "Zhong-Yin bianjie wenti de zhenxiang" [The Reality of the Sino-Indian Border Issue]. *Bianjiang Shidi Yanjiu Baogao* 5.

———. 1989b. "Suowei 'Xizang duli' huodong de youlai ji pouxi" [Analysis of the Origins of the "Tibetan Independence" Movement]. *Zhongguo Xizang* 1.

———. 1997. *Zhonghua Remin Gongheguo Waijiao Lilun yu Shijian* [The Theory and Practice of PRC Diplomacy]. Beijing: Beijing Daxue Guoji Guanxi Xueyuan. Neibuban faxing.

Yang Hongmei, and Zhou Jianming. 2003. "Dui dangqian quanqiuhua beijing xia guoji zhengzhi tezheng de ruogan renshi" [Several Thoughts about the Characteristics of International Politics under the Background of Contemporary Globalization]. *Shijie Jingji yu Zhengzhi* 3: 57–61.

Yang Jinlin. 1987. "Wang 'minzujue' pouxi" [An Analysis of "People's Self-Determination"]. *Taiwan Wenti Yanjiu Jikan* 3.

Yang Xiyu. 1991. "Shijie jingji jituanhua de tedian, yingxiang yu duice" [The Characteristics, Influence, and Policies of World Economic Grouping]. *Xiandai Guoji Guanxi* 4: 30–36.

Yang Zejun. 2001. "Qianxi Minjindang shangtaihou de dalu zhengce" [A Brief Analysis of the DPP's Post-Election Mainland Policy]. *Shijie Jingji yu Zhengzhi Luntan* 3: 70–73.

Yao Liming. 2001. "Zong zhuquan gainian, guojifa kan Zhongguo dui Taiwan yong you juedui de zhuquan" [China Has the Absolute Sovereign Right over Taiwan in the Concepts of Sovereignty and International Law]. *Taiwan Yanjiu* 1: 30–35.

Ye Zhengjia. 1996. "Sino-Indian Friendship and Cooperation Contribute to Peace and Development in Asia and the World at Large." *Studia Diplomatica* 4–5: 111–20.

Yi Ding. 1989. "Opposing Interference in Other Countries Internal Affairs Through

Human Rights." *Beijing Review*, Nov. 6.

"Yi Makesizhuyi wei zhidao shenru yanjiu renquan lilun" [Use Marxism to Guide the Further Study of the Theory of Human Rights]. 1991. *Faxue Yanjiu* 5: 13–22.

"Yi xiang zhongyao de faxue yanjiu keti" [An Important Problem in Legal Research]. 1991. *Zhongguo Faxue* 3: 5–7.

Yi Xiaozhun. 1998. "Shinian mojian: Ruhe kandai woguo jiaru shimao zuzhi wenti" [A Long Way to Go: China's Accession to the WTO is Consistent with the Country's Reform Goals]. *Guoji Maoyi* 1: 4–5.

"Yin Fatang Urges Dalai Lama to Admit Mistakes and Return." 1984. Lhasa, Tibet regional service, May 13. In BBC Summary of World Broadcasts.

Yin Weiguo. 1992. "Dulianti neibu ji yu zhoubian lingguo de lingtu zhan wenti" [Commonwealth of Independent States' International (Affairs) and the Issue of Neighboring States' Territory]. *Shijie Jingji yu Zhengzhi* 8: 44–48.

Yong Qiang. 2000. "Guojiguanxi yu 'rendaozhuyi ganyu' guoji yanjiuhui zai Beijing juxing" [International Meeting on International Relations and "Humanitarian Intervention" Held in Beijing]. *Guoji Wenti Yanjiu* 6: 48–49.

You, Ji. 1999. *The Armed Forces of China*. London: I. B. Tauris.

Yu Changsen. 2000. "Dongmeng diqu luntan mubiao ji daguo de lichang" [The Objectives of the ARF and the Big Powers' Strategies]. *Dongnanya Yanjiu* 4: 22–27.

Yu Lei. 1996. "Five-way Border Pledge Signed." *China Daily*, Apr. 27.

Yu Minyou. 2000. "Yi xin zhuquan guan yingjie xin shiji de guoji faxue" [A New Sovereignty Concept to Meet A New Century's Study of International Law]. *Faxue Pinglun* 2.

Yu Qixiang. 1993. "Jingji guojihua yu guojia zhuquan" [Economic Internationalization and State Sovereignty]. *Shijie Jingji yu Zhengzhi* 8: 27–30.

Yu Qixiang, and Jiang Yi. 1994. "Riyi shoudao tiaozhan de guojia zhuquan" [The Increasingly Challenged State Sovereignty]. *Shijie Jingji yu Zhengzhi* 7: 32–36.

Yu Qunzhi. 1994. "Xi fazhanzhong guojia diqu jingji yitihua fazhan de zhangai" [Analyzing the Obstacles to the Development of Regional Economic Integration among Developing Countries]. *Shijie Jingji yu Zhengzhi* 3: 17–21.

Yu Xiaofeng, and Jia Yajun. 2000. "Guoji yitihua jinchengzhong guojia zhuquan xin lijie [A New Understanding of State Sovereignty within the Process of International Integration]. *Taipingyang Xuebao* 4: 17–22.

Yu Zhengliang. 2000. "Guojia zhuquan cengci lilun" [The Theory of Levels of State Sovereignty]. *Taipingyang Xuebao* 4: 13–16.

Yuan, Jin-Dong. 1998a. "Multilateral Intervention and State Sovereignty: Chinese Views on U.N. Peacekeeping Operations." *Political Science* 49: 275–95.

———. 1998b. "Sino-Russian Confidence Building Measures: A Preliminary Analysis." Working Paper 20. University of British Columbia, Centre of International Relations.

———. 2001. "India's Rise after Pokhran II." *Asian Survey* 41, 6: 978–1001.

———. 2003. "China and the Shanghai Cooperation Organization." *Politologiske Studier* (Sept.): 128–38.

Yue, Ren. 1996. "Sovereignty in Chinese Foreign Policy: Principle and Practice." In Maurice Brosseau, Suzanne Pepper, and Tsang Shu-ki, eds., *China Review, 1996*, 145–75. Hong Kong: Hong Kong Chinese University Press.

Zacher, Mark W. 2001. "The Territorial Integrity Norm: International Boundaries and the Use of Force." *International Organization* 55, 2 (Spring): 215–50.

Zeng Jingliang. 1998. "Lun lengzhan hou shidai de guojia zhuquan" [A Discussion of State Sovereignty in the Post–Cold War Era]. *Zhongguo Faxue* 1: 109–20.

Zhang Hanlin. 1998. "Haoxiang yi zhang wuxing de wang" [Like an Invisible Web]. *Guoji Maoyi* 8: 31–34.

Zhang Li. 2001. "Zong gaoceng fangmian kan yinxiang jiqi Zhong-Yin guanxi zouxiang de zhuyao yinsu" [Certain Significant Factors Affecting Sino-Indian Relations Indicated in the Exchange of Visits by and between Top Officials of China and India]. *Nanya Yanjiu* 2: 7–13.

Zhang Naigen. 2001. "Lun WTO zhengduan jiejue jizhi de jige zhongyao guojifa wenti" [A Discussion of the International Legal Issues in the WTO's Dispute Settlement Mechanism]. *Faxue Pinglun* 5: 51–58.

Zhang Ruizhuang. 1982. "Meiguo xiang Taiwansheng chushou wuqi de lishi yu xianzhuang" [The History and Conditions of U.S. Arms Sales to the Province of Taiwan]. *Shijie Jingji yu Zhengzhi* 5.

Zhang Songtao. 2001. "Zhudong yingdui: Jingji quanqiuhua zai renshi qiji Zhongguo 'rushi'" [An Active Response: A Reconsideration of Economic Globalization and China's Entry into the WTO]. *Guoji Maoyi* 2: 24–27.

Zhang Wenmu. 2000. *Zhongguo Xin Shiji Anquan Zhanlüe* [China's Security Strategy in the New Century]. Ji'nan: Shandong renmin chubanshe.

Zhang Xiaoling. 1998. "'Shijie renquan xuanyuan' yu Zhongguo de renquan guan" ["The UDHR" and the Chinese Perspective on Human Rights]. *Zhonggong Zhongyang Dangxiao Xuebao* 3: 57–66.

Zhang, Yongjin. 1998. *China in International Society since 1949: Alienation and Beyond*. New York: St. Martin's Press.

Zhang Zhirong. 1988. "Ping Taiwan duli yundong" [A Critique of the Taiwan Independence Movement]. *Shijie Jingji yu Zhengzhi* 2: 42–49.

———. 1990. "Dui lishi yu guojifa de yanzhong waiqu: Ping fan Pulahe 'Xizang de Diwei'" [A Gross Distortion of History and International Law: A Critique of van Walt's "Status of Tibet"]. *Zhongguo Zangxue* 3.

———. 1992a. "Xizang renquan wenti shulun" [Review of the So-called Question of Human Rights in Tibet]. *Zhongguo Zangxue* 2.

———. 1992b. "Dangdai guoji renquan wenti qianlun" [A Brief Discussion of Contemporary International Human Rights]. *Shijie Jingji yu Zhengzhi* 1: 57–63.

Zhao Huaipu, and Lu Yang. 1993. "Quanli zhengzhi yu xianghu yicun" [Power Politics and Interdependence]. *Shijie Jingji yu Zhengzhi* 7: 36–42.

Zhao, Suisheng. 1999. "Economic Interdependence and Political Divergence." In Suisheng Zhao, ed., *Across the Taiwan Strait: Mainland China, Taiwan, and the 1995–1996 Crisis*, 21–41. New York, Routledge.

———. 2001. "China's Periphery Policy and Changing Security Environment in the Asia-Pacific Region." *Prospect Quarterly* 2, 4: 57–89.

Zhao, Weiren, and Giri Deshingkar. 1995. "Improving Sino-Indo Relations." In Michael Krepon and Amit Sevak, eds., *Crisis Prevention, Confidence Building and Reconciliation in South Asia*, 227–39. New York: St. Martin's Press.

Zhao Weitian. 1995. "Tan fuguan de libi deshi" [A Discussion of the Cost and Benefits of a Resuming Membership in GATT]. *Guoji Maoyi Wenti* 11: 20–21.

Zhao Yueling. 2002. "Dongmeng dui Nanzhonghai wenti de jieru jiqi xiaoji yingxiang" [ASEAN's Involvement in the South China Sea Issue and Its Negative Influence]. *Jiefangjun Waiguoyu Xueyan Xuebao* 6: 110–13.

"Zhao Ziyang on Death of Chiang Ching-kuo." 1988. Xinhua, Jan. 14. In LexisNexis.

Zheng Bingwen. 2000. "'Rushi' dui Zhongguo jingji de yingxiang" [The Impact of Entry into WTO on China's Economy]. *Shijie Jingji yu Zhengzhi* 1: 39–45.

Zhi Yun. 1991. "Ping fan Pulahe de 'Xizang zijue' lun" [Critique of van Walt's "Tibetan Self-determination"]. *Zhongguo Xizang* (Winter).

———. 1994. "Gao 'Xizang duli' shi meiyou qiantu de" ["Tibetan Independence" Has No Future]. *Zhongguo Xizang* 6.

"'Zhongguo-Eluosi-Zhongya' guoji xueshu taolunhui zai Beijing zhaokai" [International Conference on "China, Russia and the Central Asian States" Held in Beijing]. 1994. *Dongou Zhongya Yanjiu* [East European and Central Asian Studies] 4: 3–6.

Zhongguo Waijiao Gailan [Survey of China's Diplomacy]. 1987, 1988. Zhonghua Renmin Gongheguo Waijiaobu. Waijiaobu Bianji Shi. Beijing: Shijie zhishi chubanshe.

"Zhong-Yue guanxi zhenxiang" [The Facts about Sino-Vietnamese Relations]. 1981. *Guoji Wenti Yanjiu* 2.

Zhou Qi. 1999. "Renquan waijiao zhong de lilun wenti" [Theoretical Issues in Human Rights Diplomacy]. *Ouzhou* 1: 4–15.

Zhou Rongguo. 1997. "Jingji quanqiuhua he qucheng jingji yitihua wei woguo tigong de jiyu ji tichu tiaozhan" [Economic Globalization and Regional Economic Integration and the Challenges and Opportunities for China]. *Shijie Jingji yu Zhengzhi* 1.

Zhou Ying. 1990. "Nation Presses Ahead Despite Sanctions." *Beijing Review*, Oct. 1.

Zhou Yongkun. 2002. "Quanqiuxing shidai de renquan" [Human Rights in an Era of Universalism]. *Jiangsu Shehui Kexue* 3: 158–65.

Zhu Muzhi. 1995. "Ruhe pingjia Zhongguo renquan zhuangkuang" [How to Evaluate Human Rights Conditions in China]. *Gaoxiao Lilun Zhanxian* 4: 4–5.

———. 1996. "Properly Evaluating China's Human Rights Conditions." *Beijing Review*, Oct. 21.

———. 2000. "Bo 'renquan gaoyu zhuquan'" [Refuting "Human Rights over Sovereignty"]. *Renmin Ribao*. Mar. 3. Reprinted in *Lun Renquan yu Zhuquan*, 2001.

Zhu Ruiji. 1998. "Lun renquan he guojia zhuquan" [A Discussion of Human Rights and State Sovereignty]. Originally published in *Guizhou Daxue Xuebao* 6. Reprinted in Zhongguo Renquan Yanjiuhui bian, *Lun Renquan yu Zhuquan* [Human Rights and State Sovereignty]. Beijing: Dangdai shijie chubanshe, 2001.

Zhu Xiaoqing. 1994. "Lun Lianheguo renquan guoji baohu de zhixing cuoshi" [Discussing the Measures for Enacting the UN's International Protection of Human Rights]. *Faxue Yanjiu* 4.

Zou Jiayi. 1999. "Kesuowo weiji: Guanyu heping fazhan de jige zhanlüe wenti" [The Kosovo Crisis: Some Strategic Problems of Peace and Development]. *Shijie Jingji yu Zhengzhi* 8: 7–12.

Zu Qiang. 2002. "Jingji quanqiuhua yu fazhan zhong guojia zhudao chanye de yanti" [Economic Globalization and the Succession of Leading Industries in Developing Countries]. *Shijie Jingji yu Zhengzhi Luntan* 6: 7–11.

Zuo Dapei. 2003. "Jiu xiugai Zhongguo jiaru shijie maoyi zuzhi xiaeyi tiaokuan wenti zhi quanguo renmin daibiao dahui de gongkai xin" [An Open Letter to the NPC Concerning the Issue of Revising the Terms of China's Entry into the WTO]. www.chinastudygroup.org/articleshow.php?id=25.

Index

Integration; International Monetary Fund; World Bank; World Trade Organization
Gorbachev, Mikhail, 54, 63–64
Great Britain: and Hong Kong, 40, 93, 107–9, 142–43; and India, 74; and Tibet, 107, 113–14
Group of Seven (G-7), 197
Guofang Bao, 70
Guoji Maoyi Wenti, 199, 213–14
Guoji Wenti Yanjiu, 56–58, 67, 97
Guomindang (KMT), 36, 97; China's talks with, 96, 138; in Taiwan, 38–40, 95, 99, 124, 126, 137
Gu Yijie, 151
Gyalo Thondup, 100
Gyari, Lodi, 122

Han ethnic group, 102, 151, 243
Han Nianlong, 60
Hannum, Hurst, 166
Hanoi. *See* Vietnam
Harvard University, 182
He Fang, 213
Henkin, Louis, 166
Herzstein, Robert E., 190
Hitler, Adolf, 179
HKSAR. *See* Hong Kong Special Administrative Region
Hong Kong, 249n. 1, 255n. 1; Basic Law in, 109, 142–44, 244; China's claims to, 1, 40, 142, 227, 232; China's jurisdictional sovereignty issues in, 14, 38, 40–41, 92, 93, 107–10, 128, 133, 142–44, 226, 227, 232, 242, 244; China's territorial sovereignty issues in, 2; demonstrations against China in, 144, 227, 244; elections in, 143; "one country, two systems" formula applied to, 98, 108–9, 139, 143, 144, 244; "right of abode" in, 143–44; strategic value of, 40, 107–8, 142
Hong Kong Special Administrative Region (HKSAR), 143, 144, 249n. 1. *See also* Hong Kong
Huang Jiashi, 140
Hua Zi, 107
Hughes, Christopher, 126
Hu Jintao, 49, 87, 122, 123, 241
Human rights: analyzing China's, 2, 41–43, 146–83; award to Taiwan for, 140; China's participation in international system of, 32, 146–58, 162–85, 228, 233,

238–40, 257n. 8; China's record on, 147, 151–58, 160–64, 168, 176, 178–79, 181, 228, 233, 239, 255n. 12; China's use of rhetoric of, 151; China's white papers on, 147, 162–64, 167–68, 173, 176–77; as emerging issue, 16–17, 113; as excuse for intervention by other countries, 42, 113–15, 118, 147, 151, 152, 154, 156–59, 161, 162, 167–71, 173–77; international criticism of China's, 74, 109, 112–15, 120, 125, 142, 147–48, 150, 151, 156–62, 177, 228, 233, 243; intervention required by violations of, 17, 146, 151, 158, 166–67, 172, 177–78; motivations for China's changing views of, 94, 115, 146–48, 158–61, 165, 168–69, 176; sovereignty issues relating to, 1, 126, 146–48, 151, 156–67, 170–72, 178, 180, 184, 196, 233, 239, 240; treaties relating to, 16–17, 43, 150–52, 227–28; United States' policies on, 102, 113–15, 147, 152, 154, 156–59, 161, 163–65, 167–68, 170–71, 174–79, 181–83, 233; visits to China by representatives of, 164. *See also* Sovereign authority; Tiananmen protests; Tibet
Human Rights Watch, 17
Hu Yaobang, 101, 102, 104, 117
Hyer, Eric, 254n. 28

IBRD. *See* International Bank for Reconstruction and Development
ICCPR. *See* International Covenants on Civil and Political Rights
ICESCR. *See* International Covenants on Economic, Social, and Cultural Rights
ICISS. *See* International Conference on Intervention and State Sovereignty
Ideational influences for change, 3, 4, 26, 27–29, 31, 43, 50, 231, 234–35, 247
IMF. *See* International Monetary Fund
Imperialism (China's fears of). *See* Collective memory; Non-intervention
Independence. *See* Self-determination
India: China's border issues with, 34, 35, 37, 40, 49, 51, 56–58, 72–80, 195, 226, 232, 237–38, 253n. 22; Dalai Lama in, 40, 94, 106; as nuclear power, 72, 77–79, 237; World Bank's loans to, 258n. 6
Indivisibility and Interdependence of Economic, Social, Cultural, Civil and Political Rights (UN Assembly resolution), 152

CPSIA information can be obtained at www.ICGtesting.com
Printed in the USA
BVOW03*000911081814

362142BV00002B/2/P

About the Author

Maurice Charney, distinguished professor of English, emeritus, at Rutgers University, has published twenty-five books on Shakespeare and a wide range of other topics, including comedy, film, and modern drama. Having dealt in his three most recent books with aging, the problems of love and lust, and villainy and evil here he turns his attention to Shakespeare's style. Dr. Charney was president of the Shakespeare Association of America from 1987 to 1988 and was awarded the medal of the City of Tours in France in 1989.

Index

Finally, it is an important accomplishment of Shakespeare's art that he expresses himself with such complexity. There is no simple explanation of the meaning of any Shakespearean play. He cultivates multiple, often contradictory, meanings as a way of getting at the truth of the dramatic action. In *The Taming of the Shrew*, for example, we are never completely sure who tames whom. Petruchio is an aggressive and cocky fortune-hunter, but, by the end of the play, Kate has learned to play the marriage game, and, as Gremio says, "Petruchio is Kated" (3.2.245). In *Julius Caesar*, Shakespeare divides up our sympathies for the conspirators and the party of Caesar, so that it is difficult to tell at the end where the author's preferences lie. *Richard II* begins with an unflattering sense of the king insulting the dying Gaunt and seizing the estate that rightfully belongs to Bolingbroke, Gaunt's son, then ending the play as a Christ-like, meditative martyr being killed by King Henry IV in Pomfret castle. The same is true of Cardinal Wolsey in *Henry VIII*, who is either the king's faithful servant or a greedy, grasping tyrant in his own right. The play presents both points of view and leaves it for us to decide.

Macbeth provides another example. The Earl of Cawdor doesn't seem to hesitate in his desire to be king, but he is repelled by the idea that he has to murder King Duncan. In this he resembles Brutus in *Julius Caesar*, who wants to cultivate the illusion that the conspirators are "sacrificers, but not butchers" (2.1.166). As he says so apologetically to Cassius: "O, that we then could come by Caesar's spirit, / And not dismember Caesar!" (2.1.169–70). Lady Macbeth understands her husband's conflicted spirit with extraordinary clarity: "What thou wouldst highly, / That wouldst thou holily; wouldst not play false, / And yet wouldst wrongly win" (1.5.19–22). Macbeth doesn't need his wife to persuade him to murder Duncan; he only needs her to override his own profound contradictions.

If we are to approach a full understanding of Shakespeare's style, we need to master the art of close reading. It is my hope that *Shakespeare's Style*, with its attention to particular moments in each of Shakespeare's plays, provides a template for doing so, a template that embraces the ambiguities, complexities, and contradictions that characterize the canon. My own journey through each of Shakespeare's plays only confirms the fact that unresolved dramatic conflict is essential to his art.